THROUGH
FIRE AND
FLOOD

NUMBER FORTY-TWO:
The Centennial Series of the
Association of Former Students,
Texas A&M University

James Talmadge Moore

THROUGH FIRE AND FLOOD

The Catholic Church in Frontier Texas, 1836–1900

TEXAS A&M
UNIVERSITY
PRESS

College Station

Copyright © 1992 by James Talmadge Moore
Manufactured in the United States of America
All rights reserved
First paperback edition

The paper used in this book meets the minimum requirements
of the American National Standard for Permanence
of Paper for Printed Library Materials, Z39.48-1984.
Binding materials have been chosen for durability.

Library of Congress Cataloging-in-Publication Data

Moore, James T.
    Through fire and flood : the Catholic Church in frontier Texas,
1836–1900 / James Talmadge Moore. – 1st ed.
    The Centennial series of the Association of Former Students,
Texas A&M University ; no. 42)
        p.   cm.
    Includes bibliographical references and index.
    ISBN 0-89096-504-8 (c); 1-58544-076-0 (pbk.)
        1. Catholic Church–Texas–History–19th century.   2. Texas–
Church history–19th century.   I. Title.
BX1415.T4M66   1992
282'.764'09034–dc20   91-34327
                                                                            CIP

Contents

	Preface	ix
	Acknowledgments	xiii
1	1836	3
2	Tentative Steps, 1837–40	9
3	A New Beginning	31
4	A Bishop in Texas	65
5	Expanding the Frontier Diocese	82
6	The Immigrant Catholic	101
7	The Diocese of Galveston and War, 1861–65	121
8	In War's Wake	140
9	The Diocese of San Antonio	166
10	The Vicariate Apostolic of Brownsville	184
11	Changing the Guard in Galveston	200
12	Founding the Diocese of Dallas	222
13	1900	239
	Notes	241
	Bibliography	265
	Index	271

Illustrations

The Rt. Rev. Jean Marie Odin, ca. 1860	page 33
South wall, Mission San José de Aguayo, San Antonio, ca. 1865	45
St. Mary's Cathedral, Galveston, ca. 1860	80
The Rev. Pierre-Fourrier Parisot, 1890	102
Facade, Mission Concepción, San Antonio, ca. 1865	117
The Rt. Rev. Claude Marie Dubuis, ca. 1865	128
The Rev. Louis Claude Marie Chambodut, ca. 1870	131
Mother St. Pierre Harrington, ca. 1860	133
The Rev. Pierre Richard, ca. 1865	141
The Rev. Joseph Querat, ca. 1865	157
The Rt. Rev. Anthony Dominic Pellicer, ca. 1875	167
Altar, Mission San Francisco de la Espada, San Antonio, ca. 1890	169
Mother St. Pierre Cinquin, ca. 1885	172
The Rt. Rev. Jean Claude Neraz, ca. 1885	176
Rectory, Sacred Heart Church, Hallettsville, ca. 1900	182
The Rt. Rev. Dominic Manucy, ca. 1874	186
The Rt. Rev. Claude Marie Dubuis with missionaries, 1863	191
The Rt. Rev. Pedro Verdaquer, ca. 1900	197
Our Lady of Guadalupe Church, Laredo, ca. 1900	198
The Rt. Rev. Claude Marie Dubuis, 1887	202
The Rt. Rev. Nicholas A. Gallagher, ca. 1882	204
St. Joseph's Infirmary, Houston, 1887	221
Ursuline Convent nuns, Dallas, ca. 1880	223
St. Joseph's Church and school boys, Marshall, ca. 1890	225
The Rt. Rev. Thomas Francis Brennan	226
Interior, Sacred Heart Cathedral, Dallas, ca. 1891	229

Preface

The political and military upheaval of 1836 in Texas left Catholics north of the Nueces River cut off from the ordinary ties binding them to the larger body of their church. In the sphere of religion, they were in a real sense isolated, and this in a land first penetrated by Catholics over three hundred years before. The intervening years had produced a rich and deep legacy of faith and practice now touching the lives of thousands who waited to learn what the uncharted future might bring.

Different parts of what would become Texas after the Compromise of 1850 had belonged to several different political divisions of New Spain and Mexico, and, as Fr. Robert E. Wright, O.M.I., has pointed out, the organization of the Catholic church tended to reflect these divisions.[1] Over these decades of Spanish and Mexican sovereignty, several Franciscan provinces and three dioceses had jurisdiction over areas later included within the borders of Texas. In the sixteenth century, the area of the future "Texas" was included in the vast northern reaches of the diocese of Guadalajara. In 1620, however, in an attempt to make episcopal supervision of the area more viable, Pope Paul V established the diocese of Nueva Vizcaya (Durango), which included much of the trans-Pecos region of Texas and would continue to exercise jurisdiction over some of this region until as late as 1892.

After tentative missionary efforts among the Hasinai people of East Texas in the 1690s, vigorous missionary activities began there and in Central Texas in the early 1700s. During the same century, the development of the Catholic church was augmented by Spanish colonization efforts, particularly at San Antonio. From the 1600s onward, in various places along the Rio Grande from El Paso del Norte (Ciudad Juárez) to Matamoros, thriving Hispanic Catholic towns and parishes began to develop. The river was not a boundary then, of course, and though a town and parish church might be located on what is now the Mexican side, the parochial bounds included a large area and many people across the river. Colonization efforts in the mid-1700s led to the establishment of several lower Rio Grande towns such as Laredo, and in the 1770s, at the request of King Carlos III, Pope Pius VI established the diocese of Linares or Nuevo León. The first see city was the Villa de San Felipe de Linares, but in the 1780s the bishop moved his headquarters to Monterrey.

Later, during the tenure of Bp. José María de Jesús Belaunzarán y Ureña, O.F.M., in the 1830s, the jurisdiction was commonly referred to as the diocese of Monterrey.[2]

During the earliest years, Franciscans pioneered the church's efforts, but as the research of Robert E. Wright indicates, after 1731, diocesan priests soon joined them in furthering the development of Catholicism in Texas. The diocesan churches were sufficiently strong in such places as San Antonio, Revilla, and Reynosa that they produced a native Hispanic clergy who by 1810 were serving parishes in this northern frontier region.[3]

The political turmoil that began in 1810 and continued till midcentury destabilized in no small way the organization of the church in Texas. For instance, from 1821 to 1831 the see of Linares (or Monterrey) was vacant because the incumbent bishop had been Spanish and was therefore unacceptable to the new government of independent Mexico.[4] In spite of its having no bishop, however, the diocese, under the care of an administrator, provided what oversight it could for the churches in Texas during this period. In 1824 a vicar forane or dean, a priest who supervises a particular area of a diocese, was assigned to Texas. The first vicar forane to be sent to Texas was Fr. Juan Nepomuceno de la Peña, who arrived in San Antonio in December and set about trying to bring greater administrative order to the Texas churches. For instance, in February, 1825, he requested all priests in Texas to present themselves before him so that their authority to carry on their ministry could be reaffirmed. Peña was recalled later that year and succeeded by Fr. Francisco Maynes. It is probable that Maynes was succeeded by Fr. Miguel Muldoon in 1831.[5]

In 1830 the last of the Texas missions were "secularized." Under Spanish and later Mexican law, for a mission to be secularized usually meant that its lands were subdivided among the laity and most of its buildings turned into community buildings, with the chapel becoming a parish church. In Texas, the process of secularization began in 1794 but was not completed until Refugio and Espíritu Santo missions were secularized in 1830.[6]

In the early 1830s anticlericalism, not new to the scene, was on the rise in the Mexican political arena. Several antichurch laws were passed by the legislature of Coahuila y Tejas, the combined state of which Texas was then a part. In 1834 a law was passed that forbade the implementation of pastoral letters or directives from bishops and, in religious houses, of directives of monastic superiors without the express approval of the state governor in council with the legislature. Only disciplinary orders and matters related to penitence were exempted from this decree. Any pastoral letter or any other directive not of a private nature could not be read publicly by a pastor or superior of a religious house. Any cleric who failed to follow this procedure was to be banished for two years and permanently removed from the position he held at the time of his transgression of state law. Any person who might aid a clergyman in contravening this law was to be banished for two years as well.[7]

Between 1823 and 1836, large numbers of colonists settled in Texas. The largest number of these came from the United States, and although at least until 1834 all colonists were required by law either to be Catholics or to agree to become Catholics, the vast majority of those coming from the United States were either indifferent or hostile to Catholicism. For the Catholic church, this only complicated a situation already beset by hostility from a growing segment of Mexican political life.

Also in 1834, the state government issued another decree which stated that "the founding of edifices built by charitable donation . . . under any denomination whatever is hereby absolutely prohibited."[8] Soon thereafter, the state government granted a kind of religious toleration for the many Protestants or those of Protestant sympathies then settled in Texas. A warning therewith was given to both Catholics and Protestants, however: no one was to be molested for his religious opinions "provided, he shall not disturb the public order."[9] Since by law the construction of new churches was now prohibited, Protestants presumably would have to worship in homes or rented halls, and Catholics could not build any additional churches. Clearly, the state government was becoming increasingly antagonistic toward all organized religion.

The vast majority of Texas Catholics in 1836 continued as in the past to be Hispanic and native to the region as had been their parents and grandparents before them. However, some colonists who were genuinely Catholic by conviction did settle in Texas during the 1820s and early 1830s, mainly in the colonies founded by Martín de León, James Power, James Hewetson, James McGloin, and John McMullen.

Martín de León, a rancher and empresario from Tamaulipas, developed a colonial grant inland from the coast along the Guadalupe River. De León's Hispanic colonists began settling there in 1824. The seat of his colony was named Guadalupe Victoria (present-day Victoria) in honor of the first president of Mexico, and in the summer of 1825, a church was erected there. By 1835 more than one hundred land titles had been granted to heads of families in de León's largely Catholic colony.[10]

On June 11, 1828, the government made a colonial grant to James Power and James Hewetson. The grant lay to the southwest of Martín de León's colony, in the coastal plain between the Guadalupe and Lavaca rivers. Although Power and Hewetson were natives of Ireland, they both had resided in Mexico for several years. These empresarios launched a program to populate their colony with fellow Irish Catholics. By 1836 at least two hundred families had been granted land titles in the Power-Hewetson colony. The center of this colony was Refugio, the site of the mission of Nuestra Señora de Refugio, which was still operating when the colony was established in 1828.[11]

Two other Irishmen, James McGloin and John McMullen, residents of Matamoros, were also granted a colonial concession in 1828. This grant lay to the west and south of the Power-Hewetson colony and extended to the Nueces River. They established their headquarters and soon erected a small church at San Patricio, located on the Nueces about thirty miles from present-day Corpus Christi. While some of their Irish colonists came directly from Ireland, most had dwelt for a time in the United States. By the end of 1835, eighty-four grants had been made to individual families in the McGloin-McMullen colony.[12]

As a worldwide body, the Catholic church may not have been much concerned over the geopolitical results of the revolution of 1836, but it would have been foreign to the church's nature to long overlook the effects of that upheaval on the ability of ordinary Texans to practice their faith. A decade later, war would affect the lives of thousands of Catholics along the Rio Grande as well. The purpose of this book is to chronicle the reestablishment of ties that for a time seemed broken, efforts that became part of a mosaic of events forming around wave after wave of immigration that ultimately produced phenomenal growth and development in the life of the Texas Catholic church.

It is my hope that this volume may contribute in some small way to a far larger and much older picture, much of which has been revealed in the monumental works of Carlos Eduardo Castañeda and those of present-day historians such as Félix D. Almaráz, Jr., Robert E. Wright, Patrick Foley, and Gilberto M. Hinojosa. This book is designed to be the first of a two-volume work, the second of which will continue the historical account to these last years of the twentieth century. The present volume ends its story in the year 1900, and in a story that involves an institution now almost two millennia old, the end of a century has to be a highly artificial stopping point. It is rather more like the end of an act in a play.

What follows, then, is that act, an act filled with many different kinds of people. Many of them are courageous, and their successes, which are notable, outweigh their failures. Some are less admirable than others. They are all united, however, in their effort to live their faith in an unquiet age, an age filled with the incessant motion of unprecedented political and demographic change.

Acknowledgments

I am especially indebted to the Texas Catholic Conference and its executive secretary, Bro. Richard Daly, c.s.c., for initially making the research for this book possible. For his encouragement at the beginning of the project, I am grateful to the Most Rev. John E. McCarthy, a member of that body. I am indebted also to my wife, Linda Lytz Moore, who has once again devoted countless patient hours serving as my first editor to make this volume a reality. Sr. Dolores M. Kasner, o.p., former archivist at the Catholic Archives of Texas is due special thanks for her unfailing assistance in the initial stages of research, as are her successors, Gary Bryson, Michael Zilligen, and the present archivist, Kinga Perzynska, for invaluable assistance in the latter stages.

My special gratitude is due to my longtime friend and colleague, Félix D. Almaráz, Jr., of the University of Texas at San Antonio, for reviewing the manuscript and offering numerous helpful suggestions. The manuscript was also reviewed by the Most Rev. Joseph A. Fiorenza, who provided helpful comments, as did Fr. James F. Vanderholt, who in addition gave valuable research advice on several occasions.

Special thanks is also due to Fr. William Hoover, Gilbert R. Cruz, Fr. Robert E. Wright, o.m.i., Mary Acosta, Patrick Foley, Marilyn Rhinehart, John Carroll Eudy, Mary Lenn Dixon, and Deacon James Barnett of Our Lady of Walsingham parish, Houston, for assistance and advice at numerous levels along the way.

I wish to thank my children, Wendy, Stephen, Virginia, and Christie Moore, for accepting the limitations on my time which any research and writing effort demands.

There are others, too numerous to name here, who have enhanced the end result. Any failings are my responsibility.

THROUGH
FIRE AND
FLOOD

ONE

1836

In the fall of 1836, there remained only one regularly functioning Catholic parish in Texas north of the Nueces River: San Fernando Church in San Antonio, where in spite of isolation and the ravages of war Fr. Refugio de la Garza served as pastor. Two years before, the Franciscan pastor of Nacogdoches, Fr. Díaz de León, was killed under mysterious circumstances. After his death the laity continued to gather each Sunday in the church, where a layman led them in devotions. During the revolution, Fr. José Antonio Valdéz was forced from his pastorate at Goliad, where he also served as Mexican army chaplain, when the presidio fell to the insurrectionists. This elderly priest took refuge in San Antonio, though he does not seem to have exercised pastoral work there. Fr. John Thomas Malloy, the Irish Dominican pastor at San Patricio among the Irish colonists, was among those who successfully interceded with Gen. José Urrea for the lives of prisoners taken at San Patricio during the revolution. He may have gone to Goliad in March, 1836, in a futile attempt to save his own nephew, who was among Fannin's men taken prisoner at Coleto. He had left San Patricio by late May, 1836, when the evacuating Mexican army reported that another Irish priest, Fr. James Kelly, was then serving the congregation there. Nothing more is heard of Kelly after the summer of 1836. Father Malloy seems to have gone to the vicinity of Victoria, where he probably died in the early 1840s.[1]

Active parishes did exist that fall at Laredo and at San Elizario and Ysleta near present-day El Paso. In addition, many Catholics along what is today the Texas side of the lower Rio Grande continued to be part of active parishes centered in towns along the southern bank of the river. Although the Republic of Texas claimed these areas and much more, it was unable to exercise any real control there, and not until the Compromise of 1850 were the modern boundaries of Texas established. Only at San Antonio was Sunday mass regularly celebrated within the area under the Texas republic's control in the months and years immediately following the revolution.

Most Texas Catholics in 1836 were Hispanic, though a lesser but significant number were Irish. Hispanic Texans were divided over the revolution of 1835–36, as were some of the Irish, but those who opposed the revolution did so not so much because of how the conflict might affect the church as because they opposed a war against the national government and separation from Mexico. Texas Catholics in general, on both sides of the struggle, seem to have given little thought to what the outcome might mean for the church, although some Hispanic Catholics who sided with the revolution did have definite philosophical views about church-state relations.

When the convention at Washington-on-the-Brazos declared Texas independent on March 2, 1836, eight of the fifty-eight signers of the declaration were Catholics, and four of these went on to serve on the twenty-five-member committee that drafted the provisional constitution for the new republic. This has significance since the Texas Declaration of Independence contains some harsh references to the Catholic clergy. The document charges that Santa Anna's government had disregarded "every interest . . . but that of the army and the priesthood—both the eternal enemies of civil liberty, the every-ready minions of power, and the usual instruments of tyrants . . ."; that "it [the government] denies us the right of worshiping the Almighty according to the dictates of our own conscience; by the support of a national religion calculated to promote the temporal interests of its human functionaries rather than the glory of the true and living God . . ."; that Santa Anna had attempted to force upon Texas "the most intolerable of all tyranny, the combined despotism of the sword and the priesthood."[2]

The actual conditions prevailing in Texas during the 1820s and 1830s hardly warranted such words. The colonists from the United States certainly knew they were entering a country where there was an established church when they moved into Texas, even though an increasing number no doubt hoped for change. And on the eve of the revolution, state laws were enacted that granted a measure of tolerance to other denominations. Furthermore, during the whole period of colonization from the United States, there was almost no effort on the part of the state to force the Catholic religion into the everyday life of the settlers.[3]

It is generally accepted that the declaration's language was an attempt to affect public opinion in the United States in favor of a people portrayed to be as oppressed in conscience as in politics.[4] A sensitive chord could be struck, as it had been only sixty years since the British American colonies started a revolution that opened the way to ending the ties there between churches and government. Also, this appeal to freedom of conscience could help lessen the effect of those in the United States who were saying that the whole matter in Texas was simply a scheme to extend the influence of the slaveholding South.

Additional factors, however, should be considered: among these is the developing anticlerical mood of Mexican Federalism during this period. While by March, 1836, the Texas Revolution was no longer, if it had ever been, a struggle to reestablish Federalism within the Mexican nation, this philosophy was not dead among all Texans—including some of those who deliberated in the blacksmith shop at Washington-on-the-Brazos. Within a few days of declaring Texas independent of Mexico, this body elected as vice president of Texas one of their fellow delegates, Lorenzo de Zavala, a leading Mexican Federalist and formerly a cabinet member and diplomatic representative to the French court.

The power and influence of high church officials within the Spanish colonial administration in Mexico were resented by the Federalists. During the 1820s and 1830s one might espouse the Federalist philosophy in this regard and still consider oneself a practicing Catholic. In other words, in an important sense, a Federalist could be anticlerical without being anti-Catholic in terms of the church's faith. This seeming paradox is writ large in Mexican history. Padre Miguel Hidalgo, the father of Mexican independence, was a parish priest who in 1810 began the struggle against the domination of Mexico by a foreign Spanish government and a local aristocracy. In the Federalist view, he was a heroic cleric who was excommunicated by a hierarchy dominated by the Spanish aristocracy so that the royal authorities could execute him. Given the presence at Washington-on-the-Brazos of such a prominent Federalist as de Zavala as well as the widespread sympathy this movement had among both Hispanic and Anglo Texans, the anticlerical as distinct from a necessarily anti-Catholic influence of this movement on the writing of the Texas Declaration of Independence should not be overlooked. Interestingly, with the exception of the grievance against an established church, the declaration's references are to the clergy, not to the church per se.

With this distinction in mind, it is not so surprising that, in addition to de Zavala, two other Hispanic Catholics joined in the unanimous vote in favor of the document when it was presented to the whole convention. These were José Antonio Navarro and Francisco Ruíz. De Zavala and Navarro also served a few days later on the committee that drafted the constitution for the new republic.

Ruíz and his nephew, Navarro, both had a long history of devotion to Federalist principles. Ruíz was Navarro's mother's younger brother. Both were born in San Antonio: Ruíz in 1783, Navarro in 1795. Navarro's father served as alcalde of San Antonio in 1790. In 1813, Ruíz and Navarro joined with Bernardo Gutiérrez de Lara, a disciple of Padre Miguel Hidalgo, and Augustus W. Magee in their abortive attempt to overthrow Spanish rule in Texas. After the Spanish forces defeated the insurrection at the Medina River that same year, both uncle and nephew fled to the United States. Later, when Ferdinand VII pardoned the surviving insurrectionists, Navarro returned to San Antonio, but Ruíz remained in the United States until 1822, the year after the peaceful end of Spanish authority in Texas.[5]

After the Texas Revolution, Navarro went on to serve in the Senate of the Republic of Texas and as a trade commissioner in the abortive Santa Fe Expedition in 1841. Imprisoned by the Mexican government until 1845, he received a hero's welcome in Galveston when he returned to Texas in February of that year. He went on to serve in the convention that drew up a state constitution after Texas was annexed by the United States and later served in the state senate. Navarro County was named for him.

In 1839 and 1840 when the reorganization of the Catholic church in Texas began (see chapter 2), Navarro provided valuable assistance to both Fr. John Timon and Fr. Jean Marie Odin.[6]

After Ruíz's return to Texas in 1822, he served in the Mexican army for a time and helped put down the "Fredonian Rebellion." In 1827, he was in command of troops stationed at Nacogdoches. In 1830, Ruíz was sent to select the site for a new fort called Tenoctitlán on the Brazos River in present-day Burleson County and remained there in command until he returned to San Antonio in 1832. After the revolution, Ruíz served in the first Congress of the Republic of Texas. He died in San Antonio in 1840 and was buried from San Fernando Church.[7]

Attitudes similar to those motivating the Hispanic Federalists probably motivated the five other Catholics who signed the declaration: James Power, the Irish empresario; and Michel B. Menard, Charles S. Taylor, John White Bower, and Edwin Conrad. Power and Menard, like de Zavala and Navarro, also served on the committee that drafted the constitution.

While little is known of the Pennsylvania-born Conrad, Bower was from the Irish colony of San Patricio, where a functioning parish had once existed. Menard, a French Canadian, purchased from the Texas government after the Texas Revolution the land upon which he laid out the town of Galveston. He later provided assistance to Bp. Jean Marie Odin when Odin made the town his headquarters in the 1840s.[8] The London-born Charles S. Taylor was a delegate from Nacogdoches and later supported the work of Frs. John Timon and Jean Marie Odin when they visited East Texas in 1841.[9]

Three other Catholics were elected to the convention at Washington-on-the-Brazos but arrived after the declaration was adopted. These were Encarnación Vásquez from Goliad, and José M. Carbajál and John J. Linn from Victoria.[10]

An anticlerical attitude also surfaced in the writing of the proposed constitution for the new republic. It was not aimed specifically at Catholics, however. One member of the twenty-five-member committee that drew up the original draft, William Carrol Crawford, a Methodist minister, only narrowly defeated an effort to deny the franchise to all clergymen.[11] Even so, the draft of the document contained the following provision: ministers and priests "dedicated to God and the care of souls, ought not to be diverted from the great duties of their functions" and therefore could not serve as president or as a member of either house of the Congress. This prohibition remained in the constitution when it was adopted by the convention and later ratified by the electorate. Gracious language about their duties notwithstanding, clergy were not to be trusted with political power, and the state constitutions of 1845 and 1866 contained the same prohibition regarding the office of governor and membership in the legislature. When anticlerical forces successfully won the debate over the matter at the state constitutional conventions in 1845 and 1866, in both instances it had been years since the disestablishment of the Catholic church, and the question could hardly have been related to that church more than any other. Finally in 1868 during Reconstruction, the new constitution drawn up to facilitate reentry into the Union and the reestablishment of civil government replaced this prohibition with the stipulation that any clergyman elected to the legislature could not continue to claim exemption from military service and jury and road maintenance duty.[12]

Anticlericalism in Texas not only was fueled by factors in the history of New Spain and Mexico and American anti-Catholicism but was watered and nourished by other forces emanating from the United States as well. There it was often latent or operating just below the surface of society, but sometimes it broke to the top. For instance, at this time the New York state constitution also prohibited clerical office-holding. Fed by a nascent deism just as in Mexico, by denominational wrangling, or by what even some otherwise religious people considered the wild, frenetic displays of some frontier preachers, this was the same anticlericalism that previously had caused some of the Anglo colonists in Texas to welcome a situation where revivalists could not come and where the only legal organized religion seemed far away. The religious "burnout" some Americans experienced after the Second Great Awakening strengthened anticlericalism, making Texas seem a haven for those who wanted "no ravings" and "no ranyings [sic]."[13]

From quite a different perspective, however, it is possible that for some Texans from the United States, both in the 1830s and to a larger extent in the 1840s, there was another motivation for anticlericalism, a motivation spawned by the abolitionist movement in the North and Midwest. This movement was often led by intensely religious people, including clergymen such as the Reverend Lyman Beecher, whose daughter Harriet Beecher Stowe wrote *Uncle Tom's Cabin*, and the Reverend Elijah P. Lovejoy, who was murdered by a mob in Alton, Illinois, because of his abolitionist activities. Even in the South during the first decade of the nineteenth century, some of the frontier preachers who were quite adept at "ranting" and "ranying" did so as they exhorted their intended converts to free their slaves. At this very time of the 1830s, many northern clergymen not only had captured the attention of the press but were organizing their own publication efforts and launching speaking tours, all designed to hasten slavery's demise. For those of proslavery sentiments, a large segment of the clergy were suspect and should be kept from significant influence in the political arena.[14]

In the aftermath of the ravages committed by both sides in 1835–36, Texas Catholics found themselves isolated and virtually leaderless. While Rome had not forgotten the Texas church, in the unsettled times it was uncertain how best to go about reviving it. Should this be done through the Mexican church, which itself was caught up in the often hostile political changes occurring in Mexico? Whatever the inherent problems, this was the direction in which Rome would have to move if the Battle of San Jacinto turned out to have been only a skirmish, with Texas sooner or later being reclaimed by Mexican authorities. On the other hand, if Texas were soon to be annexed to the United States, then Catholics there would pass under the jurisdiction of the hierarchy of that country. If neither event took place and Texas remained an independent republic, then some other provision for the church would have to be made.

TWO
Tentative Steps, 1837–40

JOHN J. LINN, an early Irish colonist who turned revolutionary and later became a Texan congressman, recorded that once while encamped in the countryside he was awakened at dawn by a beautiful melody floating across the prairie, followed by the sound of prayers said in unison by a ranchero, his wife, and their three children. Linn concluded that even in those places where there was neither priest nor even a church, Catholicism was far from dead in the lives of the Texas laity. Of its work in former times, Linn wrote, "What a glorious commentary upon the blessed work of the Church!"[1]

While Catholicism was far from dead in the years after 1836, renewal had to come from some source if its ordered sacramental life was to grow and develop once more. The hierarchical structure by which Texas was included within the see of Monterrey could no longer function north of the Nueces River. The obvious major obstacle was Texas' claim to independence from Mexico. As soon as news of General Santa Anna's defeat at San Jacinto reached the capital, the Centralist government was overthrown. The new government refused to recognize the independence of Texas but was unable to extend its authority above the Nueces River. Even if this problem disappeared, the tension between church and state in Mexico was such that the Mexican hierarchy might have little means by which to strengthen the church in Texas. What the future held for the Republic of Texas no one in the late 1830s could say. But it had begun to function and act like what it claimed to be, a sovereign nation. The first president, David G. Burnet, and vice president, Lorenzo de Zavala, who had been elected by the convention at Washington-on-the-Brazos in March, resigned their offices on October 22, 1836, to make way for a new administration chosen by the voters in a general election. The new president and vice president were Sam Houston and Mirabeau B. Lamar. Frustrated in its hope of immediate annexation by the United States, Houston's administration continued to press the United States and Europe for diplomatic recognition. The United States became the first country to recognize the new nation on March 3, 1837.

Perhaps emboldened by this action, several Irish Texans in New Orleans purchasing supplies for their homes and businesses addressed a petition on

March 20 to the American bishops who were scheduled to meet in Baltimore the next month. Those who signed the petition were John McMullen, the former empresario of the Irish colony at San Patricio, now residing in San Antonio; William Hayes, Robert O'Boyle, and Andrew O'Boyle of San Patricio; Robert Hearn of Refugio; and John Linn of Victoria. The petitioners requested that English-speaking priests be sent to Texas—even though most Texas Catholics spoke Spanish. However, they also asked for help in confronting bigotry, a problem plaguing all Texas Catholics at this time.[2] Since San Jacinto thousands of settlers from the United States had been pouring into Texas, some of whom were religious zealots who took great pleasure in deriding the Catholic faith, implying that victory over Santa Anna had been a triumph over the Catholic church as well. The petitioners lamented that they had no priests to rebut this slander from the pulpit. Texas, they said, was fast becoming the haven of these self-styled preachers who represented no organized denomination.

Their charge is corroborated by the fact that at the new town of Houston that same month, a group of Protestant ministers organized what they called an "Ecclesiastical Council of Vigilance for Texas" in an attempt to prevent "rogues"—self-proclaimed ministers—from entering Texas. A committee of correspondence was formed to disseminate information on such individuals. The climate of prejudice in Texas was due as much to this class of "preachers" as to ordinary denominational bigotry.

The petitioners, after outlining their hardships, admitted that to be a priest in Texas would be "fatiguing & arduous" for anyone since Catholics were scattered over a vast area and were often poor. But in spite of bigotry, they said, Texas could well be the source of many conversions since many Texans professed no religious faith at all.

The petition was presented to officials at the diocesan chancery in New Orleans. Presumably the petitioners hoped that Bp. Antoine Blanc of New Orleans would act as their spokesman at the bishops' meeting in Baltimore. A problem in this approach was that Texas was foreign territory over which the American bishops had no ecclesiastical authority. Since no communication regarding Texas seems to have been sent by the American bishops to Rome, either they concluded that action by them in the matter was inappropriate or Bishop Blanc had already left New Orleans for Baltimore by the time the petition was submitted to his office. It is also possible that Blanc himself concluded that since the American hierarchy had no jurisdiction over Texas, it was pointless for him to present the petition in Baltimore.[3]

Nevertheless, before a year had lapsed, Rome did begin to take action to meet the needs of Catholics in the new republic. The knowledge the Vatican received concerning the plight of Texas Catholics seems to have come from a source other than this petition. In the summer of 1837 a French nobleman, Charles Comte de Farnesé arrived in Texas with high hopes. Like the earlier empresarios, Farnesé hoped to head a colonizing venture. He arrived in Houston in July, and among the proposals he presented to the president was an offer on his part to serve as an intermediary with Rome with the aim of establishing an archdiocese in Texas.[4] This would amount to the ecclesiastical independence of Texas from Mexico, by officially breaking the tie between Texas Catholics and the diocese of Monterrey. Farnesé assured Houston that this was "the sure means of making peace with Mexico through the influence of the Roman court." In addition, Farnesé asserted, the governments of Catholic European countries would readily recognize the independence of Texas. He went on to propose further that, once an archbishop was appointed for Texas, the Texas government should provide building sites at no cost for churches, rectories, and schools in all cities and towns. While not suggesting that the government directly support the clergy and the teachers in the schools, he proposed that 1,280 acres of land for each church and school be provided gratuitously in the surrounding countryside to generate funds for their support. Since under this plan, he continued, the churches, rectories, and schools were to be built by church funds, they would not be government property or available for any other than church use without ecclesiastical consent. Under his proposal, the church would be free to carry on work in all parts of Texas under the protection of the government and would be bound in all respects to the rites and canon law in effect for Catholics elsewhere in the world.[5]

As Farnesé saw it, he was not proposing the establishment of the Catholic church as the state religion of Texas, since he was not suggesting that these favors be denied to other denominations!

While much of his proposal was unrealistic, the part calling for the establishment of a separate ecclesiastical jurisdiction for Texas, independent of Mexican ties, had a fundamental attraction for Houston, which his reply to Farnesé, dated August 5, 1837, indicates:

> A separation of the religious as well as the political ties between Mexico and Texas has my entire approval, and should be followed by salutary effects producing harmony among the Catholic citizens of Texas.
>
> The Constitution of Texas assures to all sects the free exercise of their religion, and, it seems to me will not place any obstacles to your wishes in connection with the Holy Mother Church. I see no impediments at all to the establishment of the Archbishopric in Texas as in the United States of the North. However, concerning privileges, that is not within the powers of the president, but belongs exclusively to the Congress.
>
> Nevertheless, it does rest with the president to express his profound veneration for the true religion and for sound education, and his ar-

dent wishes are that their influence may abound in this new-born country. . . . if it pleases the Holy See to use your talents for the good of Texas, it will give great pleasure to [me].[6]

It was obvious to Houston that Rome's establishment of a separate jurisdiction for Texas would be a virtual recognition by the Holy See of Texas' independence from Mexico and would in turn create a more favorable climate for increased diplomatic ties in Europe.

Although nothing came of Farnesé's colonization plans, it was probably he who brought information about Texas Catholics to the Vatican's attention during the waning months of 1837 along with Houston's favorable response to the idea of the "Holy Mother Church" establishing a separate jurisdiction for Texas.[7] However, others were also attempting to do so during this same period. Word of Farnesé's proposal naturally became common knowledge among townspeople in the small Texas capital, composed of new cabins, tents, lean-tos, and an occasional cottage. A group of Houston Catholics were so encouraged that they too drew up a petition addressed directly to Pope Gregory XVI in support of the proposed archbishopric.[8]

On January 16, 1838, Cardinal Giacomo Fransoni, prefect of the Sacred Congregation for the Propagation of the Faith, wrote Bp. Antoine Blanc of New Orleans informing him of Rome's knowledge of the Texas situation and that he himself had been informed that the Texan president was very friendly to the Catholic church. He therefore requested Blanc to send some priests to Texas to ascertain exactly what conditions were like there and to make a full report to Rome of their findings so that a decision could be made as to appropriate action.[9]

Fransoni's knowledge of Houston's attitude indicates that Farnesé was the source of his information. Considering the slow pace of transatlantic travel and communication, the speed with which a response was received to Farnesé's communication is remarkable. Farnesé himself had had nothing upon which to base a communication until Houston's letter of August 5 of the previous year. Fransoni's is even more remarkable in the light of difficulties Rome was facing in its relations with Mexico. First there was an obvious political one: to move hastily toward establishing any kind of jurisdiction for Texas could be highly offensive to Mexico since it would amount to recognition by the Holy See of Texan independence. The second difficulty was ecclesiastical: for decades Texas had belonged to the see of Monterrey, earlier known as the see of Linares. Episcopal visitations were made to Texas during the early years of the century by Bp. Primo Feliciano Marín de Porras, whose travels took him as far east as the area around Natchitoches, Louisiana, then under Spanish control. Some of the French-speaking people in western Louisiana were considered communicants of his diocese until the boundary between New Spain and the United States was clearly defined in the Adams-Onis Treaty of 1819. Following Mexican independence from Spain, the bishop of Monterrey was removed from his see by those in the Mexican government who considered him too favorable to the old order, and the diocese was overseen for years by an administrator. After 1825, relations between the state and church steadily began to deteriorate in all areas of Mexico. In short, the Mexican hierarchy was in tenuous straits, and under such circumstances it was a delicate matter to summarily remove a large area from its jurisdiction. Only recently had relations between Rome and Mexico shown any hope of even a slight improvement.[10] So for Rome, then, the Texan question presented serious problems. Nevertheless, out of a sense of pastoral concern, Rome decided to take the first step toward meeting the needs of the thousands of Catholics living in a land recently ravaged by war with few or possibly no priests to lead them in the practice of their religion.

Cardinal Fransoni decided to make his request for information through a bishop in the United States. He probably decided this was the most workable course to follow in view of church-state tensions in Mexico and the hostility existing between Mexico and Texas. The nearest bishop in the United States was Blanc in New Orleans.

It was already March when Blanc received Fransoni's letter. The priest whom Blanc chose to make the trip to Texas was Fr. John Timon, rector of St. Mary-of-the-Barrens Seminary in Perry County, Missouri. Timon was also provincial superior, or "visitor," of the Vincentian province of the United States. His order was founded by St. Vincent de Paul in Paris in 1625 to consist of secular priests living under religious vows and is formally known as the Congregation of the Mission. Although Timon was not a priest in Blanc's diocese, Blanc was well acquainted with him since Timon's duties often brought him to Louisiana. Blanc also knew that in Missouri Timon had the reputation of being a priest who had caused many lapsed Catholics to return to their church. It was also said he had brought about more adult conversions than all the other priests combined in the diocese of St. Louis.[11] Timon was well known to western frontier Catholics, and the lay petitioners in New Orleans in 1837 had even suggested him by name for work in Texas.

In urging Timon to accept Fransoni's request, Blanc played directly on the Missouri cleric's missionary zeal by assuring him that a report made as a result of a trip into Texas would determine the future of the Catholic church there for years to come. Timon would have his aid and support, Blanc wrote, in carrying out any policy toward the Catholics of Texas that might result from Timon's report. Blanc urged Timon to come to New Orleans immediately, where the frequent schedule of steam packets bound for Texas would allow him to be quickly on his way. The reference in Fransoni's letter to the friendliness of Texas president Sam Houston was supported by rumor in New Orleans, wrote Blanc, and this would surely help produce a favorable climate for a Catholic renewal in Texas.[12]

As Blanc expected, Timon accepted the missionary challenge, but seminary business and lost transatlantic mail prevented his leaving as quickly as Blanc wished. It was another nine months before Timon actually set foot in Texas.

Having worked for many years in Missouri, John Timon was no stranger to the frontier. He was born in a log cabin in Conewago Settlement near York, Pennsylvania, in 1797. His parents had only recently arrived from County Cavan, Ireland. When Timon was three, the family moved to Baltimore. They moved to Missouri when Timon was nineteen, and he had spent most of the last twenty years there.

In July, 1822, Timon entered St. Mary-of-the-Barrens Seminary about eighty miles southeast of St. Louis. At the time this "aggregation of primitive log cabins," as the Vincentian historian Ralph Bayard described it, was the only Catholic seminary in the Mississippi Valley. The year after Timon's arrival, he entered the Vincentian order, and after completing four years of study, he was ordained to the priesthood on September 23, 1826. For the next nine years, Timon taught at St. Mary's in both the college and seminary, served in the administration, worked in the local parish, visited frontier villages, and gained the reputation of being a superbly effective missionary. Three different bishops requested that the Holy See make him their coadjutor bishop with right of succession to the diocese, but this was forestalled when, in 1835, Timon was appointed provincial superior of the newly erected Vincentian province of the United States. In addition, Timon was by that time both rector of the seminary and president of the college. His missionary visits to log cabin hamlets, however, continued as before. In 1838 alone, during the very time he was also involved in arranging for his trip to Texas, he helped found twelve missions on the upper Illinois River, established a parish in Cape Girardeau, Missouri, and accepted for his order the operation of two parishes and the diocesan seminary in Bishop Blanc's diocese of New Orleans.[13]

As he prepared for his Texas visit, not only did Timon have the expected problems of transferring his administrative responsibilities during his absence, but he needed to seek the advice of the Vincentian superior general in Paris, Jean Baptiste Nozo, both out of a sense of filial obedience and because he expected that, once his trip was completed and his reports submitted, the new work in Texas would become the responsibility of the Vincentian order. Both Cardinal Fransoni and Bishop Blanc had also communicated with Nozo about the proposed work in Texas, so the superior general could hardly do anything but give his blessing to the venture, and later events indicate that he did more than that. For the moment, however, Timon was left in suspense: Nozo's response to Timon was somehow lost in transit, and only in the early fall of 1838 did Timon learn through reading a French Catholic journal, *L'Ami de la Religion,* that Nozo had approved the new work in Texas. Timon continued to wait, hoping to receive an actual directive from Nozo before embarking downriver to New Orleans. Growing increasingly impatient, and with Blanc begging him to come at once, Timon made further inquiry to the Vincentian motherhouse. Then news reached him from New Orleans that a ship had arrived there on October 20 bringing nine Vincentian volunteers for work in Texas, along with a letter from Nozo indicating that Timon should long since have received the superior general's directive to proceed. Finally, on November 27 Timon received from the Vincentian procurator general, Jean-Baptiste Etienne, a synopsis of the lost instructions. Timon was directed to undertake the expedition in Texas and then make a report to both Rome and Paris, from which Cardinal Fransoni and the Vincentian superior general would formulate a policy for reorganizing the Texas church.[14]

At the end of November, Timon at last embarked by steamboat for New Orleans. As he walked the decks of the churning vessel moving slowly down the Mississippi, Timon had plenty of time to think of his destination. As with anyone who had not lived there, his actual knowledge of Texas was scanty, though he knew of recent events because the revolution had been well publicized in the United States. And Timon knew more than most Americans, for he had been in New Orleans in the early months of 1836 when the movements of the "New Orleans Grays," a group of Americans who left to join the insurrection in Texas, were followed in newspaper accounts; he was aware of public meetings, calls for additional volunteers, and efforts to raise money and equipment for those in revolt against Mexico. One of the first purchases he made on arrival in New Orleans was *The History of Texas: or the Emigrant's, Farmer's and Politician's Guide to the Character, Climate, Soil, and Production of that Country,* by a Scotsman, David Edward, to supplement what he had gleaned from newspapers.[15]

Aware that most Texas Catholics were Spanish-speaking, Timon selected in New Orleans as his companion for the Texas tour Fr. Juan Francisco Llebaría, one of the recently arrived Vincentian missionary volunteers. Seven of the recently arrived Vincentians were Spaniards who had been studying in France.[16] Though all of them wanted to work in Texas, Timon took just Llebaría since this was only a fact-finding tour of uncertain duration. The other Spaniards were given temporary assignments in the Louisiana Vincentian foundations.

Llebaría was at the Vincentian-run seminary on Bayou La Fourche when word came to report to Timon in New Orleans. The newly ordained twenty-four-year-old Spaniard made his way to New Orleans as quickly as steamboats and muddy roads allowed. It was Monday evening, Christmas Eve, when he reached the city. Llebaría had his first opportunity to hear and observe the man who was to be his close associate for the next weeks when Timon delivered the sermon that night at midnight mass. Timon informed him they would leave for Texas the very next morning. Although it was painful to spend Christmas Day aboard ship, Timon explained, they had no choice since for several days no more ships were scheduled to sail for Texas. At ten o'clock the next morning, the two priests boarded the steamship *Cuba* bound for Galveston, Texas.[17]

The journey under steam power was surprisingly short: the ship docked at Galveston at nine o'clock on the evening of the twenty-sixth. Since their arrival was after dark, Timon and Llebaría decided to spend the night on shipboard and seek lodging in Galveston the next morning. Since Timon could not speak Spanish and Llebaría could not speak English, the two priests conversed in French. During their time at sea, Timon read aloud to Llebaría from the guidebook, translating it into French as he read. The morning after their ship's arrival, the two priests were awakened by the din of the many pelicans on a small nearby island that they later discovered bore the name of its noisy inhabitants. As they surveyed the shore from the deck in the morning light, they beheld a cluster of stores, shops, and warehouses, newly constructed and almost all of wood. They decided this material had come mostly from the mainland, since they could see no sign the island had ever had trees except for three or four that jutted up from the light sandy soil and, with the buildings and new houses, barely relieved the desolate appearance of the landscape. Some of the houses were on ten-acre plots of land containing vegetable gardens that still showed signs of crops left flourishing by the mild climate. On the extreme northeastern tip of the island, near their ship, they could see a small fort occupied by a Texan army force. Some distance away, at the west end of the city, some buildings had been erected for a navy yard for Texas' minuscule navy.[18] What was completely absent from Galveston's horizon was a spire or steeple or any other sign of a place of worship.

After walking the short distance to the center of the town, the priests discovered that Galveston was crowded with immigrants and lodging was hard to find. All they could arrange for was bare shelter in what purported to be a boardinghouse. Fortunately for them, their stay there was short. About noon, as they were walking along the crowded muddy streets, Timon sighted two familiar faces, the brothers Michel and Peter Menard, whom Timon knew from years before in the missions of Illinois. This was a fortunate meeting for Timon and Llebaría, for Michel Menard had been largely responsible for the development of Galveston and both Menards were among its most prominent citizens. Michel had been a signer of the Texas Declaration of Independence and member of the Constitutional Convention, while Peter had been a member of the "Permanent Council" that briefly tried to manage the opposition to the central government in the fall of 1835. The

Menards insisted that the priests leave their present lodgings and move to their own comfortable house—an invitation the priests readily accepted. It was there on Friday, December 28, 1838, that they celebrated the first Catholic mass in the town of Galveston.[19]

Among those attending mass that day was a former student at St. Mary-of-the-Barrens Seminary, Canadian-born Dr. Nicholas D. Labadie, another old friend of Timon. Labadie had served on the medical staff of Houston's army at the Battle of San Jacinto and became a mainstay of support for the Catholic church in Galveston over the next two decades.[20]

After mass, Timon spent much of that day and the next visiting the homes and shops of the town, which reeked almost everywhere of sawdust and fresh lumber, trying to ascertain how many Catholics were in Galveston and advertising that mass was scheduled for ten o'clock Sunday morning.

That Sunday morning, in a warehouse owned by the Menards, Father Llebaría celebrated mass, and Timon preached an eloquent forty-five-minute sermon that apparently was well received by the large number present, both Catholics and Protestants. At the end of the liturgy, Timon said several prayers in English and invited everyone back at two o'clock in the afternoon for an address on Catholic doctrine. With such an inspiring speaker available to them, the Galvestonians turned out in even greater numbers than in the morning. Timon held their rapt attention for three hours, finishing just as dusk approached. Some were so moved, wrote one observer, that they wanted him to continue speaking; and the non-Catholics, thought Llebaría, were so impressed that even if they were not persuaded to enter the Catholic church, their understanding of it seemed altered for the better. Timon was so eloquent and convincing that two of his hearers, Stewart Newell, the United States consul in Galveston, and his wife, wanted to join the Catholic church on the spot.[21]

It was not difficult for the two priests to conclude that the Catholic church could have a bright future in Galveston. The next day—Monday, New Year's Eve—Timon contacted a number of prominent Galvestonians who had been in attendance on Sunday and proposed that a program be launched to erect a church in the town. The group agreed, and plans were made to begin raising funds to erect a frame structure 150 by 120 feet in size. Galveston was on the move; it was the key to Texas, Timon reasoned, the gateway through which thousands had entered and would continue to enter Texas. Galveston, located where it was, had to become for the foreseeable future Texas' great commercial center. And the people impressed him: they were all kinds, and very enthusiastic. Timon knew, of course, that enthusiasm has its limitations and often does not last—and only with much further encouragement would the small frame Galveston church be completed three years later. Texas and Texans were not yet on a stable financial footing, and the support of Catholic work in Texas could not depend on local tithes and zeal for a long time to come. For the present, these would have to come from outside sources, mostly in Europe.²²

After mass on Tuesday, New Year's Day, Timon and Llebaría boarded the steamboat *Rufus Putnam* for Houston. The route took them up Galveston Bay to the mouth of the San Jacinto, then almost immediately into the mouth of Buffalo Bayou, the narrow, tortuously winding stream that led to Houston, the 2½-year-old town that was the capital of the Texan republic. As they entered Buffalo Bayou they slowly churned past San Jacinto, with the boat almost brushing against the trees to their left where Houston's army had encamped. Elsewhere great patches of high grass, which had thus far survived the winter, hugged the stream's edge. As the hours passed and evening approached, the banks grew higher and magnolia and pine were visible among the bare oak trees that now grew along the banks. So narrow did the bayou become that some passengers wondered if their boat might become wedged between the banks or at the very least have its stacks knocked off by overhanging trees. Before dawn, the boat passed the eerie remains of Harrisburg, hardly visible in the blackness, burnt in the revolution over two years before. Finally at ten o'clock on Wednesday, the boat arrived at a small wharf at the foot of a muddy lane that seemed to be the "main street" of the mostly log cabin town. Here, too, was the only spot on the whole course of the little stream where the steamboat could turn around: a small stream, known later as White Oak Bayou, emptied here into the larger stream providing barely enough room for the boat to turn around for its return trip. As one traveler at the time put it, "While the stern of the Boat is with difficulty propelled into the . . . branch, the bow is gradually brought to, and as if conscious of having escaped a dilemma, proudly dashes down the stream."²³

The population of Houston in 1839 was about three thousand, with all but about forty of them male. However, Timon estimated the population at five thousand since Congress was then in session. In addition to congressmen and other members of the government, traders roamed in and out of town, and land speculators were there in abundance. As in Galveston, immigrants seeking land were arriving constantly. It seemed as if the least bit of rain made the mud knee-deep in Houston's streets, creating havoc for wagons trying to churn through the mire. It seemed as if every other doorway led to a saloon, and one enterprising barber decided to combine his trade with that of bartender. A sign over his shop read:

> Rove not from *pole* to *pole*—the man lives here
> Whose razor's only equall'd by his beer . . .²⁴

Thievery, brawls, and duels were common, and the famous Bowie knife was a regular part of male attire. Pickpockets were especially troublesome, and Houston's tiny police force was powerless to do anything about them.

In streets knee-deep in mud, dotted with stranded wagons and carts, the two priests walked into the town from the boat landing. For over an hour they searched for lodgings to protect them from the cold rain pelting down that day and that would also be suitable for the celebration of mass.

The weather was what, then and now, veteran residents recognize as typical of Texas. A wet norther had blown in, and balmy weather had suddenly given way to the dead of winter—at least for a time. In their search for lodging, Timon and Llebaría discovered that rooms were scarce because Congress was in session. Timon had no letters of introduction, so circumstances looked bleak until they encountered an Irish woman they had met on shipboard during the trip from New Orleans. Seeing their plight, she obtained the permission of her close friend, a Protestant woman, for the priests to use a cabin that the friend owned adjacent to her own house. The cabin turned out to be in an excellent location since cabinet members and congressmen passed that way as they went to and from the story-and-a-half frame capitol building.[25]

On January 3, 1839, on an improvised altar in their cabin, the two priests offered their first mass in Houston. Afterwards, Timon began a religious survey of the town and found about three hundred who said they were Catholics. While some were only nominal, Timon was pleased when, just as in Galveston, large crowds packed the cabin and overflowed into the street at each of two masses.[26]

By that time Timon and Llebaría had met many congressmen, among whom were several Catholics: senators Juan Seguín from the district of San Antonio and John Dunn from the district of Goliad, Refugio and San Patricio; and representatives José Antonio Navarro from Bexar County, James Kerr from Jackson County, and John J. Linn from Victoria County, a signer of the petition sent to Bishop Blanc in 1837.

These and some other congressmen invited Timon to deliver a public address in the Hall of Representatives on Sunday afternoon. A large crowd assembled, and for an hour and a half Timon explained Catholic belief to an attentive audience of politicians and townspeople, including several Protestant clergymen. Timon was pleased at the reception his hearers gave him. He was an impressive orator, and while most of his hearers did not agree with all he had to say, they made courteous and appreciative comments.[27]

One of these was the republic's first president, David G. Burnet, an adventurer from New Jersey, now serving as vice president under President Mirabeau B. Lamar. Though a Protestant, Burnet was eager to talk further with Timon and, in the course of their conversation, expressed his disagreement with certain Catholic doctrines. Timon sensed that Burnet nonetheless respected what he disagreed with, and expressed to him the view that the things that troubled Burnet most about the Catholic church were abuses and not the church's actual teachings. It seemed to Timon that his comments helped give Burnet a clearer understanding of Catholic beliefs.[28]

If Timon made any converts during his stay in Houston, Burnet was not one of them, but Timon's manner and especially his eloquence, a quality much appreciated in that age, impressed Burnet and others like him and created a better environment for Houston's Catholics. Timon soon assembled subscribers to a fund for the erection of a church, but as with its counterpart in Galveston, three years would lapse before its completion.[29]

Timon's experience in both Galveston and Houston illustrates the success an eloquent speaker could have on the nineteenth-century frontier, an era and place unsaturated with electronic communication. Timon and others like him are indicative that Catholics were not aloof from the eloquent hortatorical endeavors of the day but used them successfully to help create an improved climate for Catholics on the frontier.[30]

Timon and Llebaría briefly met the new Texan president, Mirabeau B. Lamar, inaugurated the previous month. They found him cordial but not very interested in their mission. When Timon was introduced to Sam Houston, however, the former president expressed a high regard for the Catholic church and stated that he considered himself a Catholic.[31] If that is indeed what Houston really thought, he gave no indication of a desire to practice Catholicism, and politics may have been behind his statement. Houston's aim continued to be the annexation of Texas by the United States. Diplomatic recognition from Catholic foreign powers would strengthen Texas' position and consequently cause the United States to view annexation as a means of preventing the permanent establishment of a new nation, possibly allied to a European power, on its western frontier.

From this perspective, of course, but for a different end, it would have been to Lamar's advantage to proclaim himself a Catholic also, but instead the new president only greeted Timon in passing. In contrast to Houston, Lamar desired a permanently independent Texas and was then seeking diplomatic recognition in Europe.

Although Houston later became a Baptist after his marriage to Margaret Lea, he may have harbored some favorable sentiments toward the Catholic church at the time of his meeting with Timon. As an adult, having sought baptism and been refused by several Protestant clergymen, he had received this sacrament at the hands of Father José Antonio Díaz de León in Nacogdoches in 1833.[32] Since he easily could have evaded this, Houston may have had some sincerity in the matter, at least at the time.

Although Timon spent much time with public figures who could give him valuable information about conditions in Texas, he did not neglect the pastoral needs of Houston's Catholics. Finding a dying man lying in the street, Timon took him to Houston's primitive "hospital": a cabin with large cracks in the walls that readily let in the cold north wind. The dying man was a Catholic to whom Timon administered the appropriate sacraments while trying to quiet the hospital's overseer, who kept shouting and shaking his fist at those who cried out in their agony. The only source of heat for the building was a fire in a pit located in the center of the one room, with a pot of soup hung over it. There was no chimney, and the smoke escaped through the cracks in the walls. The man died while Timon was again trying to silence the overseer. After this experience, Timon wrote his superiors of his hope that Catholic hospital work might help alleviate such conditions in the future.[33]

In a lighter vein, Timon officiated at a wedding, and he and Llebaría probably baptized several infants while in Houston.[34]

Before the end of his first week in Houston, Timon decided it would be impossible to visit Victoria and San Antonio to the west or Nacogdoches and San Augustine to the north, as he had originally planned. Winter rains had inundated Texas' primitive roads, creating only muddy torrents in their place. In addition, Victoria, San Antonio, and the surrounding ranchos, where Father Llebaría had planned to minister in the Spanish language, were on the other side of the Brazos and Colorado Rivers, now so swollen by rains they could neither be forded nor crossed by ferry. Timon and Llebaría decided they would have to rely on Catholic congressmen and businessmen they met in Houston for information on these areas.[35] Unfortunately, this meant that certain aspects of Timon's report were based on hearsay.

On January 9, Timon and Llebaría left Houston by steamboat for Galveston on the first leg of their return trip to New Orleans. While still in Houston, Timon began writing his report on his abbreviated tour, and copies were prepared for the Vincentian authorities in France, who would then forward the information on to Rome, and for Blanc in New Orleans.[36]

Timon's report on Texas was cautiously optimistic: there was much potential for the Catholic church in Texas, he wrote, but the best missionaries possible must be sent, men able to withstand adverse conditions and able to inspire the highest public confidence. Timon estimated Texas' population at two hundred thousand, including Indians.[37] He estimated that about twelve thousand of these were Catholic but that more than half of this figure consisted of former colonists from the United States who in years past had declared a Catholic allegiance only to be allowed to settle in Texas.

He reported that San Antonio was the largest center of Catholic population, a town of about sixteen or seventeen hundred, of whom fifteen hundred were Catholics of Hispanic descent. Only about fifty of the Anglos there were Catholics. Timon wrote that he was told in Houston that the two priests in San Antonio were not living in celibacy. He referred here to Fathers Refugio de la Garza, pastor of San Fernando Church, and José Antonio Valdéz, now living in retirement. Timon concluded that if this were so, it would be best not to confront these clergy until his own or a successor's authority was firmly established. In addition, the parish church building, originally quite lovely, was in disrepair; a fire some years previously had left the roof damaged. However, his information indicated that the faith was very much alive among the Hispanic parishioners. There was, Timon wrote, much potential for the church in San Antonio, although it is obvious he believed a change in pastoral leadership was necessary. The communication of this conclusion, one thus far based on hearsay, to New Orleans, Paris, and Rome served only to create a general assumption that the hearsay was fact. Later when American and European clergy arrived in San Antonio, they already believed the worst, and for some, unfamiliarity with Spanish as well as with the culture of the Spanish Empire's northern borderlands made objectivity even more elusive.

In Goliad, Timon reported, all was desolation. Only fifteen or twenty Hispanic families remained, and church property there had suffered the ravages of the recent war. Timon was told that chalices, vestments, and other ornaments of worship from surrounding churches had been placed in the church at Goliad for safekeeping during the revolution but that all had been lost.

Southwest of Goliad, in Refugio, the situation seemed less grave. The church there, a former mission, was damaged but could be restored. Approximately forty Irish families, Timon was told, lived in the vicinity and were anxious for the church to be revived and a school established. Congressmen from the region believed—too optimistically, as events proved—that church lands could provide an income for the school once the government recognized the church's title to the large tracts formerly belonging to the mission.

Farther to the southwest at San Patricio the church and adjacent hall had been completely destroyed during the revolution.

To the east of Goliad, at Victoria, conditions were better. Out of a population of about 240, 200 were Catholics, mostly of either Hispanic or Irish ancestry. Timon reported accurately that a church was still standing there: a frame structure with two bell towers.

To the east in Nacogdoches, he wrote, there were about 600 Catholics, about equally Hispanic and Anglo. An aged layman led prayers on Sundays and officiated at funerals. Since the death of Father Díaz de León, the religious situation for local Catholics had deteriorated continually. Timon had been informed that in a renewal of hostilities between pro- and anti-Mexican factions in 1838, the church building was burned, and now another religious group was attempting to erect a building on the site. Timon warned that while the constitution of the republic prohibited the favoring of one religious group over another, local officials in Texas possessed much authority and could easily discriminate to the disadvantage of Catholics. If dependable, upright priests were not sent to Texas soon to defend the church's property rights, all of it might very well be lost.

Worse, however, would be the loss of people, Timon wrote. Other religious groups were beginning to pour money into Texas from their missionary foundations in the United States. While uneducated self-proclaimed preachers abounded, it seemed to Timon that the kind of clergymen the organized denominations were sending into Texas were better educated than their counterparts he had known in the Mississippi Valley. This meant that Catholic priests sent to Texas must be exceptionally learned and well able to defend their faith without giving offense.

In addition to the areas mentioned in his report, Timon recommended that missionaries be sent to Matagorda Bay, a debarkation point for immigrants, and along the Sabine River, where he expected Catholics from Louisiana would immigrate.[38]

Timon and Llebaría arrived in New Orleans on January 14. Llebaría returned to the seminary on Bayou La Fourche and apparently was never sent by his order back to Texas. Timon, after conferring with Blanc and leading a retreat for the hospital sisters in New Orleans, returned by boat to St. Louis with the hope that soon missionary volunteers would be forthcoming for the work in Texas.

The Texan republic that Timon and Llebaría visited in the winter of 1838–39 was a land caught up in rapid change, political, economic, and social. The vast influx of immigrants was changing the face of Texas and would continue to do so for decades to come. This had been obvious to Timon in Galveston when he beheld the new dwellings, shops, and warehouses. In Houston, inland and more rustic than Galveston, the atmosphere was still the same: in the muddy streets amidst the new log buildings and incessant clamor of loquacious politicians, the land-seeking immigrant was ever present.

What may not have been so obvious that winter, at least to a visitor, was the political complexity of the new republic. Hardly more than a few days prior to the priests' arrival in Houston, Mirabeau B. Lamar had succeeded Sam Houston as president. Timon and Llebaría may have observed the new president accompanied by his special honor guard, smartly outfitted in new white-trousered uniforms. Lamar liked the guard, and it greeted the new president whenever he arrived in the capital, even when the men had to march through knee-deep mud and lose their shoes in the process.[39] Such occasions were perhaps symbolic of the insecure republic's attempt to find a place in the community of nations. The new president, Lamar, was doing his best to find this place and to make it permanent.

By January, 1839, former president Houston was serving in the lower house of the Texan Congress. The constitution called for three-year terms for the chief executive, who could not succeed himself, but the first presidential term was of only two years' duration. Lamar's term, which began in December, 1838, was the first one of regular length. In his term, however, Houston accomplished much by ending the turmoil of the revolutionary period and creating a measure of internal stability in the new republic. After virtually disbanding the Texas army when it became almost entirely made up of obstreperous newly arrived volunteers, Houston relied upon militia units and the Texas Rangers for defense against the Indians. However, his chief means of defense against the Indian tribes was to pursue a peace policy toward them and avoid the outbreak of violence. Although a small navy was created by Congress, Houston's policy toward Mexico was one that sought to keep a "cold" war from erupting into bloodshed.

Early in Houston's administration, Congress passed the Boundary Statute of 1836, which ambitiously set the western boundary of Texas along the Rio Grande to its source in the Rocky Mountains and thence northward to the 42nd parallel. During his first administration, Houston made no attempt to uphold the land claims of Texas beyond San Antonio to the west or the Nueces River to the south. To have done so would have been to transgress his peace effort, a policy best suited for a Texas that, in his view, was only waiting for annexation to the United States. Until that time, peace and a domestic strategy that would insure order best typified his policies. It was better to expend energy turning the old municipalities into counties and creating new ones than to create debts and provoke further conflict by pursuing an ambitious foreign policy.

Not all Texans favored annexation, though most did. Well before the end of Houston's first term, it was obvious that the leader of the anti-Houston, antiannexation faction was the vice president, the ex-Georgian Mirabeau B. Lamar, who announced his candidacy for the presidency in early 1838.

The election, held in the fall preceding Timon's and Llebaría's visit to Texas, was one of the strangest in the history of the republic. The Houston faction was strong, stronger than the opposition, but its guiding light could not be a candidate, since the constitution forbade consecutive terms for the chief executive. This created dissension and indecision for the Houston faction. Initially, Peter W. Grayson, a former attorney general in both Houston's and Burnet's cabinets, was selected as the Houston faction's candidate. Grayson, however, soon committed suicide while on a visit to Tennessee. James W. Collingsworth was next selected, but he drowned while traveling by boat from Galveston. A few weeks before the election, yet a third candidate, Robert Wilson, was presented to an electorate who had hardly heard of him. The result of all this happenstance was an overwhelming victory for Lamar.

Lamar's vision was of a Texas that was independent, powerful, and expansionist. He wrongly assumed from his electoral triumph that the Congress and the voters at large shared his views. While the Congress did not hesitate to show him the error of this assumption, he remained undaunted. However, his vision required money, and Texas did not have it. But his policies did have results. The capital was moved in October, 1839, to the new town of Austin, far to the west of Houston, on the Colorado River. This was done for two reasons: first, Houston was named for the former president; and second, but more important, the new site was on the western periphery of settlement where the need to protect the capital city and the government would help undergird Lamar's policy of driving Indian tribes westward and beyond the line of settlement. Anti-Indian views generally had achieved extra support when disaffected Cherokees joined Vicente Córdova of Nacogdoches in the pro-Mexican uprising in 1838 (the hostilities Timon had been told about during his fact-finding tour). The Cherokees were angry over the Texan Senate's rejection of a treaty giving them land in East Texas for which they had negotiated with Sam Houston at the time of the revolution. The uprising was put down, but the new president used the incident to support his decision to drive the Cherokees from Texas. The Cherokee chief, Bowles, agreed to move north into present-day Oklahoma, the "Indian Territory" into which the United States was then moving several of its eastern tribes. But Bowles procrastinated while he readied his forces, and on July 15, 1839, he attacked Texan forces in the Battle of the Neches. In an encounter the next day, Bowles was killed, and after another battle, the Cherokees finally retreated across the Red River into Indian Territory.

In the west, where the Comanches had been a barrier to expansion since the time of the Spanish Empire, settlers had never been safe. Oftentimes Comanche policy was to kill the men in a frontier settlement and enslave or adopt into their tribe the women and children, although occasionally such captives were sold or ransomed. Cynthia Ann Parker, mother of the great Comanche chief Quanah Parker, was captured in such a raid when she was nine years old.

In 1839, Lamar's administration became aware that a number of these captives were in the hands of various Comanche bands, but these Indians were such a formidable foe that the government saw little chance of freeing them. However, in January, 1840, several Comanche chiefs rode into San Antonio and in the name of the various Comanche bands requested a parley. A meeting was scheduled for March in the so-called Council House, the site of Las Casas Reales (the government buildings) where the town council convened in Spanish and Mexican times. The chiefs promised to bring all captured women so that sale of them could be arranged for with Texan representatives. Neither side proved honest in dealing with the other. The Indians did not plan to bring and sell all their captives, and the Texans, who suspected this, conceived a plan by which they would hold the parleying chiefs as hostages until the women were released.

In March, approximately sixty-five Comanches, including twelve prominent chiefs, arrived in San Antonio. They brought one female captive in her teens. The girl was emaciated, had burns about the face, and showed other signs of abuse. She tearfully revealed that about fifteen other women were being held west of town and that the Indians planned to ransom them one at a time. A few remarks were exchanged between the Comanches and government agents in the Council House before the plan to capture and hold the Indians was launched. A number of Texas Rangers were on hand, and a fight ensued in which most of the Comanches and some of the Rangers were killed.[40]

This event gave both sides cause for renewed rage and opened a period of even greater bloodshed in which the Comanches ranged well beyond San Antonio to places like Victoria and Linnville. Much of Central Texas was enveloped by the gory struggle between Indian and settler.

As these uncertain conditions were developing, Timon began searching for priests to go to Texas. Soon two Vincentian volunteers, Joseph Paquín and Jean Pierre Chandy, both of whom were then stationed in Louisiana, informed Timon of their willingness to go.[41] Paquín, a Missouri native and professor on leave from St. Mary-of-the-Barrens College, a school for undergraduates operated in conjunction with the seminary, was at the time serving as the school's representative in Louisiana, raising funds and recruiting students. The French-born Chandy was currently assigned to the Vincentian seminary in Bayou La Fourche. Timon laid out a route for them: towns and ranches in the west, where most of the Catholics lived, were to be visited first, except that the largest of these, San Antonio, was to be avoided since neither priest was competent to deal with the alleged irregularities that Timon believed existed there. After visiting in the west, the priests were instructed to separate, with Paquín going to Houston and Galveston and Chandy moving northeastward to Nacogdoches and San Augustine.

Having completed their Lenten and Easter responsibilities, Paquín and Chandy left New Orleans on April 12, 1839. By going to Texas when they did, they hoped to provide the Catholics they visited with the rare opportunity of fulfilling their Easter duty of going to confession and receiving Holy Communion. The period during which this could be done extended to Trinity Sunday, which that year fell on May 26. Their journey into tumultuous Texas lasted but six weeks, and while they baptized twenty-five children and three adults, they did not encounter the numbers of Catholics Timon had hoped they would.[42]

Coincidental to Paquín's and Chandy's visit that year, another priest, the Abbé N. B. Anduze, was also in Texas. Anduze was French, and years before he had served as pastor of Natchitoches, Louisiana. Now, in 1839, he was a chaplain of the French fleet that was in the Gulf because of strained relations between Mexico and France. The Lamar administration took these difficulties as an occasion to press especially hard for diplomatic recognition from France, and Anduze came to Texas to discuss the possibility, raised by Lamar, of French-Texan cooperation in a war against Mexico. Lamar communicated his offer informally to the French consul in New Orleans, who forwarded it to the commander of the French fleet, Admiral Baudin. Baudin's response was to dispatch Abbé Anduze to find out how much aid Texas was willing to offer and what was expected in return—which, of course, was diplomatic recognition. By the time Anduze got in touch with Texan officials, France and Mexico had peacefully settled their differences, but Lamar assured Anduze of Texas help should hostilities arise in the future between France and Mexico. Lamar's efforts paid off when in October, 1839, France became the first European power to extend diplomatic recognition to the Republic of Texas.

While in Texas, Abbé Anduze also discussed the affairs of the Catholic church with government officials. He later informed Bishop Blanc in New Orleans that certain Texan officials harbored adverse feelings toward Fr. Miguel Muldoon, a priest who occasionally had visited Austin's colony years before and apparently was the only priest some of them had ever seen. Anduze's letter carried allegations of immorality against the oft-maligned cleric and introduced a new one, that of atheism! The gist of his letter was that Blanc must exert all possible efforts to see that only the best of priests be sent to Texas since Muldoon had left so much to be overcome.[43]

Probably what brought up the subject of Father Muldoon was that he was back in Texas early that year. It is likely that what concerned Anduze most was that Muldoon, according to Anduze's sources, was claiming to be the bishop-designate of Texas. And he was back in the news as well: a letter he wrote to Sam Houston requesting information about the battle of San Jacinto was published in the *Galveston Daily News*.[44] The letter was apparently written as a result of Muldoon's meeting with Bernard E. Bee in New Orleans as the latter was on his way to Veracruz as an unofficial emissary of the Texan government. Bee hoped to convince authorities there to recognize the independence of Texas. Muldoon apparently offered his assistance, but Bee's mission came to nothing.

Muldoon was an enigmatic figure, loved by some, hated by others. He was called lax in religious practice by some in Austin's colony—the same ones, it is easy to suspect, who would have complained loudest if he had been strict. He was called immoral, yet all that is really known is that he drank wine and brandy just as most of the colonists did. The fact that he was a Catholic priest, of course, made him persona non grata with some. In the eyes of Texan officials, however, he should have been a hero: he had aided the imprisoned Austin in Mexico City and, hardly two years before Anduze's visit to Texas, had assisted in the escape of a Texan diplomat from prison. In April, 1837, William H. Wharton, on board a ship captured by a Mexican force off the Texas coast at Velasco, was taken to Matamoros and imprisoned. Muldoon smuggled a priest's cassock into the prison for Wharton to use as a disguise. After Muldoon taught him some appropriate Latin phrases, Wharton escaped and made his way into Texas.[45]

In direct contrast to the mood of Lamar's officials in 1839, several years later (early in the second Houston administration), when Muldoon would be back in Texas again, the Texan secretary of state would address to him the following laudatory letter:

> I embrace the occasion of your departure from the city to do myself the pleasure of expressing my very friendly regards for you personally and my individual appreciation for the many manifestations you have evinced of your kindness towards Texas and her citizens on different distinguished occasions. In these sentiments I am also happy to assure you His Excellency, the President of the Republic, unites with me in sincere wishes for your future welfare, prosperity, and happiness. The people of Texas will not cease to have an abiding recollection of the great friendship you evinced, and the valuable service you rendered our distinguished Fellow Citizen, Gen. S. F. Austin, while detained a prisoner in Mexico by the Government of that country.[46]

Whatever the truth about Muldoon's character, the allegation voiced by Lamar's officials that Muldoon was claiming to be the bishop-designate for Texas was a cause of serious alarm for Blanc and Timon. It is possible, of course, that Muldoon never made the claim attributed to him and that political factionalism was behind the allegation.[47] Probably at Blanc's suggestion, however, Anduze published in the *National Intelligencer* a statement that "the Bishop of New Orleans alone has jurisdiction over the Catholic Church in Texas and that priests who come unprovided with credentials from him have no right to exercise the Catholic ministry in the Republic."[48]

Actually the jurisdictional status of Texas was not as simple as Anduze implied, for while Blanc could commission priests for work in Texas, Rome had yet to formalize a jurisdictional structure for Texas. Aware of this and believing the charge against Muldoon, Timon wrote his Vincentian superior in Paris that prolonged delay in Rome in making further jurisdictional provision for Texas would be extremely regrettable, "because from time to time priests, uncommissioned and without faculties, enter the Republic and exploit religion for their own ends. Only recently a Mr. Muldoune [*sic*], a former Vicar-General to the Bishop of Monterrey, foisted himself upon the civil authorities and the faithful as 'the Bishop-elect of Texas.'"[49] If Muldoon ever made such a claim, nothing more was heard of his doing so, but further delay in Rome could only seem to Timon an invitation for further confusion.

Timon was pleased when he received that spring a request to go to Texas from two priests on the faculty of St. Joseph's College in Bardstown, Kentucky. Fathers George W. Haydon and Edward Clarke hoped to accompany some Kentucky Catholic families who were immigrating to Texas and to establish churches in the frontier communities they hoped to build.[50]

In December, Haydon and Clarke arrived in New Orleans and Blanc gave them the necessary faculties or credentials for their work in Texas. Shortly after Christmas, with a letter of introduction to President Lamar written by Anduze, who was then in New Orleans, they boarded a boat for Texas.[51]

Actually, there were a large number of Kentucky Catholic immigrants already in Texas, and Timon concluded that with Indian problems on the rise in the west, the priests should go first to the Kentucky Catholic settlers along the Lavaca and Navidad Rivers and then proceed farther west as conditions allowed. They arrived in Texas in the last days of December and before the end of the first week of January, 1840, were at the Brazos River, where they encountered about one hundred Catholics who had settled near Richmond. Haydon and Clarke remained there through January 6, the Epiphany, when they celebrated mass in a log cabin with as much solemnity as circumstances allowed. The people led a spartan life, Haydon recalled later, with a diet of only corn bread, beef, and coffee; they had to work hard in harsh circumstances, but their unsophisticated life, he concluded, was good.

While in the vicinity of the Brazos, Clarke became ill and remained behind in Richmond while Haydon proceeded westward to Victoria, Refugio, and various settlements along the Lavaca River. From there he went to San Antonio, where Fr. Refugio de la Garza courteously extended to him the use of San Fernando Church for the celebration of mass. Furthermore, de la Garza gave Haydon a much needed set of vestments and a chalice for use in his travels. Nonetheless, from conversations with Blanc in New Orleans, Haydon was prepared to find an irregular situation in San Antonio and later believed he had in fact found one. Though he did not speak Spanish, he wrote Blanc that both Hispanic and Anglo San Antonians assured him new pastoral leadership was required. He assumed from what he was told that neither de la Garza nor the retired Father Valdéz was honoring his vows of celibacy. Writing after his short visit, he advised Blanc that a Spanish-speaking priest should be sent to replace de la Garza.[52]

After San Antonio, Haydon went eastward to Houston and Galveston and back to Richmond.[53] In the spring Haydon set out again, this time in company with Clarke, who by then had recovered his health. After traveling three months and approximately eight hundred miles, they were back on the Brazos at Richmond in mid-June, 1840. On this journey they saw results from Haydon's earlier trip: the completion of repairs to the former mission at Refugio and the beginnings of a church on the Lavaca River at Brown's Settlement, about three miles west of present-day Hallettsville. On his first visit to Victoria, Haydon discovered Our Lady of Guadalupe Church being used by local officials as both a courthouse and a place for interdenominational worship, but now on his second visit he learned that the Catholic congressman John J. Linn had initiated proceedings to have the building returned to the Catholic congregation.

Haydon's short report to Blanc, written in Richmond in June, 1840, included this postscript: "I should be glad to hear if any thing is doing for Texas in the way of clergy—I should like to divide these long routes."[54]

Unknown to him something had been done, and help was soon to be forthcoming. Father Haydon's own tenure in Texas was short, however. Yellow fever once more struck the coast in the fall of 1841. A settlement on Galveston Bay at the present site of Morgan's Point was hit hard, and Haydon died there of the disease after going to minister to the victims.[55] Edward Clarke labored on productively in Texas until he returned to Louisville in 1856.[56]

THREE
A New Beginning

IN his report to Bishop Blanc in January, 1839, following his visit to Galveston and Houston, Timon recommended that Texas be established as a diocese to be temporarily administered by the bishop of New Orleans. Rejecting this proposal, Blanc advised Rome to immediately establish a prefecture apostolic in Texas with Timon as its head with the title prefect apostolic. Such an administrative unit may be administered by a priest rather than a bishop, and it was apparently Blanc's belief that such an arrangement would suffice until a clearer picture of the Texan situation developed.[1]

During the months of waiting for Rome to act, the Lamar administration considered advancing its own proposal for the reorganization of the church as a means of furthering Texan hopes in Europe, especially in France. The goal was the same as that of Lamar's concurrent negotiations with Abbé Anduze: French diplomatic recognition. The proposal originated with William Henry Daingerfield, a Maryland native and a Catholic, who was sent by Lamar in 1839 as a diplomatic agent to New York. Daingerfield began corresponding with the Texan minister to the United States in Washington about a proposal he hoped would be forwarded to the then unofficial Texan representative in Paris and from there to Rome. His proposal asked that an archdiocese be organized in Texas, with San Antonio, the center of the Catholic population, as the see city. If enacted, Daingerfield believed, it would increase the likelihood of diplomatic recognition in Europe by dispelling any notion that the revolution against Mexico had likewise been directed against the Catholic church and would have the added effect of increasing European Catholic immigration. The idea was presented to Lamar, who favored it, and the proposal was sent to Paris, but the matter was dropped when France extended the desired diplomatic recognition in October, 1839.[2]

Ironically, while Rome was perfecting a plan of action regarding Texas, Bp. Joseph Rosati of St. Louis was trying to get Timon named his own coadjutor bishop. This office, if accepted, would have precluded Timon's doing further work in Texas. In October, 1839, Rome notified the Vincentian superior general in Paris, Fr. Jean Baptiste Nozo, that a prefecture apostolic was to be established in Texas, just as Bishop Blanc had suggested, but that Timon should not be appointed as prefect since he was being considered for another position. Since the Vincentians had previously agreed to send priests to Texas and partially fund the work there, Rome was leaving to them the selection of the prefect apostolic. On September 7, 1839, Timon received from Rome the appointment as coadjutor bishop of St. Louis. So determined was he not to accept it, however, that the day after receiving the official documents from Rome, they were on their way back, along with a letter stating his wish not to accept the assignment.[3]

After learning that Rome was not going to insist on Timon's accepting the St. Louis appointment, the Vincentian superior general wrote Timon, his choice from the beginning, that he was appointing him the prefect apostolic of Texas. Timon did not receive these documents until April 12, 1840.

In addition to his new role as prefect apostolic, Timon was to continue as the Vincentian provincial superior for the United States. As prefect, in addition to administrative duties, Timon was given authority within the prefecture to administer the sacrament of confirmation and could, with oil blessed by a bishop, confer the minor orders, which in the Catholic church of that day preceded the major orders of deacon and priest; he could also carry out some other functions usually reserved to a bishop, such as dedicating churches and blessing chalices, patens, and cornerstones, as well as deciding certain marriage questions. He also would have authority over any church schools that might be established in the prefecture. His authority over the priests within his jurisdiction was to be much like that of a bishop: he would dispense the faculties necessary for a priest to officiate within the prefecture and could withdraw them for reason of public scandal.[4]

The establishment of the prefecture apostolic officially separated a portion of the territory claimed by the Republic of Texas from the jurisdiction of the Mexican church.[5] The prefecture did not include all of what the republic grandiosely claimed in the Boundary Statute of 1836, but only that area the republic effectively controlled—that is, the area above the Nueces River and east of the line of settlement from San Antonio to the Red River.

Simultaneously to his appointment, Timon was informed that he could appoint a resident representative in Texas if he wished, since his duties as Vincentian provincial superior would require him to be away from Texas for long periods. This special assistant was to be a fellow Vincentian of Timon's own choosing. Timon selected his friend Fr. Jean Marie Odin to fill this role with the title of vice prefect. Odin was currently on the faculty of St. Mary-of-the-Barrens Seminary and like Timon was a veteran missionary in the frontier communities of southern Missouri and Illinois. Timon had long considered Odin for work in Texas and had wanted to send him there in early 1839, but sent Paquin and Chandy when it proved impossible

The Rt. Rev. Jean Marie Odin, vice prefect of Texas, 1840–41; Vicar Apostolic of Texas, 1841–47; and first bishop of Galveston, 1847–61. Photo circa 1860, courtesy Catholic Archives of Texas, Austin.

at the time for Odin to leave his duties in Missouri. In June, 1839, he had also recommended Odin to the Vincentian motherhouse in Paris as an ideal choice to head either a diocese or a prefecture in Texas.[6]

Just as in Timon's case, however, there was opposition to Odin's going to Texas. Bp. Joseph Rosati of St. Louis, also a Vincentian, was reluctant to lose a valued priest who had worked in his diocese for almost twenty years, and Archbishop Samuel Eccleston of Baltimore and several other influential members of the American hierarchy wanted to keep Odin available for appointment to the see of Detroit.[7] In April, 1840, Timon visited Rosati in St. Louis and apparently reconciled him to the loss of Odin as well as the other Vincentians he was sending to Texas with him. Without Rosati's opposition, other bishops could not prevent Odin's leaving for his new assignment.

At the time of his appointment, in addition to his seminary duties, Odin was Timon's chief assistant in administering the Vincentian province. This meant that Timon was losing a valued colleague in one area in order to gain his services in another.

Odin was French. He was born in the village of Hauteville on February 25, 1800. In 1814, he entered a preparatory seminary at Verriere and later went on to study at the Sulpician *grande seminaire* of St. Irenaeus in Lyon. During his school days the young man excelled in oratory, which especially helped make him an effective missionary in frontier America.

As a seminarian, Odin became interested in going to America when his home village priest, the future bishop of New Orleans, Antoine Blanc, went there as a missionary. He was further moved in this direction on hearing Bp. Louis Dubourge of Louisiana when he visited France in 1816. The young Odin arrived in New Orleans in July, 1822. He was permitted to complete his studies for the priesthood at St. Mary-of-the-Barrens Seminary in Perry County, Missouri. After briefly visiting his friend Antoine Blanc at his mission station at Pointe Coupee, Louisiana, Odin journeyed up the Mississippi to the seminary in Missouri and there met John Timon, who had just begun his seminary studies. Odin was ordained to the priesthood there on May 4, 1823. While at the seminary, he decided to enter the Vincentian order.

Upon ordination to the priesthood, Odin was appointed to teach philosophy at the seminary from which he had just graduated. Unaware of the long career he would later have as a missionary bishop on the Texas frontier, Odin was disappointed that he had not been assigned to a post among either the Indian tribes or the log cabin settlements of the region. This disappointment was partly assuaged when in the years ahead he was permitted to make several missionary visits to the tribes in the area as well as weekly visits to frontier cabins. On these visits he soon learned the ways and attitudes of the American yeoman farmers as he sat by their firesides and shared their pork and cornmeal fare. Such experiences in the 1820s and 1830s were a fit preparation for his future work in Texas among a people living under similarly harsh conditions. Even in the relatively sheltered confines of the seminary, Odin did not have a soft existence. His day began at four in the morning when he celebrated mass. Even with academic responsibilities, he was subject at any time to being summoned for a sick call, and then on Saturdays and Sundays he was out riding cross-country on muddy trails visiting the mission stations for which his order was responsible. In 1825, to his sister in France, Odin wrote: "God watches over us with such paternal care and goodness, that no accident has yet occurred; frequently my horse has fallen; the branches of trees could many times have endangered my life; serpents which abound almost everywhere, are often between the legs of my horse; bears have fled before me, and amidst all these perils, nothing serious has ever befallen me."[8]

Events occurred in 1833 that took Odin to Europe and brought him notice from church officials both in the United States and in Rome. That year, Bishop Rosati of St. Louis asked Odin to accompany him to the Second Council of Baltimore as his personal theologian, and at the council's conclusion Odin was delegated to carry the council's decrees to Rome for approval. He was received there by Pope Gregory XVI as well as various officials of the curia. The pope was so interested in what Odin had to say about missionary work on the American frontier that he granted him a total of three audiences during his stay in Rome.[9]

Odin remained in Italy almost a year raising money for the Vincentian mission work in America and to pay the cost of passage for a number of volunteer missionaries going back with him to work in America. Returning to St. Mary-of-the-Barrens Seminary in September, 1835, he continued his academic and pastoral duties for the next 4½ years.[10] His success in raising money and attracting missionary volunteers plus his knowledge of Rome and the curia made him well suited for his future labors in Texas.

Odin began his journey to Texas on Saturday, May 2, 1840, when he left St. Mary-of-the-Barrens Seminary for the Mississippi River port town of Cape Girardeau, Missouri. Early Monday afternoon, he boarded the riverboat *Meteor* for the long trip down to New Orleans. Joining him at Cape Girardeau were Fr. Eudald Estany, Fr. Miguel Calvo, and Bro. Ramón Sala, three other Vincentians who planned to work in Texas. They were among those Spanish Vincentians who in 1838, along with Llebaría, had left their studies in France for work in America.

The steamboat churned its way slowly along the serpentine course of the wide river. At least the current made southbound voyages faster, and this time the current was even swifter than usual because of high water. Traveling day and night, the boat reached Memphis on the fifth and by midday Thursday was approaching Natchez, Mississippi. Suddenly, with churning blue-black clouds swirling in the sky overhead, a violent hailstorm engulfed the craft in midstream; windows in the pilothouse, dining salon, and cabins were shattered, and the missionaries and other passengers scurried for cover. The captain was forced to halt the multistoried craft in midstream. For seemingly endless minutes the huge hailstones pelted the boat and made large pockmarks on the surface of the water as far as Odin and the other anxious passengers could see. Then, almost as suddenly as it had come, the hailstorm was over. The paddlewheel turned once more, and the riverboat began its way toward Natchez, which promised to offer a respite to the passengers.[11]

As their boat approached the Natchez wharf, however, a horrifying sight confronted the passengers: a large part of the town lay destroyed by a tornado that had passed through only minutes before. Buildings were leveled; people lay dead and injured, including many who had been aboard two steamboats lying in port at the time. One was now sunk; the other still floated but had been torn apart above the waterline and was now laden with dead and dying passengers. Numerous flatboats also had been sunk. Disembarking, Odin and the other priests began ministering to the dying and offering prayers for the dead. Odin was saddened to discover that one of his acquaintances, a student at St. Louis University, was among the dead passengers from one of the other riverboats. That evening in his diary, Odin reflected that the hand of God had spared those on board his ship for had the captain not stopped in midstream for those few minutes during the hailstorm, they, too, would have been in port when the tempest struck and would have suffered the same fate as those on board the two boats destroyed at the Natchez wharf.[12]

Odin arrived in New Orleans early on Saturday, May 9; Estany, Calvo, and Sala disembarked the previous day at Donaldsonville in order to go to the Vincentian seminary on Bayou La Fourche where they were to lodge until joining Odin several weeks later in New Orleans for the last leg of the trip to Texas. In May and June, Odin visited various churches and convents in New Orleans speaking about the work in Texas and trying to raise money for it. While in New Orleans, Odin met the new French chargé d'affaires to the Republic of Texas, Alphonse Dubois de Saligny, who would later provide needed support for his and Timon's efforts. In early June, Odin even embarked for Mobile to speak there and at the Jesuit college at Spring Hill nearby. While no money was forthcoming during his Alabama trip, he did receive gifts of vestments and altar linens for use in Texas.[13]

At last, on July 1, 1840, Odin, Calvo, Estany, and Sala boarded the schooner *Henry*, which began its way toward the Gulf the next morning. The ship was crowded, and that coupled with the intense July heat made traveling unpleasant. But good company and an evening Gulf breeze helped alleviate the difficulties. Of the more than ninety passengers, Odin discovered that about two-thirds professed to be Catholics; they were mostly immigrants to Texas from Germany, Ireland, France, Holland, and the United States. Odin got on well not only with them but also with the non-Catholics, who, he noted, seemed to be free of prejudice toward him. He also met some Catholic merchants from San Antonio and Victoria with whom he discussed the state of the church in both places.

On Wednesday, July 8, the *Henry* entered Lavaca Bay on the Texas coast. After stopping at the Texan customshouse, the ship tried to move across the bay toward the port of Linnville, on the site of present-day Port Lavaca; however, the ship ran aground and part of its cargo had to be unloaded. The ship and its passengers did not reach port until late Sunday night, and it was early Monday morning, July 13, before they actually set foot on dry land.[14]

As had happened to Timon in Galveston in 1838, Odin almost immediately met two old friends in the small port town, two merchants formerly of Cape Girardeau and now doing business in Linnville.[15]

Odin and his fellow missionaries now headed for Victoria, twenty-five miles inland, which they learned was experiencing an epidemic, probably cholera. They also heard that Indians were frequently raiding ranchos in the region and attacking travelers going to the interior. For this reason the missionaries decided to travel in company with a large caravan of merchants, cart drivers, and immigrants. Arriving in Victoria on the sixteenth, Odin decided to leave Estany there to serve as pastor of Our Lady of Guadalupe Church, since the epidemic in the town increased the need for a priest. Estany was Spanish and his English was at least understandable, which well suited him to work in a community where the Catholics were either Hispanic or Irish. In addition to the Catholics in the town, there were many living out in the surrounding countryside in what had once been the Martín de León Colony. Other Catholic families resided at Goliad, which Estany was to visit occasionally.

While in Victoria, Odin met with John J. Linn, whose efforts had recently led to the city's recognizing the church's title to the parish building as an inalienable grant from the government of Mexico. Since the building was not yet cleaned and repaired, mass was celebrated in Linn's home.[16] Odin left no mention of Fr. John Thomas Malloy, possibly indicating that Malloy either was not living in Victoria at the time or was deceased.

Taking with him Calvo and Sala, Odin continued on to San Antonio with the caravan. The merchants were from New Orleans and had hired about thirty carts to carry their merchandise to San Antonio. The Hispanic cart owners for whom this was a regular business were familiar with the roads and with necessary precautions against Indian attacks. The thirty or so German immigrants increased the group's size still further, providing a measure of security in numbers. But the trip allowed few comforts: it took nine days to cover the distance to San Antonio. The travelers hoped that game along the route would be an ample food supply and therefore neglected to buy sufficient provisions for the journey. To their chagrin, only a little game was found along the trail, so an occasional dry biscuit and cup of coffee had to suffice. The precautions against the Indian threat were of no avail against hunger, thirst, heat, and exhaustion.[17]

The caravan left Victoria on Tuesday, July 21, and by evening had reached Coleto Creek. The next day early, they reached the rancho of the Fernández family, where several other Catholic families resided. They learned that Indians, probably Comanches, had stolen all the horses there just a few days before. That evening the travelers stopped for the night about six miles from Goliad. While the caravan paused in that village the next morning, Odin surveyed the condition of the presidio chapel, which had served a community of about fifteen hundred Catholics prior to the revolution. He was struck by the resilient beauty of the almost deserted village, which with its church, Our Lady of Loretto, was partially surrounded by the old and ruined fortification of La Bahía. By that hot summer of 1840, only seven Hispanic, two Anglo, and two Irish families lived at or near the site.

Odin and the others remained in Goliad all that day: the weather was too hot, and food and water too scarce, to travel farther. As the caravan went on its way the next morning, the missionaries saw the ruined Mission Espíritu Santo standing not far from the village. Over the next six days, conditions worsened for the travelers. Wagons broke down; shade trees and water were virtually nonexistent: "We were often happy if we found a little hole where we disputed with the frogs for a few drops of dirty and disgusting water." With the scalding heat and brackish water, several travelers including Odin became ill with a fever. Some medicine that Brother Sala fortunately had brought with him from New Orleans provided them some relief. Because of the heat, they began to travel only at night, but the scarcity of shade in the daytime made it difficult to rest. Relief from the sun came mainly from the shade of the carts or the hospitality of an occasional rancho such as the Rancho de San Bartólomo, about fifty miles from San Antonio, where they spent an entire day. Travel became easier as they neared San Antonio, since they encountered more ranchos. On the twenty-eighth, they enjoyed the hospitality of Don Erasmo Seguín, whose son, Juan, had commanded troops in Houston's army at San Jacinto. While there, Odin visited several other ranchos nearby and also a peaceful band of Lipan Apaches encamped in the area.

At last on Thursday, July 30, the caravan arrived in San Antonio. After obtaining lodgings at the home of the Casiano family, Odin, Calvo and Sala were impressed by the Spanish appearance of the town, with its buildings almost all of stone and adobe, bearing the indelible mark of its colonial past.

Odin soon turned his attention to the rumors he had heard about the

San Antonio clergymen, Fr. Refugio de la Garza, pastor of San Fernando Church, and Fr. José Antonio Valdéz, pastor of Goliad until forced out by the revolution. Odin carried with him documents from the bishop of New Orleans empowering him to withdraw faculties from both priests if conditions warranted it. However, Odin was not sure his authority would be recognized since he was a stranger from the United States representing a bishop in that country. Odin called at the homes of both priests and believed he saw evidence that each priest was living with a wife and children. When he announced to Father de la Garza that he and Calvo intended to celebrate mass at San Fernando Church the next Sunday, according to Odin the pastor gave his consent.

Mass that Sunday was well attended and two sermons were preached, one in Spanish, the other in English. After reaching his own conclusion about de la Garza's lifestyle, Odin found it easy to believe stories told him by some that the priest was extremely neglectful of his pastoral duties. On Monday morning he went to de la Garza's residence to inform him that he was removing him as pastor and withdrawing his faculties to function as a priest. Odin showed him the documents from Blanc giving him authority for this action. Odin then requested and received from de la Garza the parish registers and the keys to San Fernando Church.

Odin heard that Father de la Garza had sold some of the parish silver as well as some from the abandoned missions. Unfamiliar as Odin was with certain historical circumstances, this rumor suggested to him that something akin to thievery had occurred. What Odin did not understand was that under the Mexican government, when a mission was secularized, its property could be sold or otherwise disposed of by the local *ayuntamiento,* or municipal council, as the research of Félix D. Almaráz, Jr., indicates. An individual who acquired this property from the *ayuntamiento* was free to sell it. Perhaps Odin was was too ready to believe what rumor, rather than justice, laid at the aged priest's door.[18]

Matters worsened for Father de la Garza when during the same week he was arrested by Texan officials and taken to Austin due to a charge that he had written a letter to the Centralist general Mariano Arista. De la Garza was severely reprimanded in Austin but was allowed to return home in mid-August. De la Garza's political interests were not new: he had represented San Antonio in the Mexican national congress in 1824. In this period after the collapse of the government of the emperor, Agustin de Iturbide, this congress drafted a new constitution which provided for a republican form of government for the Mexican nation. That de la Garza was a diocesan priest rather than a member of a religious order had made political involvement easier for him.

Soon after Odin withdrew the faculties of the priesthood from de la Garza, he withdrew them from Father Valdéz as well.

In the years before 1840, much of the world in which these Hispanic priests had always lived collapsed. Ties to the only sources of ecclesiastical authority they had ever known were broken. Furthermore, they lived through both the collapse of the Spanish Empire, a political institution that had formed them as surely as had the church, and the collapse of Mexican authority in Texas. Their isolation was profound. De la Garza had to face the influx into his parish of people speaking a different language, with a different culture, and largely with a different religion. Most of them had little or no knowledge of the Catholic church and many were hostile to it. Yet in these confusing, uncertain, perplexing years, San Fernando Church was not deserted. On Sundays the doors continued to open. The building needed repairs, as did many others in these years; the vestments may have been threadbare, but from where were new ones to come?[19] If the ornaments of the church were in terrible condition, as Odin recorded, Father Haydon earlier that year had apparently willingly accepted some of them for his own use when the pastor offered them. In her study of the question, Sr. Mary Benignus Sheridan put the matter best when she wrote, "The miracle seems to be not that they were so bad, but that they managed to preserve any remnants of religion at all."[20]

The question will likely remain open, however, as to how guilty these priests were of the charges made against them. It seems from the existing documents that a presumption of guilt existed against these men from the time of Timon's and Llebaría's visit to Houston in 1839. One of the priests was the pastor of the parish, the other had taken refuge in the town since the revolution. As Odin had so recently witnessed, the latter's former parish was a ruin, his people forced from their homes. Yet in Timon's and Odin's correspondence the two men seem lumped together, which makes the situation even less clear. Neither Timon nor Odin seems to have examined the possibility that the charges against these priests could have been colored by factionalism. Both de la Garza and Valdéz were loyal to Mexico. Most of the Anglos and some of the Hispanics in San Antonio had supported the revolution. In other words, some San Antonians may not have been pleased to have loyalist priests in their midst. Father Valdéz, for instance, was serving Goliad and Presidio La Bahía at the onset of the revolution of 1835–36. When Goliad fell to the Collingsworth expedition in October, 1835, Valdéz and most of the Hispanic population sought refuge at Rancho de Don Carlos de la Garza on the San Antonio River between Victoria and Refugio. There Valdéz organized and probably led loyal Tejanos in attacks on Philip Dimmitt's and James W. Fannin's forces. Captured by Fannin, Valdéz and other loyalists were freed by Gen. José Urrea's army at Coleto. After San Jacinto, Valdéz's ranch, which the government granted him in 1824, was reduced to ruins by Texan troops.[21]

As for Father de la Garza, Odin may have realized that the charge of theft of church silver was untrue, and the very fact that he received from the priest a substantial amount of silver vessels and ornaments in spite of the chaos and destruction of 1835–36 indicates de la Garza exercised more responsibility than was alleged.

Odin reported witnessing the pastor's refusal to baptize a child in possible danger of death without assurance of being paid a fee. He also believed he saw evidence that de la Garza was violating his vow of celibacy since a woman and children were present in his home.[22] This might have been the case, but how far he pressed his inquiry is still a matter for conjecture. The mere presence of the woman and children does not lead to Odin's conclusion, particularly in the northern borderlands of the former Spanish Empire. The secular clergy in these often isolated areas supported themselves by farming, or as Father de la Garza did, by ranching.[23] Like de la Garza, they owned their own houses. It was not uncommon to find widowed sisters, nieces, and nephews living at the priest's residence. One such priest, Fr. Ramón Ortiz at El Paso del Norte, the present-day Ciudad Juárez, both farmed and ranched and his house was said to be like an inn. His sisters' children and grandchildren called him "Padrino" (godfather) or the nickname "Papanino." As Gilberto M. Hinojosa has observed, those unfamiliar with the culture and local customs might very well misinterpret the situation. No scandalous stories circulated about Ortiz, but he did not live in an area torn first by violence and then by factionalism and ethnic and religious prejudice. These factors make a clear picture of the San Antonio parochial situation hard to obtain.[24]

Even Odin observed that it was fear of the American Protestants that had caused de la Garza to ignore current canon law regarding baptisms and funerals: he had accepted non-Catholics as godparents, some even who were unbaptized. He also had allowed the ringing of San Fernando's bells for the funerals of non-Catholics and at the beginning of nonreligious public functions. As for the latter, Odin seemed unaware that in Spanish times it was commonplace to ring the church bells for secular purposes such as to announce a royal birth or the reading of an important proclamation. In a meeting to discuss repairing San Fernando Church, Odin asked the mayor, John W. Smith, if he or the town council had ordered the ringing of the bells on such occasions. The mayor answered that various individuals had requested this of the former pastor. After Odin stated what church policy was, Smith verbally agreed to support it. Two days later, when asked to ring the bells for the funeral of Col. Henry W. Karnes, a prominent non-Catholic citizen who had been a scout for Sam Houston during the revolution, Odin faced a storm of protest when he upheld church law and thus ran counter to what de la Garza had allowed. Odin was asked by numerous people to allow the San Fernando bells to ring for Karnes's funeral scheduled for the eighteenth. Odin explained that by church law he could not do this, that Catholic church bells could only be rung at the funerals of Catholics.

On the day of the funeral, a noisy group gathered at the front of the church, and a doctor and a lawyer went into the church and rang the bells. Odin made no attempt to stop them and said nothing. However, the noise continued for a time, and the crowd threatened to break the bells and run Odin out of town. Odin was dismayed that two Irishmen who called themselves Catholics, along with the mayor, who now had changed his mind about the bells, were among those complaining loudest. Paradoxically, two local non-Catholic judges tried to calm the group by telling them that Odin was well within his rights and that he should be praised for adhering to what he had promised to uphold.[25]

Mayor Smith, however, proceeded to call a public gathering hoping to force Odin out of town. Odin reported that only about nine youthful citizens turned out for the meeting, but resolutions condemning Odin's action were passed anyway. When the resolutions were sent to Odin, he wrote a reply stating that as a private citizen he would have been pleased to make some contribution to the solemnities of Karnes's funeral, but as an official of the Catholic church he must observe its rules or be derelict in his duty. He explained why the bells were rung at Catholic funerals and offered assurance that he would always be accommodating whenever his conscience allowed. This calmed things for the moment, but later Mayor Smith tried unsuccessfully to get the Hispanic citizens to sign a petition against Odin with the view of restoring de la Garza to the pastorate. Odin concluded that the Hispanic community supported him and was pleased that he was following the church's customs and not giving way to the wishes of many of the Anglos.[26]

Smith and his supporters had only one short-lived success, that of having their resolutions against Odin published in the *Sentinel*, an Austin newspaper. Odin immediately sent his refutation to the same paper, which published it also. Even as he did so, however, the controversy was dying down, and he soon received an invitation to the mayor's home.[27]

The ringing of bells was a small matter, but Odin believed the unpleasant episode provided him an opportunity to make what he considered a necessary statement for the time and place. Political change and frontier isolation notwithstanding, what he believed to be irregularities in the San Antonio parish now had to give way to strict observance of church law.

All was not storm and stress during Odin's initial visit to San Antonio. Odin's and Calvo's pastoral work seems to have been well received by the San Antonians. Attendance at mass was high, and when in early August Calvo publicly carried the viaticum, the sacrament of the Eucharist, to a sick man, Odin was impressed with the devotion shown by onlookers in the streets. As was then the custom, a small bell sounded as the little procession moved along the dusty street. Many townspeople watched reverently, and some of the old people wept. Rightly or wrongly, Odin believed those who told him that such religious processions had not been done for years. Yet as Sr. Mary Benignus Sheridan observed, Father de la Garza "had indeed been instrumental in keeping alive the spark of faith" in his San Antonio parish. "Had that faith been entirely dead, Father Odin and his companion would not have received so spontaneous a response to the appeals, theoretical and practical, which they made to the Catholics of San Antonio."[28]

By the end of August almost one hundred children were attending daily catechism classes, with most attending the session conducted in Spanish.[29]

The satisfaction Odin enjoyed over the successes of his and Calvo's work in San Antonio was tempered in mid-August when he received news of an Indian attack on Victoria. Estany had only narrowly escaped death when his house was the first in the town attacked and burned by an estimated five hundred Comanches. More than fifteen people were killed, and almost every house in town was either destroyed or damaged. Horses and whatever else they found useful were seized by the Comanches. Linnville, the port where Odin and his companions had entered Texas in July, was also attacked and virtually burned to the ground. It was on the afternoon of August 6 that the Indians launched their raid on Victoria, and though they retreated in the evening, they attacked again the next day. The following day they rode into Linnville, where an even greater destruction followed.

Though Estany's house in Victoria was set on fire, the priest escaped with his life but lost his clothing, books, chalice, and other items needed for the celebration of mass. Odin was able to find some clothing and spare liturgical items in San Antonio, possibly from among those Father de la Garza had preserved at San Fernando, and send them to Estany.[30]

While revenge for the Council House affair earlier in the year was among the motives for this attack, the Comanches completely bypassed San Antonio and headed for the area to the southeast. Rather than vengeance, however, their chief motive was resupplying themselves with horses, mules, and cattle, of which there were many in the vicinity of Victoria. They did well for themselves and made off with between two and three thousand animals.[31]

As the Comanches began to move westward, a company of Texas Rangers under Ben McCulloch intercepted some of them and alerted Gen. Edward Burleson and Gen. Felix Huston, who brought on an even larger force to intercept the Indians. On August 12, a battle occurred at Plum Creek and several hundred livestock were recovered. Approximately seventy-five Indians were killed, but most of them escaped. Later, a force under the veteran Indian fighter John H. Moore tracked the Comanches all the way to their major encampment hundreds of miles north of San Antonio along the upper Colorado River. In a battle there many Indians were killed and much of what they had taken was recovered. Though not always on a grand scale, warfare between whites and Indians continued in Texas over the next thirty-five years.[32]

Because of these attacks, San Antonio was tense during most of the three months Odin spent there. "We live here in constant fear," Odin wrote on August 24, 1840, and although conditions seemed safer when Texan forces assembled in San Antonio on their way to Plum Creek, an aura of fear remained. The assembled troops in San Antonio were ordered to spare neither women nor children. Odin wrote of this to Blanc: "The Indians have committed so many thefts, have assassinated so many unfortunate inhabitants, that one feels obliged not only to repulse them but to annihilate all of them, if it is possible."[33] Strange words from a man who had originally left his homeland to work among the Indians, but Odin was not immune to the gripping terror that descended on San Antonio and other frontier regions in the late summer and fall of 1840, terror fed by accounts of tortured and mutilated travelers, burned cabins, and kidnapped women and children. And San Antonians did not have to rely on the accounts of others: on October 6, a party of Indians approached the area of the Alamo and killed a townsman named Emanuel Díaz. Several days later, Odin stopped to chat with a parishioner who had come to the church for his evening prayers and was told that since January 1 of that year, about fifty people had been killed by the Comanches in the environs of San Antonio. Later in October, a young Hispanic girl from South Texas who had been captured by the Comanches was brought into town by Texan troops who had found her in an encampment from which the Comanches had just fled. The young girl was given shelter in the home of some San Fernando parishioners. The same day news arrived of the death of a San Antonian killed by Indians as he was driving cattle to the Navarro ranch.[34]

San Antonio always had been plagued by this kind of fear and the wounds ran deep, Odin wrote Etienne in Paris: "We live here in constant fear. One can not step outside the city without an escort."[35] The Comanches of Texas, who had burned Estany's house and killed Emanuel Díaz, were not the Indians Odin had visited and known before: "How beautiful Missouri is in comparison to Texas!" he wrote during this period.[36]

In spite of the fear and tension, Odin's and Calvo's work in San Antonio progressed well through the fall of 1840. Repairs were made to San Fernando Church, and Odin began to give thought to the former missions along the river south of town. In spite of the Comanche threat, one day in mid-September Odin, accompanied by José Antonio Navarro, went out to the missions to see for himself what time and change had brought to these once thriving outposts of the church, in whose environs more than a thousand Catholics still resided. The missions farthest from town were San Juan

South wall, Mission San José de Aguayo, San Antonio, circa 1865.
Courtesy Catholic Archives of Texas, Austin.

Capistrano and San Francisco de la Espada, nine and twelve miles out, respectively; their buildings were almost in ruins. San José, just five miles from town, was well preserved, however, and presented an aesthetically impressive picture; its convent, too, Odin noted, was in a good state of preservation. These beautiful and commodious structures would make an excellent site for a seminary or school, Odin thought. Mission Concepción, only three miles from San Antonio, was equally beautiful and also well preserved. The manner in which it was positioned on the river bank, he thought, made it particularly charming and a pleasant site for a boarding school for girls.

There was a cloud, however, in this otherwise hopeful picture: these well-preserved missions were not being used as churches; in fact, the church did not own San José any longer, and its legal title to Concepción was in question—unless the Texan government could be persuaded to legislate in the church's favor. The Veramendi family claimed ownership of San José Mission and its fifteen hundred acres of property, but Odin was hopeful: the Veramendis were asking ten thousand dollars for the property, but probably would take six thousand. In the case of Concepción, Odin realized that a trip to Austin would be necessary so that he could attempt to induce the government to uphold the church's title to ownership. Haste, he thought, was of the essence, else the buildings might fall into other hands and thus be lost permanently.[37]

During his months in San Antonio, Odin also pondered some of the customs Catholics there observed that were unfamiliar to him though he accepted their propriety—at least until new arrangements for Texas were made. As yet, no specific directives as to holy days and days of abstinence had been laid down for the prefecture. For instance, in San Antonio, according to the catechism books the people had used for years, there were sixteen holy days of obligation, according to Mexican usage, whereas in the United States and certain areas in Europe, only four were observed; also, according to Mexican episcopal directive, Fridays were not days of abstinence from meat, except Good Friday. Odin thought, in the first instance, that four holy days of obligation were quite enough for Texas, and such ultimately became the case. He also thought the latter practice, though very suprising to him, had a sensible origin. For over a century San Antonio had been threatened by the Comanches, making agriculture particularly difficult. Consequently, corn, beans, and other food items were exorbitantly expensive; conversely, the proliferation of Spanish cattle in that part of Texas made beef very cheap. Odin really doubted if Catholics in the region could observe each Friday in the year as a day of abstinence from meat.[38]

Odin left for Victoria and the settlements along the Lavaca River on November 9. Calvo and Sala remained in San Antonio, occupied with their pastoral work at San Fernando. Despite the Indian danger, they also occasionally journeyed to San Juan Capistrano and Espada Missions for the celebration of mass.[39]

Odin was anxious to visit Estany and his parishioners in Victoria and the Catholics to the south along the coast, since they had suffered much at the hands of the Comanches. Odin's journey was a risky, nerve-racking experience. He did not dare travel alone, but went in company with nine others.[40] They left in the early afternoon and continued into the gathering dusk until they reached Santa Clara Creek about thirty miles from San Antonio. They made their camp there in the darkness. No sooner was this done than suddenly, from out of the blackness, came the sounds of horses' hooves. Iron-cold fear gripped Odin and his companions as they peered into the night, expecting at any moment to hear the screams of Comanches on the assault. Great relief swept over the travelers when they discovered that it was only a herd of wild mustangs.

Early next morning, on reaching the Guadalupe River, Odin briefly visited the Flores rancho where a number of Catholics resided. He and the others then crossed the river and passed on through the town of Seguin, a settlement laid out only two years before. A norther was blowing in, and the wayfarers contended with heavy rains on into the night, which made havoc with their campsite set up about nine miles from Gonzales. Reaching there at noon on November 11, Odin saw that this town, where the revolution had begun only five years before, was still partially in ruin. It was burned by the Texans as they retreated upon learning of the fall of the Alamo. Its history had been turbulent, Odin learned: laid out originally by James Kerr and named for the governor of Coahuila y Tejas, Rafael Gonzales, it was soon destroyed by Indians, then rebuilt only to be destroyed again in 1836. The population dwindled, but now Odin noted that the town was beginning to grow because of heavy immigration into Texas.

From Gonzales they took the road for Victoria, which generally followed the course of the Guadalupe River. They spent a cold but rainless night on the banks of the Guadalupe, and a heavy frost covered the prairie the next morning. Odin was struck by the natural beauty along the route as the prairie grassland gave way to a border of pecan trees along the river. Now that there was no burning summer heat, perhaps the difference in beauty between Texas and Missouri appeared less to Odin. This pleasant day of travel was marred only when a rear axle broke on one of the wagons in their caravan. Rather than delay everyone, the driver and his vehicle remained behind at a ranch for the necessary repairs while the rest went on their way.

Finally on the evening of the thirteenth, Odin reached Victoria. Odin was shocked at Father Estany's emaciated appearance. Odin learned that in addition to the strain of having his house destroyed by Indians and the burden of overseeing the repair of the church while performing his regular pastoral duties, Estany had been sick also. The church had survived the Comanche raid in August and the necessary repairs were now in progress. While in the town, Odin heard accounts of its history as the center of the Martín de León colony, and that the devoted Fr. Díaz de León, who had been killed in East Texas in 1834, had once worked in this region. Before Odin left Victoria, news arrived that undoubtedly brought him reassurance as he contemplated journeying on to outlying settlements: a Ranger force had defeated the Comanches far to the north along the Colorado River, and it was even reported that some of Victoria's livestock had been recovered.[41]

Odin left Victoria at noon on Saturday the fourteenth and made his way to the nearby settlements along the Lavaca River, traveling alone since the Indian threat had subsided. Late in the evening, he arrived at the cabin of a Catholic settler where he spent the night and celebrated mass the next morning. For the next several days he moved from cabin to cabin, hearing confessions, celebrating mass, and sometimes preaching a sermon. By the end of the week, he was at Brown's Settlement, where he celebrated mass and visited with Fr. Edward Clarke, who arrived home from his own mission tour of the countryside while Odin was there. Odin was surprised and pleased to find so many Missouri Catholics along the Lavaca—several had once belonged to the parish located at St. Mary-of-the-Barrens Seminary.[42]

Odin remained at Brown's Settlement until Thursday, November 26, when he set out for Austin. He arrived there on the twenty-ninth. The weather was better and the Comanche threat seemed less, which enabled him to make the longer trip to Austin in slightly less time than it had taken him to go from San Antonio to Victoria.[43]

In Austin, Odin had much to do: he wanted to make a land purchase, and there was the matter of politics. Odin was determined to get the church's ownership of at least some of its prerevolutionary property recognized by the Texan government. As subsequent events proved, Odin was fortunate that by this time the Lamar administration had secured French recognition and both countries had exchanged diplomatic representatives. Being French himself, Odin found a natural ally in Alphonse Dubois de Saligny, the French chargé d'affaires in Austin, whom he had previously met in New Orleans.[44] Shortly after his arrival, de Saligny invited Odin to lodge at his residence, which also served as the French legation. In the days ahead Odin attended sessions of Congress and visited Catholics in the town, including Senators James Byrne, William Daingerfield, and James Miller and Representative Michael Menard, whose advice and assistance Odin needed to achieve government recognition of the church's property titles. On December 5, de Saligny hosted a dinner party where Odin met and conversed with Sam Houston in a successful effort to make the former president his ally. Amidst the politics, Odin took time out to purchase several town lots for future use and to journey fifteen miles into the countryside to visit some European Catholic immigrants.[45]

Although President Lamar was preparing to leave Austin for medical treatment in New Orleans, Odin went ahead with his petition to Congress as soon as he returned to town on the eighth. As he was pursuing his effort with Congress, a rumor circulated that Mexico was about to invade and that Juan N. Seguín had defected.[46] That Seguín had done so proved correct; he had become the victim of ethnic prejudice, a prejudice that had increased as more and more Americans arrived in Texas. Simultaneously another rumor circulated that priests in Mexico had raised two million dollars to help Mexico reclaim Texas.[47] An aura of wild uncertainty seemed to descend on Austin, and even though Odin by then had had another amicable dinner with Houston, he was fearful that this rumor might be fatal to his petition before Congress. Afraid he might become persona non grata, Odin spent much of December 19 conferring with Senator Daingerfield, discussing the possibility of counteracting any damage the rumors might create. Odin's fears proved unwarranted, however. On the twenty-first, shortly after arranging for his petition to be presented formally to the Senate, Odin was invited to serve as its chaplain for the remainder of his visit. Odin accepted, and a small altar was set up in the rude capitol where for several mornings Odin offered prayers at the beginning of the Senate's daily session.[48]

Odin's petition was presented in the House of Representatives on the twenty-first and was referred to a select House committee, which would later report its recommendation.[49]

Earlier, in December as Odin was lobbying for his petition, he had read some welcome news in a Galveston newspaper: on December 5, John Timon and another Vincentian priest, Nicholas Stehle, had arrived in Galveston bound for Austin, and from the date on the newspaper, Odin deduced they would arrive before the month was out.[50] This proved correct. Timon and Stehle arrived in Austin on the evening of the twenty-first, the day Odin's petition was presented to the House of Representatives.

Before leaving the coast, Timon and Stehle had celebrated mass in Galveston and in Houston, where Italian immigrants had recently swelled the ranks of Catholics in both towns. They then made their way northwestward toward Austin. Timon brought with him a letter for Lamar from Cardinal Fransoni in which Rome virtually recognized Texas' independence from Mexico. By the time they arrived in Austin, they had already presented the letter to Lamar: they had met him as they were en route to Austin and the president was making his way toward New Orleans for medical treatment. The letter was a formal introduction of Timon as prefect apostolic for Texas and therefore the chief pastor of Catholic Texans. As Timon translated the letter into English, Lamar could not hide his elation over the obvious implications of a document originating at the highest level of both the Catholic church, an institution of worldwide scope, and the government of the Papal States. Lamar was addressed as "President of the Texian Republic" and acknowledgment was made of his previous kindness to the clergy sent into Texas to minister to "the faithful of your country . . . the Republic over which you preside." The nations of Europe, from which Lamar was actively seeking favor, could not fail to be impressed, the Catholic courts in particular. Given Lamar's aspirations for Texas' future, his elation seemed well founded.[51]

In a communication that Fransoni knew would greatly please Lamar, the cardinal added a plea for the recognition of the church's title to its prerevolutionary property: "I earnestly entreat your Excellency . . . to aid and protect the . . . Prefect and those associated with him, and that you cause whatever property may belong to the Church, to be handed over to him, as to the lawful pastor."

Lamar, of course, away from the seat of government on a journey out of Texas, could not take immediate action himself, but he gave Timon a flattering letter of commendation addressed to Vice Pres. David G. Burnet in Austin. Lamar indicated that Timon should give both this and Fransoni's letter to Burnet as soon as he arrived in Austin.

Odin's pleasure on seeing his old friend was magnified by Timon's news of his visit with Lamar, for now Odin could be assured that his petition pending before the Texan Congress had support from the leaders of the two political factions. His own conversations with Houston had assured him of support from that quarter, and now with the goodwill of Lamar, chances were better than ever that the matter would be resolved in the Catholic church's favor.[52]

Timon and Stehle were warmly received by de Saligny and, like Odin, became guests in the diplomat's outwardly plain but sumptuously furnished legation. The year before, a wagon train carrying bric-a-brac, carpets, chairs, sofas, paintings, and even French window glass, all collected in Paris or New Orleans, had come up the muddy trail from Houston so that the French diplomat could live on the frontier in the best possible style. Even a French chef arrived to provide delectable cuisine, the likes of which had never been experienced by the vast majority of those living in the capital city of the republic. No doubt the French envoy desired and enjoyed such luxuries, but his life-style, given the circumstances, enhanced both his and his government's position with the Texan authorities.[53]

Timon, like Odin before him, was somewhat taken aback at such unaccustomed luxuries, but he soon saw how adept de Saligny was at using his contrived environment. The clergymen attended several dinner parties at which they and delighted politicians were provided with de Saligny's now famous wines and cuisine. This lobbying not only helped de Saligny's own purposes but those of his now well known ecclesiastical guests, for whose cause he actively proclaimed his support. At one such banquet on December 28, most of the guests, including Vice President Burnet, had heard Timon the previous evening when his eloquence had favorably impressed a large crowd gathered to hear him in the Senate chamber. In the banquet's more relaxed environment, Timon elaborated on his recent discourse. The largely Protestant gathering at the dinner party expressed appreciation at hearing from a Catholic priest what his church really taught instead of what rumor portrayed this teaching to be. Timon later recalled that the reaction of one senator present was to propose a toast to the unanimous passage of the Catholic property bill before Congress.[54]

De Saligny's French cuisine and fine wines coupled with Timon's charm seemed to be a winning combination: the next day the committee considering the bill reported on it favorably, and it came before the entire House the day after that. Timon and Odin trudged through muddy streets slick with ice on their way to the one-story frame capitol building to follow the course of their bill. An icy wind drove at them every step of the way, and, once inside the rude structure, they found that the board walls still let in much of the wind. However, their comfort increased as they heard several speakers come out in favor of the pending legislation; especially encouraging was the support former president Sam Houston gave the measure in his address.

Since most of the property in question had once been part of large tracts that the Spanish government had provided for use by the missions, some congressmen wanted it clearly stated that these huge tracts of land were not being returned to the church by the proposed legislation. The bill was amended by the addition of these words: "Provided that nothing herein contained shall be so construed as to give title to any lands except the lots upon which the churches are situated, which shall not exceed fifteen acres." Even so, it soon became obvious that support for the bill as amended was not unanimous. Because of its association with the revolution, Congressman Cornelius Van Ness of San Antonio moved to delete the Alamo Church from the measure. Houston immediately took the floor to oppose this exception, but to no avail; the amendment carried and soon the small minority opposing the legislation became more vocal. One congressman characterized the bill as a "Catholic privilege" act and moved that land be set aside for several other denominations in each of those areas where land or buildings were being restored to the Catholic church. This proposal was rejected, and the chair rebuked its author. It was then proposed that Mission Concepción on the outskirts of San Antonio, again because of its association with the revolution, also be excepted from the bill. Timon and Odin now began to wonder where the exceptions were going to end, and, fortunately for the bill, so did most of the congressmen; this exception was denied, and the bill, with the single amendment regarding the Alamo, was passed by a vote of thirty to four.[55]

Timon and Odin were so grateful for the aid given them by the French envoy that they both suggested to Rome that the papal court reward de Saligny with a title of nobility.[56]

On the last day of 1840, Timon and Odin left Austin to begin a mission tour over much of Texas to the east. They intended to visit Houston and Galveston and then go northeast to Nacogdoches. They traveled southeastward toward the hamlet of Comanche (not the present town of that name) where a few German-speaking Catholics had settled. Stehle, having left Austin on December 23, preceded them along the same route before moving southward, following the course of the Colorado River to visit other German-speaking settlers. The German-speaking Stehle was from Lorraine, and Timon and Odin believed he could do valuable work among the many German immigrants now arriving almost daily in Texas.

It was with a sense of accomplishment that the prefect and vice prefect rode out of Austin toward Comanche. True, the bill granting recognition of the church's ownership of property, having passed only the House, was still pending before Congress; but with friends like Alphonse de Saligny and Sam Houston and the one-sided House vote, there seemed to be no real obstacle to final enactment. And events would more than bear out their optimism: the Senate began deliberating the bill on New Year's Day and referred it to committee on January 2. The committee reported favorably on it on the sixth, the Senate passed the bill on the twelfth, and Burnet, as acting president, signed it into law on the thirteenth.[57]

What Timon and Odin had not anticipated, however, was that on January 14, with an astonishing change of conviction, Congressman Van Ness of San Antonio, whose efforts had exempted the Alamo from the legislation, proposed a bill entitled "An Act Granting the Alamo Church to the Use and Benefit of the Catholic Church." Quickly moving through both houses of Congress, it was signed by Burnet four days later. Some "arm-twisting" by Houston was probably behind Van Ness's change of heart. Houston had opposed deleting the Alamo from the original measure, apparently believing that the historic importance of the Alamo did not outweigh its initial role as a place of worship. Though of course its mission status had long since lapsed, the Alamo had continued for years under the Spanish as a military chapel.[58]

January, 1841, then, provided a milestone in the efforts to strengthen the Catholic church in Texas: the church once more had historically significant centers of operation available to it, centers that in some of the communities still had an importance in the lives of the people going back for generations. The church, since it is ultimately based on people, not buildings, could have eventually experienced renewal without the return of the properties in question, but where these buildings did exist, a disruption in the history of the locale and the lives of the people was being made right. Even where the immediate community no longer existed, because of the symbolic value some of these edifices held for wider areas, this legislation was a step in bringing about a kind of cultural healing.

The bill as signed by Burnet on January 13 read as follows:

> An Act Confirming the Use and Occupation and Enjoyment of the Churches, Church Lots, and Mission Churches to the Roman Catholic Congregations, living in or near the vicinity of the same. Sec. 1. Be it enacted by the Senate and House of Representatives of the Republic of Texas, in Congress assembled, That the churches at San Antonio, Goliad and Victoria, the church lot at Nacogdoches, the churches at the Mission of Conception, San Jose, Espada, and the Mission of Refugio, with the out-buildings and lots, if any belonging to them, be, and they are hereby, acknowledged and declared the property of the present chief pastor of the Roman Catholic Church, in the Republic of Texas, and his successors in office, in trust forever, for the use and benefit of the congregations residing near the same, or who may hereafter reside near the same, for religious purposes, and purposes of education, and none other; provided, that nothing herein contained shall be so construed as to give title to any lands except the lots upon which the churches are situated, which shall not exceed fifteen acres.

The second bill, introduced by Congressman Van Ness, provided "that the Church of the Alamo, in the city of San Antonio, be . . . yielded and granted, for the use of the Catholic Church, upon the same terms and conditions" as those churches listed in the first bill.[59]

The wording of both bills avoided a current controversy among Catholics in the United States, revolving around the question of "lay trusteeism." In some dioceses there, legal ownership of many Catholic church buildings was vested in lay boards of trustees. Conflicts between bishops and these boards had arisen periodically. Lay trustees would not own the church buildings in Texas, however. Although the legislative act granted the "Use . . . Occupation and Enjoyment" of Catholic church property "to the Roman Catholic Congregations, living in or near the vicinity of the same," the ownership of the property was by the act "acknowledged and declared the property of the present chief pastor of the Roman Catholic Church, in the Republic of Texas, and successors in office, in trust forever." All new church lots and buildings would be bought by Timon or Odin and his successors in their name as chief pastor.

The morning of New Year's Day, 1841, found Timon and Odin at the homestead of Napoleon Van Hamins southeast of Austin in the village of Comanche. Odin had already visited this family, whom he described as "Belgian-Prussian," in December. Father Stehle had celebrated mass there on Christmas Eve and baptized several family members. After mass was celebrated on New Year's Day, Timon gave an instructive talk to the family and some of their neighbors. Since January 1 was a holy day, the Catholics present were enabled to fulfill their religious duty. In a two-week period, the Van Hamins, who had not seen a priest in years, had had three masses and several baptisms celebrated in their home.

In the afternoon the priests continued on their way and in early evening came to Bastrop, situated on the east bank of the Colorado River, near a vast pine forest that to them and to later generations seemed geographically out of place. They lodged there with the Doyle family, and on Saturday, the next day, they celebrated mass at the O'Connell cabin. Saturday evening, Timon preached in the courthouse to a large gathering of mostly non-Catholics. His address, as usual, was well received, and the next morning, Sunday, almost everyone in town, including sawmill workers from the adjacent forest, came to the O'Connell house to hear him again. For most in the group, this was the first time they had ever witnessed a Catholic mass. Odin believed that most of them went away convinced that Catholic worship was not the terrible, idolatrous act they had read or been told it was. Both Timon and Odin on numerous occasions skillfully used an informal address as a means of dispelling prejudice and encouraging their hearers to witness the Catholic liturgy and see for themselves what it was really like.

After celebrating mass on Monday morning at the O'Connell cabin, the prefect and his assistant started out for the long journey to Houston. The first night out from Bastrop was spent at the home of a Presbyterian minister; not only were shelter and food provided by the clergyman, but an amicable discussion of religion as well. While no one's convictions were changed, the dynamics of serious discussion provided for the participants a welcome interlude to the drudgery of life on the frontier and the hazards of travel. Timon and Odin went on the next day to the small village of Industry, founded in 1837, one of the first communities settled by Germans in Texas. They visited several Catholics there and the next day set out southeastward over the rolling grasslands dotted with stands of small oak and cedar. By nightfall of the sixth, the feast of the Epiphany, Timon and Odin reached the still largely burned-out town of San Felipe, burned, as Odin recorded in his journal, "by order of General Sam Houston, at the time of the war." Some of the gaunt chimneys still stood as reminders of the largess of warfare. The revolution was now five years in the past, but San Felipe was never again the bustling village and governmental seat it had been in colonial times. Perhaps the missionaries considered the scarred, almost derelict San Felipe de Austin a strangely appropriate place to spend Epiphany: since the feast commemorates the visit of the gentile kings to the Christ Child and is seen by the church as symbolizing the presentation of the Christ to all the people of an often violent world, perhaps it seemed sadly fitting that such a time be spent amidst the charred signs of human conflict.

The next day, Timon and Odin began traversing the flat coastal prairie land lying between the Brazos River and Houston. They intended to visit East Texas during their journey, but since it seemed to them that, along with San Antonio, Houston and Galveston would be hubs of Catholic work in Texas, they wanted to visit those two towns again before beginning what they knew would be a laborious trek to Nacogdoches to the northeast. After spending the night in a settler's cabin, they made their way into Houston on Friday the eighth. The trip from Austin had taken almost nine days.

Houston is always wet in January. It had been wet during Timon's first visit in January, 1839, and January, 1841, was no different. The mud was a sticky mire. Wading through it, the priests made their way to a private residence where they obtained lodging. On Saturday, arrangements were made to celebrate Sunday mass in a store building. On Sunday Timon delivered an instruction on the Catholic doctrine of the Eucharist, which word he used in the title of his discourse instead of "mass." Later that day, he spoke to a large audience in the old Senate chamber of the former capitol building. Once again, a subscription list was started for a building. Church building plans had not materialized in either Houston or Galveston after Timon's 1838–39 visit, and while in Galveston in December, 1840, Timon had again begun a subscription for a church building there. Now a building committee was appointed for the new Houston parish of St. Vincent de Paul, named for the founder of Timon's and Odin's order. The parish register was opened by Odin on January 11 with the baptism of William Pascall, aged two months. In addition to Odin's duties as vice prefect, Timon appointed him as pastor of both the Houston and Galveston parishes.

In the local Houston newspaper, the *Telegraph and Texas Register,* Timon and Odin were pleased to see that the recent communication between the Holy See and President Lamar was being well covered by the press. They believed this was especially good publicity for the Catholic church to help counteract what they sensed was a growing misunderstanding of its teachings and practices due to the great influx of immigrants from areas in the United States where anti-Catholic feelings were deep-rooted.

On the eleventh, after sending their horses to Lynchburg, Timon and Odin boarded the steamboat *Dayton* and headed down Buffalo Bayou bound for Galveston. They planned to get their horses at Lynchburg on their way back from Galveston and visit along the way back into Houston. They arrived in Galveston late the next morning and remained there until the nineteenth. If Odin was to be in charge of the local congregation, it was necessary for him to become familiar with the town and meet as many people as possible in spite of the cold, rainy weather. As before, it was Dr. Nicholas Labadie and the Menards who stepped forward to help the missionaries. Peter Menard opened his home to them, and again mass was celebrated in a chapel set up in a building owned by the Menards. Dr. Labadie collected pledges once more from subscribers, and plans were drawn for a simple frame church.[60]

The missionaries reboarded the *Dayton* on January 19 intending to pick up their horses at Lynchburg. The *Dayton* arrived there at five o'clock the next morning. Timon and Odin went to the home of the Thomas Earl family, where their horses were boarded. While there they blessed the couple's marriage and baptized their four children. As the day wore on they saw that travel to Houston by horseback was impossible: rain had fallen constantly from the tenth of January to the nineteenth, and the weather was the coldest in memory. Buffalo Bayou was extremely high with a treacherous current so that the steamboats by the twenty-first could go only part way up the bayou toward Houston and even then were forced to dodge the tops of trees.

So determined were they to be on their way that after an early breakfast on January 21, they decided that where a large boat could not go, perhaps a small one could and set out for Houston in a leaky skiff. For four hours they rowed hard and bailed out the boat constantly but covered only about seven miles in the process. They abandoned the skiff, found a farmer who agreed to rent them a packhorse for their baggage, and set off across the prairie on foot. For seemingly endless hours they waded knee-deep in icy mud and water. At one point, while crossing a swollen creek, their horse fell, and all their baggage was soaked. At last, after nightfall, they arrived in Houston covered with mud and in a state of near physical collapse. Most of the next day was spent drying out clothing, altar linens, breviaries, and cassocks and attempting to replace what was ruined.[61]

Obtaining two horses, the missionaries set out northward from Houston toward the town of Montgomery on January 24 and soon discovered their ordeal from the weather was far from over. Twenty miles north of Houston, they dismounted, persuaded their horses to swim across the swollen Cypress Creek, and then crossed over themselves in a canoe; a few miles farther on, they faced the more formidable Spring Creek, where, after getting their horses across, they balanced themselves on a log and gingerly passed their baggage hand to hand to the other side. Of the entire trip northward to Nacogdoches, Odin later wrote: "What difficulties and obstacles presented themselves in this long trip! Sometimes a creek was to be crossed by swimming, sometimes [it was] a long and treacherous swamp where we ran the danger of losing our horses. At one time hunger manifested itself and [there was] nothing to appease it, . . . [and we had] heavy rain against which there was no protection or cover."[62]

In spite of the mud, rain, and cold, Timon managed to preach in various towns or in wilderness places along the road. "At different points on the road, when we stopped at night, we assembled as many as we could and explained our doctrine," Odin wrote later. After preaching in Montgomery on the twenty-fifth, they pressed on through sometimes waist-deep mud until they came to Huntsville the next day, where Timon preached to a small group gathered in a tavern.

Leaving Huntsville the next morning, they crossed the engorged Trinity River with help from some slaves and went on to Crockett, a town of about fifteen houses, where Timon again preached. Finally, in blinding rain, after nightfall on Saturday, January 30, they reached Nacogdoches. That night, Timon set out to find a hall in which to preach and celebrate mass on Sunday and obtained use of the old Stone House, or what is now called the Old Stone Fort. Before retiring they put up notices around the town.[63]

As one Nacogdoches resident, Adolphus Sterne, noted in his diary, Sunday brought "rain! rain!! rain!!!" but he nevertheless attended mass and twice heard Timon preach. A large congregation turned out for the mass and a sermon by Timon in the morning and again for another sermon by him that afternoon. Mass was celebrated again on Monday and Tuesday, and Timon preached again on February 2, the feast of the Presentation of Christ in the Temple. At each sermon there was a careful explanation of the liturgy and of Catholic teachings.[64]

The two priests discovered there were about 290 Catholics in Nacogdoches and its environs: approximately 215 were Hispanic and 75 were Anglo. The Hispanics were largely descendants of colonists who settled in East Texas in the eighteenth century. Some of the Anglos were of English and Irish ancestry, from Maryland, and had followed a frontier route, log cabin to log cabin, from there to Kentucky to Missouri to Texas. Rather than make an issue out of the ownership of the lot on which the Catholic church once stood, now claimed by another denomination, Timon and Odin were pleased to receive from a local resident, Charles Chevalier, the gift of another town site and four hundred acres of rural land. Steps were immediately taken to launch a campaign to build a church on the new site.[65]

Timon and Odin saw firsthand how prejudice against the Hispanic people had robbed many of them of their land. Some had been killed in the 1838 outbreak of violence between Anglos and Tejanos in the region, the same episode that had led to the destruction of the Catholic church in the town.[66] On February 3, Timon and Odin set out for the ranch and farm of Vidal Flores, who had managed to hold on to his land, where they remained as guests until the next day. There they baptized the children and celebrated mass.

Timon and Odin arrived at San Augustine on the evening of the fourth. Finding the Masonic Hall in San Augustine already engaged by the Methodists, Timon arranged the use of a theater called the Thespian Hall. Again large crowds turned out to hear Timon preach and observe Odin conducting a catechism class made up of children from the few Catholic families of the town. While the majority of those in the theater came more out of curiosity than anything else and probably viewed the proceedings as little different from the theatrical productions usually presented there, they were courteous, the priests noted, and seemed to give them a fair hearing.

From San Augustine, Timon returned by way of Natchitoches, Louisiana, to his headquarters in Perry County, Missouri, but Odin turned southwestward toward San Antonio.[67] Although Timon would return to Texas several times, this particular tour was probably his most effective.

After returning to Missouri, Timon received official word from David G. Burnet, the acting president of Texas, that he had signed into law the bills recognizing the Catholic church's title to its prerevolutionary buildings.[68] Timon's justly warranted elation, however, was short-lived: in early April word arrived from Bishop Blanc in New Orleans that Odin had been appointed by Rome the coadjutor bishop of Detroit. This news was devastating for all of Timon's plans for the church in Texas, and he let it be known. To Bishop Blanc in New Orleans, to Archbishop Eccleston in Baltimore, and to Cardinal Fransoni in Rome, Timon extolled Odin's special qualifications for his current work. To Blanc, he wrote that he hoped Odin would not accept the Detroit appointment unless he was put under obedience to do so should Rome carry the matter that far. In Timon's view, the appointment, if accepted, would be disastrous both for Texas and for Odin personally.[69]

Odin was unaware of his appointment to Detroit until he arrived in New

Orleans in April. Parting from Timon in San Augustine in February, Odin returned to Nacogdoches and then made his way to Victoria and San Antonio, visiting the isolated cabins of Catholic settlers along the way. On March 3 he arrived at the rancho of Don Carlos de la Garza between Victoria and the Coleto and then visited in the surrounding area until the ninth, when he set out toward San Antonio. As before, Odin traveled in company with others in this area where hostility between Comanches and settlers was once more on the rise. After visiting the Seguín ranch on the eleventh, he arrived in San Antonio the next day. He spent the next two weeks teaching catechism classes, daily visiting prisoners in the local jail, and tending to business details such as sending money to Austin for the purchase of lots there. On March 21, acting under faculties received from the bishop of New Orleans, he administered confirmation to several children in San Fernando Church.[70]

Odin left San Antonio on March 30 for Houston in the company of Antonio and Luciano Navarro. At Houston, he boarded a boat for Galveston and from there went on to New Orleans. It was his intention after conferring with Blanc to go upriver to Missouri, where he and Timon could make further plans for the work in Texas. Arriving in New Orleans on Sunday morning, April 16, Odin, after a hasty stop at Blanc's residence, went to St. Louis' Cathedral for high mass, where quite a shock awaited him. For whatever reason, Blanc chose this occasion to present the papal documents to Odin informing him of his appointment as coadjutor bishop of Detroit. Certainly another context would have been better; on discovering the intent of the documents, Odin blanched and became so disconcerted that he couldn't finish reading them. Once Odin was in Missouri, Timon reinforced his decision to return the papal documents and hope Rome would not insist he accept the Detroit post.[71]

As Odin prepared to return to Texas in June, Timon was about to leave for Europe by way of Detroit and Baltimore. To the bishops in these cities he expressed his opposition to Odin's new appointment. When he arrived in Paris in July, he was relieved to find news indicating not only that Odin did not have to go to Detroit but that Rome instead had decided to appoint him as vicar apostolic of Texas and titular bishop of Claudiopolis. This meant that Odin would be a bishop even though Texan conditions, in Rome's eyes, did not yet warrant the formation of a full-fledged diocese. Even so, as a vicariate apostolic rather than a prefecture apostolic, Texas was yet another step closer to being a diocese, and now its chief pastor would hold the rank of bishop. Since technically a bishop cannot be without a diocese, and Texas was not yet a diocese, Odin was made the titular bishop of a long vacant diocese from the past, Claudiopolis.[72]

Odin was aware of none of this, however: he was far away in his chosen land of Texas. Most of the rest of 1841 he spent in the west many miles from

Galveston. He went there in spite of war fears during this last year of the Lamar administration. Since the beginning of his term in December, 1838, Lamar had followed a policy designed to insure permanently the independence of Texas, not only from Mexico but from the United States as well. His problems were that his policies cost money Texas did not have and had irritated Mexico and further alienated the Indians in the west. Although foreign recognition was achieved and the Texan navy sailed the Gulf, relations with Mexico were at a new low, leading to war fears that did not vanish even at the end of Lamar's term that December.

The news that greeted Odin on his arrival back in Texas in late June, 1841, was that the unofficial Texan agent sent to improve relations with Mexico had been refused admittance into the country. Odin noted that this was being proclaimed at every hand as a great insult, and war fever was spreading. Many speakers, Odin observed, sounded as if Texas was the strongest nation on earth, but the truth of the matter, wrote Odin, was that Texas was "a mountain in travail." If negotiations with Mexico did not settle the matter, Odin feared for Texas' future.

In spite of the political confusion, Catholics had made some progress in Galveston, and the framework of a church was now standing. Eager to visit the west again, Odin chided the Galvestonians, telling them not to expect him back if they did not complete the building. Since Father Stehle, the priest who had come to Texas with Timon the previous December, had returned to Missouri, Odin believed he could do more good in the months ahead by visiting the Catholics of the interior than by remaining in Galveston.[73]

Odin left Galveston by steamboat for Houston on July 15. He spent several days visiting the sick and encouraging the healthy to go ahead and erect a church. On the twenty-fourth he set out for the Festus Doyle homestead on his way to the Brazos River, where he had heard that a sickness was spreading among the settlers. The purchase of a mule made his traveling easier. Travel in the region between Houston and Victoria by midsummer of 1841 was considered safe enough to be done alone. Arriving at the Brazos on the twenty-seventh, Odin spent more than a week visiting the Catholic settlers who lived along the river near Richmond.[74]

Odin set out across the Brazos in early August, and all went well until the eighth, when he began running a high fever and experiencing extreme nausea. Stopping at the home of a Catholic family, he seemed to regain his strength and set out once again two days later. Soon he found himself so sick he could not stay on the horse for which he had exchanged the mule. When he stopped to lie on the grass, the August heat was so intense he was forced to go on, but no sooner did he remount than off he came again, collapsing in the grass. Again and again he attempted to continue. Between the illness itself and the heat and dehydration, Odin believed several times that he was at the point of death. Once he dragged himself to a grove of trees, but the shade brought only limited relief, and his fever and thirst grew worse. Remounting his horse, he barely held on while the horse wandered at random. In the midst of his helpless confusion, Odin made out what appeared to be smoke from a cabin. Urging his horse on, he found a tent sheltering a newly arrived family from Michigan who took him into their care. With the tent for shelter and plenty of water provided by the Michigan immigrants, Odin's condition quickly improved. Although terribly weak, he decided to continue on the next day. For two days he traveled toward Brown's Settlement on the Lavaca River, where many of his old friends from Missouri lived. Just as he arrived there, the fever began to return, and he was confined to bed until the end of August. In early September he began with some difficulty a visitation of the various cabins scattered along the river.[75]

On September 7, after celebrating mass at the James Kerr residence, Odin left for Victoria to visit Father Estany and his congregation at Our Lady of Guadalupe Church. On the way, he was drenched in a rainstorm and decided that if only he could get to San Antonio, "the healthful air of that beautiful valley" would help restore his strength. In the company of a cart train, Odin set out from Victoria on September 9 and arrived in San Antonio five days later, after visiting Goliad and the Seguín and Cassiano ranchos along the way.[76]

This journey was typical of those Odin and his Texas missionary colleagues experienced during the 1840s, 1850s, and most of the 1860s as well. While stagecoaches became more and more common during these years and provided some improvement, the traveler was still virtually at the mercy of the elements, highwaymen, and in some places Indians, and was almost always isolated from outside assistance except for the occasional settler. Only the coming of railroads brought any real relief from these difficulties. It is noteworthy that in the fifteen months of his missionary career after setting out for Texas in May, 1840, Odin endured danger from a deadly tornado in the middle of the Mississippi River, weathered the potentially volatile controversy in San Antonio over the ringing of the parish bells, helped pave the way for the return of much church property, experienced the hardships of both August heat with little or no water and the freezing cold of a Texas norther with little or no food, crossed flooded rivers at great risk, attempted to navigate a dangerously engorged Buffalo Bayou in a skiff, waded knee-deep in the icy mud of Houston, walked for miles in incessant rain, and completed his first year in Texas by falling dangerously ill in the midst of what Texas provided most of, isolation. After all that, he decided to spend the fall of 1841 helping Fr. Miguel Calvo make repairs to the parish church building in San Antonio, which had been damaged both by a fire in 1828 and by the revolution.

After repairing the roof, the interior was replastered, five new large doors hung, a new altar and altar rail installed, and the bell tower and facade completely restored. The latter could be done only after workmen carefully filled all of the holes that cannonballs had made in the walls.[77]

This restoration was far more than a restoration of the physical fabric of San Fernando Church; it was related to something deeper, something fundamental to the religious and cultural experience of most of the San Antonio Catholics. While the French-born Odin had a way with the log cabin-dwelling frontiersman, derived from his years among the Anglos in Missouri, he showed on his second visit to San Antonio that he wanted to be sensitive to the history and metaphors of the predominant culture there. Hispanic Catholics in San Antonio had endured the cultural uncertainties produced by the revolution and no doubt wondered what would survive from their Hispanic past. As the work on the building neared completion as December approached, Odin lent his efforts to a statement of cultural and religious survival, to show by word and deed that there would be continuity.

Aware of the special place Our Lady of Guadalupe has among Hispanic people, Odin joined in planning an elaborate public display of devotion to mark her feast day on December 12. Parishioners brought everything they had that was rare and beautiful, from silken scarves, cloths, and dresses to costly jewelry, and used these to decorate the interior of the church. One hundred and fifty pounds of gun powder was purchased, and at three o'clock in the morning of Saturday the eleventh and again at noon, the church bells were rung and nine cannon shots sounded signaling that the eve of the feast had arrived. A statue of Our Lady of Guadalupe laden with jewels and necklaces was placed on an elegantly decorated litter. At three in the afternoon the bells and cannon sounded again indicating that vespers, the first liturgical service of the feast, was about to begin. A huge procession formed, and musicians with violins and a flute led the way toward the church, followed by a young girl dressed in white, carrying a festal banner, accompanied by six other young people; then came twelve girls, each carrying a candle and a bouquet of flowers. Just behind them came the statue of Mary held aloft on the litter by four older girls. Following the statue came a huge concourse of people, first women, then men. Sixty members of the local militia escorted the procession, ceremonially firing their guns at rapid intervals.

As the huge procession neared the church, Odin, Calvo, and several altar boys, two of whom carried a processional cross and censer, solemnly moved from the front of the church to meet the procession, then led it into the brilliantly lit church. After the statue was taken to a place of honor inside the church, the huge assemblage joined in singing vespers. That evening at eight o'clock, in nineteenth-century fashion, the entire city was "illuminated": in the two public squares near the church enormous bonfires were kindled and candles were placed in windows. The bells and cannon began to sound as the procession formed in the church, this time with a cross leading the way before the banner and statue, borne with the same solemnity as in the afternoon. As the procession left the church, the clergy began to lead the participants in the rosary and the singing of hymns; this was kept up as the throng wound its way through the streets and the Plaza de las Armas and Plaza de las Islas for the next two hours. The militia was again present, and at the end of each decade of the rosary, they fired a volley and the cannon sounded. This continued until ten o'clock when the procession once more reentered San Fernando Church.

The next day, Sunday, the day of the feast itself, exactly the same procession with the same solemnities as before moved around both plazas and then into San Fernando for high mass. Odin was impressed with the great care and desire for precision that had gone into this impressive celebration. The whole city seemed to participate, as well as people from near the former missions along the river south of town. Even many Anglos from Austin and other towns came to San Antonio for the celebration.[78]

This celebration, so symbolic of the long tradition of faith among San Antonio's Catholics, was a high point of Odin's activities that fall. Every day during his 3½-month stay he celebrated mass a half hour before dawn and reported never less than 130 people present! Many of the poor came at this hour in the darkness, Odin recorded, so that their lack of nice clothing would not be noticed. Catechism classes were held daily, and Odin noted that even some Protestant children of the town came running along with their Catholic friends whenever the San Fernando bell sounded.

In the midst of this daily schedule, Odin took time out to implement locally the legislation for which he and Timon had so successfully worked. The surveying of the fifteen-acre lots surrounding the San Antonio missions was carried out in early October.

Christmas was elaborately celebrated in San Fernando Church, but Odin celebrated mass that day at the altar of San José Mission, which he had decided to reopen even though it needed repair. Perhaps this act, though much simpler, was as symbolic as the elaborate celebrations on December 11 and 12. The Spanish Franciscans were long gone, but the altar lights were burning once more, and the prayers of priest and people again echoed from the missions's walls as in days past.[79]

Two days after Christmas, Odin left San Antonio to return to Galveston by way of Victoria, Houston, and the various ranchos and settlements along the way. Traveling with only one companion, not twenty miles out of San Antonio Odin came upon a hideous sight: by the side of the road lay the corpse of a young man pierced with arrows and spears. The attack had just taken place, and the man had been dead only a few moments. Odin realized that he was perhaps in greater mortal danger than at any other time since his arrival in Texas. Going to a nearby house, he learned that the young man's parents had witnessed from inside the horrifying attack on their son but had been unable to help him. Odin would have met these Indians face-to-face himself if fear of pursuit had not caused them to flee across the San Antonio River just before he reached the scene of the attack.

Several miles beyond, Odin met two travelers who begged him not to go on; not only were Indians threatening travelers, they said, but a band of about sixty outlaws were attacking cart-train drivers and anyone else who happened along.

Odin wondered later how he had managed to proceed, but he did. Fearing that Indians would come in the night and kill them in order to steal their horses, Odin and his traveling companion carefully hid the horses and then hid themselves some distance away. After an anxious but uneventful night, they continued the next day as far as Cíbolo Creek. They knew this was not a safe place because they were told Comanches had been there a few days before. They selected this spot, however, because ahead of them no water was available for a campsite except at the Coleto, where outlaws were said to be encamped. Leaving early the next morning hoping to dodge the highwaymen and cross the Coleto early in the day, Odin was about twelve miles from Goliad when he was startled to see appearing from behind a thicket a man armed with pistols, cutlasses, and a carbine. Odin decided to meet the situation head on: "I spoke to him very coldly without allowing the fear that I felt to show." Although the armed man glared at Odin and his companion, he made no attempt to harm them.[80]

After this harrowing journey from San Antonio, Odin arrived in Goliad on the last day of 1841. Since the Indian raid of 1840, Father Estany had used the Rancho de Don Carlos as his headquarters from which he visited Victoria and seven rural Hispanic communities between the Guadalupe and San Antonio Rivers. Odin arrived there on January 1, 1842, and for several days visited the scattered Catholics of this region. On the fifth he went to Victoria, where he celebrated an Epiphany mass the next day in the parish church. The year before, his first Epiphany in Texas had been spent amidst the burned-out ruins of San Felipe de Austin, but now on his second Epiphany in Texas he celebrated mass in the repaired church of Victoria.[81] This seemed to augur well for the future.

From Victoria Odin made his way to the Lavaca River and back to Brown's Settlement. From there, an uneventful four-day journey brought him to Houston, where he boarded a boat for Galveston, arriving there on February 4. Unlike in Houston, the construction of the Galveston church was almost completed. Its walls were not yet plastered and it had no steeple, but Odin gratefully offered mass there the next Sunday. The new church was already too small: people had to stand all the way out into the street during the liturgy. But it was a church nonetheless, and Odin couldn't help but shed a few tears. The building was fifty by twenty-five feet, and Odin supplied much of the money for its construction from his missionary funds. But he did not fault the Galvestonians; they were in hard economic times, and he thought they had done their best.[82] Various church ornaments were sent from donors in the United States, and these added color and dignity to the little building. It had been an anxious Galveston congregation who welcomed Odin back to their city, for they had received an erroneous report that he was near death in San Antonio.[83]

When Odin arrived back in Galveston, he had been away almost six months. Within minutes of setting foot on the island and learning that a ship was about to sail for New Orleans, Odin quickly penned a letter to Bishop Blanc summarizing his travels and hoping to hear in return how his rejection of the appointment to Detroit had been received in Rome. As he was writing, he was handed a packet of letters that had arrived in his absence. In one of these he learned that if he would not be a bishop in Michigan, then he could be one in Texas—that Rome had appointed him the vicar apostolic of Texas and bishop of Claudiopolis. For the first time Odin learned that on July 16, 1841, Pope Gregory XVI had raised the ecclesiastical status of Texas to that of a vicariate apostolic, and with the same act had allowed the missionary to remain on the frontier he loved.[84]

The prefecture, which had gotten off to such a tenuous start in 1838, was now at an end. The faith of Texas Catholics, arduous life-risking travel, and dogged determination were producing results. Most of its buildings were now returned to church ownership; some of the ancient missions had been reopened at least for occasional masses; the parish churches of San Antonio and Victoria had been refurbished; a chapel had been built on the Lavaca River and a tiny school opened there; a school had been opened also on the Rancho de Don Carlos near Victoria; and a small church was now open for worship in Galveston, the port city Odin would make his headquarters since it provided access to Europe, from which funds and personnel must come in the years ahead.[85]

FOUR

A Bishop in Texas

THE consecration of Jean Marie Odin to the episcopacy occurred in St. Louis' Cathedral in New Orleans, on March 6, 1842. Bp. Antoine Blanc served as chief consecrator and was assisted by Bishops Michael Portier of Mobile and John Chanche of Natchez. Fr. John Timon, who had arrived in New Orleans in late February, took part in the liturgy.[1]

During the ensuing weeks, Odin remained in New Orleans to lead a retreat and preach in various places. On May 11, he boarded the ship *New York* for the return voyage to Galveston, where he arrived on the thirteenth. What he met in Texas was a people living amidst problems and contradictions that seemed to bode no ready solutions. He could only repeat an earlier conclusion: "What a lot of difficulties to surmount in this sad land!"[2] Crops were failing, the economy was in acute decline, and worse still, war appeared imminent. The years of smoldering resentment between the governments of Texas and Mexico seemed about to burst into conflagration.

During the Lamar administration, which lasted from December, 1838, to December, 1841, France, the Netherlands, and Great Britain had extended formal diplomatic recognition to Texas. While Lamar thus strengthened Texas abroad, his domestic policies opened the door to uncertainties at home. Added to the increased Indian hostility, his ill-fated attempt to extend Texan sovereignty over New Mexico and divert the lucrative United States–Mexico trade through Texas and the Gulf further inflamed the Mexican attitude toward Texas. Without the backing of the Texan Congress, Lamar, in the spring of 1841, sent an expedition northwestward only to have it arrested by Gov. Manuel Armijo's troops near the present Tucumcari. The Texan troops, merchants, and trade commissioners, including José Antonio Navarro, were marched south to Mexico City, where they were incarcerated until 1844. Furthermore, the Mexican government was convinced that the Texans were in league with Federalist separatists in northern Mexico. Trying to dispel this notion, Lamar offered no aid to the separatist movement in Tamaulipas, Coahuila, and Nuevo León when in January, 1840, a convention declared the independence of the Republic of the Rio Grande and raised an army. However, when this army met defeat that March, the republic's provisional government fled to Victoria and sought Lamar's assistance. When he gave permission to recruit troops in South Texas, the Mexican government could come to only one conclusion. Then Lamar, also in 1841, authorized Commodore Edwin W. Moore to take the Texan fleet into Yucatecan waters to seek an alliance there with other separatists attempting to set up a Yucatecan republic. The Yucatecans then hired the Texan fleet to patrol their coastline. This action Lamar justified as an appropriate response to the Mexican government's refusal to negotiate with Texas.

In that same year, Gen. Antonio López de Santa Anna returned to power. While both direct and indirect actions of the Lamar administration further angered Mexico, ironically it was the succeeding Houston administration that bore the brunt of Mexico's response. It is possible, of course, that Santa Anna, having suffered the humiliation of defeat at San Jacinto in 1836, might have taken reprisals against Texas anyway, but in any event, he ordered Gen. Rafael Vásquez at Saltillo to march northward into Texas with a force variously estimated to be from eight to fourteen hundred men. Detachments were sent to occupy Goliad and Victoria, while the main body in company with General Vásquez entered San Antonio on March 5, 1842, the eve both of Odin's espicopal consecration in New Orleans and of the sixth anniversary of the fall of the Alamo. The Texans were caught by surprise, and entry was made without incident. The Mexican flag was raised, Mexican sovereignty proclaimed, the defenses inspected, and after two days, the order to retreat was given. The only action of the campaign resulted when a company of Rangers west of San Antonio harassed the army as it moved southward.

When word of the invasion spread through Texas, a war fever set in with many volunteers rushing to San Antonio. Although Houston called Congress into special session, he actually did not want all-out war with Mexico —even as a retaliation for invasion. Texas was ill-prepared militarily for such a venture, and Houston hoped that annexation would soon shift the problem of relations with Mexico to Washington. Congress even approved a declaration of war, but Houston vetoed it. At this time Houston also disbanded the navy—officially for fiscal reasons. While public outrage greeted these actions, he remained unmoved, and the war mood gradually subsided. Just as it did so, however, in the autumn Santa Anna sent a new invasion force into Texas under Gen. Adrián Woll. Once more San Antonio was taken and Mexican sovereignty proclaimed. A Ranger force began to collect around San Antonio, but Woll showed no inclination to leave. After losing about sixty men on September 18 in an encounter with the Texans along Salado Creek, Woll moved to the Rio Grande, carrying with him a number of prisoners including the entire district court—attorneys, jury, and presiding judge—which had been in session in San Antonio, as well as the Fayette County militia company, which he had captured.

Houston ordered Texan troops under Gen. Alexander Somervell to pursue Woll and make sure he crossed the Rio Grande. Somervell was ordered not to cross the Rio Grande but only to patrol it in case another invasion attempt was about to be made. Arriving in Laredo on December 8, Somervell remained there until the month was almost over and, detecting no further threat, decided to move northward. When news of his decision spread among his seven hundred troops, approximately three hundred of them refused to obey and prepared to invade Mexico. Somervell moved northward with the bulk of his force, while the others elected William S. Fisher as commander, crossed the Rio Grande to the town of Mier, and demanded a ransom and supplies. When these were denied, they attacked the town after noon on Christmas Day. They were soon surprised to discover two thousand Mexican troops garrisoned in the town. Through the night and into the next day the attack continued. Then the Mexican commander, running out of ammunition and supplies, decided he would probably have to surrender but, as one last hope, demanded that the Texans do so. Unaware of true conditions within the town and overawed by numbers, the Texans did so. After the Texan prisoners began the long march to Mexico City, most of them managed to escape. However, their freedom was short-lived: hunger and cold caused most to surrender within a few weeks. Santa Anna sent orders that one out of ten was to be executed, and the condemned were chosen by lot through the drawing of black or white beans. After the executions, the remainder continued their march to the capital, where they joined the prisoners from the Santa Fe expedition and Woll's captives.

Not all of these prisoners were released until the overthrow and exile of Santa Anna in 1844. With the aid of British diplomats in Mexico City, Houston was able to arrange for both their release and a truce with the new president, José Herrera. A treaty of recognition was hoped for, but the Herrera government lasted only eighteen months before being overthrown by Mariano Paredes, a Centralist.[3]

While Odin was still in New Orleans, rumor had it that Mexico was sending twenty-five thousand troops into Texas and that many were fleeing in front of this army. Odin believed, like Houston, that all-out war would be disastrous for Texas because of shortages in food and money. A drought in 1841 had resulted in near famine in some areas. Odin wanted to bring with him to Texas several women religious to work in Galveston and San Antonio and some priests to work among the Karankawas still living along the Texas coast, but with the invasion rumor and war scare, these plans were abandoned. Even on board ship, returning to Texas in May, Odin saw evidence of deteriorating conditions in Texas: the ship was crowded with volunteers from the United States on their way to Texas to engage in what they believed would be an invasion of Mexico. While on board ship, in spite of their bravado, Odin thought they behaved well enough, but after arrival in Galveston he saw them quickly become a lawless lot. Though he pitied the inhabitants of Corpus Christi, he sighed with relief when the volunteers went there from Galveston in early July.

> Our brave volunteers from the United States are a true scourge for the country. Unprovided with provisions they had to yield to pillage and have caused great damage. Thanks to God we have just been relieved of five companies. . . . It was a case of not being able to stand them any longer with their pistols and Bowie knives. In one single week we had four murders. Those who were already in Corpus Christi ruined the poor inhabitants of the frontier.[4]

Later Odin learned that some members of similar volunteer groups had looted, robbed, and raped in the environs of San Antonio among the Hispanic residents. That summer and fall, Odin sorrowed at the suffering of those being displaced by both armies. Many Anglo and European settlers fled eastward, while many Hispanic Texans fled southward to the Rio Grande away from the volunteers and Texan militia. Some recent immigrants left Texas entirely, fleeing through the port of Galveston. Texas was almost bankrupt, and these troops, when they received neither wages nor food, began to pillage private homes, especially in San Antonio, where many newcomer volunteers assumed that any Spanish-speaking Texan was automatically a friend of Santa Anna. At Victoria, mobs of civilians went to the Rancho de Don Carlos and forced about fifty Hispanic families to leave the region. Odin believed that the Texan troops and American volunteers did more harm that year than the Mexican armies.[5]

Odin was in Galveston only a few days when news from San Fernando parish reached him: when Gen. Rafael Vásquez entered San Antonio the former pastor, Fr. Refugio de la Garza, asked the general to recognize him as lawful pastor. Fr. Miguel Calvo protested, explaining that Rome had made jurisdictional changes in Texas. General Vásquez explained that he did not enter into ecclesiastical matters and was concerned only with his military orders. Nevertheless, according to Calvo, the former pastor did go into the church once or twice to celebrate mass but then left with the army when it evacuated the city.[6]

Amidst this confusion the new bishop and vicar apostolic tried to go on with the work at hand. While a trip to San Antonio seemed impossible under the circumstances, Galveston and Houston could profit from his attentions. Galveston itself knew little peace that summer, as witnessed by the street altercations in the opening days of June. The incoming volunteers, departing settlers, and incessant talk of invasions and war greatly added to the rawness of the new city. But work was work, and Odin concluded that "business as usual" was the only appropriate attitude for a missionary bishop.

In May Odin purchased a modest house to serve as his first permanent dwelling place in Texas. A few weeks later the sacristy of the new church was completed, but the church itself remained too small for the crowds at Sunday mass. In early July, Odin went to Houston and was delighted to find the church there almost complete. He personally supervised the installation of the altar and formally opened St. Vincent de Paul Church on Sunday, July 17, 1842. By this time Sam Houston had moved the Texan capital back to his namesake town, which gave Odin a chance to gather news from all parts and visit with the Catholic members of the government. Except for a visit to the Brazos River settlements to the southwest, Odin remained in Houston to serve as pastor until August 10. For his return trip to Galveston, Odin went by horseback as far as Lynchburg, where he baptized a newborn child, and then went on by boat to Galveston.[7]

The late summer of 1842 did not go well for Odin: for eleven days in late August and early September he was confined to bed with a fever. Then his house was robbed, and far worse, on September 19 gale-force winds struck the island city, leaving damaged and destroyed buildings in its wake. Among the latter was the recently completed St. Mary's Church. For several days before, the wind blew from the east, then late on the eighteenth it shifted to the north and blew water into the heart of the island. Many feared for their lives, believing the island was about to be submerged.

By the end of December, the Galveston church was rebuilt and in use. This time a frame steeple was added, and the following March Odin rang the bell, cast in Houston, for the first time.[8]

The confusion reigning in Texas during 1842 only reiterated for Odin the tenuous nature of both the Texan republic and his vicariate. Assistance from all quarters was needed and this included moral support as much as anything else. In the fall of 1842, Odin began efforts to obtain an invitation to the American hierarchy's Fifth Council of Baltimore, scheduled to convene on May 14, 1843. Odin, as vicar apostolic of Texas, was not part of the American hierarchy, but he was convinced he needed to be there because of the contact with other bishops such a gathering provided. Of course, he needed an invitation, so he wrote and asked for one. Archbishop Samuel Eccleston of Baltimore issued him an invitation, and Odin left Galveston by ship on March 24.[9]

The journey was not pleasant. The first day out, the ship, which went by way of Sabine Pass, was delayed there trying to get across a sandbar. Then Odin came down with chills and fever, recurrences of which plagued his entire stay in the United States.[10]

Although he was abed during most of the council's sessions, he did confer with Timon, who arranged for some extra funding for Odin's work. After the close of the council, Odin, in company with a fellow Vincentian who had served as his theological consultant during the council, visited New York hoping to raise more funds there. On his way west down the Ohio River,

Odin relapsed again and was forced to remain in a hospital at Louisville for several days. Regaining some of his strength, he went to Portland, Kentucky, where he met with Timon again. On June 19, Odin set out for St. Mary-of-the-Barrens Seminary in Missouri, where once more he was beset by illness. He became so weak that it was late September before he could start out for Galveston.[11] Odin finally arrived back in Galveston on December 16, and this time he returned to his own house, not a hired room.[12]

By mid-January, 1844, St. Mary's in Galveston seemed to be absolutely thriving. Early that month several boats loaded with colonists, many of whom were Catholics, landed in Galveston. On one boat carrying 129 passengers, Odin discovered that all except 5 were Catholics—in this instance, German-speaking. Although many immigrants were moving west, a significant number settled in Galveston and swelled the ranks of the parish. It now had seven hundred members and each day from twenty to twenty-five children came to catechism class. On Sundays, the principal mass was sung and celebrated with the Catholic church's full ceremonial. Before this mass, Odin assembled the catechism class to recite the major points of the past week's lessons. On Sundays Odin also officiated at a well-attended vespers in the early evening.[13]

With such an increase in Catholics, of which Galveston was but one instance, Odin needed additional priests more than ever. Before going to Baltimore the previous March, Odin had sought Timon's help in procuring a replacement for the late Father Haydon. While battling illness in Missouri the previous summer, Odin had been pleased to learn that two Alsatian priests had arrived for work in Texas among German-speaking Catholics. These were Jean Pierre Ogé and another priest identified only as "Schneider." Ogé went to St. Mary's Church in Lavaca County, where he worked for a time, and Schneider served in Houston and visited several German settlements.[14] But all priests who came to Texas were not suited for work there, and what appeared to be a promising situation soon faded. By April, Father Schneider, who was considered to be an exceptional orator by Odin, proved to have an irascible personality and simply could not get along with those among whom he labored. In April Schneider left Texas, leaving Odin with no help for work among the German immigrants in the Galveston-Houston area. This disappointment was soon followed by another: after Ogé went to the west, Odin received word from Strasbourg that Ogé did not have a good record in his home diocese. Furthermore, the *exeat*, or letter of dismissal from his previous bishop, that Ogé presented Odin contained false information. Odin felt betrayed and perplexed. While Ogé seemed to be doing good work, and the people liked him, Odin decided he couldn't overlook such a breach of faith. Reluctantly, in early 1845, he told Ogé to leave Texas.[15]

Other new priests arrived during 1844, however. In April, Timon dispatched two Vincentians to Texas, Joseph Paquín and John Brands. Paquín was an old friend of Odin, and both he and Brands were veterans of frontier work in southern Missouri. At last, Odin hoped, there would be a Vincentian community in Texas. He soon made Paquín his vicar general and left him in charge when he went to San Antonio that summer. Paquín also was to go once a month to St. Vincent de Paul Church in Houston. But life was especially tenuous on the frontier. In July, while in Houston, Paquín received word from Brands in Galveston that yellow fever had broken out there and his help was needed in caring for the sick and dying. Paquín immediately left Houston for Galveston, where he and Brands were soon burying as many as twenty-four victims in a single day. Some two hundred Galvestonians died in this epidemic. After a weary day among the sick and the dead, Paquín and Brands were sitting eating their evening meal in their house next to the bishop's residence when both complained of extreme fatigue. They retired for the evening and never saw each other again. Both were stricken by this disease whose origin was then so mysterious. For five days they hovered near death. Brands tried several times to leave his room to see Paquín but was stopped by those who had come to care for them. Paquín died late in the evening of August 11. Brands, who survived the disease, lamented that he had not even been able to grant absolution to his dying friend. Paquín's body was buried in front of the altar of St. Mary's Church and was later moved to the structure that succeeded it in 1847. Odin did not learn of his vicar general's death until mid-September while he was still in San Antonio.[16]

In contrast to the sufferings of Galveston, Odin was pleased at the signs of growth he witnessed that summer in western Texas. The colonists Odin previously had seen arriving in such large numbers in Galveston were mostly members of two colonizing ventures: one led by Henri Castro, which then and later drew colonists from Alsace, Switzerland, and the German states; and the other organized by the Adelsverein, or "society of nobles," which brought colonists from the German states to Texas. Prince Karl von Solms-Braunfels was a leader of this group. That summer, while Odin was in Houston on his way west, both colonizing agents called on him seeking his blessing for their respective ventures. Odin, of course, was happy to express favor for projects that would bring many Catholics into Texas. He had already loaned money to some of Castro's colonists who arrived in Galveston in dire straits, and he would do so again. In spite of ongoing tensions between Mexico and Texas, European colonists were once more coming in relatively large numbers. Ogé and Schneider were such disappointments to Odin largely because German-speaking priests were now sorely needed in Texas.

In September, Castro left San Antonio with a band of colonists and a train of eleven carts bound for his grant on the Medina River to the west. These colonists had not fared well, since they had languished for months in San Antonio in virtual poverty waiting for Castro to arrive so that their lands could be allotted.

Now Castro was with his unhappy colonists, taking them to their area of settlement, and Odin was not far behind. With all the discontent, Castro was extremely pleased to have Odin visit his colonists. While Castro's wife and children were Catholics, his own spiritual attachment to the church was equivocal, since he probably preferred his ancestral Judaism. What Castro now needed from the Catholic church was the provision of a sense of regularity and stability to his colonists' lives. The land west of San Antonio was not what even Castro had originally expected. In the greenest of times the area hardly resembled Europe, and even less so after a hot Texas summer. Poverty was to haunt these settlers for some time to come; the dry, untilled land bespoke this fact every time a colonist looked toward the horizon. The Catholic church was at least one aspect of most of the colonists' experience that could still be with them even though Europe was a world away.

Almost as soon as he arrived on the Medina River, Odin was asked to lay the cornerstone for a parish church. This was done on September 12, 1844. The new church was to be dedicated to the patronage of St. Louis, king of France, helping to make the new settlement a metaphor of the colonists' European identity. While a few of them were French, most were German-speaking, with many of these coming from Alsace, an area once part of the medieval German empire but since the 1600s a part of France. Later their little village on the frontier of Texas, with its German cuisine and language, German and French architecture, and a parish church named for St. Louis, king of France, would aptly symbolize the origins of its original settlers.

Although the land itself was a disappointment, the colonists hoped, now that Castro was on the scene, that they could own a lot more of it than they ever could of any land in Europe. And the site chosen for their village was a good one. Although only a thatched shed stood on the site at this time, Odin proclaimed it "charming."

Castro also needed something more from Odin: proof that he had indeed begun a colony in Texas, that a village had been established and land grants parceled out. This not only would attract additional colonists but would help satisfy his creditors as well. At Castro's request, Odin signed a statement, witnessed by the French consul in San Antonio, that he had laid the cornerstone of a church in Castroville and that colonists were now living and working on the site and intending to form a permanent settlement.[17]

Odin placed these colonists under the spiritual oversight of Father Calvo and Father Estany, who could visit them from time to time, Calvo from San Antonio and Estany from his work along the lower San Antonio River.

Back in Galveston by early December, Odin was pleased when John Timon paid him a visit just after Christmas. He was especially pleased to show his fellow Vincentian the year's statistics indicating increasing religious activity among Texas Catholics. During 1844, 3,150 confessions had been heard and there had been 2,850 receptions of Holy Communion. Clearly, San Antonio remained the most Catholic of areas within the vicariate: 56.4 percent and 59.5 percent of the above figures, respectively, pertained to San Fernando parish.[18]

During his visit, Timon urged Odin to go to Europe in search of additional clergy, and but for some pending engagements, Odin would have left on the boat taking Timon to New Orleans in early January. Another trip to Houston was necessary, and Father Brands had to be further prepared to serve as vicar general, since his duties would be all the more crucial during the bishop's absence in Europe. Finally on February 26, Odin left Galveston for New Orleans. Just before leaving he obtained a donation of seven lots from the Galveston City Company, adjoining another lot he had purchased six months earlier to be the site of a new St. Mary's Church, which he believed would one day become the cathedral of a new diocese.[19]

By the time Odin left Galveston in late February, word was out in both Texas and the United States that the annexation of Texas was close at hand. Houston, who had worked for annexation, had gone out of office the previous December. He had negotiated an annexation treaty that the United States Senate failed to ratify. Now, however, in the administration of his successor, Anson Jones, a series of events had led to a favorable climate in the United States for annexation. Over the years many Whigs in the United States had opposed annexation because of the existence of slavery in Texas. But now a great change had taken place. The Democrats had won the November, 1844, presidential election, and congressmen, even some Whigs, read the election returns carefully. American voters were in an expansionist mood. The Democrats' standard-bearer and the next president as of March 4, 1845, was James Knox Polk of Tennessee–like Houston, a protégé of Andrew Jackson. With their "Fifty-four, forty or fight" campaign slogan, Polk and the Democrats made a lot of noise about the annexation of the Oregon territory, jointly occupied with Great Britain since 1818. While they did want Oregon, they also wanted Texas, California, and at least a portion of New Mexico as well. The Whig candidate, Henry Clay, was equivocal about expansionism, and the Democrats won the election.

John Tyler was still president until March 4, 1845, however. The previous year it had been his and Houston's treaty which the Senate rejected, but he still wanted Texas and hoped the election results would enable him to get it before his own term expired.

Tyler, concluding that the two-thirds majority vote in the Senate required for ratification of a treaty might still be hard to get, decided to push for annexation by a joint resolution of both houses of Congress, which required only a simple majority. In a special message to Congress in December, 1844, Tyler made his proposal. Successfully passing in both houses, the resolution reached the president's desk on March 3, 1845, and Tyler signed it on his last full day in office. It still had to be ratified by the Texans, but that was a foregone conclusion.

The day Tyler signed the joint resolution, Odin's boat was nearing New Orleans.[20] The papers there over the next few days were full of news about the annexation and the new administration led by the avowed expansionist James Knox Polk. Timon was still in New Orleans when Odin arrived, and the two had opportunity to discuss the developing Texan situation, wondering what the future might hold if Mexico, as was probable, refused to recognize this annexation or if Polk, as was equally probable, began to press Mexico for the cession of other North American regions such as California.

On March 13 Odin left New Orleans for New York, where he was scheduled to sail for Liverpool. Indicative of the current technological revolution, Odin traveled to the Northeast on "the cars," the new railroad train, instead of a coastal steamer. This was certainly a different kind of travel from what he was accustomed to in Texas, and the speed made it possible for him to spend Palm Sunday in Mobile, Holy Thursday in Augusta, Holy Saturday in Charleston, and much of Easter week in Georgetown near Washington. He arrived in New York on March 29, and he and Bp. Francis Patrick Kenrick of Philadelphia embarked for Europe on April 1. After landing in Liverpool three weeks later, Odin first went to Ireland to visit the Vincentian community in Dublin and Maynooth College in County Kildare in the hope of finding volunteers for the work in Texas.

In early May Odin arrived in Paris, where he remained for a month. While there he managed to get an audience with Queen Amelia, wife of King Louis Philippe, hoping to receive a sizeable contribution for his work, but the queen, who had "a thousand questions" about Texas, promised only some liturgical items for the bishop. More successful were Odin's pleas for funds from the Society for the Propagation of the Faith in Lyon, which granted him eight thousand dollars, and the Leopoldinen Stiftung in Vienna, which provided another fourteen hundred dollars. The purpose of the latter society was to provide aid for German Catholic immigrants in the United States.[21] In Lyon Odin visited seminaries and religious houses in the region and was pleased that several priests, seminarians, and women religious of the Ursuline order volunteered for work in Texas. While on the continent, Odin also recruited two German priests and was soon pleased to learn that his visit to Ireland had paid off as well. There three priests, two of them Vincentians like Odin, were preparing to leave for Galveston. One of the Vincentians, Fr. John Lynch, whom Odin ironically considered devoted and zealous but far from brilliant, in later years became the first bishop and later archbishop of Toronto and the founder of Niagara University.[22]

Odin had a pleasant stay in Rome, where he had three separate audiences with Pope Gregory XVI to thoroughly acquaint him with the situation in Texas.[23] A far less pleasant experience was a visit he made to Strasbourg in November. In addition to Fathers Ogé and Schneider, three other priests had come to Galveston from this diocese. Deciding something was amiss, Odin had not allowed these priests to minister in Texas at all. Believing the bishop or someone in his office was using Texas as a place to send unwanted clergy, Odin knew he must go to Strasbourg and confront the bishop. The bishop of Strasbourg admitted to Odin he had signed the *exeats* for the five priests without reading them. Odin believed, however, that the bishop was probably guilty of complicity in a plan to rid his diocese of men "corrupted in every respect" by issuing letters of dismissal containing information that was simply untrue. He "indeed deserves to be rebuked," thought Odin.[24]

After spending Christmas with his family in Ambierle, Odin went by way of Paris to Brussels where he contracted for the purchase of five hundred thousand bricks for the building of a new church in Galveston. He was promised free transportation for the bricks: there were so many boats filled with colonists leaving from Antwerp bound for Galveston that the shipping companies agreed to use the brick for ballast on the ships. In February, Odin was back in Paris and this time saw King Louis Philippe and Queen Amelia—but still no financial gift was forthcoming.

Intending to embark from Le Havre, Odin and the priests, seminarians, and women religious he had recruited in France left Paris on March 9, 1846. In Le Havre Odin realized that the slower and cheaper sailing ship he was planning to take would not get him across the Atlantic in time to attend another meeting of the American hierarchy in Baltimore. Contrary winds were already delaying departure, and he had to attend this council for the sake of his vicariate. He needed no invitation now that Texas was part of the United States, and he knew the question of diocesan status for Texas would be discussed. He decided to leave his band of missionaries to the sailing ship and go back to Liverpool where he could take a faster steamship.[25]

On April 11, Odin left Liverpool on the *Great Western*, the largest steamship of its time, a technological triumph of the mid-nineteenth century. He arrived in New York after a sixteen-day crossing, in plenty of time to attend the Sixth Council of Baltimore.[26] The council went into session on May 10, and Odin was pleased when the council sent a recommendation to Rome that the vicariate apostolic of Texas be elevated to diocesan status.[27]

After the close of the council, Odin preached a mission in Philadelphia in late May and then, at the request of the Vincentian superior, made an inspection tour of the Vincentian houses in Missouri. In late June, he arrived in New Orleans and booked passage on a ship carrying volunteer troops for the United States army now in Texas. A rowdy lot, they were billeted on decks, while the civilian passengers were in staterooms. As the ship left

New Orleans, many of the troops were already lying about in a drunken stupor. Only with difficulty could others leave their staterooms, the deck and passageways were so crowded. But this was only a mild inconvenience compared to what was to come. When the ship entered the Gulf, the drunken soldiers became seasick. In retrospect, Odin considered this fortunate since it probably prevented even greater disorder. But the soldiers were not sick for the entire trip. Their officers could not control them, and the ship's captain on one occasion had to hide on his own ship to escape their threats. When dinner was served to the civilian passengers, the volunteers, who in truth were poorly provisioned, tried to force their way into the dining hall. Fortunately, the volunteers had not yet been issued firearms or else the guards could not have prevented the knife-wielding mob from entering. To disembark the volunteers, the ship had to proceed directly from New Orleans to the mouth of the Rio Grande at Point Isabel, near Brazos de Santiago. For the Galveston-bound passengers the peace they enjoyed once the volunteers were gone was almost worth the detour. On arrival at Point Isabel, Odin could see what was now in progress between the United States and Mexico: the entire tip of the point was white with tents set up for the troops. Odin noted that more than fifty small buildings and several docks had been constructed and that seven or eight troop transports were lined up.[28]

When Odin at last arrived in Galveston on July 2, he found two Jesuit priests there on their way south to join the army as chaplains. Also awaiting was a request from President Polk to send priests to the army as chaplains. To this end Odin appointed Father Estany to join the two Jesuits on their way to the army. Odin knew that many Catholics were serving in the army, mainly from the ranks of newly arrived Irish and German immigrants.[29] The fact that one of the Jesuits spoke German, the other French, and Estany Spanish would help in ministering to Catholic soldiers from Louisiana and Texas.

The war between the United States and Mexico broke out in earnest about the time Odin was returning to the United States that spring. After the joint resolutions calling for the annexation of Texas were passed in March, 1845, the Texan Congress called for a convention to meet that summer in Austin. On July 4, 1845, an ordinance of annexation was adopted and work began on a state constitution. Both the ordinance and the constitution were submitted to the voters, who overwhelmingly approved them on October 13. On December 29 President Polk signed the Texas Admission Act, and on February 19, 1846, the government of the Texan republic transferred authority to the new state government.

While this was going on, relations between the United States and Mexico deteriorated rapidly. No Mexican government could accept Polk's demand for a recognition of Texas independence with a boundary at the Rio

Grande coupled with his proposal to purchase both California and New Mexico.

With the Texan government's permission, the defense of Texas was taken over by the United States in the summer of 1845. Gen. Zachary Taylor first moved his command from Louisiana to the mouth of the Nueces River near present-day Corpus Christi. In March of 1846, Taylor advanced southward to a position near present-day Brownsville, and hostilities soon began in earnest. He used Point Isabel, which Odin visited briefly later that year, as a supply and debarkation point.

Odin was ambivalent on the war: he was pleased Texas was in the United States and was willing to send one of his few priests to serve Catholics in the army, but he feared the United States would go too far in the struggle with Mexico. He had no doubt which would win, and he regretted that the two nations had not come to an amicable agreement. Now that war had begun, the United States might not know where to stop her conquests. These sentiments he recorded in three letters that summer. The first quoted here was probably addressed to Archbishop Blanc in New Orleans, the second to Jean-Baptiste Etienne in Paris, and the third to the Society for the Propagation of the Faith in Lyon.

> Texas has again fallen prey to the horrors of war. Since it joined the United States the American government has placed troops on its borders . . . the United States has already taken possession of several small villages situated on the banks of the Rio Grande and had it not been for the great heat which stopped its march it would be well into the interior of the country [Mexico]. We continue one way or another to make great preparations for autumn, and most likely if Mexico does not decide to make peace, she will be dealt a blow from which she will have difficulty recovering.[30]

> Every day some men are sent to the Rio Grande. Already the American army includes 20,000 soldiers and they intend to increase it to 50,000 men. A detachment of 5000 men left St. Louis to attack Santa Fe and an equal force is directed to California. The zeal of the Americans is to march as far as Mexico [City], to separate part of Mexico from the central government, to form a separate republic which later by means of annexation will become part of the United States, and as a prize of war to take all of California at the same time.[31]

> They speak of seizing California and the departments of the Northeast. This issue distresses me very much for poor Mexico. It is too weak to struggle against the United States and the Americans already too greedy for lands and conquests will perhaps no longer know where to stop.[32]

Odin took heart, however, in that he believed the war would not affect the gains his European trip had secured for the Texas mission. The priests, seminarians, and Ursuline religious from France had arrived safely in New Orleans, and the men went upriver to Missouri for further study. The Ursulines were still postulants, and they remained at a convent in New Orleans until January, 1847, when they went with several professed sisters to Galveston to begin a school.[33] The Irish and German priests also arrived safely in Texas, the latter arriving in company with a large number of German colonists.[34]

Odin decided that, in spite of war and new arrivals, after a fifteen-month absence it was time for him to go west again. Now that he had German priests, he decided it was time to visit New Braunfels to start a church among the German colonists there. In New Braunfels he met with Baron Ottfried von Meusebach, chief agent of the Mainzer Verein, and other members of this society's colonization board to arrange for the founding of a Catholic church in the town. Aware that a building, parsonage, and salary had been provided by the board for the local Evangelical congregation, Odin stated that the Catholic parish would have to be administratively and financially free of the board. He assured them that a Catholic church building would be erected out of church funds but did request that a lot be donated for this purpose. The board understood his position and complied with his request.

Odin made a favorable impression in the community. As the non-Catholic Ferdinand von Roemer, a German scientist-traveler, recorded of Odin: "Bishop Odin . . . travels continually about in the country, visiting the Catholics living scattered in the various parts of the country. Fearlessly and tirelessly he traverses the lonesome prairies on horseback, and through his restless energy and unassuming, charming personality has earned for himself the universal respect also of those not of his faith."[35]

Within the vicariate at the end of 1846, there were ten church buildings in regular use, each with congregations on the increase: San Fernando in San Antonio, Our Lady of Guadalupe in Victoria, St. Mary's at Brown's Settlement on the Lavaca River, St. Louis' in Castroville, Our Lady of Refuge in Refugio, St. Joseph's at Fagan Settlement in Refugio County, Santa Gertrudis on the Rancho de Don Carlos in Victoria County, St. Peter's on Cummings Creek in Austin County, St. Vincent's in Houston, and St. Mary's in Galveston. Mass-stations where the liturgy was celebrated occasionally were located at the former missions of San José, San Juan Capistrano, and San Francisco de la Espada in Bexar County, and in the following towns or settlements: Nacogdoches and San Augustine in counties of the same name, Brazoria and Velasco in Brazoria County, Live Oak Point in Refugio County, San Patricio and Corpus Christi in San Patricio County, Cuero and McHenry Settlement in Victoria County, Brushy Creek Settlement in Lavaca County, Gonzales and Seguin in Gonzales County, Richmond in Ft. Bend County, Spring Creek and Morgan's Point in Harris County, and Liberty in Liberty County. Also, parochial schools existed in Brown's Settlement and Brazoria.[36]

There were now eleven priests in the vicariate, including Odin. According to official figures reported from all dioceses in the United States for the year 1846, the vicariate apostolic of Texas was more developed than the dioceses of Hartford, Richmond, Nashville, Dubuque, Little Rock, and Natchez as well as the archdiocese of Oregon City.[37]

In January, 1847, Odin went to New Orleans to bring back to Galveston the three novices he had brought from France the year before, along with five professed Ursuline sisters. These religious came to begin an academy for girls in the island city. On November 15 the chapter of the New Orleans convent selected a superior for the new foundation in Texas, Sr. Josephin Blin de Saint Arsene. The postulants brought by Odin from France began their novitiate upon arrival in New Orleans and were clothed with the religious habit on December 21, 1846. These were Marie Noyer, who became Sister St. Angela; Elisa Metton, who became Sister St. Augustine; and Madeleine Renard, who became Sister St. Ursula. The four professed sisters were Mother St. Arsene, the superior, and Sisters St. Bruno, St. Ambroise, and St. Stanislaus. Louis Chambodut, Anthony Chanrion, and Matthew Chazelle, recruited in France the year before, joined Odin and the sisters in New Orleans for the voyage to Galveston. The three priests had completed their studies in Missouri and were now newly ordained. The party arrived in Galveston on January 18, and the sisters set up their home in a two-year-old frame structure already in need of repair. Odin and Father Chambodut tried to make the building as hospitable as possible. Undaunted, the sisters forged ahead with organizing their school, which by May had seventy students.[38]

Meanwhile Odin proceeded with plans for the new St. Mary's Church and reserved the date of March 14 for laying the cornerstone. For this special occasion, Odin could think of no better orator than John Timon, who was then in Louisiana on an inspection tour of Vincentian institutions. Timon was pleased to come, especially since like Odin he suspected that they would be laying the cornerstone of what soon would be a cathedral for a new diocese. On March 14, 1847, the laying of the cornerstone took place as scheduled and was accompanied by impressive ceremonies consisting of a litany, psalms, and polyphonic chanting in Latin.[39]

Odin persuaded Timon to remain longer than he had planned. The laying of the cornerstone had created a heightened religious interest, and Timon was not only eloquent and affable but also a native speaker of English, factors Odin wished to capitalize on. Timon had to stay even longer when steamer traffic ceased for a time, and Odin persuaded him to lead retreats in both Galveston and Houston. When Timon failed to get a berth on the

St. Mary's Cathedral, Galveston, circa 1860.
Courtesy Catholic Archives of Texas, Austin.

first steamer that did arrive, around Palm Sunday, he gave in to Odin's new argument that he should not risk the dangers of the sea during Holy Week. Then Odin came down with a fever and convinced Timon to visit Calvo and the other Vincentians in San Antonio before returning to Missouri.[40] The following September, Timon was appointed bishop of Buffalo, New York, where he served until his death in 1867.[41]

As the weeks of 1847 slipped by, much of Odin's time was occupied with overseeing the construction of St. Mary's. He was also pleased at the steady growth of the nearby Houston parish, where he had assigned two of the newly arrived Irish priests, John Lynch and James Fitzgerald.[42]

Although Pope Pius IX approved the establishment of the diocese of Galveston and the appointment of Odin as its first bishop on May 4, 1847, it was mid-September before word of this reached Odin. Although the Sixth Council of Baltimore had requested diocesan status for Texas in May of the previous year, the death of Pope Gregory XVI and the ensuing papal election delayed decisive action on the matter for almost a year.[43]

The vicariate was now a diocese and Odin rejoiced, but Texas was still a frontier and life was hard. Joy was often tempered by sorrow. That fall word came from Castroville that Fr. Matthew Chazelle had died there on September 1 after a three-week illness. Then, at the end of September, yellow fever struck Galveston itself, and more than a hundred people died. Fr. Bartholomew Rollando, Odin's assistant and fellow Vincentian, died on October 11. Odin, too, was stricken, but survived though he remained bedridden for weeks. His house became an infirmary, although the Urusuline sisters were fortunately untouched by the disease.[44]

Work on what was now the cathedral had proceeded satisfactorily until interrupted by the epidemic. By the end of September all the exterior brickwork except the facade had been completed; the roof was on, but much interior finishing remained to be done.

Just before Christmas Odin's spirits were lifted when two more of the young men he had brought from France in 1846 arrived from Missouri. He ordained Joseph Anstaett and Charles Padey to the priesthood on Christmas Eve.[45]

The establishment of the new diocese had not changed the realities of existence in Texas. Plagues bringing suffering and death continued to come and go, and a life of privation remained the lot of the frontier Texan. Nevertheless, the Catholic presence in Texas was growing. Gone were the prefecture and vicariate: Texas had its own diocese and its own bishop, and the additional personnel Odin received in 1847 enabled him to send two priests, Louis Chambodut and Anthony Chanrion, to Nacogdoches to serve the largely Hispanic parish there, virtually untended since the death of Father Díaz de León in 1834.

For the Texas church, these events were also symbolic. The ancient roots the Franciscans had planted long ago had never died, and they were once more sending forth plants in a fertile soil.

FIVE

Expanding the Frontier Diocese

THE new diocese which came into being on May 4, 1847, was unique in that its boundaries were at the time indefinable. When Texas was annexed in 1845, the United States accepted the boundaries that Texas had defined for itself in the Boundary Statute of 1836: a boundary on the south and west following the Rio Grande to its source in present-day Colorado and thence northward into what is now Wyoming. While in its northward extremity this boundary gave Texas a claim only to a narrow band of territory, farther to the south it included more than half of New Mexico. The papal document establishing the diocese of Galveston indicated that the new diocese should include whatever territory comprised the state of Texas when its difficulties with Mexico were over—in other words, when the war between the United States and Mexico was concluded. In 1848 the United States Senate and the Mexican Congress ratified the Treaty of Guadalupe Hidalgo, in which Mexico recognized Texas independence and transferred Alta California and New Mexico to the United States.

While the war was still in progress, the United States government in 1847 indicated to Texas authorities that the new state would not have the same boundaries as those claimed by the former republic, even though these were the very boundaries Washington had recognized at the time of annexation. As Odin saw it, the federal government claimed the disputed regions "by right of conquest" whereas Texas based its claim on the annexation resolution, which accepted the republic's boundaries. Underlying the controversy was the fact that historically New Mexico never had been part of Texas. Also there was the volatile issue of slavery and its spread into the West: Texas was a slaveholding state, and slavery would exist in those areas encompassed by its boundaries. Confusion remained over Texas' boundaries until the Compromise of 1850, when the state relinquished its claim to New Mexico and the strip of land to the north and received adequate compensation in the form of ten million dollars.

During this uncertain period, Odin was obviously in a quandary: he could not really know the extent of his already unwieldy diocese until final resolution of the boundary question. Given the wording of the document establishing his diocese and the provisions of the Treaty of Guadalupe Hidalgo, it could be argued that Odin's diocese did indeed include New Mexico, an area that would be impossible for him to oversee. He was planning a trip to the lower Rio Grande Valley, where many Catholics resided in the villages and ranchos along the river, when he became aware of the full extent of the boundary controversy between Texas and the federal government.

While most of the controversy centered on New Mexico, Odin, fearing that the lower Rio Grande area, over which the Republic of Texas had exercised only tenuous control, might also be in question, decided to call off his proposed visit there and in July, 1848, wrote Rome asking for a further definition of his area of jurisdiction. It was the spring of 1849 before word came that he was to consider the entire area claimed by Texas as his jurisdiction. This meant that, rather than San Antonio, the center of Catholic population in the Galveston diocese was now the lower Rio Grande valley, where at least ten thousand Catholics resided. Some of these Catholics did not want to be included in either Texas or Odin's diocese. In the spring of 1848, city authorities of Laredo petitioned in vain both the Mexican and United States governments, asking to remain part of Mexico.

Odin received this directive just as he was leaving for a provincial council meeting in Baltimore. Since it was obvious the new diocese of Galveston was already too large even without the disputed territories, the council requested Rome to place New Mexico in a separate jurisdiction. This was realized the next year when the diocese of Santa Fe was established, the same year Texas received its present boundaries. It was three years after that, in 1853, that Odin learned that Bp. José López de Zubiría y Escalante of Durango, Mexico, still considered western Texas beyond the Pecos River to be part of his diocese. This area contained active parishes at such towns as Presidio, San Elizario, Socorro, and Ysleta along the Rio Grande. The latter two had churches that had begun as missions for the Indians who accompanied the Spanish colonists southward at the time of the Pueblo uprising of 1680 in northern New Mexico. Shortly after Odin learned of Zubiría's jurisdictional claim, he received a directive from Rome informing him that he was not to consider the area of El Paso County, which was much larger than it is today and included the parishes in question, as part of the diocese of Galveston. Most of this region was removed from the jurisdiction of the bishop of Durango in 1872 and placed within the vicariate apostolic of Tucson. However, the authority of the bishop of Durango continued at Presidio until 1892. In 1890, El Paso was transferred to the new diocese of Dallas.[1]

Even without this western region, Odin's diocese remained a vast frontier area that required an almost superhuman effort to oversee. The cathedral of the new diocese was at last opened for worship in the late fall of 1848. Joining Odin for the consecration rites were Bp. Antoine Blanc of New Orleans and Bp. John Timon, the new bishop of Buffalo, New York.[2] Certainly the new cathedral did bespeak civilization, but conditions in Texas generally were little changed from those of ten years before when John Timon first entered the republic. Until the cathedral was built, the Galveston church was little more than a hut. The roof leaked so badly that parishioners used umbrellas to stay dry during mass. And with two or three exceptions, this inadequate a church or much worse was still all that Timon's priests and laity had in most Texas communities—if they had a church at all.

Dwellings for the clergy were often in worse condition than the churches. One visitor to Galveston the year the cathedral was dedicated described the bishop's residence as "composed of three wretched huts containing seven or eight small rooms surrounded by galleries." The only thing pleasant about the place was the galleries in the evenings when Odin was at home, where fellow clerics and a few parishioners would gather round while he told of his many travels and his hopes for the future. Newcomers were invariably shocked by the number of mosquitoes and the shortage of good drinking water. Most in the island city depended on rainwater stored in cisterns, and if the cistern was above ground, the water was always warm in summer. Such water often became virtually unpotable and was often a source of disease. But not all was drab in Galveston: the beaches and Gulf breeze were pleasant as always, and by midcentury visitors remarked on the city's lovely tree- and shrub-lined streets and the flower and vegetable gardens that seemed to proliferate everywhere.

There were some things, however, that neither shrubs nor flowers could beautify. As was true with much of Texas, Galveston's southern character was increasing during the late 1840s and 1850s, and with this came an increased socioeconomic emphasis on slavery. Slaves were now numerous. Not only many of the laborers but most servants and hotel and restaurant employees in the city and some of the artisans as well were slaves. When their masters allowed them to have Sundays off, they sought respite from their oppression by gathering on the beach for recreation.

Houston lagged behind Galveston in affording modern amenities. Its small St. Vincent's Church was understandably a far cry from Galveston's cathedral, and its public buildings and dwellings on the whole appeared less prosperous than those of the busy port city. And not only did Houston have mosquitoes—though not as numerous as Galveston's—it also was plagued with ants. As one missionary noted on his way west through Houston, the "ants crawl along the streets, and through every room in endless processions; and the ceiling, the walls, the floor are traversed in every direction by the dark and ever-moving columns of their battalions."[3] At night, in order to protect themselves from ants, Houstonians set their bedposts in shallow containers of water, just as they did their cupboards and tables at all hours. If by chance an uninitiated traveler forgot to place his clothes in or on a similarly protected piece of furniture, he could be in for an unwelcome surprise the next morning.

By 1848, Odin or one of his missionaries could travel west from Houston either by horseback or on the "post," a four-horse wagon that carried both passengers and mail. The traveler on the post had to endure many dangers, not the least of which was crossing Buffalo Bayou in Houston on a six- or seven-foot-wide "bridge" constructed of two beams with tree branches laid across them. The post then headed west across the prairie, dodging mudholes and stumps.

Emmanuel Domenech was one such missionary sent west to the line of settlement in the spring of 1848. He had been among those seminarians Odin brought to the United States in 1846 who completed their studies in Missouri before coming to the Galveston diocese. From Galveston, Domenech traveled by poste wagon to San Antonio, where he was ordained to the priesthood in San Fernando Church. He left immediately for Castroville to assist the pastor, Claude Marie Dubuis, and periodically visit the communities of Quihi, Vandenburg, and D'Hanis as well as a United States army camp, Fort Inge, many miles to the west on the Leona River. Dubuis had arrived in Texas from his native France in early 1847 and was soon assigned by the bishop to Castroville. What he and Domenech endured on the frontier in and around Castroville is typical of Texas at this time, particularly in the central and western regions.

In Castroville Domenech was housed in the two-room rectory, made of stone, brick, and wood, that Dubuis and Chazelle had built with their own hands. In a small garden behind the house, near Domenech's window, was the grave of his predecessor, an ever-present reminder of the price the Texas frontier sometimes exacted from those who attempted to tame it. A barn was attached to the rectory. Behind the rectory were two small cabins, one serving as stable, granary, and hen house, with the other doubling as both kitchen and schoolroom. The latter was constructed of branches covered with thatch. The floors of all the buildings including the rectory were bare earth.

In the yard between the two outbuildings, the priests tried to grow vegetables to supplement their meager diet. Not only were ants a nuisance but scorpions, tarantulas, and rattlesnakes abounded. Their only treatment for a snakebite was cauterization of the wound. They found snakes in the schoolroom and barn and once even under the altar. The scarcity of food led Dubuis and Domenech on one occasion to skin and cook a large rattlesnake, seasoning it with cayenne pepper. Dubuis thought that if the flesh proved palatable, in the future they would have plenty to satisfy their appetites, "nay, even to exceed the bounds of moderation." At first they found it not bad, rather like frog or turtle. In spite of the acceptable taste and their hunger, however, the awareness of what they were eating prevented the priests from finishing their entrée. On another occasion, Domenech killed and cooked an alligator found in the Medina River. The priests shared it with several villagers, but no one really liked it. The wild turkeys that Domenech and a parishioner frequently hunted provided much superior fare. Food was always a problem: on one occasion Dubuis was unable to preach at mass because he had not eaten in forty-eight hours.

At midcentury, adequate clothing of any sort, let alone clerical garb, was also hard to come by for frontier missionaries. Cast-off garments from either men or women were treasured since they could be taken apart and redesigned. One West Texas missionary in this period took an old blue cotton petticoat and made from it a pair of trousers. Another working along the Brazos dressed in blue oversized trousers, a black coat, and a shapeless old hat; his only other possessions were a tin tub, a table, and a rickety bed.

Through most of the 1850s, the traveler among the western missions, particularly those at Castroville, D'Hanis, New Braunfels, and Fredericksburg, faced the threat of Indian attack. Grisly scenes are recorded in this period, as both sides committed atrocities against the other. One of Dubuis's parishioners, an Alsatian colonist named Meyer, was seized by Indians at Quihi, twelve miles from Castroville, and literally fastened to a tree with arrows through his body. Another parishioner, a Hispanic woman at Castroville, went out to gather herbs for her family's dinner and was carried off by some Lipan Apaches. She later described her experiences to Dubuis: one of her captors cut the skin around her head in order to scalp her, but before he could lift her scalp, another in the party stopped him, claimed her for his own, and carried the bleeding, bruised woman into his tent. When she fought off his advances toward her, she was severely beaten. A few days later, when she resisted him again, he angrily struck at her with a hatchet, wounding both her leg and her arm. She fainted from pain and loss of blood. The village shaman tried to help her with his prayers. She believed she would die and wanted to, but she did not. She began to recover her strength and finally escaped on horseback in the middle of the night. She had to guess the way back home. As day broke she saw her Apache captor in pursuit, but after a wild chase for several miles, she happened upon two horsemen from Castroville. They came to her aid, and the Apache fled.

During one of his trips to Fredericksburg to minister to some of the German colonists there, Dubuis suddenly found himself surrounded on the trail by some Kiowa braves. The Indians made it plain they intended to riddle him with arrows, whereupon the priest shouted out that he was a captain of the Great Spirit and a "chief of prayer." When the band's leader approached him, Dubuis asked why they wanted to kill him and said that they should seek peace with the whites. One of the Kiowas began to denounce what had happened at the Council House fight in San Antonio some years before in which their own people had been killed. For whatever reason, when he finished speaking, the Kiowas left Dubuis unharmed and went their own way.

On his way to visit the Catholic soldiers at Fort Inge, the camp on the Leona River eighty miles west of Castroville, Domenech came upon an oak and mesquite shaded chaparral about six miles from where he had just broken camp himself. Seven Hispanic cartmen lay on the grass scalped, mutilated, and riddled with arrows. Their oxen and goods had been taken. A warm ash heap showed that they had been surprised the previous night. Later the same day Domenech came upon three men and a woman who had been scalped.

The missionaries knew, of course, that all such grisly scenes had not been caused by the Comanches, Kiowas, and Lipan Apaches. One missionary cited the Texas Rangers in particular as among those who could kill indiscriminately. Once when a group of Lipans were quietly encamped near Castroville, a company of Rangers descended upon them and killed men, women, and children. They stripped the dead of their clothing, which was then donned by some of the Rangers. A mock battle was then fought for amusement.[4]

Not all contact between missionary and Indian was marked by violence. Dubuis was sometimes able to visit an encampment of peaceful Lipans near Castroville. Dubuis believed the Lipans had a vestigial knowledge of Catholicism remaining from contact between their ancestors and Spanish missionaries. He noticed that some wore religious medals dangling from their ears, but as a display of wealth, not devotion. Dubuis always carried a good supply of small religious prints to distribute to the Indians, who seemed to be especially fond of them.

Sixty Lipans entered Castroville one Sunday morning as mass was in progress. They gathered round the church, and some of them mingled with the apprehensive worshipers. But the Lipans had come in peace and seemed to be dressed especially fine for the occasion: some had on bright red garments, their silver and gold ornaments shone brightly, and their horses appeared immaculately groomed. Beautiful shellwork figurines hung from the ears of some of the Indians and added an even greater touch of brilliance to their appearance. The Indians seemed captivated by the liturgy and sought to imitate the actions of the worshipers. They were attracted particularly by the singing and tried to join in.

Far greater a danger than that of Indian attack was disease, a constant threat to the Texas missionaries during these years. Disease could strike anytime or in any place. In 1849, cholera struck Texas in epidemic proportions. James Fitzgerald, the robust twenty-six-year-old Irish priest Odin had sent to Houston in 1847, was later transferred to Victoria, where he died in this epidemic only hours after being stricken. San Antonio and neighboring towns were hit hard. Cholera first appeared in Castroville when a German immigrant, given shelter in the rectory as he made his way west to the California goldfields, came down with the disease and died. After burying the body, Father Dubuis, Father Domenech, and a parishioner came down with what they believed was cholera. With no doctor available, Dubuis concocted a home remedy—a mixture of camphorated alcohol, laudanum, pepper, and cologne water—and filled a drinking glass with it. They each consumed a third of the mixture, which burned like fire all the way down; they began to sweat profusely and then fell asleep or passed out. For whatever reason, they awoke about twenty-four hours later and felt better. A day and a half after they awakened their lives began to return to normal.[5]

If indeed they had recovered thusly from cholera, many others were not as fortunate. Scenes of horror became commonplace in many Texas communities. Of his experience after his recovery, Domenech recalled:

> At San Antonio as at Castroville, the epidemic made dreadful ravages. My day was spent in running from one bed to another, and from the church to the graveyard. I saw nothing but agony, and death, and burials.... Calls were incessant, so that I was constantly employed in dispensing remedies, as well as in consoling and praying for the dying ... the graveyard (was) as horrifying a spectacle to behold as the cholera itself, for wolves and foxes, attracted thither by the odour of the dead bodies, ransacked and violated the tombs.[6]

Fortunately, epidemics run their course, but even in good times, the Texas missionary priest had little time for rest or relaxation. In addition to being pastor and doctor, he might also have to be a carpenter or a stonemason or the practitioner of some other trade for which his seminary training had left him totally unprepared. In late December, 1849, several months after the cholera epidemic, the parishioners and their priests began building a masonry church at Castroville. Since they had no pulley in the colony, the stones and timber beams had to be lifted by hand. Dubuis decreed that both he and Domenech would become a regular part of the work force. Much of the rough carpentry work fell to them, which they carried out at the direction of those more skilled than they. Their "instructor" would make a mark on a felled tree, and the priests would saw away at the appropriate spot. At other times they gathered stone at a nearby quarry, which took ingenuity. Driving an ox-cart as near the large stones as possible, they then removed the wheels, allowing the bed of the cart to rest on the ground, and with oak levers pushed the stone over wood rollers into the conveyance. After filling it as much as they dared, they lifted one of the axles as much as they could and placed a stone under it, then proceeded to do the same at the other axle, and so on. Over and over the process was repeated until the axles were high enough for the wheels to be replaced, and then off to the building site they went.

Dubuis was forced to search for appropriate trees to supply the pillars for roof supports that would line the aisle down the middle of the nave.

Such large trees were not common in the area, but eight were finally located, felled, and placed in carts in the same manner as the stone. When the eight timbers had been set upright, the roof was then set in place. An Irish merchant passing through Castroville in early 1850 drove up to the partially finished church looking for the pastor. Finally he approached a man dressed in dirty blue trousers, a red flannel shirt, and a mauled old hat who was busily mixing mortar. The workman walked to a water trough to remove the grime from his face and hands and announced that he was Dubuis.

The determination of the priests and congregation paid off: they celebrated mass in the new edifice on Easter Day, 1850.[7]

The sacrifices and deprivations the Texas frontier exacted from those who lived and worked there were used as an allurement by Bishop Odin in recruiting additional personnel for the diocese. Texas symbolized challenge to many of the young clergymen and women religious Odin met in his travels outside the diocese. Providing for the religious needs of the thousands of Catholics along the lower Rio Grande, an area now clearly within the new diocese's bounds, made the recruitment of additional priests and religious more important than ever. Meeting the needs of this region would remain uppermost in Odin's mind throughout the 1850s.

In April of 1849, after the conclusion of the Seventh Council of Baltimore, Odin went north to Montreal in search of recruits. Two Ursuline sisters and five members of the Oblates of Mary Immaculate agreed to return with the bishop to Texas.[8]

Shortly after their arrival that fall in Galveston, the two Ursuline sisters were given positions of leadership in their order's community there. Sister St. Chantal was elected assistant superior of the convent, and Sister St. Thomas was made treasurer and directress of the Ursuline academy.[9] Odin asked two of the Oblates, Fr. Augustin Gaudet and Bro. Paul Gelot, to remain in Galveston to work at the cathedral. Fr. Pierre Telmon, Fr. Alexander Soulerin, and Bro. Joseph Menthe were assigned to the lower Rio Grande Valley. They left Galveston by ship and reached Point (now Port) Isabel at the river's mouth in early December.

A U.S. army officer, Lt. Julius Garesche, a native of France, gave the Oblates his rooms and provided them with meals during their brief stay at Point Isabel. After celebrating mass in an improvised chapel, the Oblates, accompanied by Garesche, journeyed on the next day toward Brownsville, thirty miles inland.[10] A merchant provided them with a place for the celebration of mass, and they made it into a rather elegant little chapel. At first, only a few attended mass. The French-speaking Oblates worked to perfect their English and Spanish, however, and by March of the next year, their chapel was filled on Sundays. By that time they were able to preach in both English and Spanish. Telmon particularly impressed his hearers, for he was a former professor of scripture at seminaries in Marseilles and in Ajaccio on Corsica. His sermons usually consisted of his reading a portion of scripture and then exegeting it and using it as a basis for doctrinal explanation. Sometimes clergy of other denominations attended mass in order to hear him.[11]

Most of the Catholics were not in Brownsville, however, but living on ranchos in the countryside. Many were hesitant to attend mass in a church in Brownsville, a new town dominated by the recently arrived Anglos, some of whom exhibited bigotry toward the Hispanic Texans, or Tejanos. Responding to this situation, the Oblates began a ministry to the Catholics at Santa Rita, then known as Rancho de Santa Rita, thus inaugurating a long-standing ministry by this order to communities along the river.[12]

In April, 1850, Odin left Galveston overland for the Rio Grande Valley, the journey he had intended to make two years before but which expedience had caused him to postpone. A ship would have been easier, but this way he could visit various churches along the way. He traveled first to Victoria, San Antonio, and Castroville and then west to visit an army camp on the Arroyo Seco. For fear of Indians and outlaws, the officer in command provided Odin with a military escort as he went on to visit the larger encampment on the Leona River, which the Castroville priests occasionally visited.

On the Leona, Odin visited a captain seriously wounded by the Comanches, and he gladly accepted another military escort for a journey to an encampment of Texas volunteers. From there an escort of Texas Rangers accompanied him to Eagle Pass, which he reached in late May. Odin learned there from military scouts that a band of over six hundred Comanches were nearby, and he decided the safest way for him to proceed downriver was on the Mexican side. Crossing the river at Eagle Pass, the bishop visited Presidio del Río Grande, adjacent to the sites of Missions San Juan Bautista and San Bernardo, from which in Spanish times expeditions had set out to found missions and settlements in the land of the Tejas to the north. Odin recorded that he received a warm welcome and was asked to administer confirmation. With some difficulty, Odin refused, explaining that he was out of his jurisdiction and lacked the authority to do so.[13]

Heavy rains prevented his departure for three days. Finally he set out toward Laredo accompanied by several townspeople and a Mexican military escort. When he reached Laredo on June 12, he discovered that Comanches had killed one man and wounded six others there just prior to his arrival. In Laredo, he met Fr. José Trinidad García, the pastor of San Agustín parish there since 1832. This visit was quite different from his first visit to San Antonio ten years before. This time the bishop left García as pastor of the parish, extending to him the full faculties of a priest in the new Galveston diocese and even increased these faculties regarding certain marriage questions. After remaining there several days administering confirmation and celebrating mass, Odin proceeded downriver on the Mexican side to the town of Guerrero, Tamaulipas.

In Guerrero the pastor asked Odin to administer confirmation, and when the bishop stated that he had no authority to do so out of his diocese, several offered to go with him to the Texas side of the Rio Grande to be confirmed there. Odin might have done this except for fear of the Comanches: the day before he arrived in Guerrero, Comanches were reported to have killed three men and taken sixty horses between the town and the river. Odin was persuaded to remain long enough for a courier to go to the administrator of the Monterrey diocese to get permission for Odin to administer confirmation. The Monterrey diocese over long periods had had no resident bishop. For instance, shortly after assuming the leadership of the diocese in 1834, Bp. José María de Jesús Belaunzarán y Ureña, O.F.M., had been forced to leave under government pressure. Long periods without a bishop had, of course, prevented the ordinary administration of confirmation. The current bishop was Salvador Apodaca Loreto, whose permission was apparently received several days later. "Then I had to put myself to work," wrote Odin to one of his priests. Over a six-day period, Odin reported that he confirmed 2,200 persons. Each of these days he preached two or three times in Spanish and administered confirmation to several hundred people. In order to hear all the confessions, priests each day were in the confessionals from four A.M. to midnight.[14]

All told, Odin recorded that he confirmed about 11,000 people in the towns and cities of the Rio Grande Valley: in Guerrero, Mier, Camargo, Reynosa, and Matamoros in the Mexican state of Tamaulipas, and in Laredo, Roma, Rio Grande City, and Brownsville in Texas. This large number of confirmations was probably due to the church-state tensions in Mexico that had either prevented bishops from visiting their parishes regularly or caused their absence entirely; in addition, war between the United States and Mexico had disrupted travel in the region. Even during these years, however, the many Catholics along the Rio Grande did have priests available to them in the larger towns such as Matamoros, Camargo, Reynosa, Mier, Laredo, and Guerrero.[15]

Odin at last reached Brownsville in early August. For the next three weeks he celebrated mass, administered confirmation, and preached there and in Matamoros, Santa Rita, and Santa Rosalia. At Santa Rita there was a small chapel constructed like the dwellings of most of the valley's inhabitants, with a thatched roof and with walls of upright stakes covered over with mud plaster. The chapel was dedicated to Our Lady of Guadalupe. On Odin's arrival there on the evening of August 21, about eight hundred people greeted him. A large procession formed and moved around the public square of the village as the rosary was prayed. A cross led the way, then came the women of the village followed by a richly decorated statue of Mary borne by four young girls dressed in white. The clergy and men of the rancho came last. The procession finally made its way to the chapel where the assembly joined heartily in singing several litanies. The next day, Odin celebrated mass and administered confirmation. Evidently moved by the celebration at the rancho, Odin wrote, "This ceremony was for me and for all the people a source of unspeakable consolation."[16]

On August 28 Odin left Brownsville for Brazos de Santiago on his way to Corpus Christi. He traveled by way of Padre Island, going up its entire length, rather than by the road on the mainland, because of the Indian threat. Fortunately for the bishop, his traveling companion on this trip was a Hispanic South Texan who knew what to expect on Padre Island. As Odin and his unnamed companion traveled its 140-mile length, they met no other person, and drinking water for man or horse was not to be found except by digging for it in the sand. Odin's companion had brought along a spade for this purpose, and they dug a five- or six-foot well each evening that supplied drinking water and enabled them to brew coffee.[17]

Arriving in Corpus Christi in early September, Odin found there about thirty Catholic families, mostly of Hispanic descent. He heard confessions, celebrated mass, and administered baptism. From Corpus Christi he went to San Patricio and then to Refugio, where he found Fr. Jacques Giraudon weak from illness but apparently out of danger. The old mission at Refugio, built originally for the Karankawas, was still standing but in a state of great disrepair. The altar was gone and Odin celebrated mass on a table. The walls bore heavily the marks of desolation left by the violence of the Texas revolution fourteen years earlier.

A few days after reaching San Antonio on September 20, the exhausted Odin fell violently ill with a fever and almost died. A United States Army surgeon came to his aid and nursed him back to health. By October 13 the resilient bishop was able to administer confirmation and within a few more days was traveling again: back to Castroville, then to New Braunfels, to the settlements along the Lavaca River and Cummings Creek, then northeastward to Nacogdoches, and finally home to Galveston by way of Houston in early December.[18]

This very successful trip might have caused Odin to view the closing year with a high degree of satisfaction but for the fact that distressing news awaited him in Galveston: his own Vincentian order, responding to a shortage within their ranks after the return of a number of priests to Europe, had decided after ten years to cease its work in Texas. If this were not enough, another letter awaiting him in Galveston informed him that the Oblates he had recently visited in Brownsville in August were likewise being withdrawn from his diocese. These blows were staggering: the eight thousand Catholics in the San Antonio area and the ten thousand or more in the lower Rio Grande

Valley would be deprived of clergy. Furthermore, he discovered that Galveston, the see city, had already been without priests for five weeks. They had left in obedience to their respective superiors. In the case of the Vincentians, finances may have been the reason, but Odin found this hard to accept. As a priest, Odin had been devoted to his order, but now he felt resentment and a sense of abandonment. In a December letter to Etienne, the Vincentian superior general, the resentment came out:

> This measure seems neither just nor honorable to me. . . . It was a contract in my eyes. . . . The city of San Antonio and its environs include nearly eight thousand Catholics. Was that not a sufficient number of souls to excite the zeal of the children of St. Vincent? . . . Texas is a country that is more vast than France, its population is rapidly increasing; each week more than six thousand new colonists arrive. Before ten years it will be one of the most prosperous states in the union. Why then abandon such a vast field? Why withdraw from such forsaken souls? Where are [Vincentian] priests to be placed? In the wealthy cities of the United States where priests are already so numerous![19]

As for the Oblates, their superior, Bp. Charles de Mazenod of Marseilles, was doubtful from the beginning about the advisability of his order taking on responsibility of new work in Texas. By the end of January, 1851, all of the Oblates had been withdrawn from Texas.[20]

Sixteen new priests were needed if the vacated posts were to be filled. Odin realized that he must once more tax all available European sources and begin to plan for the day when men could be trained locally in Texas. In the waning days of the year he penned a letter to Emmanuel Domenech, then on leave in his native France, asking him to present the now even more urgent needs of Texas to the Europeans and to refuse nothing offered him: "ornaments, chalices, prayer books, ciboriums, rosaries, *etc., etc.,* take everything."[21]

Fortunately for the Spanish-speaking Catholics of San Antonio, Fr. Miguel Calvo remained there on into 1852. To provide some assistance in the San Antonio parish, Fr. Claude Dubuis in the spring of 1851 began to visit there every ten days or so from his post at Castroville. Since he could not yet speak Spanish, his pastoral effectiveness was limited to those who spoke English, French, and German. The assistance of Fr. Jacques Giraudon, who was proficient in Spanish, helped alleviate this situation in the fall of 1852, and Odin himself served the parish for a time that year while Dubuis was in Europe.[22]

This serious readjustment for the diocese of Galveston demanded that Odin go again to Europe to search for more priests and to personally implore Bishop de Mazenod to reassign the Oblates to Texas. Before leaving for Europe in the summer of 1851, Odin made what provision he could for the lower Rio Grande Valley: when Domenech returned from Europe in May, instead of sending him back to assist the overtaxed Dubuis, Odin assigned the young priest to the Catholics along the lower Rio Grande. Dubuis had wanted Domenech sent to Fredericksburg on his return, but the bishop realized that the thousands of Catholics along the Rio Grande posed a greater need.[23] When Domenech objected that he was not proficient in Spanish, an unmoved Odin responded that a Spanish-speaking priest would be sent as soon as one was available. It was better to send a priest who could speak only broken Spanish than to send no priest at all.

When Domenech arrived in Brownsville in May, 1851, he was befriended by the same Lieutenant Garesche and his wife who had previously aided the Oblates. Domenech set about learning Spanish as quickly as possible. To increase his credibility with the Hispanic Catholics who attended mass in the Brownsville church, he had his letter of appointment translated into Spanish and read aloud at Sunday mass.

The picture of life in Brownsville and the lower Rio Grande Valley left by Domenech in his published account of his experiences there is not altogether a pretty one. The officials of the new Texas county and town governments were sometimes an unsavory lot, Domenech recorded. Some were given to violence and other acts of intimidation toward those under their authority, particularly those of Hispanic, Irish, or German origin—and of these, especially Hispanics. Executions and lynchings were common. Of Brownsville's officials, Domenech declared that "were those that deserved it most brought to the gibbet, the very functionaries would be the first, and they would be followed by a goodly number of judges, barristers, and doctors, headed by the sheriff himself."[24] The sheriff was particularly brutal toward Hispanic prisoners, though his sadism and readiness to hang prisoners extended to his fellow Anglos as well. Domenech was not immune to danger either. The priest, who went armed because of the sheriff, shot one of his vicious attack dogs when it assaulted him. Domenech then had to prevent this brutal official at pistol point from beating him with a whip in attempted reprisal.

Spanish land titles were supposed to be respected under United States and Texas law, but with officials of this caliber on the scene, Domenech recorded, many native Hispanic Texans were losing their lands during this period.

In order to get a clearer understanding of life along the Rio Grande, Domenech visited Matamoros soon after his arrival in Brownsville. There he met the town's young priest who was using his own private inheritance to relieve the sufferings of the poor and complete his parish church. Shortly after this, in late June, 1851, Domenech decided his Spanish was developed enough so that he could journey upriver as far as Mier. He visited both sides of the river and met the pastors of the Mexican parishes in Reynosa, Camargo, and Mier. At Reynosa, where there was a large stone church with a massive steeple, the pastor obtained a guide to assist Domenech along his way, and at Mier the pastor gave him shelter and entertained him with chocolates, sweet cakes, and cigarettes. On his return trip, Domenech stayed for a time with the pastor at Camargo, whose house, like those of his parishioners, was constructed like the thatched-roofed chapel at Santa Rita. At Camargo Domenech celebrated a sung mass accompanied by local musicians playing violins, clarinets, a trombone, and a drum. Near Reynosa, his horse ran away, and the pastor there came to his aid once more by supplying a replacement.

In addition to Reynosa, Camargo, and Mier, Domenech also visited Rio Grande City, Roma, and Álamo as well as numerous ranchos along the way on both sides of the river. On his return, he visited Rancho de la Palma on the Mexican side of the border where a large gathering celebrated a fiesta in honor of Santiago, or St. James, on July 25. Many of the participants arrived on horses with saddles and bridles set with silver. The women wore beautiful dresses and had mantillas over their heads or draped over their shoulders. Festive lanterns were hung, and musicians accompanied a grand ball. Later, Domenech attended a similar fiesta at Rancho Santa Rita near Brownsville in honor of Our Lady of Guadalupe. At that fiesta, after devotions similar to those Odin participated in during his first visit to the valley, a fireworks display was held before the music and dancing. As Odin had before him, Domenech concluded the fiesta at Santa Rita the next morning by celebrating mass and preaching.

In fiestas such as these, held on major Christian feasts such as Christmas and certain saints' days, Catholic commemorations remained alive among the rancheros even if a priest was available only occasionally. On one isolated rancho Domenech visited, he was surprised when, during a pause in his sermon, an elderly voice took up his theme by relating an allegory. The voice belonged to an aged Mexican priest, between eighty and ninety years old, who was living out his life among the people of the rancho.

Later that year, Odin sent Domenech an Irish priest to be his assistant. Domenech later lamented that the assistant "had not youth enough . . . to support with impunity the excesses of the climate. I was often obliged to leave him alone, and go by myself to the more distant ranchos and villages; and as he knew no Spanish, his position in my absence was painful and critical enough."[25]

Odin's trip to Europe was quite successful. Almost miraculously, he was able to persuade Bishop de Mazenod to send the Oblates back to Texas. With this victory, Odin was able to write Domenech in 1852 that three Oblate priests would arrive to replace him in September of that year. The Irish priest had already left because of health problems.[26]

The Oblates did not arrive in Brownsville until mid-October. This new

Oblate community consisted of Fathers Rigomer Olivier, Pierre Keralum, and Jean-Marie Gaye and Bro. Pierre Roudet. Also arriving with them was Fr. Jean-Maurice Verdet, the superior of the Texas Oblates, who came to oversee the reestablishment of their order's work in the Valley.

Just three months later, in January, 1853, the Oblates were joined in Brownsville by the Sisters of the Incarnate Word and Blessed Sacrament. These sisters resided first in a small borrowed house where on March 7, 1853, they opened a school. Their residence was like a barn, with such shoddy doors that they had to tie them shut "with the strings of their aprons."[27] However, later that month, the work began on a permanent convent, the very first one for this order in America. Father Verdet was a skilled mason and directed the construction of this building himself. In November it was opened as both convent and school.

At Odin's request, the Oblates sent one of their number, Fr. Jean-Marie Gaye, to Laredo in March, 1853, to install two diocesan priests, recently arrived from France and newly ordained, Fathers Claude Dumas and Louis-Marie Planchet, to be in charge of San Agustín parish. With their petition to remain in Mexico having proved unsuccessful, many Laredoans moved to the Mexican side of the river to what became Nuevo Laredo, and in 1851, Father García began celebrating mass there as well as in Laredo. That same year, however, García was succeeded by Don Timoteo Frías. The Nuevo Laredo parish, of course, was not under Odin's jurisdiction, but Frías began functioning in both parishes since his predecessor had done so. This change occurred while Odin was in Europe; thus Frías never formally received faculties to work as a priest in the diocese of Galveston. When Odin returned from Europe, he received negative reports about Frías's work in Laredo and apparently directed that he leave the parish. Thus it was as Frías's successors that Dumas and Planchet arrived in Laredo in March, 1853. For the Laredo parishioners, with the installation of French priests of the Galveston diocese, annexation must have seemed complete.[28]

In Brownsville, the Oblates soon found inadequate the small wooden chapel built there in 1850, and in 1856 they began the erection of a brick church in the Gothic style so popular in the nineteenth century. The Brownsville Oblates had an abundance of talent. Father Keralum, who had been an architect in France prior to entering the order, drew the plans, and Brother Roudet supervised the making of 250,000 bricks. The new church was to be dedicated to the patronage of Mary of the Immaculate Conception. The church was not completed until 1859, but its magnificence seemed well worth the wait: nine bronze and crystal chandeliers brought from Paris lighted the interior with its black and white marble tiles, eight fluted columns, vaulted ceiling decorated in blue with gold stars, and altars and pulpit designed by Keralum. News of the wonder of such a building in the lower Rio Grande Valley traveled far and wide. As beautiful and impressive as the new Brownsville church was, however, of greater importance was the Oblates' work among the ranchos in the countryside. It was there that most of the Catholics lived, worked, and died. With their dirt floors and thatched roofs, the mud-plastered chapels along the river surpassed the splendid new structure in reflecting the heart of the Oblates' mission in the valley. In these chapels, for the rest of the century and into the next, the Oblate priests on the ranchos carried on their mission, not waiting to be sought after but living out their lives among the people.[29]

Bishop Odin returned to the Rio Grande Valley in 1854. Fearing Indians south of San Antonio, Odin went by ship to the valley at the end of July, 1854, and spent many weeks there. He was anxious to meet Bp. Francisco de P. Verea y González, the new bishop of Monterrey, who had quickly gained the reputation of being an excellent pastor and administrator. Verea was visiting the towns along the Mexican side of the river in his diocese, as Odin did on the Texas side. The two prelates met at a rancho when their confirmation visits brought them together. It was a productive meeting since they were able to work out jurisdictional problems resulting from the flood-induced shifting of the Rio Grande, which left small isolated pockets of Texas and Mexico on the "wrong" side of the river.

The meeting between the two bishops went well and perhaps helped dispel a negative image Odin had of the clergy of Mexico, an image contradicted by much of the evidence. For instance, Father Domenech, in his description of the Mexican clergy he met during 1851–52 as he worked along the lower Rio Grande, presented a positive picture of these priests: they readily gave him shelter; the Matamoros pastor sacrificed his own money to care for the poor; the pastor in Camargo lived like his people and had an active congregation, some of whom supplied instrumental music for the parish liturgy. And although the large El Paso County to the west was not to be included within Odin's diocese, there in the El Paso Valley, on both sides of the river, Catholic parishes were also flourishing. Perhaps the most notable of the priests in that area at the time and for years thereafter was Don Ramón Ortiz, pastor of El Paso del Norte, today Ciudad Juárez. Father Ortiz actually ministered on both sides of the river, and in the 1850s founded, along with his assistant, Father Vásquez, a church on the Texas side of the border at the village of Concordia.

Rather than being based on his own first-hand observation, Odin's views of the Mexican clergy during the 1840s and early 1850s seem at times to have been formed by the opinions of others and by his own lack of understanding of the culture and conditions of life in northern Mexico and New Spain. On occasion, he seems also to have been overly concerned about how these priests were viewed by the newly arrived American settlers, whose objectivity should have been suspect. On the other hand, prior to meeting Bishop Verea, Odin had encouraged the Oblates to continue their friendly relations with the priests on the Mexican side of the river and had expressed pleasure over a visit Father Verdet had already made to the bishop in Monterrey. Also, on his first visit to Laredo, he had left Fr. José Trinidad García as pastor and had even increased his faculties pertaining to marriage impediments.

Now, in his meeting with Verea, a member of the Mexican hierarchy, Odin came face to face with a man he later referred to as a "good and saintly bishop." And when the Monterrey bishop ran afoul of the anticlerical Mexican government, Odin gave him sanctuary in the diocese of Galveston. For a time in the 1860s, Verea lived with the Oblates in Brownsville and from there ministered as best he could to the people of his diocese.[30]

After his meeting with Verea, Odin visited Reynosa, Tamaulipas, Mexico, at the invitation of the mayor and the local pastor. Probably going back to Galveston by the route he had followed in 1852, Odin arrived there in November of 1854 after four months of travel, riding a mule and wearing a tattered suit spattered with mud.[31]

In San Antonio and its environs, the church continued to grow during the 1850s even though the withdrawal of the Vincentians was a tremendous blow. To make administration more efficient for this area, after Dubuis became pastor of San Fernando Church in 1852, Odin appointed him vicar general for the western part of the diocese, which made him the bishop's official representative.[32]

Circumstances in San Antonio brightened in 1851 with the arrival of a community of Ursuline sisters. Odin had previously had a convent constructed there, and the Ursuline communities in Galveston and New Orleans supplied sisters to live there and open a school. Dubuis met the sisters in Galveston and escorted them as they traveled by stagecoach to San Antonio. Of the seven sisters forming the new community, three were from Galveston while the others, including the superior, Mother Marie Trouard, were from New Orleans. They arrived in San Antonio on the night of September 14. Other than construction of the house, little else had been prepared for them: the house was unfurnished and littered with wood shavings and other rubbish left by the carpenters, and to the sisters it appeared full of spiders and scorpions. That night Dubuis managed to find for the sisters mattresses that were their only furniture for the succeeding six weeks. Their school would not open for some time, and they consequently had no income. Gifts of food and other necessities from San Fernando parishioners kept them going until they were ready to open the school on November 3. Announcements from the pulpit of San Fernando Church publicized the event, and quite a crowd of young girls assembled at the convent that day. Soon over three hundred students were enrolled, and when facilities for boarding students were completed, the number increased even more as families in other parts of Texas as well as Mexico began sending their children to the school.

With the increase in numbers, it became evident that more sisters and additional buildings were needed. Since no more sisters could be spared from either Galveston or New Orleans, Odin looked to Ireland for help, and the Ursulines of St. Mary's Convent in Waterford agreed to send two sisters to San Antonio. Another sister also came from Brignoles, France. The year after opening the school, the Ursulines were able to add a small chapel, refectories, and dormitories to their original convent. The sisters, who had been starving shortly after their arrival, had such favorable public response to their school that in August, 1852, Odin pointed to their thriving educational enterprise as worthy of emulation by other religious orders. The Ursuline schools in both San Antonio and Galveston continued to grow throughout the 1850s in spite of sporadic outbreaks of religious prejudice.[33]

When Odin was in France in 1851, he arranged for four members of a teaching order of men, the Society of Mary or Brothers of Mary as they were popularly called, to come to Texas to open a school for boys in San Antonio. Odin was particularly concerned that a Catholic boys' school be available to the Hispanic Catholics of San Antonio, who comprised the majority of the bishop's seven-thousand-member flock in that city. Other religious groups were making inroads into this segment of the Catholic population, and Odin believed that schools might change this situation. Brothers Nicholas Koenig, John Baptist Laignoux, and Xavier Mauclerc were sent from France and were joined in Texas by Bro. Andrew Edel, previously a professor at St. Mary's Institute in Dayton, Ohio. The Society of Mary first began work in the United States at Dayton in 1849 and had three schools in operation by the time the brothers came to San Antonio. They arrived there in the spring of 1852 and lived first in the rectory of San Fernando Church. They opened their school in the fall with twelve students in an old shop building on the southwest corner of Plaza de Armas, or Military Plaza. Classes were offered in both Spanish and English. From these very modest beginnings the present St. Mary's University eventually evolved.

Odin soon purchased a lot on the east bank of the San Antonio River, and construction began on a two-story school building to which the brothers moved their school in March, 1853. By this time, enrollment had reached 120.[34] Until the city later built a bridge, a rowboat was used to ferry day students back and forth across the river each day.[35]

The first director of the school was Bro. Andrew Edel. Although his stern approach to education sometimes brought complaints from both parents and parish clergy, the school nonetheless prospered under his leadership, which continued until 1866. In 1855, the brothers took possession of the lands around Mission Nuestra Señora de la Purísima Concepción de Acuña, 2½ miles south of the city, where they began to raise vegetables for the dining hall of the school in town. Edel made regular boat trips from the school to the mission to bring back produce for the school. In 1859, the brothers came into actual ownership of the mission property. They refurbished the mission church and on May 28, 1861, solemnly reopened it as a place of worship. By the eve of the Civil War, the brothers were providing an education for over two hundred students in San Antonio.[36]

Meanwhile, parochial life in San Antonio was also changing during the decade of the 1850s. Largely because of European immigration, the aging parish church of San Fernando grew too small for its many parishioners. Although San Fernando was vastly enlarged during the 1860s and later became the cathedral of a new diocese, the decision was now made to erect an additional parish to serve primarily the Anglo and German Catholics of the city, rather than build a new and larger San Fernando. Some immediate action, however, was taken to hold together San Fernando's rapidly deteriorating building. The winter of 1855–56 was severe in San Antonio, and the cold produced large cracks in the roof of the church. Rain poured in over the altar, tabernacle, organ, and statuary. During one downpour water rose to the height of two feet in the church.

Work on the foundations for a second parish church, to be known as St. Mary's, began in late 1855. Through the next year and into the next, the work continued; by February, 1857, the structure and its exterior were virtually complete. The expenses required for the new structure and for repairs to San Fernando pressed Dubuis to turn again and again to the Catholics of the city for additional funds. The Hispanic population was generous, noted Dubuis, while others, who tended to have more money, were less so.[37]

The efforts of Bishop Odin, his priests, and the men and women religious to meet the needs of Texas Catholics particularly in those areas where they were concentrated enjoyed significant success in the 1850s. However, the situation was an ever-changing one; continuous immigration made this inevitable. Furthermore, forces were at work that gravely complicated this generally hopeful picture. The 1850s were tumultuous and strife-torn over slavery; violence in some places was commonplace. The continued attempt by many to justify slavery created fertile soil in society for all forms of prejudice. At another level during the same decade, increasing immigration was met by a rising nativism with its accompanying anti-Catholicism, and some Texas Catholics were hit by bigotry from both sources.

SIX

The Immigrant Catholic

BETWEEN 1850 and 1860 Texas' population nearly tripled, increasing from 212,592 to 604,215. The majority of Texans in 1850 were natives of the Old South, and of the thousands entering Texas during the 1850s, southerners continued to predominate. Most of these were Protestants, but immigration during this decade nonetheless brought a significant rise in Texas' Catholic population, enabling it to keep pace with the total increase. There were approximately 40,000 Catholics in Texas in 1850, and while no official figures for 1860 exist, it can be estimated from later figures that the Catholic population was between 100,000 and 125,000 that year. European immigration steadily increased during the decade so that by 1860 there were over 43,000 Texans of European birth. Of these the Germans were the largest group with 20,553. While Czech, German, Irish, and Polish immigration was responsible for much of the increase in the Catholic population in the central and western parts of the state, many Mexican Catholics immigrated into the Rio Grande Valley during this same decade. As early as 1852, Odin wrote to Archbishop Blanc of New Orleans that "many Catholics particularly from Mexico and Germany are arriving. All our priests will have to speak English, Spanish and a little German."[1]

When Bishop Odin returned to the valley in 1856, growing political unrest in Mexico, stemming from the wars of La Reforma, was already sending many refugees to the Texas side of the border. The river was at flood stage, and Odin was not able to reach all the places that he wanted to visit. This time he journeyed overland from Galveston. He was using a mule to pull his buggy, but after reaching Laredo, the animal died. The only horse he could obtain was a high-spirited one, and soon afterward, as he was attempting to cross an engorged stream, the horse shied and overturned the buggy. Odin almost drowned and was fortunate to come out of the accident with only scratches and a black eye.[2]

Two years later, Odin conducted what turned out to be his last visit to the growing number of Catholics along the Rio Grande. In the late summer and fall of 1858, he made confirmation visits all the way from Port Isabel to Laredo. By that time he was fifty-eight years old and had been on the Texas frontier eighteen years. His strength in the face of harsh existence still

The Rev. Pierre-Fourrier Parisot, O.M.I., circa 1890.
Courtesy Catholic Archives of Texas, Austin.

held. At least, that was the conclusion of the missionary priest, Pierre Parisot, who accompanied him one day on a thirty-mile trip over a muddy trail. At one point, Odin spied a dried-out piece of corn bread that Parisot had forgotten to remove from his luggage. He asked if he might have it, but Parisot warned him that he might break his teeth on it since it was two weeks old. Odin ate and enjoyed the bread, remarking that he often carried a piece of corn bread with him while traveling in case he could find no cabin in which to spend the night. "I always found a piece of corn bread to be a delicious supper, seasoned with a good appetite." During that particular trip Odin traveled almost two thousand miles and confirmed 3,413 people.[3]

Beginning in 1852, Czechs from Moravia and Bohemia, then part of the Austro-Hungarian Empire, began entering the state and settling in the fertile black land of Central Texas. Most reestablished themselves as productive farmers in their new land, as they had once been in the heartland of Europe.[4] A few Czechs were in Texas as early as the 1830s. One Czech, Frederick Lemsky, was with Houston's army at San Jacinto and was part of the impromptu "band" that played "Come to the Bower" as the Texans attacked.[5]

Approximately 70 percent of Czechs immigrating to Texas in the 1850s and on into the twentieth century were Roman Catholics. About 25 percent were Protestants, usually members of the Brethren Church, which had historical ties back to Jan Hus who lived a century before Luther. Since the Czech language was then forbidden in Austrian-controlled Bohemia, many Czechs also spoke German. The Rev. Bohumir Menzl was probably the first Czech Catholic priest in Texas; he arrived with a group of Germans in 1845, and for several years worked in the area around Fredericksburg and at New Braunfels, before returning to his homeland in 1856. In 1852 and 1853, at least thirty-two Czech families arrived in Texas, forming the vanguard of the thousands more who would come in the years ahead. While many Protestant Czechs in the 1850s settled in the vicinity of Nelsonville west of Cat Spring in Austin County, Catholic Czechs settled farther to the west in Fayette County. Fayetteville in the eastern part of this county is sometimes called the "cradle of Czech settlement in Texas." Some of these early Catholic immigrants moved on to a village originally called Bluff, about five miles southwest of La Grange, and soon changed its name to Hostyn. Ironically, it was situated on land once belonging to Fr. Miguel Muldoon. Many years later, in 1889, the Czech Catholic benevolent society known as the *Katolicka Jednota Texaska* was founded there. In November, 1856, Czechs began settling in Navidad, a community in the blacklands of southern Fayette County about five miles northeast of present-day Schulenburg. Soon, the community became known as Dubina, which means "oak grove" in Czech. There, in 1858, Joseph Peter, Sr., erected a log structure where mass could be celebrated for the community's Catholics. Czechs settled as well at the community of Mulberry, also in southern Fayette County, and changed its name to Praha (Prague) in 1858. Fr. Joseph Bittowski formed St. Mary's Church there in 1866.[6]

Like other newly arrived Texans, the Czechs found their first years hard. Their first houses were often temporary shelters until the first crops were planted. One early Czech Texan remembered life at Dubina in 1856–57 thusly:

> With shelter provided, all began clearing the land, made rail fences and prepared the land for tilling. In the following fall only one small bale of cotton was made by the whole group. It was loaded on a sled and pulled by oxen to La Grange, where it was sold. Indeed this first struggling effort at making a living was filled with forebodings. By now, the savings brought from Europe were spent. Flour was $20.00 a barrel, and an epidemic broke out, caused by hard work and contaminated water. It was truly a fight for survival. But God was with us. The following year crops were better and with the kind help of those of English speaking extraction, we became firmly established.[7]

Polish immigration into Texas was simultaneous to that of the Czechs.[8] One of the priests whom Odin interested in coming to Texas while in Europe in 1852 was Fr. Leopold Bonaventure Maria Moczygemba. Odin visited the Franciscan community at Schonau near Würzburg in southern Germany. Moczygemba, a native of the village of Pluznica in Prussian Poland, was twenty-seven years old at the time. After studying at gymnasiums in Gliwice and Opole, he entered the Order of Friars Minor Conventual, or "Black Friars," whose black habit distinguished them from the then blue-grayish-clad Friars Minor Observant. Moczygemba set out for Texas with three other Franciscans from Schonau: Bonaventura Keller, who served as their superior, Dominic Mescens, and Anthony Muller. Moczygemba was the lone Pole in the group; the others were Germans, and all were to work among the then increasing number of Texas Germans. Odin referred to the entire group as "German priests" since Moczygemba's birthplace was then part of the German kingdom of Prussia. Moczygemba was assigned to St. Peter's Church in New Braunfels as its first resident pastor, while the others went to Castroville, D'Hanis, and Fredericksburg. Moczygemba remained in New Braunfels until February, 1854, when he was transferred to Castroville.[9]

Texas impressed the young Polish priest. He liked the openness of the society and the economic progress the Germans were already experiencing in Texas. Moczygemba began to write his many friends and relatives in Upper Silesia in Prussian Poland telling them of the opportunities he believed Texas could offer them. His letters were addressed to whole families and even to entire villages. To some, these letters offered a glimmer of hope for a better life at a time when the farmers of Upper Silesia were experiencing extraordinarily hard times: their landholdings had been reduced in size by the Prussians early in the century; epidemics and floods had wreaked their toll during the early 1850s; and beginning in 1853, the Crimean War caused Russia to stop the export of grain to Europe, thereby drastically inflating the price of wheat and other grains in Prussia and its domain. Although charitable programs throughout Germany brought some aid to the Poles in Upper Silesia, their problems were exacerbated by the increasing social gap between the small landholding Polish farmers and the mostly Prussian large landholders.

As T. Lindsay Baker points out in *The First Polish Americans: Silesian Settlements in Texas*, it was from these small landholders that the Catholic Polish immigrants to Texas came in the 1850s. In September, 1854, the first group of immigrants from Upper Silesia began their long journey to Texas, traveling by train first to Berlin, then on to the port of Bremen, where in October they boarded the wooden ship *Weser* for a two-month voyage to Galveston. A few of the party followed some days later in the ship *Antoinette*. The *Weser* reached Galveston on December 3, 1854. From Galveston, the Poles took ship for Indianola and from there either walked or hired the services of the Hispanic cart drivers to take them and their belongings overland to San Antonio, where they arrived a few days before Christmas. Moczygemba, who by then was the superior of his order in Texas, hastened from Castroville to meet them.

Moczygemba had first thought of settling his countrymen at a site near

New Braunfels but had decided on two other sites: one in Karnes County southeast of San Antonio, and the other, the already existing town of Bandera, northwest of San Antonio. The land chosen in Karnes County was owned by John Twohig, a Catholic businessman in San Antonio. He and Moczygemba inspected the land together, and Twohig agreed that until the settlers could buy the land from him, he would reserve it for them. Most of the newly arrived Poles chose to go to the Karnes County site, which thus became the location of the first Polish colony in the United States. On Christmas Day, 1854, Moczygemba offered mass under an oak tree at what soon was named Panna Maria, which in Polish means Virgin Mary. In Baker's definitive study of these first Polish settlements in Texas (and in the United States), three theories are given as to why the settlement was so named. First, the same year the colony was founded, Pope Pius IX proclaimed the dogma of the Immaculate Conception of the Blessed Virgin Mary; therefore, the colonists thought it appropriate to place their church under the patronage of Mary of the Immaculate Conception and name their settlement "Virgin Mary." Another theory is that the immigrants were so impressed with the beauty of St. Mary's Church in Krakow in their native land that they named their new home after it. Yet another theory revolves around the story that Father Moczygemba, while on a preaching mission in another frontier village, had a vision of St. Mary's Church in Krakow encircled by a bright light and interpreted this as a sign that the new settlement should be named Panna Maria.

In the spring of 1855, Moczygemba began selecting stone for the new village's church. Work soon commenced, and the cornerstone was blessed on August 14, 1855. The new edifice was consecrated and officially opened on September 29, 1856. Long before its completion, however, the settlers began to use it as a place of worship. In the spring of 1856, a figure of Christ brought from Upper Silesia was affixed to a large cross erected by parishioners at the entrance to the incomplete church.[10]

Of those who arrived in 1854, about sixteen families chose not to settle in Karnes County but to go northwestward to Bandera, a town established only the year before their arrival in Texas. But settlers had not rushed to the area because it was on the outer edge of the frontier, exposed to Indian attack. The town's promoters were more than eager to attract the newly arrived Poles to their would-be town—so eager that in February, 1855, they arranged for wagons and teamsters to carry the settlers and their baggage to Bandera. The drivers were instructed not to charge for their services, and under no circumstances were they to allow any of the settlers to return to San Antonio in the wagons. Once the immigrants were in Bandera, they had no way to leave except on foot. The Poles worked in the sawmill and when able bought land from their employers and erected houses. Over the next three years, the Polish population of Bandera grew as a few families from Panna Maria moved there, believing the area afforded a healthier climate.

The Polish settlers at Bandera erected their first church, a log structure, in 1858. They used this church until after the Civil War, when a masonry building replaced it.[11]

Some of these first Polish settlers chose to live neither at Bandera nor at Panna Maria but in San Antonio. They were mainly artisans for whom life there promised a better means of support than in the rural settlements. Their numbers increased throughout the decade, and they gravitated toward the southeastern quadrant of the city. These Polish Catholics worshiped at San Fernando until 1866, when they converted a former warehouse and bakery in their neighborhood into a church, St. Michael's, the third oldest parish in San Antonio.

Some of the Poles who arrived in 1855 had disassembled their farm wagons and brought them along on their voyage and thus had their own means of transportation for the overland journey to San Antonio. While most of these new arrivals chose to settle in the already established Polish rural communities, with some staying in San Antonio, about thirteen families decided to pioneer a new farming community.[12] A German by the name of John Demner advised them to investigate some land about eighteen miles east of San Antonio on Martinez Creek. They did so and were favorably impressed. Their settlement was first called Martinez after the stream by that name. The settlers named their first church, a log structure built in either 1856 or 1857, St. Hedwig's, for the patron saint of Silesia.[13] In the 1860s the village came to be known by this name. This was ironic since about that same time the name of the church was changed to the Annunciation of the Blessed Virgin Mary.[14]

The settlers were pleased to discover a fellow Pole living nearby, John Dirstyn, who had been in Texas since about 1835. He had married into an Anglo family and was a great help to the Polish settlers in their relations with local Anglos in the years ahead. Many years later, one of his daughters entered an order of Polish-speaking nuns known as the Sisters of the Immaculate Conception, or "Blue Sisters" from their blue habit. These sisters taught at both Panna Maria and St. Hedwig.

Other Polish settlements sprang up in the 1850s as a result of either continued immigration or the movement of settlers from the original Polish communities. For instance, east of Panna Maria, in DeWitt County, the towns of Yorktown and Meyersville became the sites of new Polish communities about 1856. Germans were already settled in each, and while relations between the two ethnic groups were generally amiable, a disagreement arose in Meyersville over what language would be used in the sermons at mass. Consequently most of the Poles there moved to Yorktown, where their fellow countrymen were in the majority. Later several families founded a Polish-speaking parish farther to the east at Coleto.[15]

Some other Polish communities in existence by the late 1850s were located in Victoria, Inez, and St. Francisville, near present-day Bay City, and at Gaina (from its original name, Las Gallinas), south of San Antonio.[16]

Like other central Texas farmers, the Polish settlers suffered extreme hardship in the Texas drought of 1856–57. A series of wet northers lasting from December, 1855, until late March, 1856, delayed the spring planting, and by the time the crops of 1856 were ripening, drought had begun. At Panna Maria no rain fell for over a year. Food prices drastically increased, and corn was imported from as far away as Ohio. Like many others, some of the Poles began to question the wisdom of locating in Texas. At Panna Maria, some of the settlers decided that John Twohig and his partner, Col. W. J. Hardee, had overcharged them for their land. They suggested that Twohig's apparent generosity in holding land for the settlers until it could be paid for was a mask for exorbitant prices. The drought brought their discontent to the surface, and since Father Moczygemba had been instrumental in beginning Polish immigration to Texas, much of their anger was aimed at him—in spite of the fact that the priest had purchased 238 acres from Twohig and parceled out most of it to colonists who could not afford the prices. Moczygemba reserved 25 acres of this tract to serve as the church site and for other ecclesiastical uses since he had purchased the land with money provided him by his order for the establishment of a religious foundation in Texas.[17] One group of families became so disgusted with Texas that they went north to Franklin County, Missouri, west of St. Louis on the Missouri River.[18]

Moczygemba, in addition to his work in the Polish settlements, had oversight over his fellow Franciscans working in New Braunfels, Fredericksburg, and Castroville. With anger and resentment increasing against him, Moczygemba left the Polish settlements for Castroville and later New Braunfels. He left Texas, probably in early 1858, to consult with his superiors in Rome. Moczygemba apparently intended to return to Texas, for before his departure for Rome he had informed Odin of his willingness to assume the administration of St. Mary's College and Seminary in Galveston, which the Oblates had just left. In response, Odin requested additional personnel from the Franciscan superior general in Rome, who promised to send to Texas six priests for the school. In 1859, additional Franciscans did arrive to work in the school, but Odin concluded they were ill-suited for academic work: "[The Franciscans] sent here two priests of the Order, three young scholastics and nine aspirants of various nationalities who had scarcely begun their studies. I made all possible sacrifices to encourage them in their enterprise, and having need of study themselves they . . . [were not able] . . . to begin this good work. It was impossible for me to keep them."[19]

Odin's disappointments increased when he learned in the summer of 1859 that Father Moczygemba was not returning to Texas. After conferring with the superiors of his order in Rome, Moczygemba accepted oversight of his order's administration of several New York state parishes. This led to Moczygemba's withdrawing from Texas the remaining priests of the Order of Friars Minor Conventual. Odin was bitter over this turn of events, for he could ill afford their loss. Not all the reasons for Moczygemba's decision are known, but his difficult experience in Texas was no doubt one of them.[20] Not only had he borne the brunt of the anger and disillusionment of his fellow Poles, for whose condition he no doubt felt great responsibility, but before leaving Texas he had pleaded in vain to his superiors for Polish Franciscans to serve the Texas settlements. Moczygemba resided and worked in the North until his death in 1891. It was twenty years after his departure from Texas before he returned to visit his brothers and their children.[21]

It is from Father Moczygemba that we have the first population figures for these early Polish settlements in Texas. While on his way to Rome in 1858, he gave the following statistics to correspondents of two Polish newspapers: Panna Maria, 120 families; San Antonio, 50 families; Martínez, 25 families; and Bandera, 20 families. T. Lindsay Baker points out that while these figures indicate that the area of major Polish settlement had a population of 1,002, the total number of Polish Texans was greater since only parishioners in the major communities were included in Moczygemba's figures given to the reporters.[22]

Two other Polish priests were serving in Texas at the time of Moczygemba's departure for Europe: a fellow Franciscan, Fr. Anthony Rossadowski, and Fr. Julian Przysiecki. Rossadowski, originally from Russian Poland, had served as a chaplain for Poles fighting unsuccessfully for independence in 1830 and later for United States forces in the Seminole War. He supervised the construction of the first church at Bandera but left in 1860 to join Moczygemba in New York state when the latter recalled the members of his order in Texas. Przysiecki arrived in Texas in 1857 and remained until his death in 1863.[23]

A school may have existed at the church in Panna Maria as early as 1858, and Moczygemba and Rossadowski at one time even hoped that a college would develop there as well. One source indicates that the first teacher at the school was Peter Kiolbassa, whose father had been a deputy from Silesia in the Prussian parliament.[24]

The late 1850s saw continued German immigration into Texas. Most came to establish farms but some to join the even greater number of Irish immigrants drawn to Texas to labor as construction workers on Texas' small but expanding rail system. The Houston and Texas Central Railroad Company began expanding its trackage north and westward from Houston during the 1850s. By early 1861, it had reached Millican north of Navasota and had built a roadbed as far north as Booneville (present-day Bryan). At Hempstead a line went west across the Brazos to Chappell Hill. By the time the Civil War began in 1861, other lines connected Houston with Galveston;

with Richmond and Alleyton, near Columbus, to the west; and with Orange to the east. A line in East Texas ran from Marshall to Shreveport, Louisiana. Odin expressed concern over the welfare of the hundreds of immigrant workers involved in this relatively new industry in Texas in one of his last reports to the Society for the Propagation of the Faith:

> The need for a hospital for our poor sick patients is being felt more and more. Railroads which are being constructed in Texas lure to us a great number of Irish and German workmen. Exposed to the intense heat of a burning sun, poorly nourished and deprived of healthful water they are often attacked by fever. During epidemics our sick people do not know where to seek refuge. Therefore I long to be able to offer them a place of refuge.[25]

Most of the Germans in this period continued to settle in Central Texas and to the west in Gillespie County as had their predecessors of the previous decade. When the Conventual Franciscans withdrew from Texas, not only the Polish settlements were deprived of most of their clergy but the Germans west and north of San Antonio as well. Consequently, Odin was especially pleased when a German Jesuit, Fr. Francis Xavier Weninger, arrived at Galveston in 1859 to lead a series of preaching missions in Texas. Odin had hoped that the Jesuits would assume the administration of the Galveston college-seminary. In this he was disappointed, but he was glad nonetheless to have Weninger in his diocese. Weninger was an effective preacher in the German language, and Odin had wanted for years to get him to come to Texas.[26] His missions were quite successful, although he created some controversy among non-Catholics around the state, since other denominations tended to resent his oft-repeated admonition that the Catholic canonical requirements regarding baptisms, mixed marriages, and the children of such marriages be strictly observed. Weninger did try to lessen this resentment at times by either verbal or published explanations of these requirements. After preaching in Galveston, he went to Houston in late March, 1859, and remained into early April when he departed for Victoria, San Antonio, Castroville, Fredricksburg, and New Braunfels. By late June he was in Austin. He was struck by the lack of priests, particularly among the Germans. He encouraged Odin to seek help from the newly-founded Benedictine Abbey at St. Vincent, Pennsylvania. Odin had twice previously asked help from these German-speaking priests, but Weninger urged him on to a third attempt. In addressing his repeated plea to the Abbot, Boniface Wimmer, the bishop offered San José Mission and the adjacent plot of five hundred acres of farm land to the Benedictines to be their headquarters. Five German congregations, he wrote, needed their efforts immediately.[27] Still the Benedictines refused, citing as reason their needs in Pennsylvania. Weninger advised Odin to go to Pennsylvania and personally plead for priests.

Since the Benedictines had several foundations in Pennsylvania, at Weninger's suggestion Odin stopped in New Orleans and used the telegraph there to locate the abbot before going north. Odin arrived at the abbey in St. Vincent in June, 1859, and was successful in luring the Benedictines to Texas. On July 1, Frs. Alto Hoermann, the prior for the new foundation, Peter Baunach, and Aemilian Wendel, and Brothers Michael Boehns and Norbert Rossberger set out by train for Cairo, Illinois, where they boarded a riverboat for New Orleans with San Antonio as their ultimate destination.[28] Other Benedictines soon followed.[29]

Establishing their headquarters at San José, they began to work in the new St. Mary's parish in San Antonio and in Castroville, D'Hanis, Fredericksburg, and New Braunfels. They also took charge of Mission San Juan Capistrano near San Antonio. Odin began sending funds to the abbey in Pennsylvania to help train future priests and brothers for work in Texas, and he purchased a lot in San Antonio on which he hoped a house would be built for the priests working at St. Mary's. A contribution for the Benedictines' work in Texas was even received from King Ludwig of Bavaria. Fr. Peter Baunach's work at St. Mary's in Fredericksburg progressed so well that the cornerstone for a new stone church was laid there on June 1, 1861, just as the Civil War was beginning. Things went so well that the prior, Alto Hoermann, in 1861 believed great changes lay ahead: "From here our influence shall be felt far and wide. We will be able to preserve the faith in the whole of Texas, and we ought to follow the immigrants who are moving westward to California, and finally through the Mexican population in our locality [we] may come in contact with the people in Mexico itself."[30] Future events, however, left this prediction unfulfilled.

There was another group of immigrants to Texas in this decade which, though small in number, had the potential to challenge Catholic missionary endeavor to a greater degree than any of the others. These were a colony of "Fourierists" who immigrated from France to North Texas in the mid-1850s. They came hoping that frontier conditions would enable them to implement the teachings of the French socialist Charles Fourier, who lived from 1772 to 1837. Fourier taught that private property should be eliminated and the economy and society based on small, self-sufficient agricultural communities. The movement was not only anticlerical but atheistic as well.

The Fourierists came to Texas under the leadership of Victor Considerant, who took them to the environs of the village of Dallas. Odin was especially interested in them not only because they were organized atheists but because like him they were French and therefore, in his view, Catholic by birth. In June of 1856, he wrote to the Society for the Propagation of the Faith in Lyon: "Since the origin of this colony I have felt great anxiety for these poor compatriots and a great desire to consider the means of bringing them back to the practice of their [religious] duties. To this end I charged Reverend Chambodut with traveling over the entire northeastern part of Texas."³¹ Chambodut, Odin's vicar general, was away from Galveston two months and reported on this assignment about 200 Fourierists living in the vicinity of Dallas. He also found seven Catholic Anglo families in this village and reported them eager to have a church opened for them. He hoped these could form the nucleus of a Catholic community in Dallas that might have some impact upon the Fourierists. Chambodut visited all of the latter, both the main group of 164 still aligned with Considerant and a smaller group farther from Dallas that had broken away from the others. Chambodut was reportedly well received by his compatriots, especially, he said, by the children, who seemed happy to see a French priest.³² Later Odin sent Claude Dubuis among the Fourierists, whom Dubuis reported increasingly dissatisfied both with life on the frontier and their social experiment. Some made plans to leave Texas entirely, while the rest soon abandoned their social experiment and settled down to follow their own pursuits. Dubuis advised them on how best to come to terms with life in Texas and was successful in persuading many to resume the practice of their religion. By 1859, a Catholic church was functioning in the town of Dallas, even though the perpetual clergy shortage meant a priest had to be shared with Nacogdoches.³³

Anti-Catholic sentiment in the northeastern United States increased with the arrival of many Catholic immigrants during the 1840s. In New England some parishes used armed guards to protect themselves from mob violence during this period. Scurrilous literature circulated in many places, leading to convents being raided and in some instances burned to the ground, as were several Catholic churches. Philadelphia was the site in 1844 of the most notorious outbreaks of violence: in May and July, there was mob violence in the streets, and many Catholic homes and two Catholic churches were destroyed. In the early 1850s, the Know-Nothing party became the political vehicle for this antiforeign, anti-Catholic sentiment. "Vigilance committees" were formed in many American towns and cities for the express purpose of countering what was considered to be foreign and/or Catholic influence. In the northeast it was the Irish immigrants, coming in vast numbers, fleeing famine in their homeland, who usually fell victim to the Know-Nothings' hate campaign.

It was the summer of 1854 when Know-Nothing activity began in Texas. Bishop Odin was aware of the Know-Nothings' activity in Galveston as early as July. They first stirred up resentment against Galveston's German community, who were speaking out indignantly at their attackers. The bishop was uneasy about the future, for he knew of the violence in the Northeast and the readiness on the part of some to listen to the Know-Nothings' prejudice. To Blanc in New Orleans he wrote: "What will they do? I hope God will thwart their sinister projects. This unfortunate society [the Know-Nothings] already produces a very sad effect on minds. It embitters souls and completely divides our small community."³⁴ The party even won some local elections in San Antonio, with its large number of Catholics, where their anger was aimed largely at Hispanics but also at Germans and Poles. Of the sixty-one newspapers in Texas at the time, the Know-Nothings eventually claimed the allegiance of twelve. The Democrats retained the adherence of thirty-two, twelve were independent, and the others were literary or religious in nature. Since annexation, as in the rest of the slaveholding South, the Democratic party had been dominant in Texas politics. It was immensely strengthening to the Know-Nothings, however, when for a brief period in the 1850s Sam Houston, who once had seemed so favorably disposed toward the Catholic church, joined them. Houston justified his new stance by saying he was not against the faith of Catholics but against what he considered to be the "foreign allegiance" they held to Rome. In the *Texas State Gazette* of September 1, 1855, Houston is quoted as saying that "the design of the . . . [Know-Nothings] is not to put down Catholics, but to prevent Catholics from putting down Protestants. The membership of the Order [Know-Nothings] would not, nor do they intend to interfere with the Catholic religion or their model of worship, but at the same time we are not to place power in the hands of those who acknowledge or owe temporal allegiance to any foreign Prince, King, or Potentate."³⁵

Whatever Houston's understanding of the Know-Nothing aims may have been, these aims did interfere "with the Catholic religion . . . [and] their mode of worship," as witness the previously cited arson and violence. His real reason for joining the Know-Nothings was his break with Texas Democrats over the Kansas-Nebraska Act in 1854. This law furthered the interests of the slaveholding South by repealing the Missouri Compromise line of 1820 and thereby permitting the possible spread of slavery to areas where it had previously been forbidden. The Kansas-Nebraska Act was viewed in Texas as a great victory on the national level for the slave-based economy that dominated much of the state. The bill was enacted and became law in the spring of 1854. Sen. Sam Houston of Texas voted against the bill, however, believing that a bloody contest would result between North and South for control of the territories, particularly Kansas, and ultimately pull the Union apart. By the fall of 1854, many believed this was already happening in what soon became known as "Bleeding Kansas," where pro- and antislavery forces were in guerilla warfare over control of the new territory.

Houston believed he might have a better future politically in Texas with the Know-Nothings, who paradoxically preached prejudice and hate against Catholics and foreigners but were much less committed to the institution of slavery than were the Democrats, one simple reason being that much of the party's national support came from the North where immigration was making the biggest impact. As the controversy between North and South grew even more volatile in the late 1850s, the Know-Nothings began to fade away, but only after they had created festering wounds of fear, suspicion, and hate.

On June 16, 1855, at a mass meeting of Democrats in Austin, a resolution repudiating Know-Nothing principles was adopted:

> That the true test for qualification for office is the test declared by Mr. Jefferson, "Is he honest; is he capable; is he faithful to the Constitution?" and that any party that prescribes a different test, and requires no positive declaration of principles other than that the candidate is opposed to placing in Office citizens of foreign birth, and those professing the Roman Catholic religion, is not in accordance with the genius of the American Government, and violates all the fundamental principles of free speech, free press, and free conscience, upon which this Republic was founded.[36]

Other meetings of Democrats in San Antonio and Galveston also strongly condemned Know-Nothing principles. At one meeting of Hispanic Democrats in July, José Antonio Navarro denounced the Know-Nothings as those who "proclaim equality" and "offer asylum and liberty" to many, but deny it to Catholics. "The Texas-Mexicans are Catholics and may be proud of the belief of their fathers; they will defend themselves against such infamous aggression." In August, voters in Bexar County voted against the Know-Nothings overwhelmingly.[37] The Galveston meeting accused the Know-Nothings of a willingness to violate the Constitution's prohibition of the establishment of a religion or of a religious test as a qualification for holding public office.

In May, 1856, Texas' Democratic governor, Elisha M. Pease, who later opposed secession and after the Civil War joined the Republicans, came out on record in favor of distributing public funds to all Texas schools regardless of affiliation as an expedient means of remedying Texas' woeful lack of educational facilities. The Know-Nothings immediately attacked the governor for wanting to "establish" denominational schools and "Jesuit education." In this assault, Catholic teaching orders were attacked as purveyors of a kind of education that sought to prepare "the American mind for the world of despotism."[38]

Catholics were not attacked only in the press, however. A young French-born priest, Antoine Borias, ordained by Odin in Galveston in 1854 and transferred from Beaumont, his first assignment, to Goliad in 1856, was attacked and severely beaten by some of the local Know-Nothings.[39] Ethnic and religious prejudice had smouldered in Goliad for years, and it had been only two years before the attack on Borias that Odin with some difficulty had regained the use of the church there. This building originally had been the church for the Presidio de Nuestra Señora de Loreto de la Bahía del Espíritu Santo. The climate of prejudice already there was fertile ground for the Know-Nothings. In January, 1841, the government of the Republic of Texas had given to the vicar apostolic, John Timon, title to the buildings of the former Franciscan missions in Texas and the presidial church at Goliad. But in 1852 Odin encountered a volatile situation at Goliad. During the war between the United States and Mexico many Hispanic families there had fled southward, but Odin reported that by 1852 nearly sixty families had returned to reestablish themselves. Tragically, of their former village only the presidial church remained standing. In 1847, several Anglo families had established a new settlement on the other side of the river, obtained a charter for a new town from the legislature, and then claimed for it the property of the older municipality, including the presidial church. The new city government had then proceeded to dispose of this property as it wished. The church had been first conveyed to the secretary of the town council and then to a non-Catholic congregation. When Odin visited Goliad in the fall of 1852, he found many Catholics but no church in which he could celebrate mass. He used a private home for this and made no public mention of the church property. He believed that some of the Anglos of the new town were now ashamed to have been party to such an unjust transaction. He told town officials that he had no intention of suing for the building's return but would seek redress through the state legislature. He believed a lawsuit might be successful but feared the costs and time involved. He hoped, too, that a sense of justice would cause the council to return the church. Odin discovered, however, that the matter would be more complicated than that, since another religious body now had what it considered legitimate possession of the building. Finally, in dealings involving both the town council and the religious body, Odin by a payment of five thousand dollars once more obtained the use of the Spanish presidial church for Goliad's Catholics. By the summer of 1854, mass was being regularly celebrated there and some restoration work was in progress, but the attack on Father Borias two years later demonstrated that tension had only subsided momentarily.[40]

Know-Nothingism victimized Hispanic Texans in other areas as well and spread its influence to many who in a formal sense had no connection with it as a political party. It cast a long shadow over the Texas landscape. Perhaps the worst example of this in the 1850s involved the cart drivers who for years had carried freight between the port of Indianola and the inland towns of Victoria and San Antonio; according to Bishop Odin it involved the Hispanic people of the western frontier in general. What is usually called the "Cart War" erupted in 1857, after a "vigilance committee" in San Antonio had been stirring up resentment against Hispanic residents, when word was spread that one freight company hired only Hispanic drivers. Odin wrote in July:

> San Antonio is in great distress and they fear a famine. To complete the misery the Vigilance Committee sheds fear everywhere and raises on the entire frontier a horrible persecution against the poor Mexicans. The inhabitants of Helena and Goliad no longer wish to permit . . . [the] carts to go to port. Deprived of this feeble resource they will have to leave the country or die of hunger. Today more than sixty came back that they did not allow to pass. How beautiful is the liberty that is so vaunted in this country.[41]

Attacks continued into the early fall and as many as seventy may have been killed. Gov. Elisha M. Pease, who already had taken a stand against the Know-Nothings, went personally to San Antonio at the end of September to organize a company of seventy-five Texas Rangers to protect the cart drivers back and forth between San Antonio and the coast. Odin was in San Antonio during Pease's visit and was pleased to report this new turn of events to the clergy at Galveston.[42] But while goodwill motivated the governor, and violence did subside, the freight company that had hired only Hispanics fired them, and what Odin had originally feared was the outcome for many of the San Antonio drivers.

As Arnoldo De León points out in his study of Anglo attitudes toward Hispanics, *They Called Them Greasers,* the prejudice against Hispanics fanned by the Know-Nothings coincided with that from another source during this volatile decade. The opposition to slavery exhibited by many Hispanic Texans helped cause Hispanics as a whole to be suspect in Anglo eyes. While there were notable exceptions, such as the future Confederate officer Santos Benavides of Laredo, who more than once returned escaped slaves to their masters, numerous Hispanics in the antebellum period helped slaves escape to freedom in Mexico. In 1854 a convention at Gonzales called for the formation of vigilance committees to prevent contacts between Hispanics and blacks, and in 1856 in Colorado County, Hispanics were accused of involvement in a slave insurrection and given five days to leave the county. In 1857 a resolution passed in Uvalde County requiring any Hispanic traveling through the area to have a pass issued by an Anglo official.[43]

De León points out that it was injustice of this nature that was behind the activities of Juan Cortina at the end of the decade. In July, 1859, Cortina shot the Brownsville sheriff in response to an ethnic epithet. Cortina then launched an insurrection along the border, issuing proclamations enumerating the injustices committed against Hispanics in South Texas since 1848. Paramount among these were land thievery and unequal treatment before the law. Cortina, who was forced to retreat into Mexico, at one point hoped in vain for help from Sam Houston when the latter made a political comeback in 1859.⁴⁴ In spite of Cortina's grievances, a Brownsville Oblate priest at the time, Fr. Pierre Parisot, sympathized with the Anglos and considered Cortina "ignorant and unprincipled."⁴⁵ The record of the 1850s however, can leave no doubt but that the injustices were real.

The Know-Nothings also tried to cause trouble for the Ursuline convent and school in San Antonio. In the early summer of 1857, a student there died, a girl of about fifteen. Prior to her illness she had asked Father Dubuis to receive her into the Catholic Church; Dubuis had refused since her father in Austin would not give his consent. Later, as the girl lay dying and again requested reception into the Catholic church, this was granted. She was buried in the convent cemetery. Soon stories began to circulate in Austin, fanned by anonymous letters published in certain newspapers, to the effect variously that the girl was not dead but had been secretly sent by the sisters to another convent, or to France, or that she had been locked in a cell to force her to join their order; in a more sinister version, there was the implication that Dubuis had caused her death to prevent her from telling the world that baptism in the Catholic church had been forced upon her. In the face of such publicity, the girl's father came from Austin, had the body exhumed, and identified it as that of his daughter. Also, a note she had written left no doubt as to her wish to join the Catholic church.⁴⁶

With such stories being spread by the Know-Nothings, a group of tourists in San Antonio even went to Fr. Pierre Parisot, at the time serving in Dubuis's place while he was in Europe, and asked to be allowed to see the inside of the Ursuline convent, "examine its secrets," and have opportunity to converse with the sisters. Parisot agreed to their request, met them at the convent door, conducted them to the community room, and introduced them to the sisters. For some time they visited with the sisters and were then invited to tour the convent and go into all its rooms. After making the tour, they seemed satisfied that Catholic convents contained no secret passages, dark dungeons or chambers, and no secret caches of arms. Parisot assured them as they were leaving that "you have seen one cloister, and in seeing it you have seen them all." They responded that their impression of the nuns was that they were "very amiable and highly educated ladies."⁴⁷

Problems related to church property that surfaced in the 1850s were inspired, if not by direct Know-Nothing influence, by the same temporal ambiance. In March, 1856, the city of San Antonio attempted to seize the rectory of San Fernando Church for nonpayment of taxes. The pastor, Claude Dubuis, learned the exact course of action the city planned to take when he saw in the newspaper his house advertised for sale by the city. Rather than threatening legal action, Dubuis gathered signatures on a petition and presented it to the city council. In spite of all their previous bluster, the mayor and council agreed to place the rectory in a tax-free category.⁴⁸

Facade, Mission Concepción, San Antonio, circa 1865.
Courtesy Catholic Archives of Texas, Austin.

The bishop did have to go into court during this period to obtain use of some of the mission property at San Antonio. Odin hoped to put both Concepción and San José missions into the care of religious orders: Concepción for the Brothers of Mary and San José for the Franciscans. Both sites were excellent for educational facilities. Before he could proceed with these plans, he was forced to bring costly lawsuits against others who were claiming ownership. Individuals had seized some of the mission property, and the City of San Antonio itself initiated claim to the Mission San Antonio de Valero, the Alamo. In the latter case, proceedings dragged on for five years. In 1846, when the United States–Mexican War began, the federal government had asked Odin for permission to use the Alamo buildings as a military depot. Odin had consented since San Antonio's Catholics were not using it at the time. The army proceeded to repair the dilapidation that had prevailed at the Alamo since the siege of 1836, and the present familiar form of the chapel's facade dates from this time. Odin used the rent money for the Catholic schools in San Antonio.

What seemed to be a fortuitous circumstance soon led to a debacle, however. When the City of San Antonio realized that the army had agreed to pay rent to the Catholic church for use of the Alamo property, it went to court in an effort to claim the property for itself. It was not until January 5, 1856, that the ownership of the missions was once more decided. At that time the Texas Supreme Court ruled in Odin's favor. The matter was finally put to rest, but only after the diocese had spent nine thousand dollars on court costs in a case whose conclusion should have been obvious from the start because of the legislation of 1841.[49]

By 1858 the diocese of Galveston had grown to the extent that the bishop concluded the time had come for the first diocesan synod. The clergy were duly notified that it would convene in the Galveston cathedral on Sunday, June 13, 1858.[50] A synod is a diocesan assembly of all the clergy under the presidency of the bishop. While the bishop is the sole legislator, the clergy discuss and advise the bishop on the various issues before the synod.

A solemn pontifical mass began the proceedings. The laity and general public were invited to those sessions of the synod devoted to worship and the reading of the synodal statutes.

As was then the custom, after the mass the bishop read the decrees of the Council of Trent and then proceeded to read regulations regarding clerical life-style as defined by the various Councils of Baltimore and the council of the province of New Orleans, of which the Galveston diocese was a part. These and the synodal decrees provide insight into Catholic life on the eve of the Civil War. The conciliar decrees on clerical life directed priests always to dress in clerical attire—a black cassock if possible, and when not, street clothing of the same color and with no adornment—an indication of changing frontier times from even a few years before when getting clothing of any kind could be an insurmountable problem. The clergy were forbidden to enter gambling halls and saloons unless out of grave necessity in the exercise of their pastoral duties. Should any priest have the temerity to drink in these establishments, he was to be reprimanded by the bishop and suspended.

In each church or chapel, once on each Sunday and major feast day, mass was to be celebrated with music, a choir if possible, and the use of incense. Sermons were to be preached at these masses and were encouraged at other times as well.

The synod decreed that the Society for the Propagation of the Faith, from which the Galveston diocese and the vicariate before it had received so much financial assistance, was to be an established entity in the diocese, and the clergy were to urge the laity to contribute to its international missionary work.

Among the other decrees were those pertaining to the administration of church property, the keeping of parish records, the care of sacramental vessels, occasions when priests might be absent from their parishes, the building of confessionals, mixed marriages, and contributions for seminary education. Fees were set for various dispensations regarding marriage, such as when there was not time enough for the public reading of nuptial banns or when a marriage was not in accord with the church's rules of consanguinity and affinity. In the latter instance, the fees were to be commensurate with the petitioner's financial condition. All such fees collected were to be applied to a seminary education fund.

The synod also declared that the Blessed Virgin Mary was to be honored throughout the diocese by special devotions, especially on the feast of the Immaculate Conception since under this title the Blessed Virgin had been declared the principal patroness of the United States. To this end, the synod recommended that every congregation have a chapter of the Archconfraternity of the Immaculate Heart of the Blessed Virgin Mary.

In order to encourage Eucharistic devotion, permission was granted for having Solemn Benediction, with the appropriate number of candles and incense, after mass or vespers on each first Sunday of the month and each holy day of obligation.

The clergy present requested, and the bishop agreed, that an annual requiem mass be offered by each priest for all deceased clergy of the diocese and that upon receipt of the notice of the death of a priest, each priest was to offer three masses for the decedent's soul.

As part of the synodical business, Bishop Odin announced the establishment of a diocesan chancery and the appointment as chancellor of Fr. Louis Chambodut, since 1852 the diocesan vicar-general.[51] It would have been obvious at this synod, even to a stranger, that the diocese of Galveston was too large. For instance, because of distance and poor traveling conditions, only seventeen of the diocese's forty priests were able to attend the synod. Realizing this, Odin announced a plan to decentralize the diocesan administration. Already in 1851 he had appointed Claude Dubuis in San Antonio as his vicar-general for the western part of the diocese. Now, in 1858, the synod decreed in addition that there would be three vice-chancellors as well in various parts of the diocese to help in the administration of church law. Claude Dubuis was appointed for San Antonio, Augustin Gaudet, O.M.I., for Brownsville, and Jacques Giraudon for Laredo. Since the death of Jean-Maurice Verdet, O.M.I., which occurred in 1856 when his New Orleans–bound ship *Nautilus* sank during a storm in the Gulf of Mexico, Gaudet had been the Oblates' superior in Brownsville. Giraudon had worked in Laredo since 1855.[52]

As the turbulent decade of the 1850s came to a close, Texas Catholics could nonetheless look back on a period of remarkable progress. There were still gaps: even though in 1859 Odin permitted six dissident Ursuline sisters to leave the Galveston convent and go to Liberty to begin a girls' school, the future of the enterprise appeared uncertain, and besides, much more work needed to be done in East Texas; and more money and personnel were needed along the Mexican border. In Brownsville, for instance, the Sisters of the Incarnate Word were in dire need of additional school buildings for their growing student body, which by 1860 numbered about two hundred. Their school provided an opportunity for education where no other was available. In spite of the limited resources, the sisters nonetheless were preparing in March, 1860, to begin a similar work in Laredo.[53]

In spite of the Know-Nothings and what they represented, by 1860 there were in Texas forty-five Catholic churches or chapels and sixty-four mission stations where mass was regularly celebrated in temporary structures, private homes, or other buildings. Four new chapels were constructed in 1859 alone. Forty priests worked in the diocese. There were now five boys' schools: one that was part of St. Mary's College and Seminary in Galveston, temporarily under the direction of diocesan priests and laymen pending the arrival of the Christian Brothers; St. Mary's College in San Antonio, under the Brothers of Mary; and three smaller schools at Brownsville, Laredo, and Brazoria. Three academies for girls existed in the diocese: those at Galveston and San Antonio, operated by the Ursuline sisters, and the school at Brownsville, operated by the Incarnate Word sisters.[54]

This growth probably would have continued unabated but for the impending national collapse which in its fury eclipsed even the turbulence of the 1850s.

SEVEN

The Diocese of Galveston and War, 1861–65

WITH the fragmentation of the Democrats in the spring of 1860, the victory of the Republicans in the presidential election that year was virtually assured. Although the Republican party was not officially abolitionist in its 1860 platform, it was nonetheless perceived as being such by the vast majority of the white population of the South.

Despite Abraham Lincoln's assurances throughout 1860 that while he opposed the extension of slavery into the territories, he would not tamper with the institution in states where it was legal, he was viewed by most whites in Texas as an abolitionist. While significant numbers of Catholics in the Hispanic communities and those of recently arrived European colonists did not concur in this view, many other Texas Catholics did. Certainly their bishop concurred in this estimation of Lincoln and the Republican party. In a letter to the Society for the Propagation of the Faith in Lyon, France, written immediately after the November election, Odin referred to the president-elect as an abolitionist whose election had put all of the South in a state of anxiety.[1]

In 1856, the new Republican party had sought support from Irish Catholic immigrants by publishing an account of how an Irish Catholic allegedly joined the party when he decided that its position on slavery was more acceptable than that of the Democrats from the standpoint of Catholic morality. This effort probably did not result in very many Irish immigrants joining the Republicans, but publicity such as this had helped further convince most Catholics of the South that the new party was ineluctably opposed to their economic interests.[2]

The influence of the Catholic church in some areas of the South tended to mitigate some of the barbarities of slavery: the church insisted, for example, that the slaves of Catholic slaveholders be taught the church's faith, that the sacraments must be available to blacks as well as whites, and that slave marriages were as inviolate as those of its white members. This influence occurred, of course, precisely because Catholics were involved in slaveholding. Sometimes the clergy themselves were slaveholders. For instance, the cook and servants for Bishop Odin at his residence in Galveston were legally his slaves. The Vincentian order owned slaves who served as cooks and maintenance workers at several of its religious institutions in Missouri and Louisiana. In 1847, Odin purchased an entire family, the husband, whose name was Clem or Clement, and his wife, Emily, together with their children, who previously had worked at the Vincentian school at Cape Girardeau, Missouri. But although the Vincentians participated in the institution of slavery, it should be pointed out that some of them, such as John Timon, developed over the years a strong antipathy to it.³

It would be a mistake to see Bishop Odin or his successor in the diocese of Galveston, Claude Marie Dubuis, as partisans on the question of slavery; like other southern bishops they simply accepted it as part of the society in which they lived. Bp. John England of Charleston, South Carolina, for instance, held that while slavery was an evil, the abolitionists were wrong to call for its sudden removal since this would produce an equally evil social disruption. The French-born bishop of Savannah, Georgia, Augustine Verot, proclaimed slavery to be both a duty and a burden for slaveholders: that slaveholders were morally bound to feed, shelter, and properly clothe their slaves; that Catholic slaveholders were also bound to see that their slaves were trained in the Catholic faith and to respect their marriages as inviolate. He condemned the separation of families and other evils of the slave trade.⁴

Since the Catholic slaveholder was supposed to provide religious education for his slaves, this meant that on some plantations priests and catechists were allowed to hold instruction classes for them. Some slaves even learned to read and write this way. However, while the Catholic church in the South improved the lives of some slaves, it did not fight the institution of slavery as such. Occasionally there were problems of conscience over the slave system, but these could easily give way to a spirit of accommodation. For instance, when the French Daughters of the Cross established their convent and school at Cocoville, Louisiana, in 1855, their superior was repelled by the institution of slavery, but as time passed, she came to terms with the social order and purchased some slaves for her community.⁵

It is not surprising, therefore, that Bp. Jean-Marie Odin viewed negatively the results of the 1860 election. He perceived Lincoln's victory as the catalyst for the disruption of society, the harbinger of disunion and war. In the early months of the war, Odin would speak of Lincoln's "maliciousness," since the new president was determined to subdue the seceded South: "Lincoln's maliciousness increases every day . . . and it is believed that he would like to vent his wrath upon the maritime cities exposed to the gunfire of his boats."⁶ When the war came, the bishops of the province of New Orleans readily supplied chaplains for the Confederate army and blessed its banners. In their churches prayers were regularly offered for the Confederacy and Jefferson Davis.

Neither Odin nor his successor in Galveston, Claude Marie Dubuis, wanted a war fought to perpetuate slavery, but they subscribed to the typical southern view: that the South only wanted its independence, and the North brought on the war to prevent it. They saw the North, then, as standing for disruption and war, and war ran counter to the interests of the church and society. They had little sympathy for the southern "fire-eater" on whom they might with more justice have blamed the war, but in their world after the spring of 1861, the blockade along their coast was a Union blockade and the invader wore a blue uniform.

Texas officially seceded from the Union on March 5, 1861; the secession convention lacked a quorum on the originally intended date of March 2. On March 17, Gov. Sam Houston was deposed from office because of his refusal to swear allegiance to the new Confederate States of America: the legislature declared the office of governor vacant, and Lt. Gov. Edward Clark assumed the office. During the previous year, Houston had fought to keep Unionist sentiment in Texas alive by backing the presidential candidacy of the Constitutional Union party nominee, John Bell of Tennessee. This party had been formed in the aftermath of the Democrats' collapse to give the southern voter a Unionist alternative to the "fire-eater"-backed Democrat, John C. Breckinridge of Kentucky. Some of Houston's finest oratory was spent in support of the Bell ticket in a courageous effort to thwart the promoters of secession. He spoke at a campaign rally at the San Jacinto battleground: supporters wore lapel ribbons and distributed handbills urging their fellow Texans to come out to San Jacinto for one more cheer for "Old Sam." There was a cheer, but it wafted weak amidst the din of a surging tide of secession.[7]

To complicate matters further for Catholics in the Galveston diocese, as war broke out on the heels of secession, Jean-Marie Odin, the only bishop they had known, left Galveston to assume his new position in New Orleans. The see of Galveston became vacant at one of the most vulnerable times imaginable.

The year before, on June 20, 1860, Archbishop Antoine Blanc of New Orleans had died.[8] This was a personal loss to Odin, for Blanc had been a good friend and loyal supporter through all Odin's years in Galveston. Odin, as senior bishop in the province, set about to poll the other bishops of the province for suggestions regarding a successor for Blanc. And because New Orleans was an archdiocese, the other American archbishops were asked to submit candidates as well.[9] Odin's own choice was the bishop of Natchez, Mississippi, William Henry Elder. Well known in Louisiana, Elder was energetic and in the prime of life. But some of the other bishops expressed strong support for Odin, so his name was among those sent to Rome. As Archbishop John Baptist Purcell of Cincinnati pointed out to Odin, Blanc's successor should be of French origin and familiar with conditions in the archdiocese of New Orleans. Odin fulfilled both these requirements.[10]

Odin probably did not want to be Blanc's successor. In part, this was because he was sixty years of age. But there was another reason as well. Odin liked Texas in spite of the hardships; he wanted to live and die there in the midst of what he had helped to build, working with familiar priests and religious in whom he had high confidence. Also, he believed the Galveston diocese would suffer without him: its financial structure was always tenuous, but he understood it and feared it might collapse under someone unfamiliar with it. Nonetheless, on Thursday, April 18, 1861, a papal appointment to the provincial see of New Orleans arrived at the bishop's residence in Galveston.[11]

The appointment was forwarded there by Archbishop Francis Patrick Kenrick of Baltimore. It arrived at no ordinary time. As the document was in transit from Baltimore, Fort Sumter was fired on on April 12 and surrendered on April 14. President Lincoln issued a call for volunteers to form an army to save the Union, and in response Virginia seceded on April 17. Had the appointment come a few months later after the blockading of Galveston and the rest of the southern coast by the United States Navy, it might never have reached Galveston at all, and like the see of Little Rock, Arkansas, New Orleans might have remained vacant until the end of the war.

After some hesitation, and at the urging of Archbishop Kenrick, Odin resolved to accept the appointment to New Orleans.[12] Prior to leaving Galveston, Odin appointed Fr. Louis Chambodut as the administrator of the diocese to serve until a new bishop could be appointed and arrive on the scene. During this period, however, as archbishop of New Orleans, Odin continued to exercise oversight of the diocese to the degree that war and distance allowed.

By June, 1861, Odin was in residence in New Orleans. One of the first problems he had to face was the process of filling the vacancy in the Galveston diocese. Already for those within the Confederacy communication was difficult with areas outside the seceded states. In some instances, Odin had to depend on private individuals to carry his letters to fellow bishops in Union states. In late June, he was able to get letters through to Archbishops Purcell in Cincinnati and Kenrick in Baltimore.[13] To the latter, he wrote, "The Mission of Texas needs a man acquainted with the English, Spanish and German languages, and ready to lead a life of privations and hardships." The vast majority of Catholics in the diocese of Galveston lived in scattered villages of five, ten, or fifteen families. A bishop must be prepared to visit these villages as well as the large towns; therefore, wrote Odin, he must be an experienced frontier missionary. To that end, Odin told both Purcell and Kenrick that he wished to submit to Rome the names of Fathers Claude Dubuis, Pierre Parisot, and Louis Chambodut for consideration as his successor in Galveston. All three of these men met Odin's standard of being "able to lead a life of privations and hardships." Dubuis, like the other nominees, was a native of France. He had served on the western frontier of the Galveston diocese since 1846.[14] Parisot was a member of the Oblates of Mary Immaculate and had served in Galveston, the missions of East Texas, and Brownsville. Parisot had first arrived in the diocese in 1852.[15] Chambodut, now the administrator of the diocese, had served as vicar-general for several years. He had first arrived in the diocese in 1846 and had served as a missionary in East Texas before going to Galveston to assist the bishop.[16]

For the diocese of Galveston, the absence of a bishop only compounded other problems caused by the war. The United States Navy began a blockade of the Texas Gulf coast that summer. Galveston was Texas' main port of entry. The fact that blockading ships could be seen in the Gulf off Galveston was a source of concern not only there but for those living hundreds of miles inland as well. Sister St. Marie, writing from her Ursuline convent in San Antonio to Odin in New Orleans, described the impact the blockade of the Gulf coast was already having on the life of San Antonio during the summer and fall of 1861. Many families were leaving. Businessmen were going to Monterrey where, under the protection of a neutral country, they could carry on their enterprise as usual, importing goods freely through the unblockaded Gulf ports of Mexico. Many workmen now unable to find jobs in San Antonio were going to Monterrey as well. There was a general fear that Texas, in spite of its long coastline, would be cut off completely from the outside world. Rumor was rife: it was told in San Antonio in mid-July that two blockade ships sitting off Galveston had recently taken five blockade-runners in one day. All mail would cease, the San Antonians feared. And since the Ursuline sisters deposited much of their funds in New Orleans, as did the Galveston diocese itself, Sister St. Marie feared her order's school might become destitute. Prices were already rising: coffee was up to a dollar a pound in San Antonio, she wrote, and other more necessary goods were becoming scarce. In October rumor had it that Union troops were going to invade at Indianola on the Gulf and also by way of New Mexico in the west. Since most of the Ursulines were French, they were considering obtaining a French flag to fly over their school and convent. One of the few bright spots in Sister St. Marie's experience that fall was that, paradoxically, her order's boarding school enrollment unexpectedly increased when many Mexican students arrived. For these students, civil turmoil was nothing new; what San Antonians feared, they had already learned to live with in their native land.[17]

In a short postscript to Odin in a letter of October 14, 1861, Sister St. Marie asked, "Where, then, is the Bishop of Texas?" Little did she know that it would be more than a year and a half later before a new bishop arrived in the Galveston diocese.[18]

Odin tried to exercise at least some oversight of the Galveston diocese by communicating by mail with Chambodut and other diocesan officials in Galveston. For instance, in September, 1861, Odin directed the diocesan chancellor, Fr. Joseph Anstaett, to cease all church-related building construction in Galveston since coastal cities were in danger of naval bombardment. Whether such directives reached their intended destination, of course, depended on whether the blockade could be penetrated or military conditions allowed mail to be transported across western Louisiana into Texas.[19]

Claude Dubuis, Odin's first choice as Galveston's next bishop, had accompanied him to New Orleans in the spring of 1861. Dubuis was ill at the time, and Odin believed he might have a better chance of regaining his strength quickly in Louisiana. Whatever the case, Dubuis was soon able to work in the parish at Mandeville, north of New Orleans across Lake Pontchartrain. He was there by June 10 when he performed his first recorded baptism in the parish and worked there at least intermittently until May, 1862.[20] During his year of work there, Dubuis officiated at numerous baptisms and several weddings. Among those married were two slave couples who, as Dubuis noted in the parish records, "had the licence of the Master."[21]

Health problems still plagued Dubuis, however; in September, 1861, he asked Odin's permission to visit his native France, where he believed his health would further improve; he could also recruit new missionaries for the Galveston diocese. Such a trip would require leaving New Orleans on a blockade-runner that could successfully elude Union ships. He wanted to embark in April, 1862.[22] Events occurred, however, that made an April departure date impossible, even for an intrepid Texas frontier missionary.

While Dubuis was still in Mandeville in the late winter and early spring of 1862, a large Union naval flotilla under the command of Adm. David G. Farragut and Adm. David D. Porter assembled off Ship Island about ten miles from the Mississippi coast out in the Gulf. Its object was New Orleans, the Confederacy's greatest port, by which the Confederacy effectively controlled the lower reaches of the Mississippi River. In addition to the flotilla, Union troops were assembled at a fort on Ship Island to be placed on transport ships to follow the navy into the mouth of the Mississippi. These troops were to become an occupation force for the city of New Orleans and as much of the rest of south Louisiana as might fall into Union hands. Everyone in New Orleans knew the force was forming there and for what reason. But Confederate New Orleans felt secure. Lake Pontchartrain did not afford proper access to the city for such a force; only the river could do that, and the Confederates believed they had successfully closed the vast stream to the invader. South of New Orleans were two forts on each side of the river: Fort Jackson and Fort St. Philip. Between these a giant cable had been stretched across the river, and all kinds of flotsam, from old steam boilers to half-wrecked barges, had been pushed against it by the current. Gen. Mansfield Lovell, Confederate commandant at New Orleans, assured Richmond that the forts' guns, the cable, and the flotsam guaranteed the safety of the city. And they almost did, but for the determination of David G.

Farragut. In April, his strategy led to the penetration of the barrier across the river and the surrender of the forts. By the end of the month, New Orleans and its environs were in Union hands.[23]

Although the Union occupation of New Orleans was a serious blow to the Confederacy, it did make it possible for Dubuis to go to Europe (but not to Galveston) unhindered by the blockade. Odin decided to join Dubuis in his journey; they could both recruit priests and religious for their respective areas, and Odin could go on to Rome to press the urgency of filling the vacancy in the Galveston diocese and to urge the appointment of Dubuis as well. In Rome in September, Odin was delighted to learn unofficially that Dubuis was indeed to become the next bishop of Galveston. On October 22, Pope Pius IX issued the necessary documents to this effect.[24]

In Lyon, France, on November 23, 1862, in a chapel of the major seminary, Odin, along with the former bishop of Toronto, Armand de Charbonnel, and the current bishop of Valence, Jean Paul Lyonnet, consecrated Dubuis to the episcopacy.[25] A French newspaper account of the ceremony described Galveston as "this episcopal town of Texas occupied and menaced by fire and pillaged by the brutal army of the North."[26] While such language reflects the prevailing French attitude toward the Union, the account may also indicate that news of the shelling of Galveston by Federal gunboats in October and the subsequent evacuation of its small Confederate garrison had reached France by the time of Dubuis's consecration.[27]

On February 4, 1863, Dubuis and fifty-nine priests, nuns, and seminarians left Le Havre on a French ship bound for New Orleans. Their crossing took sixty days. The sea was bad in the English Channel, which alone took eight days to get through. Taking a southerly route, the ship soon encountered balmy weather, and Dubuis was able to have a religious community on shipboard during the long crossing: the breviary was prayed in common on the deck, and courses in English and theology were taught each morning. One missionary later recalled, "In the evening, because of the heat, we stayed up very late on the bridge and took part in some very agreeable talks. [The bishop] . . . spoke to us of Texas, of his first years, of the dangers that he was able to overcome. He told us of different medicines for this hot country. Then would come different games in which . . . [the bishop] took an active part, which made our evenings . . . [joyful]."[28] On the solemnity of the Annunciation, a sung mass was celebrated on the bridge. When no thurible was found for the incense, a missionary emptied a tin of preserves and fashioned it into one.

Because of French attitudes toward the Confederacy and Napoleon III's activity in Mexico, Dubuis feared that the French ship on which he was traveling might not be allowed to land in New Orleans. However, as his ship entered the Gulf, three French warships were sighted, and Dubuis concluded from their positions that they had called at the port of New Orleans.

The Rt. Rev. Claude Marie Dubuis, bishop of Galveston, 1862–81. Photo circa 1865, courtesy Catholic Archives of Texas, Austin.

He may have been correct, for on April 4, Good Friday, the new bishop of Galveston arrived in New Orleans without incident.[29]

Since Dubuis and his retinue of missionaries gave their ultimate destination as Texas, it was necessary for them to take an oath before Federal authorities in New Orleans that they would never take up arms against the United States. They had no hesitation in doing so, but the entire process was troublesome and consumed one whole day in the lives of the weary, hungry travelers. Dubuis learned from Odin that only a few people remained in Galveston; most had gone inland to Houston to escape the clash of forces that the coastal seaport invited. Although he learned that Galveston was by then back in Confederate hands, he wondered what changes had occurred there, especially when Odin told him that in New Orleans some had had their houses and furnishings seized and were then exiled into the countryside because of their pro-Confederate stance.[30] Odin summed up his view of current conditions thusly: "Hate increases every day. The North wants the destruction of the South, and the South, rather than give in, is determined to fight to the last drop of blood."[31]

At the very time the new bishop of Galveston arrived in New Orleans, thousands of Union troops were upriver near Vicksburg, involved in the ultimately successful effort to wrest that city from the Confederates. Dubuis feared that skirmishing might break out over wide areas of Louisiana outside the environs of New Orleans. In view of this, he decided not to attempt to go overland to Galveston. He could not get there directly by ship either, since Galveston was blockaded. The only thing to do was embark across the Gulf for the Mexican city of Matamoros and then cross the Rio Grande to Brownsville. Leaving the seminarians and religious in New Orleans, the new bishop, following this route, finally reached Brownsville and his diocese on April 24, 1863.[32]

When he arrived in Brownsville, Dubuis discovered a terrible drought, with many horses and cattle dying, so for thirty days he had public prayers for rain offered in the Brownsville church. He recorded that ample rains began to fall during this time. As for the rest of his diocese, he was told that most places had enough food, but the economy was suffering because of the continuing decline in value of the paper Confederate dollar, down by then to twenty-five cents. Everything had two prices, he discovered, one in specie, the other four times higher in paper.[33]

The French, Dubuis discovered firsthand, had troops along the border at Matamoros. The new bishop recorded no displeasure at seeing them there. Indeed, most Texans were pleased since the French presence strengthened Confederate hopes of ultimate success.[34]

By the time Dubuis reached Texas, Union and Confederate troops had clashed several times along the Texas coast. In August, 1862, Union troops were repelled when they attempted to land at Matagorda Bay and Corpus

Christi. The following month, Union troops destroyed the fortification at Sabine Pass, moved up briefly as far as Beaumont, destroyed the depot there and two railroad bridges, and then retreated to the Gulf. And, of course, Galveston had been lost and then retaken by the Confederates.[35]

During this uncertain period, Fr. Louis Chambodut had done his best to maintain the diocesan administration. Though communication with the outside world was difficult, whenever mail did make it through the blockade from New Orleans, there was often a packet of newspapers sent by Odin to Chambodut. For many people along the coast these packets became the only source of news from the outside.[36]

Chambodut was not aloof from politics: he was an ardent Confederate. For instance, on August 15, 1861, a colorfully impressive ceremony took place in St. Mary's Cathedral in the presence of a company of troops about to leave for Virginia where they later became part of Hood's Texas Brigade in the Army of Northern Virginia. This particular company was made up of Southeast Texas Catholics of French ancestry. The cathedral was packed that day to witness the blessing of their banners by Father Chambodut, who delivered a stirring patriotic address.[37] Chambodut was later rumored to have been the only Catholic priest ever to pull the lanyard of a field piece in defense of the Confederate cause. If he did so, it was either when Galveston was lost or retaken by the Confederates.[38]

Since there could be no doubt about Chambodut's loyalties, it is not surprising that the Confederate military authorities held him in high regard. Gen. John B. Magruder was sent by Richmond to take command in Texas in October, 1862. Although the Union navy forced Confederate troops off Galveston Island that same month, they did not send their own troops into the city until December. This enabled Confederates to be in constant contact with Galveston, and one of those whom they contacted was Chambodut. He seems to have been informed beforehand as to when Magruder intended an attempt to retake the island. According to a preconceived plan, Magruder sent an orderly to Chambodut who had lain awake awaiting him on the morning of New Year's Day, 1863. About three o'clock in the morning, Chambodut heard the tinkling of spurs outside his door, and the orderly called out, "Father Chambodut, General Magruder—the convent." This was to alert Chambodut that the operation was in motion and that the Ursuline convent and academy were needed as a hospital.[39]

During the ensuing violence of January 1, 1863, the sisters at the convent impartially served the wounded of both sides. Chambodut went from cot to cot trying to bring some comfort to the wounded regardless of creed or politics. For many months to come, the bloodstained floors of the convent were mute but grim reminders of the suffering that had gone on there. The ceilings too were stained in places where blood had seeped through into the first floor.[40] Among those who died in the hospital during the fighting

The Rev. Louis Claude Marie Chambodut,
vicar-general of the diocese of Galveston during the Civil War. Photo circa 1870,
courtesy Catholic Archives of Texas, Austin.

was a young Confederate lieutenant from a Catholic family well known to the Ursuline sisters. He was Sidney Sherman, Jr., son of Gen. Sidney Sherman, the celebrated veteran of the Texas Revolution. The convent was filled with dying men in both blue and gray, but Mother St. Pierre Harrington, who had known young Sherman for much of his life, would not allow the youth to suffer alone and attended him until he died, as the horrified students of the Ursuline academy looked on from an upper balcony. As Civil War battles go, this was a minor engagement, but for many in Galveston that morning the war became "hell."[41]

Galveston remained under Confederate control until the end of the war. Magruder's successful strategy involved moving troops across the railroad bridge from Virginia Point on the mainland and using several riverboats and barges loaded with troops protected by cotton bales to attack the Union fleet in Galveston harbor. When one Union gunboat was captured and another ran aground, the Union fleet evacuated the harbor. About six hundred Union troops were captured by the Confederates.[42]

St. Mary's Cathedral was shelled during the fighting, as was almost every other building in Galveston more than one story high. Until the war's end either streaks of sunlight or streams of rain greeted those who attended mass there. The Strand, which Odin called "the most beautiful street in Galveston," was now lined with pockmarked buildings.[43]

Following the Confederate victory at Galveston, more Union than Confederate wounded convalesced in the convent-hospital, mainly from the Forty-second Massachusetts Regiment. The island was in Confederate hands, but the blockade was still very much a reality. Several days after the battle, a Union ship decided to open fire on the white building on the beach which was that part of the Ursuline convent used as a hospital. Since some weapons were stacked on the grounds, the convent must have been mistaken for a military installation. The floors shook and the beds rattled at several near misses. A patient who was a Union officer told the sisters to get some yellow cloth, the military hospital color, so he could display it from the building. When no such cloth could be found, Mother St. Pierre ran to the chapel. While she prayed, some of the other sisters found an old yellow petticoat, and the officer raised this "flag" on the roof of the building. The ship's guns turned in another direction, and the convent made it through the entire war intact, saved, as the Ursuline historian Sr. S. M. Johnston put it, "by a quick-witted Yankee, a yellow petticoat, and a prayer."[44]

It was during the following April, almost four months after the Confederate recapture of Galveston, that Dubuis arrived in Brownsville from New Orleans on his return trip from France. After remaining there several weeks, Dubuis began a tour of the western area of the diocese. Many European colonists lived in this area of Texas. Only the year before, some of the Germans had lost relatives when a group from Gillespie, Kerr, and Kendall

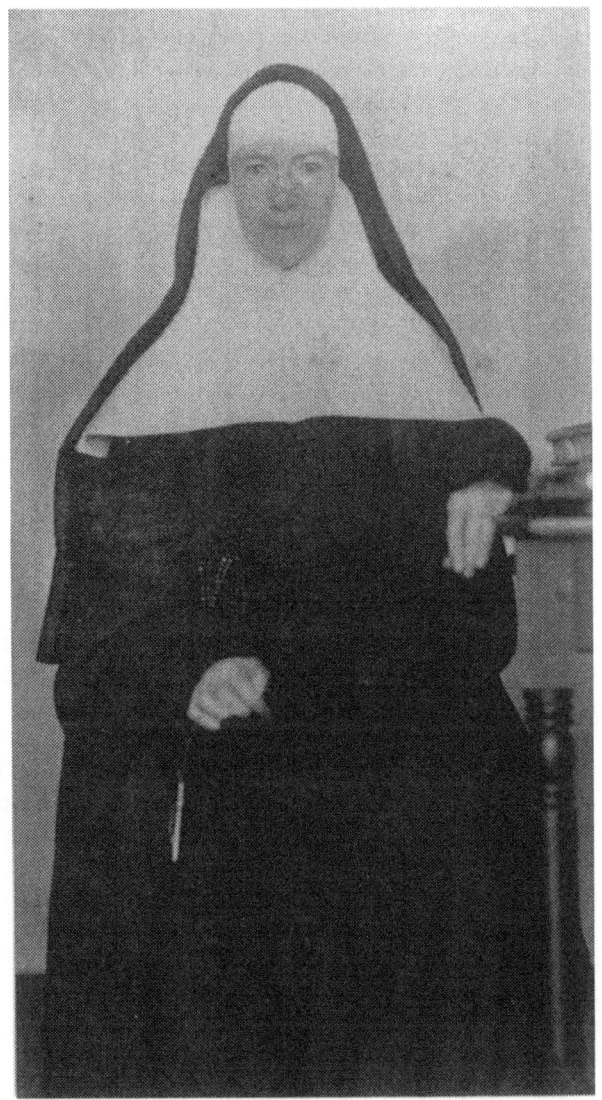

Mother St. Pierre Harrington,
Ursuline convent in Galveston, circa 1860.
Courtesy Catholic Archives of Texas, Austin.

counties, trying to get to Mexico in order to join the Union service, was ambushed and massacred by Confederate partisans sent by the governor to suppress Unionist activity. On his return to Brownsville by way of Laredo, Dubuis fell ill with a fever for three weeks at the village of Roma. By early October he was back in Brownsville.[45]

Several weeks before, on September 8, 1863, while Dubuis was returning to Brownsville, a four-thousand-man Union force under Gen. Nathaniel P. Banks had converged by sea on Sabine Pass, far up the coast, in an attempt to invade and occupy southeastern Texas. By that time, the fortification at Sabine Pass was back in Confederate hands. This invasion attempt resulted in a battle in which forty-six Confederates under the Irish-Texan tavern owner Lt. Richard Dowling, after sinking a boat in the right place in the channel, turned back the entire Union force and thoroughly thwarted General Banks's invasion plans. Dowling was a parishioner of St. Vincent's Church in Houston, and the banners of his men had been blessed there by Fr. Félix de Connobio, a Franciscan who was also a Confederate military chaplain.[46]

Although he was a fellow Catholic and a Confederate, and they doubtlessly admired his heroism, the Oblate Fathers of Brownsville did not appreciate all the fruits of Dick Dowling's victory, for now Banks aimed his efforts along the Gulf coast in their direction. Bishop Dubuis had once more left Brownsville for San Antonio, this time on his way to Galveston, when Banks invaded the lower Rio Grande Valley. Brownsville fell on November 6, and a Texan cavalry unit in Union service under the command of a former Texas judge and future governor, Edmund J. Davis, cleared the river of Confederates as far up as Rio Grande City. Some of the men under Davis's command were Hispanic Catholics from South Texas, a reminder to the Brownsville clergy as well as the bishop that not all of the flock were in agreement on the issues at hand.[47]

Dubuis finally entered his battle-scarred see city and cathedral in December, 1863.[48] Had he still been at Brownsville when it fell into Union hands, he might not have been allowed to leave. The commander of the Union garrison there was convinced that the Catholic clergy were so extremely pro-Confederate that they might resort to spying for the South. Perhaps this was because the Confederacy favored the presence in Mexico of the French, who were aligned there against an anticlerical republican government, and because the Oblate clergy of Brownsville, like Dubuis, were natives of France. Summoned to make a sick call twelve miles from town soon after the beginning of the Union occupation, Fr. Pierre Parisot had great difficulty in getting a pass to leave Brownsville; when he finally did so, he was stopped by four sets of pickets, sent, he later learned, to see if a message was concealed beneath his cassock.[49]

In contrast to the Oblates, the Sisters of the Incarnate Word and Blessed Sacrament in Brownsville seem to have been shown respect by both armies.

The wives of officers from both sides were often housed in the convent, and the sisters were left in peace.[50]

General Banks himself visited the Oblates' residence on one occasion, saying that he wished to learn Spanish. The fathers gave him a lesson, but he never returned for another. The priests discovered later that Banks believed they were keeping government property in their house. Later, only with difficulty did they prevent a search party from breaking down several doors in their residence. Following this episode, the Oblates in Brownsville were ordered by Banks to pray for the president of the United States as the Catholic and Episcopal churches in the North did at the appropriate places in their liturgies. Parisot responded to the authorities that since the bishop of Galveston had ordered him to pray for Jefferson Davis, he was conscience bound to do so until directed otherwise by him. The general finally decided to let the Oblates pray as they would.[51]

In this result, the Brownsville Oblates were fortunate: in the summer of 1864, the Catholic bishop of Natchez, Mississippi, William Henry Elder, was arrested and told to pray publicly for the president and Congress of the United States or be exiled from his diocese and have all his churches closed. He refused and was briefly sent out of the diocese, but his churches were not closed. After some months, he was allowed to return.[52]

Brownsville was retaken by Confederates under Col. John S. Ford on April 30, 1864. Brazos de Santiago, at the mouth of the Rio Grande, however, remained in Union hands until the end of the war.

Participating in the Confederate effort to drive Union forces from South Texas were men under the command of Col. Santos Benavides, a Catholic and member of a prominent Laredo family. The fact that Hispanic troops fought on both sides in the contest for control of the valley illustrates the division existing among Hispanic Texans. While more Texas Hispanic soldiers served in Confederate service than in Union, the division was significant. In April, 1861, for instance, a number of Hispanic residents of Zapata County declared for the Union, refused to acknowledge Confederate state and county officials, and went as an armed force in an attempt to prevent precinct officials from taking an oath of allegiance to the new Confederacy. They were defeated by a Confederate force, and some of their leaders were executed. The Benavides family were among those who supported secession and the Confederacy. Basilio Benavides, Col. Santos Benavides's uncle, as a state legislator from Webb County supported secession, as did Refugio Benavides, who like his brother Santos commanded troops in the war along the Rio Grande. In February, 1864, Col. Santos Benavides turned back a Union military threat to Laredo and continued to patrol the river until the end of the war. Among those he opposed in this contest was Capt. Octaviano Zapata of the First Texas (Union) Cavalry.[53]

While Federal troops were losing ground along the Rio Grande, General

Banks, who had gone to Louisiana, was planning another attempt to invade eastern Texas. With a force of twenty-five thousand, Banks moved up the Red River in Louisiana toward Texas. General Magruder and General E. Kirby Smith, the Confederate commander of the Trans-Mississippi Department, hastily assembled an army to stop the new Union threat to Texas. At Mansfield, Louisiana, near the Texas boundary, on April 8, 1864, Confederate troops under Gen. Richard Taylor successfully stopped Banks's invasion effort.[54]

In this time of renewed hostilities, Bishop Dubuis made a daring overland trip through eastern Texas and Louisiana to New Orleans in order to increase the manpower of the Galveston diocese. He went there to bring to Galveston the seminarians and religious he had brought from France and left in New Orleans to study the year before. Although Dubuis at that time had gone by ship from New Orleans to Matamoros to avoid the blockade and possible military action in Louisiana, this time he decided to brave the difficulties of a trip through western Louisiana and the Union lines. It would be quicker than the other route, which also involved a long overland trek from Brownsville to Galveston. Dubuis set out from Galveston just as Banks's army began to move up the Red River toward Texas. He managed to avoid encountering these forces, as well as the gangs of thieves who took advantage of the public chaos and operated as close to New Orleans as New Iberia. He also had to be careful of Union troops in the occupied areas, since he believed he would be arrested if it were discovered he was coming from Confederate Texas. In spite of all, Dubuis safely arrived in New Orleans on Easter Day, March 27, 1864.[55]

Remaining there only a few days, Dubuis, accompanied by the seminarians and religious, began to retrace the long, dangerous trek back to Galveston. In spite of travel and wartime difficulties, Dubuis's health held up surprisingly well, and his stay in New Orleans allowed him to enjoy briefly the hospitality of his mentor, Archbishop Odin, and to gain strength for the return trip to Galveston.

What Dubuis learned in New Orleans about Union operations aimed at Texas may have caused him to shorten his stay there. On the return trip, Dubuis and his party were two days on board a steamboat on the Mississippi, then for two more on a flatboat that had no provisions on board. They disembarked at a small hamlet where Dubuis knew a priest was ordinarily in residence, hoping to get food there. The priest was away and his house empty, but Dubuis instructed everyone to make themselves at home, and soon chickens from the priest's coop were roasting in the kitchen.

By April 25 the party had reached Grand Coteau, Louisiana, where both a convent of the Religious of the Sacred Heart and a Jesuit residential house were located. There they received word of the "good news" of Banks's defeat at Mansfield. Dubuis managed to buy a horse and wagon so the women religious traveling with him would not have to walk and also to provide a means of carrying the baggage. Later on the journey, the wagon got stuck in a stream, and two of the seminarians had the miserable experience of falling into a hog wallow in the middle of the night while going for help.

Food was a problem on the entire trip: both armies had carried away so much of it. Once while they were still in Louisiana, a wealthy Creole woman, a Catholic planter named Le Blanc, saw the group from afar, recognized their clerical attire, and sent one of her slaves to make certain the travelers came to her house so she could feed them.

Just after they entered Texas, a Confederate cavalry unit, their weapons at the ready, bore down suddenly on them. The troopers assumed that a group traveling together must be soldiers. As it turned out, the captain was an acquaintance of the bishop and treated them all quite hospitably.[56]

After returning to Galveston, Dubuis went west to San Antonio in June, 1864, and remained in that part of his diocese until fall. He reported an abundance of food everywhere in the diocese: generous rains had helped provide a lush harvest. Hardly anyone had any money, however. Confederate paper was virtually worthless now and specie was scarce. The presence of French troops at points along the border continued to cheer the spirits of many in Confederate Texas, however. "The most cordial understanding holds sway" on the Rio Grande, Dubuis believed. On every hand, he reported, there was "but one cry—'honor and glory to the French.'"[57]

Despite the abundance of food and encouragement from the French presence, disease took a severe toll in the Galveston diocese during the last half of 1864. Yellow fever broke out in Galveston and along the surrounding coast. Inland, in an area running from Alleyton west of Houston to San Antonio, then south to Brownsville on the coast, cholera and typhoid took their toll. Three Ursuline sisters and one of the Christian Brothers who were operating St. Mary's College and Seminary, died from yellow fever in Galveston. Dubuis himself came down with "choleric fever" for two months while in San Antonio during the summer.[58]

In contrast to circumstances faced by those making trips to the outside world, travel conditions and communication remained surprisingly good within the Galveston diocese during 1864. The few railroads remained in good working order. Houston, forty-five miles from Galveston, was the hub of this mode of transportation. That fall the bishop rejoiced that the company of Sappington, Risker and Hall opened a new stage line from Alleyton near Columbus all the way to Brownsville. The stage line connected with the railroad at Alleyton, which provided service through Houston on to Galveston and Beaumont. The stage trip from Alleyton to Brownsville took four days and cost forty dollars, but mail carried this way had a good chance of reaching New Orleans. This was another reason Dubuis welcomed the French presence at Matamoros: so long as the French were on the Rio Grande, the mails would be allowed to move across the border and avoid the blockade.[59]

Early in February, 1865, Dubuis reported to Odin in New Orleans that peace was now the ardent desire of his fellow citizens. One Polish Texan later wrote of this time, "At last God took pity on us: the Confederacy was defeated."[60] Galveston itself bore the scars of war and war-imposed neglect more than any other city in Texas. In early 1865, its shell-damaged cathedral narrowly escaped a fire that destroyed many buildings around it. Also, during heavy rains that fell along the Texas Gulf coast in the winter of 1864–65, the vaulting over the cathedral's Chapel of the Blessed Virgin gave way, causing the supporting arch between the chapel and the nave of the building to shift, threatening to bring down the entire structure. Dubuis obtained some strong iron bars from Houston and was able to restore the arch to within an inch of its original position, thus avoiding further danger either to the building or to the worshipers who continued to use the damaged building in spite of shot, shell, and weather.[61]

As the fortunes of the Confederacy faded during February of 1865, Dubuis noted what he thought was a commensurate increase in religious fervor in the Galveston diocese. He was also convinced that much anti-Catholic prejudice, left over from the Know-Nothings of the previous decade, was being dispelled.[62]

After Lee's surrender at Appomattox, Gen. E. Kirby Smith and Gen. John B. Magruder, supported by Texas' Gov. Pendleton Murrah, issued a call to continue the war in Texas. To that end, a meeting was called by Murrah in Marshall in May. There it became evident that everyone but a few fanatics wanted the war to end. On May 13, at Palmito Ranch near Brownsville, the last skirmish of the Civil War in Texas was fought; ironically, the Confederates routed the Federal troops.[63]

Ardent Confederate though he was, Fr. Louis Chambodut, vicar-general of the diocese of Galveston and its administrator from 1861 to 1863, wrote of the war's end: "Thank God the war is over! It is impossible to describe how the people have suffered for four years. I will not talk of the last two weeks of the Confederation in Texas."[64] What Chambodut would "not talk of" was the anarchy that spread through the state when the collapse of the Confederate government became known and a simultaneous flood of hungry, disillusioned, often angry Confederate veterans began returning to their home state. By early June, state and local government in Texas collapsed. Governor Murrah and a number of army officers fled the state for Mexico. There were no Federal forces as yet in Texas except at Brazos de Santiago, so anarchy had no opposition. Hungry veterans, many of whom had been unpaid for months, broke into buildings believed to contain Confederate military provisions that they reasoned belonged to them. Of course, some did not stop with the looting of government property.[65]

On June 19, 1865, Federal troops under Gen. Gordon Granger arrived at Galveston. There the Emancipation Proclamation was read publicly declaring all slaves in Texas to be forever free. Reconstruction had begun.

EIGHT

In War's Wake

AVAILABLE statistics indicate that the Galveston diocese made a rapid recovery from the Civil War. By the end of 1866, there were fifty-five Catholic churches or chapels functioning within the diocese of Galveston, an increase of ten over the reported number in 1860. There were now sixty-five priests, reflecting an increase of twenty-five. Bishop Dubuis was once more off to Europe in 1866 to recruit additional priests and religious for his diocese. At least ten men were ordained to the priesthood that same year, and twelve more were preparing for ordination. There were eight schools for girls and eight for boys, an increase of five and three respectively over the prewar figure. The diocese of Galveston not only had survived this worst of American wars but was once more on the move.[1]

In spite of the gains, however, there were some losses: the Benedictine fathers, seeking to build a foundation at Mission San José near San Antonio to be the center for their work in the area, were hard hit by tuberculosis during and just after the war. Their ranks were so severely depleted that their plans for a center never materialized. Another Benedictine, Fr. Peter Baunach, who had labored so fruitfully at Fredericksburg during the war, became ill from the same malady and was forced to leave Texas for the motherhouse in Pennsylvania, where he died in 1868.

During the war the Benedictines had worked very successfully among the Germans of the west. They constantly had to ward off charges of disloyalty to the southern cause because their parishioners, the Germans, were often either lukewarm or opposed to the Confederacy and because they themselves not only were Germans but were from the North as well. As one of their Fredericksburg parishioners recalled, "The people in our district who are mostly Germans, sided with the Union. This tendency became very critical in our development. Still we preserved our attachment to the Catholic Church, the most magnificient Union on earth."[2] But they held to their task through the war and on into the period of Reconstruction: at St. Mary's in San Antonio and St. Louis' in Castroville, with stations at Quihi, D'Hanis, and Bandera; at Sts. Peter and Paul in Fredericksburg, with stations at Boerne, Comfort, and Llano; and at St. Peter's in New Braunfels.

Work began on a new stone church in New Braunfels in December, 1867,

The Rev. Pierre Richard, pastor,
St. Louis' Church, Castroville, 1868–80. Photo circa 1865,
courtesy Catholic Archives of Texas, Austin.

but Fr. Columban Schmidtbauer, the priest who initiated this work, became the last Benedictine pastor in Texas during this period. He too contracted tuberculosis and left for Pennsylvania in April, 1868.[3]

Until the spring of 1867, the Benedictine abbot of St. Vincent, Boniface Wimmer, had no intention of closing the work in Texas. Their work had survived the war, so surely good times were ahead. In April, 1865, Wimmer wrote King Ludwig of Bavaria, who periodically contributed to the order's American work, of their plans for a college at San José and that same year communicated his plans to Rome. In 1866 Wimmer met Dubuis in Rome. Apparently the meeting went well, for Wimmer soon dispatched two more priests to Texas. In early 1867, however, continued reports of illness and death from tuberculosis created discouragement at the motherhouse, and the abbot put the matter before his confreres at St. Vincent's in March. The ill Peter Baunach had already arrived from Texas and pleaded before the gathering that the Texas work be continued, but when the vote was taken, the majority decided against him.

This was distressing news to the bishop of Galveston. Dubuis suspected that the debt incurred at San José had influenced their decision and wrote that he would help remove this burden. Since the rains had weakened the structure of San José and collapsed the cupola, he was willing for them to abandon it and move into the city. It would be acceptable to make only enough repairs to keep out the rain and thus forestall further deterioration to San José's walls.

Financial considerations probably were not the determining factor in the Benedictines' decision to close their Texas work. With so much illness and death in their ranks, they decided to keep their missionary efforts closer to home. Wimmer informed Dubuis that the withdrawal would be gradual, so it was 1868 before Father Schmidtbauer, the last Benedictine from St. Vincent's, was withdrawn. Schmidtbauer never reached St. Vincent's, however. Severely ill by the time he reached St. Joseph's Priory at Covington, Kentucky, he could go no farther and died there in September.[4]

The work of another order in San Antonio, the Society of Mary, had a happier ending. All through the war, Bro. Andrew Edel had directed the brothers' work at St. Mary's Institute and their agricultural work at Mission Concepción near the city. In contrast to the Benedictines, disease had been less prevalent in their ranks. Unlike the Benedictines, Brother Edel had been overtly loyal to the Confederacy. Edel wrote to his European superiors early in the conflict that they should beware of northern propaganda: "Do not impute this distress as a crime of the South, though the black Republicans would have it so. Do not believe what these latter say, for they are hypocrites and liars. Long life to the Southern Confederacy!"[5]

The school's enrollment increased during the war, but since outside communication had been at a minimum, Edel decided in 1865 to travel both to his order's provincial headquarters in Dayton, Ohio, and on to the general headquarters in France. Among the requests he intended to present to his superiors were these: that a school be opened in Corpus Christi, an orphanage at Mission Concepción, and a separate day school at St. Mary's in San Antonio; that a priest of their order be sent to San Antonio; that a separate province be established for their work in Texas; and that he himself be replaced as superior of their San Antonio house.

Edel's trip to Dayton and Paris largely brought disappointment. After his return to San Antonio on October 15, 1865, some of the brothers expressed the opinion that their work should be abandoned. While St. Mary's Institute had come through the war rather well, it had reached such a size that it probably could not continue if additional personnel were not forthcoming. Bishop Dubuis understandably urged the brothers to continue their work anyway.

Meanwhile, their superior in Dayton also concluded that the order's work in San Antonio should be abandoned. Edel insisted that the superior visit the area before making a final decision. The superior, Fr. John N. Rheinbolt, agreed and arrived in San Antonio in February, 1866. For twelve days Rheinbolt visited classes, met with each brother individually, conversed with students, and sponsored faculty discussion sessions. Then he changed his mind. The brothers' work should indeed continue, and he would help it do so. His previous opinion, he concluded, "certainly showed an absence of due reflections."[6] Rheinbolt did grant Edel's request to step down and appointed his assistant, Bro. Charles Francis, to succeed him. Francis presided over the brothers' work in San Antonio until 1882.[7]

In both 1866 and 1867, Dubuis made the long journey to Europe, again in 1867 seeking recruits for Texas. All the while, of course, Texas was going through the vicissitudes of Reconstruction. With one branch of the Federal government at odds with the other, it seemed for a while that Washington could not make up its mind. When Abraham Lincoln was assassinated in April, 1865, Andrew Johnson of Tennessee became president of the United States. This pro-Union Tennessee Democrat had been put in second place on the Republican ticket in 1864 only as a ploy to win the votes of some northern Democrats more devoted to the Union than to their party. But Johnson was no Republican. Like them, he opposed slavery, but his opposition arose from his hatred of the southern aristocratic planter class. Johnson saw slavery as the chief support of this class's dominance of southern society. The aristocrats were also Democrats, but Johnson was from East Tennessee, where many mountain people had strong ties to the Union and held Johnson's attitudes toward the planter class. Once slavery was abolished, however, Johnson saw little reason to further the social advancement of black Americans.

Johnson's views were soon the basis of a widening gulf between himself and the Republican congressional leadership, who wanted to extend civil rights to the former slaves. Glad to be rid of slavery, Johnson was nonetheless a white supremacist. Johnson wanted the former Confederate states to have a rather easy time of getting back in the Union and going about business almost as usual. In terms of Federal policy, his view prevailed from the end of the war until March, 1867, when Congress took Reconstruction out of his hands.

Like most other ex-Confederate states in this first phase of Reconstruction, Texas elected public officials (in the summer of 1866 following a constitutional convention) and tried to resume its place in the Union. Because of Johnson's attitude toward the wealthy planter class, only those from this group who had aided the Confederacy were disfranchised. After the implementation of congressional Reconstruction, however, in March, 1867, a great many more whites in the South lost their right to vote. Anyone who had voluntarily aided or supported the Confederacy was in danger of being turned away from the polling place.

One such individual was the Very Reverend Louis Chambodut, Dubuis's vicar-general in Galveston. Chambodut, though French-born, had become a naturalized citizen before the war. A friend of Gen. John B. Magruder (the general gave him his sword as a memento at war's end), the vicar-general was well known along the coast as an ardent Confederate partisan. As Reconstruction began, Chambodut urged like-minded citizens of Galveston to participate fully in the electoral process and not to leave the field to others. It was exactly this kind of participation in southern state politics which the Republican congressional leadership intended to prevent as they sought through such measures as the Fourteenth and Fifteenth Amendments to bring about greater social justice for blacks. On one occasion when Chambodut presented himself at the polling place, he was publicly turned away on the grounds that he had been a well-known supporter of the Confederate cause. Reportedly, the vicar-general "laughed heartily as he declared that he was sorry for the effect, but did not regret the cause."[8]

Regardless of his political loyalties, Chambodut was a priest first, and his sacerdotal work went on as usual even though he might bear the opprobrium of the Union authorities. As his bishop took measures to further the church's work in the diocese, the vicar-general was there to do his part.[9] The ex-Confederate rejoiced not only at the diocese's renewed life but at that of the city and state around him as well. Four years after the war's end, the vicar-general wrote with pride to his niece in France of the changed city, which she had last seen from the deck of a Confederate blockade-runner: "Galveston is growing fast to be a city . . . changed for the better in every way. The buildings are more substantial than in your time. Some of them are really magnificent . . . we have street cars (horse-drawn) and for 5 cents you go where you please, so I do not keep a horse, for I have no use for him."[10]

While Chambodut and other pro-Confederates suffered the loss of civil rights during the congressional phase of Reconstruction, some other Texans either enjoyed them for the first time or were strengthened in the exercise of them. Black Texans, of course, were foremost among these, but some of the Hispanics, Czechs, Germans, and Poles presented themselves before the registrars and took the "ironclad" oath that they had never supported the Confederacy. They could then vote and hold office while others around them could not. These and the Anglo Unionists joined former governor Elisha M. Pease and Judge Edmund J. Davis in forming the new Texas Republican party. Just as blacks fell prey to nightriders and other vigilante groups typified by the Ku Klux Klan, so did many of the Hispanic, European, or Anglo Unionists. However, Hispanics and Europeans, with their different names and accented speech—or inability to speak English at all—were easy marks, and, of course, prejudice against these groups was nothing new.

As they had been during the war, many Hispanic Texans continued to be divided over the questions that dominated the period of Reconstruction. Many had favored the Union and therefore supported the Republicans and their policy of extending civil rights to the former slaves. Others, such as José Antonio Navarro in San Antonio, a signer of the Texas Declaration of Independence, supported the Democrats in their opposition to radical social change. Some of San Antonio's old and prominent Hispanic families tended to have the same attitudes in these matters as did their Anglo counterparts. Their influence in the Hispanic community insured the existence of significant division. The Republican faction was strong enough, however, to have its own newspaper, *El Mexicano de Tejas*, which pushed for racial equality. The Republican factionals organized the "Mexican Texan Club" under the leadership of Epistácio Mondragón, Juan M. Chávez, and Juan E. Barrera, among others.[11]

As T. Lindsay Baker indicates in his thorough study, *The First Polish Americans: Silesian Settlements in Texas*, the Polish Unionists in Karnes County were particular targets for reprisals from ex-Confederates.

> They knew very well that we Poles held with the side of the North, so that was why they considered us their enemies.
> . . . they began to make every effort to drive them [the Poles] from the country, even by force of arms. . . . When they saw a Pole without knowledge of the language, a peasant with no education, these southerners looked upon him as they did upon the Blacks, and felt that they had the same right to deny him his human rights as they did the Blacks.[12]

These are the words of Fr. Adolph Bakanowski, a Polish priest who arrived in Texas in November, 1866. He came with five other Poles, four priests and one seminarian, to work in the Polish communities. Since the death of Julian Przysiecki in November, 1863, the Poles had had no Polish priest in their midst except briefly in 1865–66. It was fortunate for them that Bakanowski and the others arrived in time to provide leadership during the trying times of Reconstruction.[13]

The coming of these priests to Texas was due to the efforts of Bishop Dubuis during his 1866 visit to Europe.[14] While traveling through France, Dubuis happened to meet two exiled members of the Polish nobility, Darius and Denise Poniatowski, who told him of a Polish religious order known as the Congregation of the Resurrection, headquartered in Rome but with a number of members working among the Polish exiles in Paris.[15] The background of the Congregation of the Resurrection made it especially suitable as a source of help for the Poles of Texas during violent times. Through the nineteenth century and into the twentieth, Poland was partitioned between Russia, Austria, and Prussia (Germany after 1871). In 1830 the Poles in Russian Poland rose in revolt and were ruthlessly put down. Many Poles took refuge abroad, and three such emigrés founded the Congregation of the Resurrection, which Rome officially recognized in 1842. For obvious reasons, the priests of the new order were very popular among Polish exiles.

After learning of the order from the Poniatowskis, Dubuis went to Paris where he met with the superior. Sagaciously, the bishop knew what to say to the superior to get the Polish priests he needed for Texas: "If I heard of ten thousand souls outstretching their hands for priests and if I knew their language, I would come to them through fire."[16] A Polish priest, whose countrymen had endured fire again and again, could hardly ignore ten thousand Polish souls anywhere on the face of the earth. The skillfully proffered challenge was accepted by the Paris superior, who immediately wrote his order's father-general in Rome, an ex-revolutionary himself, recommending that the Texas work be pursued. Permission to proceed with the venture was soon forthcoming, and two priests, Fathers Adolf Bakanowski and Vincent Barzynski, and seminarian Felix Zwiardowski were selected to go to Texas.

Bakanowski was made superior of the new work. Both he and Barzynski were former revolutionaries themselves. In 1863 Poles in Russian Poland had once more risen in revolt and again had been put down. Bakanowski, born to a well-to-do family, had joined the revolt shortly after his ordination that year. Soon he was forced to flee to Austrian Poland and from there went to Rome. Barzynski likewise had participated in the insurrection. When the Russian authorities discovered that he was involved in smuggling arms to the rebels, he, too, fled to Austrian Poland. There, the Austrians incarcerated him for illegal entry into their empire, but finally allowed him to go to Paris.

From there, he went to Rome where he applied to join the Congregation of the Resurrection and actually took his vows a short time after Dubuis's visit to Paris.

It is unknown whether or not the seminarian Zwiardowski had participated in the 1863 insurrection or not: born in Lublin, he was in Rome in 1865 when he joined the order. Like the others, he was still in his twenties when he left for Texas.

While in Paris, Dubuis managed to recruit three other Polish priests. Although not members of the Congregation of the Resurrection, they agreed to go work in Texas Polish communities under the Resurrectionists' direction so that there could be better coordination of priestly work in the Polish parishes and mission stations. The six Poles arrived in New York on October 11, 1866, and since Texas did not yet have a rail connection with the East, they then set sail for Galveston. Their coastal voyage to Galveston was a dangerous one: they encountered storms and some of the ship's windows were broken and a mast was snapped in two. They finally arrived in Galveston on November 1.

Barzynski went to work among the Poles of San Antonio, while Bakanowski and Zwiardowski went to Panna Maria in Karnes County. Bakanowski sent the non-Resurrectionists to the Polish communities of Martínez (soon renamed St. Hedwig) and Bandera and to the Czech settlement of Praha in Fayette County.

By the time the priests arrived, some of the Texas Poles had already suffered various acts of violence. Much of this up to 1866 was a result of the general lawlessness following the Confederacy's collapse in 1865. But as resentment by many Texans grew over the course of Reconstruction, the violence was more often related to the pro-Union sentiment of many Polish Texans. This was particularly true for those in Karnes County, where pro-Confederate sympathies among settlers of southern background remained especially intense for a frontier county.[17]

Baker recounts that in August, 1867, as voter registrars were at work in Panna Maria, horsemen rode in to disrupt the proceedings. They threatened the registrars and assaulted two Poles who were there to take out naturalization papers; the Poles were accused of trying to turn themselves into "damned Yankees," and death threats were made. Although the military came to investigate, this incident was only the beginning. Soon horsemen began riding through the village shooting at the houses and at the feet of pedestrians and trying to rope children as if they were calves. Cowboys rode into the church, behaving obscenely as they did so, on at least one occasion while Bakanowski was celebrating mass. At times armed men tried to instill fear at weddings and village parties. Farmers in the countryside were threatened; one farmer's daughter had her life threatened and the cow she was milking shot down next to her.

Baker points out that not all Anglos in the region joined in the harassment of the Poles, and a few Poles and other Europeans joined in with the lawless gangs. However, the reality was that the Unionist majority of Catholic Poles found themselves virtually a besieged people by August of 1867.

Given his background, the new parish priest in Panna Maria was not one to take the abuse of his people and his church in a placid manner. Following the army's investigation in August, 1867, Bakanowski prepared his parishioners to defend themselves against further threats. He had taken up arms before; he could do it again. The priest announced that the ringing of the church bell at any unscheduled time was to be the signal to gather for action. In the meantime, he wanted the people in the town of Helena, the source of much of the lawlessness, to know that the Poles of Panna Maria could give troublemakers more than they bargained for. He gathered the men together with their guns and led them to Helena, where they rode back and forth through the streets with the surprised inhabitants looking on.

For a time the trouble ceased at Panna Maria, but in November a hostile gang rode into town. But Bakanowski's leadershp paid off. As Baker recounts it:

> The trouble began while Father Adolph, inside the church, was ringing the evening Angelus bell. Hearing noise and the sound of gunfire outside, he rushed out the door of the church to find a party of mounted cowboys shooting at the tower bell. As the priest began running toward the rectory to get his revolver, one of the southerners with his horse barred the way and fired his gun. Undaunted, the clergyman tried to hit the troublemaker in the head with a wooden pole. At this point a group of armed peasants came to the rescue, driving the southerners from the scene. The troublemakers did not fully retreat, however, until they had shot and injured a man and a woman. A band of angry young . . . [Poles] pursued the attackers toward Helena as far as Cibolo Creek, where a brief gunfight erupted in the twilight. As the cowboys swam their mounts across the stream, the Poles fired at them. Two of the riders were hit and "sank into the river." The others disappeared into the darkness.[18]

A short period of peace followed, but the harassment soon began anew. In early 1868, certain Anglo Unionists in San Antonio began to try to obtain aid for the Poles. Bexar County Judge William W. Gamble was among the first to do so. He wrote the Texas secretary of state that some local Karnes County officials were in collusion with outlaws in opposition to the Polish settlers: the very future of the colony was in jeopardy. Simultaneously, Gen. John S. Mason in San Antonio advised his superiors to send troops into the county, but over a year went by before a permanent garrison was established there.

In the interim, harassment continued with a serious confrontation occurring at Panna Maria on March 28, 1869, Easter Day. As the parishioners left the church after mass, they were met by approximately eighty armed, mounted men, with a number of women in carriages who had come to watch the "show" at the Poles' expense. One of the men pointed a shotgun at a group of Polish women in front of the church and pulled the trigger. For whatever reason, it did not fire. Upon hearing the women in the carriages laughing and applauding over the atrocious act, Father Bakanowski took his gun, went to the second floor of the adjacent school building, and fired over the heads of the women in the carriages. The marauders left, but a few returned later to exchange insults with the Polish defenders of their village.

Soon thereafter Bakanowski and Zwiardowski, unable to get anyone to go with them for fear of reprisals, went by back roads to San Antonio to seek immediate military assistance. They took with them a petition signed by their parishioners. They stopped to see Fr. Vincent Barzynski long enough to learn that Bishop Dubuis was in the city, and in company with him went to see the local commander, General Mason. Mason assured them that he knew of the situation and had arranged to have troops sent there in about a month. Bakanowski responded that by then they probably all would be dead. The general, evidently moved by the priest's words, summoned the officer in charge of the troops destined for Karnes County and told him to take his men there as soon as possible. In a matter of days they arrived, and while all trouble did not cease, the army provided a presence that worked to end the large-scale harassment of the county's Polish population.[19]

Bakanowski and his fellow Resurrectionists did more than lead the resistance against outlaws and fanatics. Virtually without sacerdotal care for three years upon their arrival in 1866, the parish churches had few furnishings and deteriorated vestments. One of Bakanowski's first acts was to order from his superiors in Rome a painting of the Blessed Virgin for the church in Panna Maria. Stations of the cross were ordered next from Europe, and after their loss in transit, a second set finally arrived in early 1870. The chief importance of these objects, of course, pertained to their use in religious devotions, but for a frontier people the carvings and paintings also helped bring color and beauty into a harsh and often tedious existence. Likewise, for these Polish Catholics such objects were reminiscent of familiar European scenes left behind years before. By 1870, the violent times were largely over, and the erection of the stations of the cross in the Panna Maria church occasioned one of the largest celebrations held there in the 1800s. Baker records Father Bakanowski's description of the event, which occurred in February of that year:

> Little girls, from six to ten years old, carried the stations, two of them to each station. All of them wore white dresses with one band

across the shoulder like a sash and another band of the same color worn like a belt. On their heads they wore garlands made from green leaves and white roses. In front of the maidens went others in similar white dresses carrying banners. After them followed three small girls, five years old, dressed in the following manner: The first one had on a violet dress, with the bands and all ornaments in the same color, and she had a crown of thorns on her head and was carrying a cross in her hand. The second one wore a green dress, a laurel crown on her head, and at the side of the green sash hung an anchor. The third one had on a pink dress, a garland of roses on her head, and at the side of the pink sash hung a heart with golden rays. Farther on in the procession came the girls with the stations. Next came the priests. Behind them came singers, both men and women. Still farther on were fifty riflemen, who celebrated every adoration of the cross with gunshots. At the entrance to the church, Rev. Vincent Barzynski heartily welcomed the solemn procession. Inside the church he explained the stations of the cross. . . . He preached for three hours, but we listened with tears in our eyes until the very end.[20]

Remarkably, the Polish Catholic communities thrived during this period. In San Antonio the Polish parish of St. Michael dedicated its first building in January, 1868. A new edifice was completed that same year at St. Hedwig, the former Martínez, and over the next decade, new churches were erected in Bandera, Coleto, and Yorktown.[21]

Whatever the sentiments of clergy and laity may have been over the recently ended war, and whatever alterations in Texas society the changing course of Reconstruction might bring as the balance of power shifted in Washington, the bishop of Galveston was faced with the ongoing task of raising money and manpower for a diocese that in spite of all sociopolitical changes was continuing to grow. With the end of the war and the Federal blockade, Europeans began once more to see Texas as a land of promise, and hundreds and thousands of Mexicans began to seek refuge in South Texas as the forces of Maximilian and Benito Juárez collided in the struggle for control of Mexico. Some Catholics there who had no special love for the French-backed Maximilian were shocked at the violent hostility toward the church exhibited by some of Juárez's generals and sought refuge in Texas. Many others did so just to escape the demands of opposing armies. Whatever their motives, the general population as well as the number of Catholics in the Rio Grande Valley was on the rise during the late 1860s.

The Catholic population in East Texas, though smaller than in any other inhabited portion of the state, was also on the rise in this period. In 1865, Dubuis sent Fr. Jean Giraud, a young priest he had ordained and brought with him from France in 1863, to Nacogdoches. By year's end Giraud wrote him that the Catholic population, particularly around Marshall and Jefferson, was increasing due to immigration both from Europe and from other parts of the United States. By 1867 Giraud became the first resident pastor in Jefferson and in less than two years saw his congregation increase from twenty-two to fifty. Jefferson then had a population of twelve thousand and was larger than Dallas.[22] After the war, when railroad construction began again, many Irish and German railway workers were drawn to East Texas causing significant Catholic communities to spring up in the larger towns of the area.

Although Bishop Dubuis's trip to Europe in 1866 had excellent results for the diocese, that year did not begin well for him personally. In spite of illness he went west to San Antonio in cold, damp January weather. West of Alleyton the stage coach in which he was riding was hurled over on its side when a wheel collapsed. When Dubuis finally arrived back in Galveston, he came down with pneumonia. He also was stricken with neuralgia that later turned into chronic rheumatism, which afflicted him the rest of his life. He was in bed for several weeks. His condition was not helped when during this time thieves attempted to break into his room. On hearing them, Dubuis grabbed what was at hand and ran out into the night after them, but the would-be burglars fled from the hatchet-wielding bishop into the darkness. By mid-March, Dubuis was able to walk along the beach or go oyster fishing in Galveston Bay, and in early April, he embarked for Europe.[23] He believed he could delay his departure no longer since he wanted to be back in the United States in the fall to attend a plenary council of the American hierarchy in Baltimore set for October 7, 1866.

The council had been called by Archbishop Martin John Spalding of Baltimore. Spalding, as archbishop of Baltimore, like other nineteenth-century occupants of this the oldest of episcopal sees in the United States, was virtually the American primate. This 1866 council was known as the Second Plenary Council of Baltimore since it was the second such gathering of the entire American hierarchy. Such gatherings were not annual or even very frequent, and for each one special permission from Rome was required.

In addition to deciding certain questions of church law, Spalding quickly saw that such a council would help soothe wounds left by the war. Presumably if the Confederacy had forced the United States government to recognize its independence, Rome would have made certain ecclesiastical adjustments to the new political reality. Since there were not to be two nations but only one as before, there was a need to give outward witness to this and to get on with the business of the church in America. Clearly the hierarchy, North and South, had not been entirely apolitical, and such a council provided an opportunity of healing the wounds of war.

Only two months after Appomattox, Spalding wrote Rome seeking permission to call such a council.[24] In September, 1865, Spalding wrote Odin, his fellow metropolitan in New Orleans, of his desire for a plenary council. "The holding of the plenary council," responded Odin, "will be gratifying to all the bishops of the South. Everything seems so gloomy in the future, that it will be beneficial for all."[25] And John Timon, now the bishop of Buffalo, responded to Spalding's suggestion with his typical enthusiasm: "I thought that *your* idea was an inspiration from on high."[26] In his official request to Rome, Spalding listed the following as his main reasons for desiring a council: first, to be a great witness to the Catholic church's unity in a country where there was a proliferation of denominations, where new divisions over theological questions frequently occurred, and where most of the major religious bodies had divided over the sociopolitical questions that brought on the war; second, to provide for the erection of new dioceses in a country changed by four years of war; third, to provide for more uniformity among the church provinces; fourth, to discuss the evangelization of blacks in America; and fifth, to organize monetary contributions to the Holy See.[27] Concerning black Americans, Spalding wrote: "I think it is precisely the most urgent duty of all to discuss the future status of the negro. Four millions of these unfortunates are thrown on our Charity, & they silently but eloquently appeal to us for help. It is a golden opportunity for reaping a harvest of souls, which neglected may not return. It is imperative on us to see immediately what is the most practical means of saving their souls. . . ."[28]

The decision was made to convene the council in October, 1866, for fear that an earlier or later date would put it during a very acrimonious session of Congress. The conflict between the president and Congress was coming to a head, and the course of Reconstruction was part of the controversy. Since the bishops, like the country in general, were not in agreement over the issues dividing the government, it was deemed better to keep the council as insulated as possible from a conflict that might counteract any good the conclave might produce.[29]

Dubuis embarked from New York on May 5 and by May 17 was in sight of Brest, where he entrained for Paris.[30] On this trip, in addition to the Polish priests of the Congregation of the Resurrection, Odin recruited several secular clergy and a number of women religious to staff a hospital in Galveston. Dubuis made his way to Rome in June but was back in France by early July. By early August, he thought he had successfully arranged for several hospital sisters to return with him to Galveston.[31] A short time later, he learned to his chagrin that the nursing sisters for the proposed hospital had decided they could not fulfill their original commitment to this work. Never one to give up easily, Dubuis sought the help of Mother M. Angelique Hiver, the superior of the Monastery of the Incarnate Word and Blessed Sacrament in Lyon.

Dubuis knew this order well because of its work in Brownsville. It was not a nursing order but was dedicated to education and was cloistered. Its rule did not lend itself to the kind of regimen necessary for round-the-clock care of the sick. Dubuis's persistence still paid off, however. The bishop decided that if he could only find some religious nurses who would agree to go to Galveston, then with Mother Angelique's assistance he could in effect found a new nursing order for work in Texas. Mother Angelique was agreeable to the bishop's plan, and when three religious nurses at the Hospital of the Antiquaille accepted Dubuis's invitation, they entered the Monastery of the Incarnate Word and Blessed Sacrament; in less than a week they received the habit from Dubuis for the new congregation, which was to be based on the rule of the order of the Incarnate Word and Blessed Sacrament but with the necessary adaptations for a life dedicated to nursing the sick. The new community was known as the Congregation of the Sisters of Charity of the Incarnate Word.[32]

The original members of the new congregation were Nanette Mathelin, who took the religious name Sr. Mary Blandine of Jesus; Lucine Roussin, who became Sr. Mary Joseph of Jesus; and Josephine Escude, who took the name Sr. Mary Ange of Jesus. Sister Mary Blandine became the first superior.

On September 29, Dubuis embarked on the *Europa* for New York with thirty priests and religious for the Galveston diocese and fourteen for Odin in New Orleans. Their crossing was rough and at times dangerous, but they arrived in New York on October 11. There Dubuis separated from his missionaries to go to the council in Baltimore while they went on to Galveston. The group took different ships but all experienced the same perilously stormy weather. Most of the missionaries including the nursing sisters arrived in Galveston on October 25, while the Polish Resurrectionists did not arrive until November 1.[33]

For the obvious reason that they needed a hospital, the citizens of Galveston, regardless of their religious affiliation or lack thereof, welcomed the three nursing sisters enthusiastically. As evidenced by an account in the *Galveston Daily News,* Catholic religious orders for women were held in high repute in both North and South because of their humanitarian endeavors during the late war:

> Welcome them! . . . These holy women have a worldwide reputation and deservedly so. We have seen them, under trying circumstances in the field hospital of the army, or private establishments, always devout, always indefatigable in their attention to the sick and wounded, seemingly never weary in well doing. Many of our gallant Texas boys owe, at this moment, their lives to the Sisters at the hospital of St. Francis de Sales, Richmond, where they were attended to during the war and which was set apart solely for the Texas troops. A hospital

here, conducted on the plan of similar institutions where the Sisters preside, is much needed; indeed is absolutely required.[34]

Before the sisters' arrival, construction of a hospital began on block 487 in the eastern end of the city, a site purchased by Bishop Odin in 1860 for this express purpose. What the sisters saw when they first visited the site in the fall of 1866 was a 2½-story frame building with a small octagonal chapel attached to it and an adjacent story-and-a-half residence, all still under construction. Until their residence was completed, the sisters stayed at the Ursuline convent. The main hospital building was completed in early 1867.[35]

As the new missionaries to Texas were making what proved to be their perilous way to Galveston in October, Dubuis was in attendance at the council in Baltimore. Because of his delay in leaving France, he was a week late arriving at the council. In addition to various preliminary meetings, Dubuis missed what was in all probability the most colorful religious ceremonies the country had ever witnessed. Archbishop Spalding had been appointed by Rome as the apostolic delegate to preside over the council sessions, which he referred to as "the largest conciliary assemblage of Bishops which has been convened since the Council of Trent."[36]

> The opening day, October 7, was crisp and clear. No effort or expense had been spared to make the first solemn session as impressive as possible. Forty-five archbishops and bishops and two mitred abbots in full regalia, some 120 council officials and theologians, a host of ceremonial officials and acolytes gathered at the rectory and proceeded with solemn step around the block to the main entrance to the cathedral. Sidewalks, windows, and rooftops were packed by the devout and the curious, who alike received the blessing of the apostolic delegate as he strode majestically in the midst of his attendants.[37]

As the procession entered the cathedral, an orchestra struck up the grand march from Wagner's *Tannhauser*. Later the orchestra accompanied a choir in a rendition of Mozart's Twelfth Mass, the liturgical music for this opening service of the council.

The business of the council moved so slowly that Dubuis did not miss very much by arriving late. Archbishop Spalding later wrote, "I verily believe that if four or five of our fathers had been asleep, or in a state of devotional extasy [*sic*] during the deliberations,—for some of them were very pious & devoted—we would have made twice the speed, & done much more business, in a much more satisfactory manner."[38] This council should have accomplished more than it did, for an important question was before it: how best to reach out to the former slaves. But the task of evangelizing the freedmen was left to the provinces concerned rather than receiving the national response the question merited. On other matters, the decrees of the council did provide "a distinctly American statement of doctrine as well as discipline and a replete and practical guide for the consolidation and strengthening of the Church, particularly in such areas as diocesan organization, sacraments, worship, education, pious associations, and Catholic publications."[39]

Rome had informed the American bishops prior to the council that it desired positive action to evangelize American blacks. In the debate on this question, Bishop Dubuis did not support the appointment of a vicar apostolic whose purview would have crossed diocesan lines to include work among blacks throughout the country. Dubuis was not alone in his opposition, for this proposal—which might have borne momentous results—received strong support from only two bishops: Verot of Savannah, Georgia, and Whelan of Wheeling, West Virginia. Archbishop Odin stated that no new action was required since in his view everything possible was already being done.[40]

Much public attention centered on the Catholic church because of the council. Its colorful and solemn closing on October 21, 1866, was witnessed by a huge congregation that included Pres. Andrew Johnson, who, although he belonged to no church, reportedly had a respectful interest in Catholicism.

Soon after his return to Galveston following the council, Dubuis set out on a trip across Texas. He had to arrange for the erection of new church buildings at Indianola and Port Lavaca on the Texas coast, where, now that war was past, the tide of European immigration was once more swelling the ranks of Texas Catholics. The bishop also spent several days in Victoria, where a group of five Sisters of the Incarnate Word and Blessed Sacrament from the convent in Brownsville had recently arrived to establish a school, Nazareth Academy.

In 1865, Dubuis had asked the Sisters of the Incarnate Word and Blessed Sacrament to begin educational work in Victoria. They complied, though at great cost. Since more personnel were needed to begin such work, the superior, Mother St. Ange, and the convent's council decided to send Mother St. Claire, their previous superior, to Europe to seek additional sisters and aspirants to the religious life for their order's work in Texas. Money was short, and Mother St. Claire volunteered to make the trip alone. She managed to find twelve volunteers in Ireland and France. They had to make their return trip to Brownsville by way of Veracruz, where they had to wait several weeks for a northbound ship. During this interval, tragedy struck: yellow fever broke out and four of the sisters died, reducing the number of new religious for the Brownsville community to eight.[41]

In spite of this disaster, the resolve to open a school in Victoria remained strong: on August 22, 1866, the chapter of the community voted unanimously to go ahead with the new work and selected five sisters to undertake the venture. These were Mother St. Claire, selected to serve as superior, and Sisters Mary of the Cross, Mary Louise, Mary Paul, and Justine. They arrived in Victoria on December 21, 1866, shortly before Dubuis's arrival. Fr. Augustine Gardet, the pastor in Victoria, and his parishioners enthusiastically welcomed the sisters, whose arrival meant educational opportunity for the young girls of the town and surrounding area. Father Gardet took new lodgings in order to give over his entire house as a temporary convent for the sisters and from his own personal inheritance provided a significant portion of the funds required for the construction of the academy building.[42] On January 7, 1867, the new community opened its school in Victoria with fifty-five students beginning an educational work which continues to the present.

Leaving Victoria, Dubuis went on to Panna Maria, where the Polish emigré priests were just beginning their work. From there, he went to San Antonio and Austin where in the latter he saw with satisfaction that the new convent of the Sisters of Divine Providence was nearing completion. These sisters had taken up the administration of the parochial school of the Austin parish, which the pastor, Fr. Nicholas Feltin, had begun in 1866. Feltin changed the name of the parish that same year from St. Patrick's to St. Mary's of the Immaculate Conception, the name the church bears today as the cathedral church of the diocese of Austin.[43]

In Houston in January, 1867, on his way back to Galveston, Dubuis was pleased to learn that a small group of Ursulines recently arrived there from New Orleans already had forty young girls in the school they had reopened at St. Vincent's Church. Their combination school and convent was a two-story frame building at the corner of Franklin and Caroline streets, built in 1861 by Franciscan priests. These priests had done much work among Houston's poor during the Civil War years, and education was part of their work. But the last of them, Fr. Augustine D'Asti, died in March, 1866, and the school ceased to operate – at least on its previous basis. With her financial support apparently cut off, Miss Mary Brown, the headmistress of the school, opened a new school at another site, but many could not afford it. Dubuis, some months before his January visit, had named Fr. Joseph Querat, then at Refugio, as the new pastor in Houston. Querat, like Dubuis, was anxious that the school reopen on a basis that would make it available to rich and poor alike. It was this mutual desire that led to an invitation to the Ursulines to take up this work in Houston.[44]

By the time Dubuis arrived back in Galveston in early 1867, the workmen were finishing the mansard roof of the sixty-by-forty-foot two-story hospital building.[45] Oversight of the construction for the hospital, convent, and chapel for the Sisters of Charity of the Incarnate Word was in the hands of Father Chambodut, the vicar-general, who, because of his long residence, genial nature, and pro-Confederate stand during the recent conflict, may

The Rev. Joseph Querat, French missionary priest in Cuero, San Patricio, Refugio, Houston, and Galveston, 1855–89. Photo circa 1865, courtesy Catholic Archives of Texas, Austin.

indeed have been "the most popular and the most beloved man" among the white residents of post–Civil War Galveston.[46]

On February 23, 1867, the three nursing sisters left the Ursuline convent, where they had stayed since their arrival in October, and moved into their new residence. Since the hospital building was not yet complete, the sisters opened a temporary clinic in their convent. In January and February laudatory newspaper articles called for local financial support for the sisters and the new hospital. Finally, on April 1, 1867, the hospital opened with a medical staff of five physicians under the leadership of Dr. James Nagle. Nagle was Dubuis's own physician. Father Anstaett wrote to Odin about this time, "Doctor Nagle is the physician in whom Monsignor [Dubuis] has the most confidence; because he is the only one who always restores him [to health], a man of firm faith with a profound knowledge of the human body and of the different maladies which have come out of the box of Pandora."[47]

In February, 1867, after remaining in Galveston for only a few weeks, Dubuis set out for Corpus Christi and the lower Rio Grande Valley. In the valley, Dubuis found that the population had increased by the thousands as Texas remained a refuge for those fleeing the war in Mexico between the supporters of Maximilian and those of Benito Juárez.[48] While the influx of immigrants merited many more, Dubuis was able to send only two additional priests to the valley that year.

Back in Galveston by early March, Dubuis was planning another trip to Europe. Two purposes beckoned him: he needed more priests and religious, and Pope Pius IX had invited all the bishops worldwide to attend in Rome that year the commemoration of the eighteenth centenary of the martyrdom of St. Peter and St. Paul. Five hundred of them, including the bishop of Galveston, accepted the invitation.[49]

When Dubuis left Galveston, as spring began, he had of course no way of knowing about the impending disasters that would strike the Texas coast before his return late in the year. On June 29, newspapers on incoming ships brought word to the now twenty thousand Galvestonians that "yellow jack" or the dreaded yellow fever was raging in Cuba. Two days later on July 1, they received word that the disease was as close as Indianola down the Texas coast on Matagorda Bay. Three-fourths of Galveston's population had arrived since the war's end: Czech, German, Irish, and Polish immigrants, as well as Americans from other states. Those who had survived the disease during the last outbreak in 1864 had a degree of immunity, but many of the newly arrived did not. This fact caused fear that a new epidemic might be the worst in memory. Those who could leave Galveston did so. While it was not known yet that the disease was carried by mosquitos, some suspected that filthy conditions related to stagnant water somehow contributed to the outbreak and spread of the disease. Consequently, some efforts to alleviate such conditions in Galveston were made during the first days of July, and all ships from Indianola were denied entry to the port. But it was too late: travelers from Indianola in whose bloodstreams the disease was incubating had already arrived on the island and there was enough stagnant water left to allow for the ample breeding of the disease-carrying variety of mosquito. Over the next months the new hospital of the Sisters of Charity of the Incarnate Word and another hospital run by the city government received hundreds of yellow fever victims. When a norther in November finally cleared the Texas coast of mosquitos, the disease abated, but by then 1,150 in Galveston alone had succumbed to yellow fever. Among them was Mother Mary Blandine, the hospital sisters' superior, who died on August 18 after a three-day illness. Sister Mary Ange came down with the disease but recovered. With the loss of their superior, the sisters worried over the future of their work, but they were encouraged when a letter arrived from the bishop in Europe announcing that five sisters would be coming to Galveston to join the nursing community.[50]

The epidemic drained the sisters' hospital of funds. Fortunately, James P. Nash, a longtime benefactor of the diocese who had operated a business school in Galveston before the war, initiated a newspaper campaign that brought in contributions from around the state.[51]

Hundreds died in Houston as well, including the Confederate hero Dick Dowling, who had begun during the epidemic to raise funds there for the sisters' new hospital in Galveston. In Corpus Christi the disease hit in July also; Fr. Anthony Miconleau died in August and Fr. Jean Gonnard in September. Father Gonnard and the other priests of the area had nursed the sick during the epidemic. In all, over three hundred died in Corpus Christi.

In their ignorance of what caused the disease, physicians tried various treatments for yellow fever. One Corpus Christi physician devised a treatment in which the patient's feet and legs were submerged in a tub filled with ashes and hot water. The patient was then rolled in blankets to bring on a sweat, which was supposed to get rid of the disease. The claim was made that if a patient did not sweat during the first eight hours after the onset of the disease, death was inevitable. Gonnard received this treatment and did not respond; the same was also true of the physician who devised it.[52]

By early October, Dubuis, having attended the commemoration in Rome, was in Coutouvre, France. He had already obtained several seminarians and religious for work in the diocese and was expecting to have several more before his trip was over. For this purpose, he left Coutouvre by rail on the night of October 6 bound for Nancy and Strasbourg. As the bishop was making this journey through France, far to the west in his diocese another disaster was about to strike.

On the morning of October 7, 1867, a devastating hurricane struck the lower Rio Grande Valley. Matamoros suffered damage and three-quarters of the city of Brownsville was leveled; not even the Civil War had brought a tenth of such suffering as this. Brazos de Santiago, Clarksville, and Bagdad in Mexico simply disappeared when a tidal wave swept over them and in places for miles into the interior.[53]

The convent and school of the Sisters of the Incarnate Word and Blessed Sacrament in Brownsville were a total loss. Mother St. Ange wrote a few days after the storm that in one "awful night of horror, all the fruit of fifteen years' savings" were lost, and one building was lost on which the sisters still owed a sizable debt at 18 percent interest. The storm raged on into the early hours of the next day while the sisters and their students took refuge in the chapel. Only with daylight on the eighth did the sisters venture out to behold the shocking devastation all around them. It was then they discovered that two little girls were missing, but a frantic search revealed them relatively unharmed, sleeping in a pool of water in what was left of the dormitory![54]

The Oblate Fathers in Brownsville offered the sisters the use of one of their buildings, a new one that had come through the cataclysm unscathed. As soon as he returned to the United States, Dubuis went to Brownsville to survey the devastation. Some feared that the bishop might send the sisters elsewhere in the face of such destruction. But Dubuis arranged for a new site for the sisters' work, and soon a contract was signed to begin new construction.[55] Dubuis left Brownsville in February, 1868, and went upriver to Laredo. He confirmed forty-two hundred people on this one trip alone. Returning to Brownsville in mid-March, he then set out for New Orleans, where he made financial arrangements to cover the new school building in Brownsville.[56]

In September, 1867, the Vatican had officially approved the decrees of the Plenary Council of Baltimore held the previous year. To implement these decrees relating to church law and custom, each province in the United States was required to hold a council of its own. Dubuis and the other bishops of the province of New Orleans met there in early December, 1868, under the presidency of Archbishop Odin. As soon as the week-long meeting was over, Dubuis hastened to Galveston to summon a diocesan synod, the second in the diocese's history. This was necessary to discuss the proceedings in New Orleans and also to give Dubuis the opportunity to make changes designed to improve the administration of his ever-growing and already far too large diocese. In recognition of the latter condition, the synod met in two sections, one in Galveston, the other in San Antonio.

The Galveston section met on December 14, 1868, and the San Antonio section on January 4, 1869. This synod approved a decree changing the organizational structure of the diocese; this decree in part foreshadowed the future division of the Galveston diocese.[57]

Under the arrangement, the bishop was to appoint two archpriests, one each for two administrative sections of the diocese. One section was the area from the eastern boundary of Texas to the Colorado River; the other section included everything to the west of the Colorado River. Whenever the bishop was absent from the diocese, each archpriest was to govern that part of the diocese to which he had been assigned. The diocesan vicar-general, Louis Chambodut, was appointed archpriest for the eastern half, and Joseph Anstaett, theretofore the diocesan chancellor resident in Galveston, was sent to San Antonio as archpriest for the area west of the Colorado River. Four chancellors were named: Frs. John B. Bellaclas for Galveston, Louis Chaland for San Antonio, Augustin Gaudet for Brownsville, and Jean C. Neraz for Laredo. The new office of rector general of religious was created to oversee the affairs of certain religious orders. Fr. Stephen Buffard was named to this position. Two vicars forane or rural deans were also appointed: Fr. Matthew Sarry for the San Antonio region and Fr. Augustin Gaudet, the superior of the Oblates, for the Brownsville area.[58]

After the close of the respective sessions of the diocesan synod, Dubuis began once more to make preparations for a European trip, this time to attend the First Vatican Council. Leaving Galveston in early May, he stopped in New Orleans to encourage Odin to join him for the trip to Europe since he was going early enough to spend some time at Vichy; he believed this would be helpful to the almost seventy-year-old archbishop, who was now in failing health. Odin's physician approved, and he and Dubuis left New Orleans together for the five-day rail journey to New York. The journey was exhausting for both of them, especially Odin, who found it impossible to sleep "on the cars."[59]

They set sail from New York on May 15, and at last Odin was able to rest. Arriving in France, Dubuis and Odin went to Vichy, but the latter's health could not be fully restored. The First Vatican Council opened in December, 1869, with both Dubuis and his mentor in attendance, but Odin soon had to retire to his native village of Ambierle in France. Like Dubuis, Odin supported the call for a definition of papal infallibility and wrote Spalding in Rome during this period, "Had I been in Rome, I would have signed the *Postulatum,* asking for a definition of the infallibility of the Sovereign Pontiff."[60] His health continued to weaken, and he died on May 25, 1870. He was buried beneath the south transept of the large, sixteenth-century village church at Ambierle, near the house he had been born in seventy years before.[61]

Following the First Vatican Council, which formally ended on October 20, 1870, Dubuis returned to Texas and soon set out once more for a tour of his vast diocese. Visiting both the eastern and western parts of Texas, he confirmed approximately fifteen thousand people in the months subsequent to his return from Rome.[62]

During the Reconstruction period, in addition to the hospital in Galveston, several other religious foundations began operation in the vast Galveston diocese. In the 1860s the Sisters of St. Mary of Namur came to Waco at the invitation of the bishop. This order, originally founded at Namur in present-day Belgium in 1819, arrived in the United States in 1863 at the behest of the former prefect apostolic of Texas, John Timon, by then the bishop of Buffalo, New York. At the end of the Civil War, after opening their first American foundation in Lockport, New York, a group there led by Sister Mary Angela set out for Waco, where they established a school that later became the Academy of the Sacred Heart. These sisters went on to establish several schools in areas of North Texas that after 1890 became the diocese of Dallas.[63]

In Galveston, the Sisters of Charity of the Incarnate Word began an orphanage in 1868, and about the same time a request from a number of San Antonio citizens urged them to send several sisters to open a hospital in that city. In March, 1869, at a time when they were enlarging their Galveston hospital (soon to be known as St. Mary's Infirmary), the community sent three sisters to San Antonio to begin work that eventually became Santa Rosa Hospital. In April, 1871, a small group of these sisters opened a hospital at Hearne for the Houston and Texas Central Railway Company, which was fast completing its line from Houston to Dallas. At Hearne the Texas firm's line crossed that of the new International and Great Northern Railroad Company, and about a thousand workers were employed there by early 1871. The existence of this hospital, known as St. Therese's, was brief: by 1872, railway construction had moved on, and it closed. Also in early 1871, Dubuis made arrangements for the Sisters of the Incarnate Word and Blessed Sacrament in Brownsville to begin another school, this time in Corpus Christi. They commenced their work there in March of that year when they established Incarnate Word Convent and Academy.[64]

It was also about this time that the Congregation of the Holy Cross came to Texas. St. Mary's College and Seminary in Galveston during the 1860s had a tenuous existence, and for a time Bishop Dubuis hoped that the Benedictines at Mission San José near San Antonio would establish a viable college and seminary there. By 1867, with the Benedictines leaving Texas, he realized help would have to come from another source. For this reason, in 1869, Father Chambodut, the diocesan chancellor, requested Fr. Edward Sorin, the provincial superior of the Indiana province of the Congregation of the Holy Cross, to send religious to Galveston to administer the college-seminary. The diocese offered to donate over two thousand acres of land in Bee County that the order could then sell to support its work in Texas.[65] Sorin was the founder of the University of Notre Dame and was French like Dubuis, Odin, Chambodut, and a majority of the Texas clergy. Sorin and Dubuis both attended the First Vatican Council and reached an agreement, later confirmed by the provincial chapter at Notre Dame, by which the Congregation of the Holy Cross came to Texas.

A group of religious were selected for the new venture and put under the leadership of Bro. Boniface Muher, who arrived in Galveston in September, 1870. He wasted no time and was soon teaching a class of twenty-four boys. It was decided to postpone the opening of a seminary, and St. Mary's was referred to as a "commercial college." Others arrived from Notre Dame as the scholastic year progressed. Soon Dubuis suggested that Holy Cross take over the operation of St. Joseph's College in Brownsville, which the Oblates had founded and thus far maintained. In 1873 three members of Holy Cross went there for that purpose, but they remained only a year. The order continued their work in Galveston for several years but by 1878 had withdrawn to concentrate on establishing a school in Austin.[66]

In 1871, Sorin himself went to Austin, where Dubuis had promised some downtown land for an academy. In 1872, before this project developed, Mrs. Mary Doyle, a widow in Austin, offered to make available her 398-acre farm across the Colorado River three miles south of the city for a Catholic boys' school. Dubuis informed Sorin of the proposal, and he accepted it provided that the Congregation of the Holy Cross could also have control of the Austin parish, St. Mary's of the Immaculate Conception. Dubuis agreed, and both he and Sorin went to Austin in the spring of 1872. Sorin obtained the Doyle property for the nominal sum of $995, which sum Mrs. Doyle bequeathed to the Congregation of the Holy Cross at her death. An adjacent tract of 123 acres with a prominent hill located on it was obtained from a former Confederate colonel, William Robards, who donated 20 of the acres.[67]

The next step did not prove so easy. Fr. Nicholas Feltin was still pastor of the Austin parish, and he had invested personal funds in the parish and did not want to leave. Saying that the school for boys should actually be in operation before he vacated the parish, he also demanded financial remuneration. Apparently an appropriate settlement was reached with Feltin through the efforts of the bishop. Feltin left Austin in May, 1874, to become pastor of St. Joseph's Church in San Antonio. In early 1874, Holy Cross priests, sisters, and brothers arrived in Austin to begin their work there. The sisters operated two parish schools, one for boys and the other for girls. The brothers were in charge of operating the farm south of town where the future St. Edward's College was to be located. A member of the Congregation of the Holy Cross, Fr. Daniel Spillard, succeeded Feltin as pastor of St. Mary's and had the additional responsibility of getting the college in operation. This was the same year the diocese of San Antonio was formed with a boundary along the Colorado River, and until 1948 the Austin parish was in one diocese and St. Edward's College (University) in another.[68]

Other Holy Cross sisters had already begun work in Texas in 1871. As

Dubuis was returning from Europe in the fall of 1870, he met on shipboard Mother Mary Euphrosine, who had been on a visit to her order's motherhouse in France. The bishop told her of the need for teaching orders in Texas, and instead of returning to her convent at Notre Dame, she and another sister went on from New York to Texas. Establishing themselves briefly in Corpus Christi, they moved to Nacogdoches at Dubuis's request in April, 1871, and opened a school in the building of the former Nacogdoches College. This school operated until September, 1872, when all but one member of the community moved to Clarksville in North Texas to open a school there.

Without the approval of her superiors, Sr. Joseph Potard remained behind to teach the children of the town. Born Renée Françoise Potard into an aristocratic French family, she was determined to devote her energies to those who needed her. For her school, she rented halls and for several years taught in a log cabin while providing free education to those who could not pay. In 1878, she purchased a house in Nacogdoches but two years later moved to the church in El Moral to work among its Hispanic parishioners, descendants of colonists who settled there in the 1700s. Sister Joseph was tireless and resourceful. In the absence of a bell, she used a cow's horn to announce classes or devotions in the church. She visited the sick and dying and, in the absence of a priest, buried the dead. When circumstances required, she traveled long distances by horseback, often alone, to visit those in need or get supplies for her students. She lived thus until just before her death at the age of seventy-one in 1893.[69]

The year 1874 was one of change for Texans. In January, the Democrats regained control of the executive branch of the state government for the first time since 1867. The state was allowed formally to reenter the Union in 1870, and Republican Edmund J. Davis was elected governor with a Republican controlled legislature. In 1872, however, the Democrats regained control of the legislature. According to the 1869 state constitution, elections were to be held over a four-day period, but the Democratic controlled legislature passed a law limiting voting to a single day. Davis signed the bill, and when the 1873 gubernatorial election was held on one day, Democrat Richard Coke won. Davis, citing the constitution, appealed to the judiciary. The Texas Supreme Court, in the controversial Semicolon Decision, upheld the arguments of the government lawyers and ruled that the one-day election law was illegal. Despite the decision, the Democrats announced their intention to take over the office. In January Governor Davis barricaded himself in the ground floor of the capitol on the night before inauguration day. He telegraphed Pres. Ulysses S. Grant for military aid in holding on to his office, but the White House refused. As morning approached, the Democrats used ladders to reach the legislative chambers and proceeded to inaugurate Coke. Davis had no choice but to retire peacefully. He practiced law in Austin for years thereafter and was active in state Republican party affairs, but Reconstruction had ended and a new political era had begun.

The Reconstruction years witnessed renewed growth and change in the diocese of Galveston. The postwar violence did not vanish overnight, but renewed immigration, railroad building, and the slow revival of commerce all contributed to an eventual return to normality. To meet the increasing demands of a burgeoning population, the bishop of Galveston continued to look to Europe, particularly to his native France, for priests and religious. He did not look in vain. By the end of 1873 there were eighty-seven priests serving a Catholic population of 180,000, and religious foundations existed in Galveston, Houston, Victoria, Nacogdoches, San Antonio, Corpus Christi, and Brownsville.[70]

In a compact area, one diocesan structure could have served well the needs of the Catholic population, but the diocese of Galveston was hardly compact. And incoming immigrant ships at Galveston and Indianola, as well as Mexican immigration along the Rio Grande, insured a steady increase in this population. The railroad building of the early seventies indicated that in the future most areas of the state would be accessible by rail, but even so, the bishop of so large an area would have to continue to be an incessant traveler.

As in the area of politics, 1874 was a year of change for Texas Catholics. Having already laid the groundwork for a division of the diocese at the second diocesan synod, Dubuis petitioned Pope Pius IX to divide his large diocese. On August 27, 1874, a papal decree declared the area between the Colorado and the Nueces Rivers to be the new diocese of San Antonio. The boundary on the west generally followed a line from Rock Springs in Edwards County west to the point where the Pecos joins the Rio Grande, which then proceeded along the Rio Grande to the El Paso County line, a much larger county than it is today, then west northward to the southern border of New Mexico. The boundary then moved eastward along this line into Texas to the Colorado River. The large El Paso County remained under the jurisdiction of the bishop of Durango, Mexico, until 1872, when it became part of the vicariate apostolic of Tucson, and the town of Presidio on the Rio Grande remained in the diocese of Durango until 1892.[71]

On September 18, 1874, three weeks after erecting the diocese of San Antonio, Pope Pius IX erected the vicariate apostolic of Brownsville to consist of that area lying between the Nueces River and the Rio Grande.[72] The Catholic church in Texas had indeed entered a new era.

NINE

The Diocese of San Antonio

Rome appointed Fr. Anthony Dominic Pellicer of Mobile, Alabama, as the first bishop of the new diocese of San Antonio. Some weeks later when the vicariate apostolic of Brownsville was established, Pellicer's cousin and fellow priest in Mobile, Fr. Dominic Manucy, was appointed the first vicar apostolic of that jurisdiction. Both Pellicer and Manucy were consecrated to the episcopacy in the same service in the Mobile cathedral in December, 1874.

Pellicer, born in San Augustine, Florida, was fifty years old when he went to San Antonio. Ordained to the priesthood in 1850, he had first been sent to St. Peter's Church in Montgomery, where he remained until 1866 except for time spent as a Confederate army chaplain during the Civil War. In 1866 he became rector of the Cathedral of the Immaculate Conception in Mobile, and he also served as vicar-general for the Mobile diocese.[1] Having built a substantial church in Montgomery and founded a large orphanage for boys in Mobile, Pellicer had attained the reputation of being a builder and successful administrator. In spite of his apparent energy, by the time he was appointed bishop Pellicer had been diagnosed as a diabetic. But since the disease had not yet become debilitating, he was optimistic as he set out for San Antonio, where he arrived on December 23, 1874.[2]

San Fernando Church, the original parish church of San Antonio, became the cathedral of the new diocese. By the time of Pellicer's arrival, San Fernando was no longer the original eighteenth-century Spanish structure. In 1868 the cornerstone of a new structure had been laid at the site of the old. But instead of the original building being torn down, the new structure was built around and over part of it. Not until the new structure was nearly completed was a portion of the old church removed, with the remaining section becoming the sanctuary or altar area of the large new edifice. Symbolically for the new diocese, its cathedral was an architectural blend of the old and the new, even as the diocese itself, though new, had its roots firmly planted in the region's Spanish past.[3] The enlarged church had been open for use a little over a year when Pellicer arrived to make it the cathedral of the new diocese.

It was in San Fernando on December 27, 1874, that the new bishop for-

The Rt. Rev. Anthony Dominic Pellicer,
first bishop of San Antonio, circa 1875.
Courtesy Catholic Archives of Texas, Austin.

mally took possession of his diocese. The Incarnate Word sisters at their new hospital on Military Plaza provided a banquet for their new bishop and the clergy after the service of installation.

San Antonio at this time was a city of between twelve and thirteen thousand people and was second only to Galveston in size. Although the city was multiethnic, its population continued to be predominantly Hispanic in heritage. Within the city itself there were now four parishes: San Fernando Cathedral, with a predominantly Hispanic congregation; St. Mary's, founded originally to serve both English- and German-speaking congregations; St. Joseph's, which by now had been organized for the ever-increasing number of German Catholics; and St. Michael's, which served the city's Polish Catholics. The Ursuline Academy and St. Mary's College continued to thrive, and there were also now two parochial schools: one at the cathedral, staffed by the Incarnate Word sisters, and another at St. Joseph's under the direction of the Sisters of Divine Providence. Also in the city was Santa Rosa Hospital, staffed and directed by the Sisters of Charity of the Incarnate Word, who also operated St. Joseph's Orphanage. The Spanish missions in the environs of San Antonio were then under the direction of Mexican Jesuits exiled in 1873 by the anticlerical government of President Sebastián Lerdo de Tejada. Bishop Dubuis had agreed to take them into the diocese prior to its division. They held a regular schedule of masses at Concepción, San José, San Juan Capistrano, and San Francisco de la Espada. They also served churches at Blas Herrera, Las Gallinas, and Graytown, and another church located on the Medina River.[4]

In 1877, at the request of the vicar apostolic of Brownsville, several southern counties of the San Antonio diocese including Live Oak, Bee, Goliad, Refugio, Aransas, and San Patricio were put in the Brownsville jurisdiction, while an area along the Rio Grande and upper Nueces River including Kinney and Maverick counties was transferred to the diocese of San Antonio.

The changes notwithstanding, the size of Pellicer's new diocese—90,909 square miles—remained formidable. When Pellicer arrived, the railroads had not yet sufficiently penetrated the area to revolutionize travel as they had in some other parts of the state. There was some improvement when on February 19, 1877, rail service between San Antonio and Houston commenced. Yet two-thirds of the diocese remained accessible only by stagecoach, on horseback, or on foot.

In spite of such rigorous frontier conditions, by the late 1870s there were about eighteen parochial schools throughout the new diocese, such as those taught by the Sisters of Divine Providence in Castroville, Fredericksburg, New Braunfels, and Wenzel. Also at the time, in addition to their order's San Antonio school, the Sisters of the Incarnate Word and Blessed Sacrament were operating a small parochial school at Graytown near San Antonio, where one of the Mexican Jesuits served as pastor.[5]

Altar, Mission San Francisco de la Espada, San Antonio. Photo circa 1890, courtesy Catholic Archives of Texas, Austin.

The concern over education was such that in several parishes, with no teaching sisters available, schools were taught by the parish priests, who sometimes complained with good reason that little time was left to devote to regular pastoral duties. Sometimes an educated lay person in the parish was willing to take on either some or all of the teaching responsibility and thus free the pastor for other duties.

Fortunately additional teaching sisters entered the diocese during the waning decades of the century so that even some towns in sparsely populated areas had parochial schools by the 1890s. In 1894, for instance, a community of the Sisters of Mercy began a school in West Texas in Martin County at Stanton, then called Marienfeld. They eventually opened schools as well in Pecos, Fort Stockton, and Menard. Their schools in Pecos and Fort Stockton were specially designed to serve the Hispanic children of the area.[6]

In 1875, in an attempt to meet the educational needs of the Polish communities in his diocese, Bishop Pellicer approved the founding of a new community of teaching sisters known as the Order of the Immaculate Conception of the Virgin Mary. When a popular lay teacher at St. Joseph's School in Panna Maria, John Barzynski, left for Missouri in 1872, the pastor, Fr. Felix Zwiardowski, conducted classes for a time but soon discontinued them because of conflict with his other duties. He was chagrined when, in the absence of any school, justice of the peace Emanuel Rzeppa arranged for a public school to open in Panna Maria with a non-Catholic teacher. Verbal warfare resulted between Zwiardowski and Rzeppa over the existence of the public school. When the pastor announced that anyone sending his children to the new school would not be granted absolution, Rzeppa entered a complaint against Zwiardowski in court. The district judge ruled that if no parochial school could be maintained at Panna Maria, then the public school must remain open, but if St. Joseph's School could operate on a regular basis, then the public school could be closed.[7]

In some desperation, Zwiardowski went to Castroville to seek the aid of Mother St. Andrew, superior of the Sisters of Divine Providence, who agreed to allow three Alsatian sisters to set up a community in Panna Maria and reopen the school. They were so successful that soon five young Polish women entered the convent at Castroville because of their exposure to the order's work in Panna Maria.

In 1869 the Sisters of Divine Providence, under the leadership of Mother St. Andrew Feltin, had gone from Austin to Castroville, where they established their motherhouse. They opened a day school in conjunction with their convent. Their community and school grew and buildings were added. Mother St. Andrew made three trips to Europe and eventually obtained approximately ninety-five sisters from France, Germany, and Ireland for their work in Castroville and in San Antonio at St. Joseph's School.[8]

However, Father Zwiardowski soon received information that Mother St. Andrew was seeking to have Bishop Dubuis, on the eve of the establishment of the San Antonio diocese, place all parochial schools in the Polish and German communities in that area of Texas under the care of her order. As much as he valued the order's work in Panna Maria, Zwiardowski apparently believed this would promote the "Germanization" of the Polish communities since the order had numerous members who were German-speaking Alsatians. Zwiardowski's solution was to propose to Bishop Pellicer the founding of a new teaching order around the five Polish sisters in Castroville. With the approval of both the bishop and Mother St. Andrew, these five sisters and two Alsatian sisters formed the new teaching community, known as the Order of the Immaculate Conception of the Virgin Mary, in April, 1875.

The order was successful for several years, but it remained small, and in 1881 the sisters disbanded and joined other orders. Several members of the Sisters of Charity of the Incarnate Word went to Panna Maria from San Antonio that same year, thus beginning their order's association with the school that spanned many decades. At first teaching was done entirely in Polish, since few if any of the children spoke English. However, by the turn of the century, the sisters, wanting their students to become bilingual, invited English-speaking teachers from a nearby public school to teach some of the courses in English.[9]

The staffing of the Panna Maria school by sisters of an order founded primarily to provide health care was part of a policy the order had embarked upon in response to Bishop Pellicer's acute interest in furthering parochial school education. Without abandoning its primary mission of health care, the order had already taken up teaching for a time in Houston, and, of course, teaching was involved in running St. Joseph's Orphanage in San Antonio. In 1875, at Pellicer's suggestion, the sisters agreed to open their school at the orphanage to others. Pellicer then transferred to their care about three hundred Hispanic students who previously had attended a free day school run by the Ursulines in conjunction with their girls' boarding academy; he did this because the day school was not compatible with a cloistered order such as the Ursulines, since its students did not live in community.[10] Also in 1875, the Sisters of Charity of the Incarnate Word opened their school in Graytown near San Antonio.

In 1870, Bishop Dubuis had made the San Antonio community of the Sisters of Charity of the Incarnate Word independent of the original foundation in Galveston, largely because of distance and the fact that no railroad had yet connected San Antonio with Houston and Galveston. This independence made it easier for the San Antonio sisters to respond affirmatively to Pellicer's urgings to incorporate teaching into their work. By 1884 they were conducting eleven schools and two orphanages, as well as Santa Rosa Hospital. In 1893 they began Incarnate Word Academy in San Antonio, which in the next century evolved into Incarnate Word College. By 1900 this San Antonio–based order had over three hundred members and was in charge of twenty-nine schools, orphanages, and hospitals in Texas, Missouri, and Mexico.[11]

Meanwhile other women religious were pressing forward the work of their own educational enterprises. At Victoria, the Sisters of the Incarnate Word and Blessed Sacrament continued successfully to operate Nazareth Academy. By 1875 additional sisters from both France and Ireland had joined the Victoria faculty. Serving both boarding and day students, the school achieved such goodwill in the area that parents petitioned the state to declare Nazareth Academy a "public" school and grant it public funds. This was possible under state law at the time. To qualify for state aid, a private school's faculty had to pass a qualifying exam, and salaries were then paid for a certain number of months depending on the size of the student body. From 1874 until 1895 Nazareth Academy received state funds equivalent to a state teacher's salary for each of its teachers for four months of the year. In a successful attempt to exclude most Catholic private schools from state assistance, the law was changed in 1895 to require faculty of such state-aided schools to wear ordinary attire, thus ruling out teachers who wore the religious habit.

During the 1870s the sisters added a separate chapel to their original convent and school complex. In the 1880s an additional frame building was added to help accommodate the increasing number of boarding and day students attracted to the varied curriculum offered in Nazareth Academy's elementary, middle, and upper divisions, a curriculum that included mathematics,

Mother St. Pierre Cinquin, superior,
Incarnate Word convent, San Antonio. Photo circa 1885,
courtesy Catholic Archives of Texas, Austin.

astronomy, geography, Latin and English grammar, art, drawing, penmanship, and needlework.

The sisters in Victoria also briefly attempted to educate the black children of the area. With the end of Reconstruction in the 1870s, virtually any impetus toward integration ceased in southern society for decades to come, and the sisters taught black children separately. Had their work survived, however, it would have provided an opportunity for black children in Victoria that was virtually unavailable from any other source. The sisters arranged to have this school receive state funds also, but it had hardly begun to operate when it was forced to close in response to a campaign against it by non-Catholic clergymen in the black community.[12]

During the tenure of Bishop Pellicer, St. Mary's College in San Antonio continued under the leadership of Bro. Charles Francis, who had succeeded Bro. Andrew Edel in 1866. This school, which evolved later into St. Mary's University, was the most prominent educational institution in San Antonio, and Pellicer was a frequent visitor there. As the intellectual center of the city, it was an important social center as well. A few days before Christmas, 1876, the bishop attended what was billed as the "first grand literary and dramatic" event in the school's hall. The *San Antonio Express* for December 23 carried an account of the evening stating that "music, addresses, orations, readings, recitations, dialogues, and dramatic renditions" made up the program.[13] The school's orchestra played for such occasions as well as commencement exercises, which in those times were entertainment events as much as anything else. When dignitaries visited San Antonio, the natural place for Pellicer to take them was St. Mary's. When the bishop of Monterrey, Nuevo León, Mexico, visited the city in March, 1878, a courtly public reception with an address in Spanish and orchestral and vocal music was arranged at the school. Such events at St. Mary's were in stark contrast to much of what went on in a city whose economy was based on cattle, with streets lined with saloons and often clogged with herds starting out on the long drive northward to railheads in Kansas or pastures in Wyoming.[14]

In spite of its growing prestige, St. Mary's was not designed to fulfill another educational goal Pellicer had set: that of providing seminary training for priests for the new diocese. For this the bishop turned to the Mexican Jesuit refugees within the diocese. This was natural since from the time they arrived in San Antonio in 1873, these Jesuits had been conducting an informal seminary for the benefit of their own members. Pellicer began sending a few men to them for training, and in 1876 arranged for them formally to open a seminary as well as a men's college in Seguin, near San Antonio. The town was already connected by rail to various parts of East and North Texas, making it an ideal location for a school.

The building of a recently closed girls' school was purchased, and in late September, 1876, the Jesuits and their seminarians arrived in Seguin. The local parish, St. James, was turned over to them by Pellicer, and since most of the parishioners were English-speaking, an Irish member of the community was appointed as its pastor. In addition, the Jesuits were given the churches in San Marcos, Lockhart, and Gonzales as well as those along the railroad line between Luling and Cibolo.

The college-seminary was named for Our Lady of Guadalupe, and classes formally began on October 16, 1876. The Jesuits and the bishop were eager for the college to be well received by the public, since if it succeeded financially, it could help support the seminary. But events proved disappointing. The total enrollment by the end of the year 1876 was only twenty. During the second year, 1877–78, the faculty was increased by four, and during the third year of operation, a tract of land was obtained for raising vegetables to help cut expenses. But still the enrollment rose only to thirty-five. Fees were reduced and the Jesuits continued advertising as they had all along in both Texas and Mexico, seeking students.[15]

The hard economic times worked against the new institution, and when changed conditions in Mexico made it possible for the Jesuits to return there in the summer of 1880, all but one did so. They reopened their novitiate in Mexico City and their college and seminary in Saltillo. One remained behind for a time to continue pastoral work in Seguin and San Marcos.[16]

The apparently bleak future for diocesan seminary education was made even bleaker that year with the death of the bishop, its chief proponent. In spite of his diabetes, Pellicer had not spared himself in administering his diocese. Like Dubuis and Odin before him, Pellicer was often absent from his residence at St. Mary's Church in San Antonio. In 1875, his first calendar year as bishop, Pellicer visited almost all of the parishes and missions in the diocese. He left San Antonio in Easter week for a two-thousand-mile trek — all of it by stage or "ambulance," the common wagon-like vehicle of the time with two seats for passengers, each running the length of the vehicle, with a top to shield from sun and rain. In addition to the settled regions of the diocese, Pellicer traveled westward across the southern Staked Plains to reach the military posts and sparse settlements of the far western part of his diocese, at a time when wagons and stagecoaches moving across the plains were still attacked by Indians.[17]

The pace of travel never really let up for very long during his tenure of five years and four months. Confirmations had to be administered, cornerstones blessed, and churches consecrated. In 1876 alone, new churches were built at Praha, Meyersville, High Hill, and Cicero. One was consecrated at Bandera, and cornerstones were blessed for the new building at St. Mary's College in San Antonio and for a new church in Panna Maria. And in addition to all his travel in the diocese that year, he also went to Rome. Under such a schedule and in a time prior to the discovery of insulin treatment, his health could not last. He did seek treatment — such as was available. At times when he was exhausted he would go to Mobile for a short vacation, but in 1878 when more was needed than a rest, he tried other means. In July he journeyed to a health resort in Waukesha, Wisconsin, known as Bethesda Spring and advertised as "Dunbar's Wonderful Discovery." He remained there into September. Even there the problems of the diocese were not far away since his correspondence indicates that he continued to administer the diocese through his vicar-general, Fr. Jean C. Neraz.[18]

He visited the resort several times, and his health on such occasions seemed to improve. Even so, as he once wrote from Dunbar's, he was "by no means well." In March, 1880, a small bump appeared on Pellicer's neck and quickly developed into a large inflamed sore. The bishop kept to his duties and officiated in San Fernando Cathedral for the blessing of the oils on Holy Thursday and at High Mass on Easter, but the inflammation refused to heal—and it was but one manifestation of his diabetes. He died on April 14, 1880, and was buried in San Fernando Cathedral. A large procession of clergy and laity along with a military honor guard from the local U.S. Army post accompanied his body through the streets. His cousin, Bp. Dominic Manucy, vicar apostolic of Brownsville, celebrated the requiem mass.[19]

At the time of the death of its first bishop, the diocese of San Antonio contained forty-seven thousand Catholics, forty-five priests, fifty churches, and eight chapels.[20]

During the years of his tenure as bishop, Pellicer had the administrative assistance of Fr. Jean Claude Neraz, who served as his vicar-general. Throughout the remainder of 1880, Neraz was the administrator of the diocese, and in early 1881 he received word from Rome that he was to be Pellicer's successor. Neraz was fifty-three years old and like Odin and Dubuis was a native of France from near Lyon. It was in Lyon in 1852, while studying for the priesthood, that Neraz met Odin and decided to volunteer for the Texas missions. Ordained in St. Mary's Cathedral in Galveston in 1853, Neraz set out for Nacogdoches, where he worked over a wide area for the next eleven years. Like the rest of the frontier clergy, he lived a spartan existence, often having only the corn his people donated for him to live on. His missionary work sometimes took him a hundred miles or more from his headquarters in Nacogdoches.[21] In 1864 he was sent to Liberty in Southeast Texas but two years later was transferred to San Fernando Church in San Antonio as assistant pastor. From there he went to Laredo. With Fr. Michael Souchon, he supervised the building of a new St. Augustine Church and the completion of a convent for the Ursuline community founded there in 1868 by Mother St. Joseph Aubert and Sr. Tereza Pereda. By virtue of the decrees of the second synod of the diocese of Galveston, Neraz became the chancellor for the Laredo district in 1869. In 1873, he returned to San Fernando Church in San Antonio as its pastor.[22]

Neraz's consecration as a bishop took place in San Fernando Cathedral

The Rt. Rev. Jean Claude Neraz, bishop of San Antonio, 1881–94. Photo circa 1885, courtesy Catholic Archives of Texas, Austin.

on May 8, 1881; the chief consecrator was the bishop of Little Rock, Arkansas, Edward Fitzgerald. Bishop Dubuis of Galveston was also present at what was one of his last appearances at public worship in Texas. The very next day, while still in San Antonio, Dubuis addressed a circular letter to the clergy of his diocese giving instructions as to how the diocese was to function following his imminent departure for Rome. In Rome he asked to be relieved of all diocesan administrative duties.[23]

One of the first problems Neraz had to face was that of providing for the education of future clergy. With the Jesuits' college-seminary at Seguin now closed, Neraz sought to found a seminary at St. Joseph's College in Victoria, then under the administration of a newly arrived Irish priest, Fr. Lawrence Wyer. It was under his leadership that the reconstituted seminary took shape. Wyer was energetic and determined that the seminary would succeed; he even used his own personal funds for the support of students when diocesan funds ran low. Under his guidance the seminary became a vital contributor to diocesan life for the rest of the century. At least forty priests were educated there over the next twenty years. Wyer became pastor of St. Mary's parish in Victoria in 1891 but continued to be the mainstay of the seminary. The seminary became so dependent on Wyer that it closed shortly after his death in 1902. Though it had lasted only a little over twenty years, the Victoria seminary had been invaluable in its service to the young diocese. Its closing left an educational void that was filled the following year by the founding of St. Anthony's Seminary in San Antonio.[24] The school for boys in Victoria was revived in 1906 by the Society of Mary.

The 1880s and 1890s witnessed continued advancement by the various religious orders in their commitment to education and charitable activities. On the very edge of the diocese, across the Colorado River from Austin, St. Edward's College experienced significant development during the 1880s. In 1879 a frame building was erected for classes previously taught in the farmhouse that stood on the property. In 1881 a second frame building was erected to accommodate boarding students, and the school received a full-time president, Fr. John Lauth. The school was officially given the name St. Edward's at that time, and an official charter from the state for St. Edward's College was obtained in 1885. Under Lauth's successor, Fr. Peter Hurth, the site of the campus was moved to its present hilltop location when in 1888 construction began on a large masonry building designed by the prominent Galveston architect, Nicholas Clayton. In 1891 a wing was added to the main building, and by the end of the century another addition and a separate auditorium were completed.[25]

The Sisters of Divine Providence moved their motherhouse to San Antonio from Castroville in 1896. Their educational efforts in San Antonio led to the founding of Our Lady of the Lake University in the twentieth century. As Sr. Angelina Murphy shows, the sisters had managed to conduct their work during the 1880s and early 1890s in spite of frayed relations with Bishop Neraz, a situation that produced grave concern for both the sisters and the bishop. Indeed the sisters came to view him as a tyrant. When Neraz made his *ad limina* visit to Rome in 1883, he went to the motherhouse of the Sisters of Divine Providence in St. Jean-de-Bassel and requested the separation of the Texas province, headquartered then at Castroville, from the French community. The exact nature of the response he received is ambiguous. What the bishop wanted was to have the Sisters of Divine Providence in his diocese totally independent of the French motherhouse and completely under his authority. The congregation in Texas, since its arrival there, had been led by Mother St. Andrew Feltin.

It was Mother St. Andrew who began the enlargement of the convent at Castroville and purchased land near St. Joseph's Church in San Antonio for use as an academy. Mother St. Andrew was French like the bishop and, also like the bishop, very strong-willed—a trait she also shared with her brother, Fr. Nicholas Feltin. It was he who somewhat reluctantly finally gave up the pastorate of St. Mary's in Austin to the Congregation of the Holy Cross in 1874. He was then made pastor of St. Joseph's Church in San Antonio, where in 1877 Mother St. Andrew sent four sisters to do educational work. A controversy arose between two of the religious who also happened to be blood sisters. After the matter was brought to the attention of Mother St. Andrew in Castroville, she decided in favor of one and transferred the other out of St. Joseph's parish. His sister's action infuriated the pastor, Father Feltin, who said the truth was with the other sister. But Mother St. Andrew refused to change her decision. This rather petty disagreement soon attained enormous proportions when the father of the two sisters entered into the dispute, sided with Mother St. Andrew, and proceeded to attack Feltin, charging him with trying to win the affection of his daughter and attempting to poison him. He went to the police, swore out a warrant, and had the pastor arrested. All of the San Antonio papers, of couse, carried the story. The charges were deemed groundless and the case thrown out of court, but the public scandal had enormous repercussions. In the minds of some, particularly a number of the clergy, the blame did not fall on either of the two nuns or the pastor or even the sisters' father but on Mother St. Andrew in Castroville, the logic apparently being that if Mother St. Andrew had reversed her decision when the pastor of St. Joseph's objected, then the public scandal would have been avoided! Even when the newspapers came out with stories upholding the pastor's innocence, the resentment by some of the clergy against Mother St. Andrew did not go away. For her own part, Mother St. Andrew found it hard to forget how priests had denounced her when she was only carrying out her duty as superior of her community. It had not been she who had impugned her brother's character, yet now she bore the blame. Bishop Pellicer tried to bring about a reconciliation between all parties in the controversy but with very limited results. The two sisters at the heart of the dispute left the order and were followed by three others as a reaction to the event. Relations between Father Feltin and his sister, Mother St. Andrew, never returned to normal, although she was at his bedside when he died the next year in 1878.

At the time of the scandal, Bishop Neraz had been the vicar-general under Pellicer. Mother St. Andrew believed that Neraz later sought the separation of the order in Texas from its motherhouse at St. Jean-de-Bassel in France because of resentment he held against her stemming from this scandal. After his return from Europe in 1883, Neraz told Mother St. Andrew that a separation was imminent. Mother St. Andrew herself had visited St. Jean-de-Bassel, also in 1883 but before the bishop's visit, and had brought fifty-two volunteers from the motherhouse back to Texas with her. She had received no indication that a separation was pending and believed she could never have brought so many back with her if a separation had been planned. As late as the early summer of 1886, Sister Florence, visiting from Texas at St. Jean-de-Bassel, received no indication there that a separation had occurred three years before or was then pending. The only communication Mother St. Andrew received from St. Jean-de-Bassel concerning the matter was an account that while Neraz was there in 1883, he asked if the Texas congregation "depended on" the motherhouse and was told that because of distance it couldn't. Mother St. Andrew saw this as a statement of the obvious and not as an indication of a formal separation. Bishop Neraz, however, believed otherwise, although he waited until the summer of 1886 before acting on the matter. That year the story went around that Mother St. Andrew had told all of her sisters, and some of the laity as well, that they were to "beware of all priests without exception." This was later firmly denied by Mother St. Andrew, but her days as superior were numbered. On June 29, 1886, four priests signed a statement sent to the bishop that they would not work in the same parishes with sisters of the order as long as Mother St. Andrew was in charge. On July 28, Neraz appointed an investigative commission, and although Mother St. Andrew denied making the disparaging remark about priests, the bishop and his council concluded on August 16 that Mother St. Andrew would have to go.

The next day, the sisters at Castroville were informed in writing that Mother St. Andrew must resign and a successor be elected. The bishop arrived at Castroville on August 27 to supervise the election, but the sisters were determined to resist what they believed was unwarranted interference in their community. When the ballot was taken, Mother St. Andrew was unanimously reelected. Neraz then declared that Mother St. Andrew was deposed and a successor must be elected or the community would cease to exist as such. At this threat, Mother St. Andrew told her bewildered community to vote for Sr. Florence Walter, who was quickly elected. Neraz accepted the election even though the new superior was Mother St. Andrew's choice.

Sister Florence, now Mother Florence, was not in Castroville but was returning from France when the election occurred. When her train passed through San Antonio, Bishop Neraz came aboard long enough to inform her of her election and to state that henceforth he was her highest superior. To reiterate his point, he went the next morning to Castroville and formally presented the new superior to the sisters. He also privately instructed Mother Florence to burn Mother St. Andrew's papers and refuse her any administrative or advisory responsibility. He also wanted her sent away from Castroville.[26]

Mother St. Andrew remained for a while in the diocese, but she could not always be obedient to the bishop, who was now her order's real superior. For a time she was out of the order entirely, caring for her brother's children, but when Neraz died in 1894, Mother Florence telegraphed the following message to Mother St. Andrew, by then in California: "Bishop Neraz died Nov. 15. May he rest in peace. Please feel free to come home now, if you can. We want you here."[27] Because of family responsibilities, Mother St. Andrew did not return to Castroville until 1900; she died there five years later.

Later, during the administration of Neraz's successor, John Anthony Forest, the Texas congregation of the Sisters of Divine Providence received a papal constitution by which it governed itself within the normal bounds.

Neraz, after his death in 1894, would not be remembered only for his rigidity—some would remember that during the smallpox epidemic of 1883 he had visited the patients quarantined in tents set up outside the city so that his priests would not be exposed to the disease.[28] And some would remember that he had fostered the evangelization of black people in San Antonio after a long period of woeful neglect in this area. Virtually every other ethnic group in the city—but not the blacks—had a Catholic church that it considered its own. In September, 1887, Neraz asked that appeals be made in all San Antonio churches for funds to erect a church for black Catholics. He received enthusiastic support from the Oblate priest, Fr. Richard J. Maloney, who volunteered to lead the effort in founding the new parish. Maloney was joined in his effort by Margaret Healy Murphy, the widow of a Corpus Christi judge, who ultimately donated her fortune and devoted the remaining years of her life to work among the black Catholics of San Antonio.[29]

Early in 1888, a site for a church and school was obtained and construction began almost immediately. The church was dedicated by Bishop Neraz on September 16, 1888, and named for St. Peter Claver, the seventeenth-century missionary among the African slaves of Colombia. St. Peter Claver had been canonized in 1885, and this was the first parish in the United States to be put under his patronage. Maloney was named pastor and worked there until his death.

Margaret Healy Murphy's work in the new parish eventually led to the founding of a new religious order known as the Sisters of the Holy Ghost, whose special purpose was to work in parishes and schools among black Catholics. Bishop Neraz gave his formal approval to the new order in 1893. As the years passed, these sisters expanded their work into several southern states and into New York, not only teaching but caring for orphans and the elderly as well.[30]

Shortly before Neraz's death in 1894, *The Southern Messenger* was founded and became the leading Catholic journal in the state for the next sixty years. In 1890 the Oblate pastor at St. Mary's Church in San Antonio, Fr. C. J. Smith, had begun a publication called the *Monthly Review of St. Mary's Church*. It met with wide acceptance, soon became the *St. Mary's Weekly Review*, and by 1892 was known as *The San Antonio Messenger*. A layman, L. William Menger, took over the publication in 1893 and gave it the name it bore until its demise in the 1950s, *The Southern Messenger*.

After Neraz's death on November 15, 1894, the diocese remained vacant for about ten months.[31] During this period Fr. Stephen Buffard served as its administrator. In August, 1895, Fr. John Anthony Forest, pastor of St. Mary's Church in Hallettsville, was named as the third bishop of San Antonio. Like his predecessor, Forest was French. Born in 1838 at Saint Martin-La-Surete, France, Forest was one of the volunteers Dubuis brought with him to New Orleans in 1863. Ordained there soon after his arrival, he went almost immediately to Texas by way of Matamoros, where he was given charge of St. Mary's Church in Lavaca County, four miles west of Hallettsville. Soon all the missions in Lavaca, Fayette, and Gonzales Counties were placed in his care, and in that area he labored for the next thirty-two years.[32]

Forest was consecrated a bishop by the archbishop of New Orleans, Francis Janssens, on October 28, 1895, in San Fernando Cathedral. One observer recorded that literally thousands took part in the procession that winded its way toward the cathedral for the consecration. The number of bishops participating in the rite was greater than usual since a number of the eastern prelates, including the archbishop of New York, happened to be passing through the city returning from a special celebration surrounding the picture of our Lady of Guadalupe in Mexico City.[33]

Forest had an excellent record as a missionary. When he arrived in 1863 in the area where Fr. Edward Clarke had begun work among the Missouri Catholics along the Lavaca River in the 1840s, the log cabin was still the common structure for both church and dwelling. After the war, Czech immigrants arrived in increasing numbers. During the thirty-two years he spent in the region, numerous new churches and schools were built, including St. Mary's near Hallettsville, Sacred Heart in the town of Hallettsville itself,

Rectory, Sacred Heart Church, Hallettsville, circa 1900.
The Rev. Louis P. Netardus, pastor, is on the porch.
Courtesy Catholic Archives of Texas, Austin.

St. John the Baptist at Antioch, St. Joseph's in Yoakum, Saints Cyril and Methodius in Shiner, and St. Joseph's in Moulton. His reputation as a builder was no doubt one of the reasons his name was sent to Rome recommending him as a candidate to succeed Neraz.[34]

During Forest's fifteen-year episcopate, the scope of Catholic education continued to grow, and several religious orders entered the diocese for the first time. In 1897 the Sisters of Our Lady of Charity of Refuge arrived in San Antonio to establish Our Lady of Victory School for delinquent and neglected girls. The Claretians or Sons of the Immaculate Heart of Mary entered the diocese in 1902 and took charge of San Fernando Cathedral. The Society of St. Joseph or "Josephites" arrived in 1904 to work at St. Peter Claver parish among the black Catholics in the city. In this parish, three years before, Forest had opened a home for the aged and the poor, which now the Josephites began to administer. These priests continued their work there into the next century and by 1910 had been so successful that they opened a second parish among the city's black Catholics.[35]

At the end of the century, the twenty-six-year-old diocese had a Catholic population of about seventy-five thousand served by seventy-three priests. Services were scheduled on a daily or at least weekly basis in seventy-three parishes and missions, and mass was celebrated on an irregular basis in at least eighty mission stations. Immigration was continuing and ensured that the diocese's phenomenal growth would continue into the twentieth century.[36]

Forest was the last of the line of French prelates, beginning with Odin in 1840, to work in the Catholic church in Texas. With his death in 1911 this "French" epoch came to an end. Such an epoch was not unique to Texas. French priests had immigrated to the United States, mainly to Maryland and Kentucky, as refugees during the French Revolution. Their ranks had been augmented by an even greater number of clergy who in the post-Napoleonic era, already filled with zeal to reclaim for France its former position as "first daughter" of the papacy, looked westward to a wilderness challenge even greater. Between 1800 and 1850, of the twenty-three bishops appointed to areas west of the Appalachians, eleven were French. These clergy tended to couple their zeal to rigidity and ecclesiastical triumphalism, and according to a study by Fr. Barnabas Diekemper, this tendency can still be seen reflected in some of the buildings constructed during the period. Their rigidity helped make them strict disciplinarians, and they sometimes could not understand either the laity or the non-French priests with whom they came in contact. Because of this, early in the nineteenth century, some of the laity in Louisville, Kentucky, petitioned their bishop against having more French clergy sent among them. When these clergy came into the Southwest, as was the case at least first with Odin, they sometimes exhibited little understanding of Hispanic Catholicism and culture. Their answer was often to attempt to lay a French Catholic veneer over what they encountered. The enlargement of San Fernando Church in San Antonio, where a Gothic addition was built around the preexistent Spanish colonial structure, was a metaphor of this approach. On the other hand, these priests were on the scene at a time when otherwise there likely would have been no one. Furthermore, with many of them there was a positive side to both their rigidity and their triumphalism, in that these tendencies reinforced a determination that pushed them onward in spite of grave hardships. The result was not always what it might or should have been, but at the end of their era, the Catholic presence was writ large across the face of the land.[37]

TEN

The Vicariate Apostolic of Brownsville

THE year that marked the beginning of the see of San Antonio, 1874, also marked the beginning of the vicariate apostolic of Brownsville. Although as originally constituted the jurisdiction's northern boundary did not extend as far northward as the Nueces River, at the request of its first vicar apostolic, Bp. Dominic Manucy, the jurisdiction was enlarged in 1875 to include the entire region between the Rio Grande and Nueces River.

Before he came to Texas, Bishop Manucy's career had virtually paralleled that of his cousin, Anthony Pellicer, San Antonio's first bishop. Both were born in Saint Augustine, Florida, in 1823 and studied at Spring Hill College near Mobile, Alabama. Both worked in the same parishes at various times in the diocese of Mobile.[1]

The total population of the new Brownsville jurisdiction was about sixty thousand in 1875, out of which there was a Catholic population of approximately forty-two thousand.[2] Approximately forty thousand of the Catholics were of Hispanic descent.

After his consecration to the episcopate in the Mobile cathedral on December 8, 1874, Manucy prepared to embark across the Gulf for the Rio Grande Valley of Texas. Dangerous weather plagued his voyage, causing him not to arrive at the mouth of the Rio Grande until February 8, 1875, four days behind schedule.

By this time a railroad was operating between Brownsville and Point Isabel, where a Brownsville delegation awaited Manucy as he disembarked. After Manucy and the assemblage boarded the train, a telegraph message notified the city, and the bell of Immaculate Conception Church there began to peal. This was the signal for a gathering to form at the depot to welcome Manucy when his train had traveled the short distance from Port Isabel.[3]

At the depot, the town's Hispanic citizens had constructed a huge arch in honor of the new vicar apostolic. As the bishop stepped off the train, another welcoming committee, this time headed by the mayor, stepped forward officially to welcome Manucy and escort him to the church. As a band played and two twelve-pounders began firing nearby, accompanied still by the ringing of the church bell, a procession guided by the sheriff of Cameron County made its way from the depot toward Immaculate Conception

Church. At the entrance to the church, two speakers welcomed Bishop Manucy: A Brownsville attorney, F. E. McManus, delivered an address in English, and M. A. Venero delivered one in Spanish.

Manucy responded to the proceedings in both Spanish and English. He seemed moved by the town's welcome but appeared worn out from his long and dangerous trip. He stated that he would enjoy seeing the throngs regularly at mass more than he did in this triumphal reception.

Manucy took up residence with the Oblates, and on Sunday, February 14, was formally installed as vicar apostolic of Brownsville by Bishop Dubuis of Galveston. Again a huge procession formed, this time moving from St. Joseph's College, the Oblates' parochial boy's school, to the church. After the mass and service of installation, Manucy and about two hundred guests returned to St. Joseph's for lunch prepared and served by some of the Catholic women of Brownsville.[4]

This was an auspicious beginning for Manucy in Brownsville, but the good times did not last. The storms the bishop's boat had endured in the Gulf were the more accurate portent for his career in this border city. There was opposition to Manucy's presence in Brownsville emanating from two sources. First, Manucy learned, not everyone in Brownsville wanted him there. Some had opposed the reception the city administration gave him on the day of his arrival. After the plans were first publicized, an anonymous letter was sent to Fr. Pierre F. Parisot, the Oblate missionary most active in preparing the grand reception. Its threatening language read in part:

> Sir: I am delegated by the W. L. of W.M.G.R.P.A.O. of & C. . . . to announce that if you attempt to have a procession through the public thoroughfares of our city there is a bullet ready for your worthless carcass and another for your d—— Bishop. And if you erect a throne for your d—— Prince of the Church. . . . Remember, sir, that in this grand Republic there is no room for such trash as a Prince sitting on a throne. Bullets are in readiness, look out.[5]

What the initials meant, Parisot didn't know. But soon someone publicly compared the festivities planned for Manucy's arrival to "dancing the bolero and fandango."[6] Then a pamphlet was circulated denouncing the city's plans, and a group scheduled a ball, apparently hoping to detract from the public celebration of Manucy's arrival.

The second source of opposition to Manucy's presence in Brownsville was within the bishop himself. Right from the start, he had not really wanted to be there, even before he had ever laid eyes on the city. Upon receiving news of his appointment as vicar apostolic of Brownsville the previous September, Manucy had written his friend James McMaster, editor of the New York Catholic newspaper *Freeman's Journal,* that he viewed the assignment "as the worse [sic] sentence that could be passed on me for any crime! I

The Rt. Rev. Dominic Manucy,
first vicar apostolic of Brownsville, circa 1874.
Courtesy Catholic Archives of Texas, Austin.

had reason to believe, if I had been proposed for any see, it was for San Antonio. The change was made, no doubt, to advance the interests of some favorite!—Indeed I scarcely believed my name had been sent in at all for any place; though I was positively assured, by one who professed to know, it went in for San Antonio."⁷ Manucy's disappointment may have only increased when he learned that the "favorite" who received the coveted position in San Antonio was his own cousin. Manucy went on to bemoan the fact that the vicariate's Catholics were mostly Hispanics, whom he then proceeded to disparage in language more appropriate to a bigot than a priest. Furthermore, they didn't have any money: "Brownsville district is a country without resources. The Catholic population is composed almost exclusively of *Mexican greasers*—drovers and *ladrones*. No money can be got out of such people—not to bury their fathers!" He then cited how a priest in Brownsville recently had to appeal "to the charity of the faithful abroad" just to build a schoolhouse. He seemed unaware that Dubuis and Odin had had to appeal to "the faithful abroad" for the past thirty-five years to keep the church alive in all parts of Texas. But there Manucy saw another problem:

> Worse than all, the only priests in the country are the O. M. I.—Oblates of Mary Immaculate. They most likely own what little church property is in the place; and in consequence will be masters over the bishop—all a bishop will be useful for, then, will be to ride the circuit, like a Methodist preacher, administer confirmation, and be *the laughing stock of Religious Men!* A fine prospect surely for a man, who has already spent twenty-four years of his life in arduous duties! . . . If there were any hope of doing any good for the glory of God [I would] welcome the sacrifice, but I see no possible means before me. All that I have conversed with, that have visited that part of the country, speak in the most discouraging manner of that people. Surely if that district of country presented any advantages one of the Oblates would have been appointed bishop!

Disdain for most of the laity, engendered by ethnic and racial prejudice, and jealousy toward most of the clergy clearly could not bode well for the future of the new Brownsville vicariate. At least one person in Brownsville was aware of Manucy's inner conflict even before the bishop's arrival. The previous December, the Oblate superior, Fr. Florent Vandenberghe, had gone to Mobile for Manucy's consecration to the episcopate and had easily seen that Manucy was anything but happy about moving to Brownsville. The superior had concluded, however, that the new bishop was "pious . . . learned . . . a man of God" and that his "kindness and simplicity" made up for the fact that he was difficult to approach. Still, Vandenberghe had wondered how Manucy, who had been happy as the parish priest of "six hundred select Catholics" in Montgomery, Alabama, would fare in his new missionary role in the Rio Grande Valley, where presumably he did not consider the Catholics "select." And when Manucy had become ill at ease at the mention of the Oblates of Brownsville, their work, their property, and then had burst into tears in front of Vandenberghe, the picture had been crystal clear.[8]

Many of the Oblates in Brownsville had been shocked at this report, and they were even more shocked at the attitudes expressed by Manucy in the days following his arrival. Manucy told some of the Oblates that the new vicariate was comparable to those in Africa and Asia where a bishop was good only for administering confirmation. He continued to weep before them and to declare that he should have a bigger and better assignment. He seemed to want to have little to do with the Hispanic laity but sought out rather the Anglos, declaring to them that he was one of them and not a Frenchman like Dubuis and Odin! "Until now you have been administered to by foreigners, but I know the rights of the American citizens."[9] Sadly, unable to free himself from the racial attitudes of the antebellum South from which he came, Manucy was ill-suited to the important task that lay before him, and even more sadly, he left scars lasting well into the next century.

The current Oblate superior, Vandenberghe, could not help the bishop change his attitudes, for in contrast to most of his brothers, he shared some of them himself: the vicariate of Brownsville was to him a "Sahara," and while Manucy preferred Montgomery, Vandenberghe would much rather have been in Canada.[10] Most of the Oblates, such as Jean-Marie Clos, could never make peace with a bishop who harbored such prejudices and resentments. For them, the place for the church's major work was not amidst the relative comforts of Brownsville but among the people of the ranches and towns of the valley.

Manucy's increasingly open disgust at being where he was soon alienated not only the Hispanic laity but some of the Catholic Anglos as well. This loss of support created a favorable climate for anti-Catholic bigotry, which had existed among some of the Anglos all along. In a strange twist of circumstances, the anti-Catholic faction used the zeal of some of the Catholics to create havoc for Manucy. During this period, the Mexican government was enforcing various restrictive laws against the Catholic church and its religious orders. In the last week of February, 1875, twenty-three Sisters of Charity arrived in Brownsville after being deported from Mexico. The townspeople were gracious in their welcome to the sisters. On learning of their arrival, many of them, along with some of the Oblates, went down to the boat dock and formed an escort for the exiles as they made their way to the church. The bishop greeted them there and celebrated mass for them, including an impressive homily. In the days following, a movement began among the townspeople to persuade Manucy to provide a permanent residence for these sisters renowned for their care of the sick. Delegations called on the bishop, and the city agreed to support the sisters for a number of months in exchange for their efforts in caring for the sick.

Manucy's response was negative and definite: the sisters could not stay. He lacked the funds, he said, to provide a permanent residence; their presence under such circumstances would interfere with the work of the Oblates and the convent already established in Brownsville; and without the permission of their superiors, the sisters could not stay in Brownsville anyway. With no other alternative, the sisters prepared to leave on March 3, but bad weather prevented their departure and it was postponed for several days. This gave the anti-Catholic element an opportunity to fan the anger at Manucy's intransigence into a public demonstration against the bishop whose presence they had resented from the start.

Around four in the morning of the day the sisters were to leave, a crowd began forming at the railroad station. When the sisters arrived about nine o'clock, they simply told the crowd they could not remain in Brownsville without the bishop's permission and proceeded to seat themselves in the car. Soon the crowd began shouting "Vaya el obispo" or "Away with the bishop"; the car was uncoupled from the rest of the train and carried by the crowd several yards away from the track, where it was put down. Angry speeches followed. Later, a crowd marched to the Oblates' residence where the bishop lived. Manucy went out to meet them and managed to calm their anger. However, he apparently refused the mayor's request to go to the station and try to persuade the mob to put the car back on the track. The mayor himself finally convinced them to do so. The police were watchful for the next day or two, but there was no further disturbance. The sisters left Brownsville. And soon after so did Manucy, to make his first visitation tour of the vicariate.[11]

In spite of his attitudes toward place and people, Manucy did set out to perform his pastoral duties. Taking two Oblate priests with him, he made his way to such towns as Encantada, Santa María, Capote, Lomita, Davis, and Roma. Fr. Jean Lagier from Laredo met the bishop at San Ignacio and accompanied him the rest of the way to Laredo. From Laredo, Manucy took the stagecoach to San Antonio, arriving in mid-May. After a visit there with his cousin, Manucy went to Corpus Christi by way of Victoria and the port of Indianola. He remained in Corpus Christi almost a month and then made other stops on his return to Brownsville. By late July, he was back in Brownsville after traveling well over a thousand miles in a 3½-month period, much of it over roads and trails little or no better than what had previously greeted Odin and Dubuis. He had confirmed over twenty-six hundred people. He estimated that the vicariate contained about forty thousand Hispanic Catholics and probably no more than twenty-five hundred Anglo Catholics, if that many. It was easy for Manucy to conclude that the main problem in the new vicariate was the same one that had faced his predecessors: a lack of priests. The communities of San Diego, Concepción, and Brackettville, for instance, each had in its environs a Catholic population Manucy estimated at between two and three thousand, each with no priest, though in San Diego, where a resident priest had served from 1867 to 1872, a small chapel stood. In spite of the obvious need for a bishop in the Brownsville area, Manucy concluded almost immediately after his return to Brownsville, if he had not already, to move his residence to Corpus Christi. It was more "becoming," and earlier hostilities lingered on in Brownsville.[12] He also wanted to be out of a situation where he had to be dependent on the Oblates, who owned the church property in Brownsville. His sojourn in Corpus Christi as he returned to Brownsville from his tour of the vicariate contributed to his decision, for he had decided at least by August 3 to move there.[13]

Manucy made this decision in spite of his discovery on returning to Brownsville that a fund had been started to erect a residence for him that would enable him to live apart from the Oblates. Three thousand dollars had already been subscribed when rumors of Manucy's intended move began to circulate. Nevertheless, in early September, the move was announced officially, and on September 20 Manucy officiated publicly for the last time in Brownsville before moving his residence to Corpus Christi.[14] According to one source, only two or three laymen of the Brownsville parish came to bid him farewell as he departed the city.[15] Resentment compounded into bitterness in his wake.

On the other hand, Manucy did take measures to meet the pastoral needs of the valley with the limited resources at his command. It seems likely that Manucy was back in San Diego shortly after his move to Corpus Christi to fulfill a request of the town's large Catholic population, which had no priest—a situation typical to most areas of the new vicariate. Although he thought Corpus Christi's fifteen hundred Hispanic and four hundred Anglo Catholics were in need of additional priests, Manucy nevertheless took Fr. Claude Jaillet with him on his return to San Diego. Jaillet, a native of Lyon, France, had come to Texas in 1866 immediately following his ordination to the priesthood by Bishop Dubuis, who was in France seeking missionary volunteers. Jaillet had been stationed in San Diego from 1866 to 1872 and for the past two years had ridden a circuit out from Corpus Christi to numerous ranches and villages, occasionally including San Diego. In doing this Jaillet had followed a daily routine common to most of the priests in the vicariate: mass at about seven in the morning, then on horseback to the next ranch, often a day's ride away, where in the evening he would teach the catechism, lead devotions, and give a homily on church teachings afterwards.[16]

When the people of San Diego asked during Manucy's first visit that Jaillet reside there again, the bishop agreed, on the condition that their

The Rt. Rev. Claude Marie Dubuis with missionary volunteers at their departure from Le Havre, France, for Texas on February 4, 1863. Seated (*from left*): Claude Fauvre, Étienne Marie Buffard, Bishop Dubuis, Stephane Savoye, Jean Antoin Forest (later the third bishop of San Antonio); standing (*from left*): Jacques Chaland, Louis Chaland, Joseph Martiniere, Emile Chapolard, William McSweeney, Pierre Richard, Claude Martiniere, and Claude Jaillet. Courtesy Catholic Archives of Texas, Austin.

small chapel be replaced by a larger edifice. The people gave their promise and later, with great difficulty, they and Jaillet accomplished this task. It was made no easier by the fact that while Jaillet was to spend more time in San Diego than before, he could not be there all the time. The lack of personnel gave Manucy no choice, so in addition to Jaillet's responsibilities as pastor in his place of residence, he was put in charge of all the missions in an area about one hundred miles long and about sixty miles wide, running from the Nueces River to the north, all the way south to a point about twenty miles below the village of Concepción, and comprising all of Duval and portions of Nueces, McMullen, Live Oak, and Jim Wells counties. When a seminary graduate from France, Pierre Bard, arrived in Corpus Christi the next year, Manucy immediately ordained him a priest and sent him to San Diego to share Jaillet's heavy duties. This allowed at least one priest to be in San Diego at all times while the other made the rounds of this six-thousand-square-mile portion of the Brownsville vicariate.

What Jaillet and Bard had to do to visit the Catholics of this area was not unique—it was simply the way things were in the vicariate. It took from one to two months to visit the entire region. First the priest went north toward the Nueces River, then west, then south, then last of all to the east. In the late 1870s there was only one chapel in this region outside San Diego, at Concepción; otherwise, just as the Oblates did along the Rio Grande, mass was celebrated at an altar set up in the home where the missionary was staying. The custom was that someone, usually a small boy, would go from house to house ringing a little bell signaling the residents to come to where the priest was staying. Once the people were assembled and if it was morning, mass was celebrated; if it was evening, catechism, the rosary, hymns, and a homily followed.

By 1886 the endeavors of these two missionaries had helped produce congregations with chapels to the southwest of San Diego at Benavides, Realitos, and Hebbronville on the new Texas-Mexican Railway; to the south at Guajillo, Palito Blanco, and Falfurrias; to the west at Rosita; to the north at Tío Mendieta; and to the east at Alice. Though Jaillet's duties eventually took him elsewhere, Bard remained in San Diego until his death in 1920 during the worldwide influenza epidemic and is buried there in San Francisco de Paula Church.[17]

While the vicariate in the late 1870s and early 1880s was experiencing the fruits of missionary labors, the vicar apostolic apparently was attaining no greater satisfaction at being in South Texas than at the beginning of his tenure. He tried to carry out his duties, however, and to the extent that he did so he endured the hardships they required. Father Parisot in his memoirs recounts an arduous trip made with Manucy in 1879. They began their trip from Corpus Christi to visit some of the missions to the west, including San Diego, and were to be joined along the way by Fr. Jean Bretault, an Oblate like Parisot, who was in charge of a large number of ranches to be visited in the Rio Grande Valley. They traveled in an overloaded ambulance, a four-wheeled covered conveyance with a seat for a driver and two passenger seats facing each other and running the length of the vehicle. The second day they bogged down in a marsh, and Manucy asked Parisot what they should do. Parisot stated that they must send for help in Corpus Christi, which they did. But shortly after getting out of one marsh, they bogged down in another. The ten or twelve boxes and trunks made the load too much for the two mules pulling the ambulance, and according to Parisot the bishop's driver, who had been hired as an act of charity on Manucy's part, was too sick to handle the mules properly. Manucy once more asked the Oblate what to do. Parisot's response, after removing his boots and socks and rolling up his trousers, was to jump into the mire and begin unloading the ambulance. Afterwards he began pushing the vehicle from behind, but to no avail. Then, looking up at Manucy, who had remained all the while seated in the ambulance, Parisot exclaimed, "Bishop,—*salva reverentia,*—take off your boots and come down behind the ambulance!" Then, according to Parisot, "His Lordship put his dignity aside for a few minutes and came down into the mire and united his efforts with mine."[18] When they were unable to free the vehicle, the bishop wanted to send to a village for help and then return to Corpus Christi. They could start out again, he said, the following week when the roads might be drier. Parisot countered that Bretault was already on his way to meet them at the first ranch served by the Oblates on their itinerary and that necessary planning had to be done there for their visit to the others. To delay as Manucy wanted was to risk not meeting Bretault and possibly to destroy the entire purpose of the visitation. Still Manucy insisted, but the Oblate was not to be silenced. Turning to the bishop, he said, "Place your confidence in God, and say a short prayer to the Blessed Virgin Mary, asking her to aid us, and we shall conquer the elements." But the unmoved bishop responded, "My dear Father, your theology is correct, but it will not dry the roads."[19] By this time Manucy had put his boots back on and was once more seated in the ambulance. Soon a group of mounted vaqueros driving a herd of livestock appeared, but even their help failed to free the stranded vehicle. Now more distraught than ever, the bishop again demanded to return to Corpus Christi, but somehow Parisot once more persuaded him to get down into the mud and push. As Parisot recalled, they urged the driver to whip the mules harder, said three Hail Marys, and then gave an especially strong push as they prayed again, "Mary, help us," and finally the ambulance began to move and was soon free. With this success, the bishop gave in to Parisot's pleas and went ahead with his visitation tour.

During the next two months it was almost a daily occurrence for their conveyance to get stuck in the mud, but they did not return to Corpus Christi until the appointed time. They never wanted for meat on this trip, for Manucy was an excellent shot with an old musket he carried and valued highly. Parisot recounted that after arduous efforts for two and a half months, visiting more than eighty ranches, the bishop arrived in Brownsville, rested for two weeks, and then went upriver to visit more towns and ranches, working now "as hard as his priests."[20]

Whatever the bishop's shortcomings, his trip must have been a success: the people came to know their bishop better and reportedly were impressed with his homilies; and he confirmed 2,862 children and adults.[21]

In spite of this, Manucy seems never to have adjusted to life in the vicariate. Whereas Odin and Dubuis, like the Franciscans before them, had begun their priesthood with a definite missionary zeal for work on the frontier, Manucy's entire priestly experience before coming to Texas had been in parishes of small cities where at least the rudimentary comforts of nineteenth-century life were the rule and not the exception. At St. Mary-of-the-Barrens, Odin's life among the frontiersmen had been an apprenticeship for his work in Texas, whereas Manucy's preparation for Texas had been twenty-four years of service in comfortable city parishes. That coupled with his own inner prejudices led to discontent.

In 1884 Manucy was appointed bishop of Mobile but retained jurisdiction over the Brownsville vicariate. On his departure for Mobile, he appointed Claude Jaillet, the missionary at San Diego, as vicar-general and administrator of the vicariate *ex officio sed non in titulo*–that is, the actual administrator on the scene, but without the title "administrator." By this time, Manucy was in ill health, and Mobile, with grave financial problems, was not what he had hoped–or rather, perhaps, as he had remembered it. He resigned his new see that same year and actually requested to return to his old vicariate. The Vatican agreed, but Manucy died in Mobile on December 4, 1885, without ever returning to Texas.[22]

Jaillet was reappointed administrator of the vicariate following Manucy's death by Archbishop Francis X. Leray of New Orleans. Leray first offered the position to the Oblate priest Pierre Parisot, who requested that Jaillet be reappointed. In 1887 Bishop Neraz of San Antonio was given the added duty of administrator of the vicariate. Little changed for Jaillet, however, since Neraz made him vicar-general with powers of administration, just as Manucy had done. Jaillet remained in this position until 1890 when a new vicar apostolic was appointed for Brownsville.[23]

Jaillet was well suited to his new responsibilities during these years, for obviously he was no stranger to the realities of life in South Texas. For years his diet had been that of the vast majority of the people: tortillas, the round flat bread made of finely ground corn flour, and frijoles (beans), with coffee when available. The difficulties of travel through the mesquite thickets, devoid of ample water, had been his almost daily companions during the years he traveled alone from ranch to ranch. To him and to every priest in the vicariate the story of the Oblate father Pierre Yves Keralum was a familiar one. This priest after twenty years service in South Texas had disappeared on his way to visit a ranch on November 12, 1872. It was ten years before his remains were discovered in a mesquite thicket by vaqueros searching for stray calves. He had lost his way and died of hunger and exposure.[24]

Once the same fate almost happened to Jaillet. Losing his bearings in the brush country, he wandered aimlessly for several days without food and water. Finally, he discovered a mudhole whose murky water saved him.[25]

Jaillet had to combine his new duties as administrator with his duties as pastor of St. Patrick's Church in Corpus Christi. Previously, under Bishop Manucy's direction, a new church had been erected there to replace the adobe structure built in 1854. Mistakes had been made in its construction, however, and Jaillet was burdened with having to launch extensive repairs: the brick foundations for the interior support pillars were only two or three inches deep, causing the center of the church to sink several inches; and the original tin roof, exposed to the seacoast environment, had rusted through in many places allowing the rain to enter "as through a sieve."[26]

With the appointment of Bishop Neraz of San Antonio as administrator of the vicariate in 1887, nothing really changed for Jaillet since the day-to-day administration remained his responsibility as vicar-general. Neraz visited the vicariate to administer confirmation in both 1887 and 1888.[27]

For an area containing so many Catholics, it was indeed unfortunate that no chief pastor resided there for slightly over half a decade. The reasons for this are unclear. The area's first and thus far only resident vicar apostolic had not really wanted to be there, and the vicariate's tenuous circumstances were now only compounded by this protracted vacancy. It speaks well of the priests, laity, and religious of the vicariate of Brownsville that matters progressed as well as they did.

In a summary by Jaillet in January, 1888, Brownsville, Rio Grande City, Roma, Laredo, San Diego, Corpus Christi, San Patricio, Aransas, Papalote, Lamar, and Refugio are cited as the main centers of Catholic activity. Areas around each of these centers comprised a "mission." Missionary responsibility at Brownsville extended throughout Cameron County and into half of Hidalgo County. At that time seven Oblate fathers were in charge of Brownsville and about two hundred ranches within an adjacent area about 40 miles wide and 150 miles long. There were about eighteen thousand Catholics in this mission alone. Father Parisot headed the Oblates who worked in the Brownsville mission at that time. The Sisters of the Incarnate Word and Blessed Sacrament had by then been in Brownsville for over thirty years and continued to operate the second oldest school for girls in Texas. The major church edifice of this mission was, of course, the Church of the Immaculate Conception in Brownsville. In addition, there were six chapels located in various villages and ranches of the mission. In most places, masses were celebrated in homes or other buildings.

Upriver and adjacent to the Brownsville mission was that of Rio Grande City, also staffed by the Oblates, which consisted of the western half of Hidalgo County and the eastern half of Starr County. The western half of Starr County and all of Zapata County made up the mission of Roma upriver from Rio Grande City. It also was under the care of the Oblates.

There was a well-proportioned church in Laredo, as well as the Ursuline convent and girls' academy administered by sixteen sisters. About six thousand Catholics lived in the Laredo parish and mission, which included Webb County, out of a total population of approximately seven thousand. By 1888 the territory of the mission of San Diego, once so large it took a month or more for the priest to visit it all, consisted only of Duval County and three-quarters of Nueces County. The priest now had a five-room house, and three new chapels were in use in various parts of the mission. There were between six and seven thousand Catholics in this mission.

In Corpus Christi, the Catholic population was about fifteen hundred.

In addition to the new St. Patrick's Church, the one Jaillet had had to repair, a new convent and academy for girls had been built by the Sisters of the Incarnate Word and Blessed Sacrament in 1885. In 1888, at the request of Jaillet, these sisters opened St. Joseph's school for boys.[28]

In the area north of the Nueces River containing San Patricio, Bee, Refugio, Goliad, and Aransas counties, which had been added to the vicariate at the request of Bishop Manucy in 1877, four missions were now functioning that in contrast to the other missions were composed virtually entirely of Anglos. These were San Patricio, which also included Garrettville; Aransas and Papalote; and Refugio, which also included the old mission at La Bahía. Church buildings were in use at each of these places.[29]

In 1890 Fr. Pedro Verdaquer de Prat, pastor of the Church of Our Lady of the Angels in Los Angeles, California, was named the next vicar apostolic of Brownsville. Born in Torello, Spain, in 1835, Verdaquer had come to the United States as a young man and had been ordained in San Francisco in 1862. For a time he worked among the Indians of the West Coast. Verdaquer was in Europe at the time of his appointment and was consecrated a bishop in Barcelona on November 9, 1890.

Recognizing the need for Spanish-speaking priests, Verdaquer visited several Spanish seminaries in late 1890 and early 1891 to recruit volunteers for the vicariate. In company with six seminarians, Fernando Caballero, Benedict Donado, Ramón Monclus, Luis Plana, Michael Puig, and Amelio Ylla, the new bishop set out from Barcelona in the spring of 1891. On arriving in the United States, the seminarians were sent to the seminary in Cape Girardeau, Missouri, to continue their studies. Later they transferred to St. Joseph Seminary in Victoria.

On May 21, 1891, Verdaquer formally assumed the administration of the vicariate. Since Laredo was a larger city than Corpus Christi and also closer to the heart of the Catholic population centered along the Rio Grande, Bishop Verdaquer moved his headquarters there in August of 1892.

Like Odin and Dubuis, Verdaquer was a missionary. He accepted the challenge life in South Texas offered, and he used this challenge to attract priests who, like himself, were missionaries. To one applicant he wrote, "[If you are] willing to submit yourself to a poor mission life, in my most poor Vicariate, you may come. . . . even in Laredo the best Parish, the Priest cannot have a regular monthly salary, some months they get ten dollars, some eight, some five, but never . . . more than ten."[30]

Pedro Verdaquer administered the vicariate for twenty years. His long tenure provided a stability the vicariate needed, to experience the kind of development its sizable Catholic population required. In Laredo three more parishes were established during this period, as well as St. Peter's parochial school and the Academy of Our Lady of Guadalupe, both administered by the Ursulines.

The Rt. Rev. Pedro Verdaquer, vicar of Brownsville, 1890–1911. Photo circa 1900, courtesy Catholic Archives of Texas, Austin.

Our Lady of Guadalupe Church, Laredo, circa 1900.
Courtesy Catholic Archives of Texas, Austin.

An orphan's home was opened in Laredo in 1907 by the Servants of the Sacred Heart of Jesus and of the Poor, an order founded in Mexico in 1885 by Fray José María Yermony Parres as a means of alleviating the desperate plight of street children.[31]

The Sisters of Mercy, both a teaching and a nursing order, first began work in the vicariate at Refugio in 1875. In 1894 at the encouragement of Verdaquer, they moved to Laredo to begin work that led to the establishment of Mercy Hospital.[32]

Shortly after the turn of the century, Bishop Verdaquer was given land and a hospital building in Corpus Christi recently constructed from funds donated by the citizens. He invited the Sisters of Charity of the Incarnate Word in San Antonio to take charge of the project, and on July 26, 1905, Verdaquer blessed Spohn Hospital, named for the doctor who donated the land.[33]

During Verdaquer's tenure new parishes with resident pastors were established in Alice, Goliad, Kingsville, Mercedes, Mission, Riviera, Rockport, San Benito, and Skidmore. A number of missions, some with chapels, were opened and attached to these parishes.[34]

At the end of the century, at the midpoint of Verdaquer's tenure, the vicariate of Brownsville had a Catholic population of about sixty-three thousand, which made it second in size to the diocese of San Antonio. The vicariate had only twenty-two priests to serve this vast number. For this to be accomplished in even the remotest way, priests almost constantly had to be on the move, and Verdaquer was no exception. As he toured the ranches of his vicariate, Verdaquer emphasized preaching, believing that the people wanted not just to see their bishop but to hear him as well. Many evidently responded well to this and to him personally; those in Laredo, who knew him best, called him simply "Padre Pedro." Verdaquer continued traveling throughout his vicariate, often on horseback, throughout his long tenure.[35]

ELEVEN

Changing the Guard in Galveston

WHILE the division of the diocese of Galveston in 1874 provided Bishop Dubuis with a much smaller territory to oversee, this was true only in a comparative sense. The diocese still included most of Central Texas, all of East Texas from Galveston to Texarkana, and all of North Texas from Texarkana to the Panhandle. It was still too big, particularly for a bishop whose health had begun to fail. Rheumatoid arthritis would plague Dubuis from now until the end of his life. Even with rail transportation a reality over more and more of his diocese, it was increasingly difficult for the veteran missionary to accomplish the visitations his diocese required. Furthermore, Dubuis began to spend more time in Europe, where he believed the climate made his disease easier to bear.[1]

Change was needed in the diocesan administration, but unfortunately the right changes did not occur for several years. Consequently, the diocese of Galveston began to attain the reputation of being rife with unrest and clerical bickering, to the extent that the reputation of the Catholic church itself was damaged among the general public, particularly within the city of Galveston.

In 1878, at the request of Bishop Dubuis, Rome appointed a coadjutor bishop for the diocese, with the right of succession. This was Bp. Pierre Dufal, the former vicar apostolic of Eastern Bengal in India. Dufal was then fifty-five years old. Born in France in 1822, he joined the Congregation of the Holy Cross and was ordained a priest in 1852. Dufal was consecrated a bishop eight years later in 1860 and was made the vicar apostolic of Eastern Bengal, where he had served since 1858. In 1866 he returned to France to become superior general of the Congregation of the Holy Cross. Two years later, he resigned to assume his former position in India but did not return there until after the First Vatican Council.[2]

Dufal, with eighteen years of experience as a bishop, might have been just what the diocese needed. But it was not to be. Dubuis no doubt was glad to have the assistance of another bishop, but it probably irritated him when the new coadjutor bishop asked to be consulted in the decision-making process. After all, for over fifteen years Dubuis had been the only master on board the diocesan ship.[3]

By March, 1879, Dufal was already considering resigning. Dubuis was then preparing to leave Texas again for Europe. On March 5 he gave Dufal power of attorney to transact business during his absence, and some of his comments hinted that he did not plan to return. Unless Dubuis changed his mind, Dufal would thenceforth be bishop in fact. But Dufal was on the verge of seeking a way out of his still-new situation even as Dubuis was leaving for Europe. He was dissatisfied with the way the diocese was being administered and wondered whether it would be possible to change things without great difficulty. Those who saw nothing wrong with the status quo would resent efforts to effect change and would become a continuing source of opposition to Dufal. And, of course, Dufal realized that Dubuis might return after all.[4]

Dubuis was hardly out of the diocese before Dufal decided to submit his resignation to Rome. During the months he awaited Rome's response, he continued to administer the diocese. A pastoral letter to the diocese announcing Pope Leo XIII's jubilee on the anniversary of his election was issued in March, followed in June by a directive to all diocesan clergy regarding special collections, wedding dispensations, and the wearing of the clerical collar in public.[5]

In December, 1879, the Vatican wrote Dufal informing him of the acceptance of his resignation. Dubuis in France was simultaneously advised of Dufal's resignation and asked to offer suggestions for the future of the Galveston diocese.[6]

On January 20, 1880, Dufal, citing "the interest of the diocese and . . . my poor health," officially announced his resignation.[7] According to instructions he had received, he issued with this announcement a statement that Dubuis, presumably until his own return to Galveston, was appointing the vicar general, Theodore Buffard, as administrator of the diocese. Dufal's own authority ended immediately, and he left Galveston in early February. From 1883 to 1888 Dufal served as procurator general of the Congregation of the Holy Cross in Rome. Retiring in 1888 to the congregation's motherhouse at Ste. Croix de Neuilly-sur-Seine, he lived there until his death ten years later.[8]

Bishop Dubuis returned to Texas following Dufal's departure. During this last visit to Texas, he ordained four men to the priesthood in St. Mary's Cathedral: two on November 21, 1880, and two others on January 30, 1881.[9] But Dubuis did not intend to remain in Texas and probably would not have returned at all but for Dufal's resignation. A document conveying his power of attorney to the diocesan chancellor, Louis Chaland, was drawn up in Galveston in April, 1881, enabling him to conduct business and sign contracts in the name of the bishop.[10] Dubuis then went to San Antonio to attend on May 8 the consecration of Bishop Neraz.[11] The next day he addressed a circular letter to the clergy of his diocese announcing his immi-

The Rt. Rev. Claude Marie Dubuis,
titular bishop of Galveston, in retirement in France, 1887.
Courtesy Catholic Archives of Texas, Austin.

nent departure for Rome and the reappointment of the vicar-general, Theodore Buffard, as the chief authority in the spiritual affairs of the diocese. He announced, however, that the chancellor, Louis Chaland, would be in charge of finances.[12] After arriving in Rome, Dubuis officially resigned the administration of his diocese on July 12, 1881, but retained his title.[13] This meant that jurisdiction over the diocese was permanently out of Dubuis's hands although he remained the titular bishop.

The Vatican now appointed the Reverend A. J. Meyer, C.M., as apostolic administrator of the diocese of Galveston.[14] Meyer, the president of the College of St. John the Baptist in New York City, was a Vincentian like Odin, and had he accepted the appointment, he would have been consecrated as a bishop. His appointment would have made him bishop of Galveston in every way but in name. Apparently Meyer did not reject his appointment immediately, for he sent word to Galveston that Buffard's authority conveyed by Dubuis was reaffirmed and that he should administer the diocese until Meyer's own arrival there.[15] Soon thereafter, however, Meyer asked the Vatican to withdraw his appointment. It may be that stories of dissension among the upper echelon of diocesan clergy were already current in the Catholic circles of New York City. Perhaps also Dubuis's long absences and Dufal's short tenure gave Meyer pause as he considered the appointment.

By the fall of 1881, it was known in Rome that another appointment would have to be made for the diocese of Galveston, and in mid-December the Very Reverend Nicholas A. Gallagher, vicar-general and former administrator of the diocese of Columbus, Ohio, was asked to become the administrator of the Galveston diocese.[16]

Meanwhile, conditions there were deteriorating further. Some of the diocesan clergy were chafing under what they considered Buffard's high-handed administration of the diocese, and Meyer's rejection of his appointment had only added to the tense, uncertain atmosphere. Some of the clergy held that Buffard's authority was now questionable since his original appointment had been made by Dubuis, who later had resigned all administrative authority, and reconfirmed by Meyer, who then had rejected his own appointment to the Galveston diocese. It was also argued that while Dubuis's original appointment had actually divided authority between Buffard and the chancellor, Louis Chaland, Buffard was now acting as administrator, a role envisioned only by Meyer.

The dissatisfied priests presented their case to the archbishop of New Orleans, Napoleon J. Perche, who on December 20, 1881, issued a long letter to both the clergy and laity of the diocese. In his letter, Perche completely set aside Dubuis's letter of May 9, 1881, and made it clear that until a new bishop arrived, all authority in the diocese flowed from his office as archbishop of the province of New Orleans. Perche then declared that Buffard was "the canonical, lawful and legitimate Vicar-General of the Diocese of

The Rt. Rev. Nicholas A. Gallagher,
administrator of the diocese of Galveston, 1882–92, and bishop, 1892–1918.
Photo circa 1882, courtesy Catholic Archives of Texas, Austin.

Galveston." Dubuis's chancellor, Louis Chaland, was also declared the legitimate chancellor. Perche appointed diocesan counselors to sit under the presidency of Buffard until the arrival of a new bishop. The effect of the letter was to clarify the chain of command in the diocese, but it did not remove the dissatisfaction some felt toward Buffard's conduct of diocesan affairs.

Buffard printed a cover letter entitled "Circular to the Clergy" that was distributed throughout the diocese along with the archbishop's letter. In his cover letter, Buffard stated that he had gone to New Orleans to present his case to the archbishop and that Perche's letter spoke for itself—which it clearly did.[17] Symbolic of the confusion was the fact that although Perche declared in his letter that Dubuis's authority ceased with his resignation, Buffard used Dubuis's seal on his cover letter.

Father Gallagher in Columbus soon became aware of Galveston's problems —even before receiving official notification from Rome of his appointment.

Bp. John Quinlan of Mobile was in Rome at the time of Gallagher's appointment in December, 1881. The subsecretary of the Propaganda, what is today known as the Congregation for the Evangelization of Peoples, visited Quinlan on Saturday, December 24, to tell him of the decision of the previous Monday appointing Gallagher to Galveston, since Quinlan's diocese was in the New Orleans province also. Quinlan wrote Gallagher the news of his appointment in a letter dated Monday, December 26, stating that the official appointment would not be mailed until later that week. Aware of the turmoil in the diocese of Galveston, Quinlan urged Gallagher to accept the appointment "like a man." To reassure Gallagher, Quinlan added, "I congratulate you on your appointment because I believe it to be an excellent one—this is no *blarney!* but my sincere conviction."[18]

Gallagher was soon to need all the reassurance he could get. In the opening weeks of January, a plethora of letters began arriving on his desk. The contents of them were disconcerting. Quinlan had hardly mailed his letter in Rome before word of Gallagher's appointment reached Galveston. Apparently someone in Rome cabled the message to the United States days before the papal decretals ever left Rome. The news reached Galveston by telegraph on Tuesday morning, December 27.[19] And before the day was out, Fr. Anthony M. Truchard, the president of St. Mary's University in Galveston, penned a letter to Gallagher leaving him no doubt about dissension among the Galveston clergy:

> Although a stranger to you, I take the liberty of addressing you today in order to humbly request you to come to us as soon as possible. Our dear Diocese has suffered so much and for so long a time for the want of a good head that now time is precious. The condition of affairs has grown of late from bad to worse. The present Vicar General has

brought religion into ridicule in the whole city. The Catholic population is so disgusted with his doings that, had the good news of your appointment been delayed a little longer, I fear that grave scandals would have occurred.[20]

Truchard went on to assure him that had he come to Galveston only two years before, he could have had "an easy task"; now he would "encounter some difficulties" but the "greatest number of priests" would support him.

During the first week of January, Gallagher received a letter from the archbishop of Cincinnati, William Henry Elder, his own metropolitan. Elder encouraged him to accept the appointment to "poor Galveston [which] has been long suffering from the bad health and absence of Bp. Dubuis."[21] A few days later, Elder received a communication from the pastor of St. Patrick's Church in Galveston, Fr. Jean Louis Bussant, who wrote that while the diocese of Galveston might "have a bad name," it was only because it had been without a bishop for so long. He feared these reports about the diocese might prevent Gallagher from accepting the appointment and implored Elder to use his influence to the contrary. Elder did exactly that, forwarding Bussant's letter to Gallagher with a cover letter assuring Gallagher that should he refuse or even delay his acceptance of the appointment, he would take on his conscience the responsibility "for the evils that follow."[22]

If by now Gallagher did not understand why Bishop Quinlan referred to the appointment as one he should accept "like a man," he soon would. The prominent Catholic paper *Freeman's Journal,* published in New York City, carried at this time an article on the ills of the Galveston diocese.[23] Its lay editor, James Alphonsus McMaster, always at home with controversy, now took upon himself the role of confidential advisor to Gallagher, even though he was a total stranger. This was not odd conduct for the strong-willed editor: because of his anti-abolitionist views during the Civil War, a conflict in which freedom of the press was narrowly interpreted, he had personally attacked Pres. Abraham Lincoln, and as a result had had his paper closed for eleven months and had spent some of this time in prison. He clashed with his bishop over Irish politics and quarreled with the prominent Catholic intellectual Orestes Brownson over philosophy, so to publicly and privately enter the controversy over conditions in the Galveston diocese was a relatively small matter for McMaster.[24]

McMaster's correspondence with Gallagher in early January highlights the fact that although by then Gallagher's appointment was common knowledge, no one on this side of the Atlantic, including the appointee, knew the exact nature of the appointment. McMaster was certain that it was a clear-cut appointment as bishop of Galveston. Yet the diocesan vicar-general, Buffard, had referred to Dubuis as "titular bishop" in his recent circular letter to the clergy. The New Orleans archdiocesan newspaper did the same thing. McMaster informed Gallagher that the confusion probably resulted from Meyer's appointment and hasty resignation before he ever took the office.[25] Later in the month, when the papal decrees finally reached Gallagher, it was made clear that while he was to be elevated to the rank of bishop, he was to be the "administrator" of the diocese of Galveston. Dubuis in retirement in France was to retain the title "bishop of Galveston." As administrator, however, Gallagher was to be the chief authority in the diocese, governing it in every way as if he had the title the Vatican had allowed Dubuis to retain. Yet the confusion over the exact nature of Gallagher's new position, aided and abetted by a segment of the Catholic press, only heightened his apprehension over the assignment to Galveston. There was no doubt some disappointment over not receiving the title "bishop of Galveston," if for no other reason than a fear that without it the confusion in the diocese might be harder to dispel.

Certainly Gallagher's awareness of the diocese's internal administrative problems increased almost daily during January. McMaster wrote again on the seventh to inform Gallagher further of the troubles he was about to face.[26]

In the second week of January, Gallagher, still unaware of the precise nature of his appointment to Galveston, received a disturbing letter from the diocesan chancellor, Louis Chaland, which not only made the same charge against the vicar-general as Truchard had made in his letter of December 27, but made it obvious there was deep hostility between the diocesan chancellor and the vicar-general, the two highest officials in the diocesan administration. After outlining the problems resulting from Dubuis's "insomnia, nervousness and acute rheumatism," then Dufal's resignation and the episode with Meyer, Chaland wrote: Now, we have had and have for Vicar General a priest—the Very Rev. Father Buffard who by his authoritative ways and by his unreasonable denunciations from the pulpit, etc., etc., has brought things to such a critical condition that he is the object of severe criticisms and even ridicule in many of the best Catholic families in Galveston."[27] In spite of this the chancellor urged Gallagher to accept the post, assuring him "that all is not lost, nor is the difficulty insurmountable. On the contrary, I believe that after your arrival—which I hope in the Lord will be in a few weeks—all things will right themselves again with both priests and laity." The financial conditions of the diocese, he wrote, were sound.

It was perhaps some small comfort to Gallagher that, simultaneously with Chaland's letter, another arrived from the vicar-general, Theodore Buffard, also urging him to accept the appointment to Galveston. Buffard sent along a copy of his recent circular letter to the diocese and wrote that Gallagher should not be apprehensive about coming because of the dissension in the diocese, a dissension he explained as follows: "Rome was so long before speaking that a few priests questioned whether there was any authority; and the

Metropolitan of the Province had to . . . decide the question, as your Lordship will see it by the Circular which I enclose."[28] Buffard also urged Gallagher to be consecrated a bishop in Galveston and not in Columbus: it would be "the greatest spectacle ever witnessed in Galveston, and you would be more and more endeared to your people." Gallagher would take this advice, hoping that a grand occasion might serve as a rallying point for the sense of unity that his new diocesan administration so drastically needed.

Soon after Buffard's letter, another communication arrived in Columbus from Truchard, further impugning the behavior of the vicar-general.[29] This letter was an answer to Gallagher's request for more information about the situation in Galveston. Truchard's account was essentially what McMaster in New York had conveyed to Columbus, and Gallagher's subsequent action regarding Buffard indicates that he found it to be accurate. As Truchard described it, the trouble began soon after Dubuis's departure. Dubuis had appointed Buffard as vicar-general with authority over spiritual affairs and had made Louis Chaland chancellor with authority over the temporal affairs of the diocese. According to Dubuis at the time, no changes in clerical appointments were to be made without his permission—apparently to be obtained from him in Europe. However, Dubuis resigned the administration of the diocese upon arrival in Rome. Father Meyer was then appointed to the diocese and apparently wrote Buffard that he was to administer the diocese until his arrival—which, of course, never occurred. In the meantime, Buffard removed Fr. Pierre Chandy as chaplain to St. Mary's Infirmary in Galveston without either publishing Meyer's letter or consulting with the diocesan counselors. Chandy complained to Archbishop Napoleon J. Perche in New Orleans who reinstated him in his position at the hospital, whereupon Buffard went to New Orleans and apparently showed Perche proof that Meyer indeed had conveyed to him the powers of administrator of the diocese. At this point, Perche issued his circular letter of December 20, 1881, in effect confirming Buffard both as vicar-general and administrator of the diocese until a new bishop was named.

The situation was further confused when Perche changed the composition of the diocesan counselors on Buffard's advice but subsequently reversed the action.

At some point during the early weeks of 1882, Gallagher must have also heard Buffard's side of the story. His version is contained in a letter dated February 9, to Bp. Francis X. Leray of Natchitoches and coadjutor to Archbishop Perche of New Orleans.[30] From Buffard we learn that the sisters at St. Mary's Infirmary refused to accept his appointee as their chaplain and sent a delegation to Perche in New Orleans seeking redress. The archbishop's response was to replace Buffard's appointee with the priest the sisters had requested. Buffard refused to accept Perche's decision, but the new chaplain took up his duties anyway. Furthermore, several priests, some of whom were members of the diocesan priests' council, sent complaints to Perche; their complaints were related both to Buffard's appointment of a new chaplain for the hospital sisters and to changes in composition of the council. Buffard considered this a "rebellion," the leader of which in his view was Fr. Louis Bussant, pastor of Galveston's St. Patrick's Church. Buffard indicated that he believed a protest to Rome was in order over what he considered Perche's meddling in Galveston's diocese's affairs—that is, when the archbishop had acted on the side of the "rebels."

Gallagher's thoughts can easily be imagined as he struggled with the decision before him. Probably something McMaster had written about the diocese rang in his head: "so grand in promise and so wretched in fact."[31] Certainly Gallagher displayed fortitude when he accepted the appointment as administrator. As such, he was to be consecrated a bishop and possess the same authority over the diocese as if he possessed the title, a title that was to be retained by Dubuis until 1892. But as long as the authority was in his hands he believed he could handle the job.

Once he accepted the appointment, Gallagher wisely decided to visit Galveston almost immediately. He had to show both factions that there would soon be a bishop in Galveston again and settle once and for all the question of who possessed chief authority in the diocese. As he saw it, this could best be done in person: too many letters already had been written. Certain people needed to see the source of authority for the institution they served.

Rail travel allowed Gallagher to go from Columbus, Ohio, to Galveston in about two days. He arrived there near the end of February and met Buffard, Chaland, Bussant, Truchard, and the rest of the local clergy, as well as some of the laity and religious. Though he was yet to be consecrated a bishop, his authority as administrator of the diocese had commenced with his acceptance of the appointment. Therefore, before returning to Columbus, he sent a circular letter to all priests in the diocese stating what he had already told the chancery officials in Galveston. In this letter of March 3, Gallagher announced that he had assumed "entire jurisdiction over this Diocese." In his absence and "until otherwise ordered by us," all requests for marriage dispensations were to be directed to the vicar-general, Buffard. And this was all that was to be directed to the vicar-general. Chaland, the chancellor, was to continue to conduct the diocese's financial affairs in Gallagher's absence. As for anything else: "All other causes which on account of urgency cannot be deferred until our permanent abode amongst you, may be referred to us at Columbus, Ohio, until Easter."[32]

Gallagher's consecration as a bishop took place in St. Mary's Cathedral in Galveston on April 30, 1882. Although he was ill, Archbishop Perche came from New Orleans to act as chief consecrator, but he was so fatigued that his place was taken by Bp. Edward Fitzgerald of Little Rock. Bishop Neraz of San Antonio and Bishop Manucy, the vicar apostolic of Brownsville, served as co-consecrators. A seventy-five-piece orchestra accompanied the choir in a liturgy that lasted about five hours. The congregation filled the cathedral as well as the churchyard and surrounding streets.[33]

Soon a power of attorney affidavit signed by Dubuis arrived from France. Since diocesan property was held in Dubuis's name, such an affidavit was needed to give Gallagher complete authority over it.[34] Bishop Gallagher thenceforth was in every sense the chief ecclesiastical authority within the diocese of Galveston. Until he received the title "bishop of Galveston" in 1892, the Vatican gave him the title "bishop of Canopus and administrator of the diocese of Galveston." By making him "bishop of Canopus" the Vatican was fulfilling the traditional requirement that a bishop possess title to a see. Canopus was an ancient but defunct diocese.

At the time of his consecration, Gallagher was thirty-six years old. He was born on February 19, 1846, in Temperanceville, Belmont County, Ohio. His parents, John and Mary Gallagher, were born in Ireland but had lived in the United States from a very early age. When he was ten, his parents placed him in the care of Fr. J. M. Jacquet of Coshocton, Ohio, who for the next six years saw to the boy's education. In 1862 young Gallagher entered Mount St. Mary's Seminary of the West in Cincinnati. After completing his studies, he was ordained to the priesthood in Columbus, Ohio, in 1868.

Only three years out of seminary himself, Gallagher was appointed president of a new diocesan seminary in 1871. When lack of financial support forced this school to close in 1876, Gallagher became pastor of St. Patrick's Church in Columbus. He served there until the death of Bp. S. H. Rosecrans in 1878, when he became the administrator of the diocese. After the installation of a new bishop in 1880, Gallagher served as vicar-general until his appointment to Galveston.[35]

Gallagher moved carefully but decisively to end the factional infighting in Galveston. For a few months Buffard remained the vicar-general, but in 1883 he was sent to Denison in North Texas, an area he had once served in. Chaland remained chancellor for a time and served at the cathedral until 1884, when he returned to France. Chandy was reinstated by Gallagher as the chaplain for the sisters at St. Mary's Infirmary and remained there until 1883. For a time he served at the cathedral, but by 1884 he was in Jefferson. Fr. Louis Bussant, pastor of St. Patrick's Church, whom Buffard had considered the leader of the "rebellion" against him, remained as pastor there for several years. Truchard remained at St. Mary's University until 1884, when the Jesuits began administering the school and an Irish Jesuit succeeded him. For several years Gallagher seems to have had neither a vicar-general nor a chancellor; for the latter he relied on a board of judicial advisors, among whom in the late 1880s was Buffard's nemesis, Bussant. By 1893 there were no French priests left in the diocesan administration.[36]

This absence was in line with Gallagher's policy: that of bringing into the diocese clergy and religious for whom English was their native language. Gallagher was not particularly anti-French—as a youth he had had for his mentor a French priest, and he both read and understood this language—yet he appeared so to the French clergy and religious as increasingly he brought into the diocese either native-born American clergy and religious or at least those whose first language was English. Since most of the English-speaking foreign Catholics were in Ireland, and most English-speaking American Catholics were of Irish extraction, most of those Gallagher brought in came from these two groups. Since he was himself of Irish descent, the charge naturally arose that he favored the Irish, particularly as more and more of the French priests were allowed to retire to France.[37]

In line with his policy, Gallagher moved quickly to forbid the sisters at St. Mary's Infirmary from recruiting any additional candidates for their order from France. While the Sisters of the Incarnate Word and Blessed Sacrament in Brownsville, Victoria, and Houston had previously recruited candidates from Ireland to serve in their teaching order, the Galveston hospital sisters had not. In 1882, they had only one sister born in Ireland, Sr. M. Clare Malone, and another, Sr. M. Rose Cashin, born in Kentucky of Irish parents. While a few other sisters in the community were not French, the majority were, and the community's records were written in this language. Since most of the sisters were French, most of their contacts were in France and therefore most of their candidates came from there. The problem for them now was how to recruit in areas where they were largely unknown. Some Irish candidates did enter the community at the end of 1883, however, possibly through Gallagher's own efforts.[38]

When the community's elections were held in January, 1883, the bishop's influence was felt: Gallagher himself presided when the community met at St. Mary's Infirmary, and for the first time the record of the proceedings was kept in English, not French. As the historian of the order, Sr. Mary Loyola Hegarty, states, "The official act of election shows an almost total exclusion of the French sisters from office." Furthermore, when the sisters became deadlocked for three successive days over choosing a superior, the bishop made his own choice and insisted that the sisters approve—which they did.[39] The new superior was not French.

The bishop's choice as the new superior, Sister M. Augustine, was born Henrietta Edwards in 1855 in San Antonio and was the daughter of Canadian immigrants. Her final profession in the order had occurred only about thirteen months before her election as superior.

From 1883 until 1888, the bishop removed from the hospital sisters the care of St. Mary's Orphanage in Galveston and put it into the hands of the Sisters of Charity of the Incarnate Word, whose motherhouse was in San Antonio. The reason given was the Galveston community's lack of adequate personnel to administer the orphanage. However, the real reason was the bishop's view that the community lacked enough English-speaking sisters.[40]

The size of the Galveston community increased in the mid-1880s. In 1883 and 1884, five Irish candidates entered the community. 1884 also was the year Mother M. Augustine made her first recruiting trip, to Canada and New York. Two Irish from New York and seven Canadians returned with her to test their religious vocation. The superior was soon in correspondence with several Irish convents, and in October, 1885, three sisters arrived to join the community. In 1887 Mother M. Augustine went on a recruiting trip to Ireland and brought back nineteen postulants for the Galveston community. This growth enabled the community to extend its work: in 1887 the sisters began to operate St. Joseph's Infirmary in Houston, and in 1888 they returned to St. Mary's Orphanage in Galveston.[41]

Prior to his short visit to Galveston in late February of 1882, Gallagher visited the Dominican sisters of Sacred Heart Convent in Somerset, Ohio, and began to make arrangements for bringing a Dominican community to Galveston to open a school. The Dominican sisters arrived by train in Galveston in September, 1882. Bishop Gallagher accompanied them on the trip from Ohio. Their convent was a two-story residence at the corner of Sixteenth and Market streets that had also been the home of the Sisters of Mercy, who had until recently operated a school at the cathedral.[42]

The school building that Gallagher had arranged for was completed in time for the opening of the new Sacred Heart Academy on October 9, 1882. The student body then consisted of 20 girls and 11 boys; by Christmas this had increased to 250 girls and 100 boys. In 1884, boys over the age of twelve began attending a Jesuit school that opened in the city.

The course of instruction in the new Sacred Heart Academy was probably the same as that followed by the Dominicans in Ohio: "The plan of instruction in this Institution is the same as adopted in all leading Catholic schools. The solid essential branches of a thorough English education are taught in each department by the most competent teachers. The Sisters pay the strictest attention to the refinement of manner and personal neatness of their pupils."[43]

Life in Galveston during the mid-1880s was not easy for the Dominicans or for anyone else. A dengue fever epidemic struck the island in 1884; this mosquito-borne, flu-like disease caused illness throughout the general population, and at least one Ursuline sister and one Dominican died as a result.[44] And on November 15, 1885, much of the east end of Galveston was destroyed by a fire driven out of control by high winds. The Dominican convent remained unharmed, however, although just across the street the fire raged for many blocks in all directions.[45]

In 1887 the bishop asked the Dominicans to extend their work in Galveston by opening a school for black children. The Sisters of Mercy had begun a school for black children there in 1881, but it had been closed when these sisters left Galveston prior to the arrival of the Dominicans. Gallagher obtained a house at the corner of Twelfth Street and Avenue K in which the Dominicans opened Holy Rosary School with thirteen students in September, 1887. Over the next months, so many additional students began attending the sisters' school that the bishop arranged for the construction of larger facilities at the corner of Twenty-fifth Street and Avenue I. Holy Rosary School opened there in the fall of 1888 with an enrollment of over two hundred. On this same site, the bishop opened a parish for black Catholics, also called Holy Rosary, that same fall. The new parish was made a mission of the cathedral, and Gallagher served as its first pastor.[46]

Some in Galveston did not look kindly upon the Dominican sisters when they opened Holy Rosary School. Even before this, there had been some resentment at having a community of nuns from the North in Galveston. While an uncle of Mother Agnes Magevny, the superior of Sacred Heart Academy, had been a colonel in the 154th Tennessee Infantry, C.S.A., this was eclipsed by the fact that one of the community's members, Sr. Imelda Rosecrans, niece of the late bishop of Columbus, Ohio, was also the niece of a Union major general, William S. Rosecrans. Not all ex-Confederate citizens, of course, shared such prejudices. One ardent friend of the sisters put her view of General Rosecrans thusly: "We did not admire General Rosecrans . . . [only because] he wore a uniform we didn't like."[47] It also annoyed some within the diocese that the new bishop, who had brought this northern religious community to Galveston, was himself a northerner, and that two of his brothers had served in the Union army.[48]

The Ursuline community in Galveston, the oldest in the city and diocese, did not share the amicable relationship that the Dominicans had with the new bishop. Gallagher did not get on well with the Ursulines, and would not do so for many years. For one thing, the community was very "southern" in sympathy well into the 1880s: in 1885, for instance, Fr. Abram Joseph Ryan, the "poet-priest of the Confederacy" and a personal friend of Jefferson Davis, was an honored guest of the community and read aloud his then famous poem "The Conquered Banner," a valedictory to the "Lost Cause." However the bishop and these sisters may have differed over the Civil War, this was probably not the major cause of their problems. As in the bishop's relationship with the sisters at the infirmary, each associated the other with what each considered a different order of things. Gallagher equated the sisters with the years of Odin and Dubuis; the sisters equated the bishop with an administration that seemed opposed to all things French. Also, Gallagher could be very abrasive at times. Perhaps he did not intend to be, for he was a shy man, and shyness can produce what appears to be abrasiveness. The dissension at the onset of his administration, coupled with the fact that he did not yet possess the title "bishop of Galveston," may also have contributed to his authoritarian manner.[49]

In the late summer of 1882, Gallagher called on Mother St. Augustine, the superior of the Ursuline community. As the sisters recorded the interview, the bishop does not appear in the best of lights. After an exchange of greetings, Gallagher first announced that he did not entirely approve of the sisters' devotional regimen and that thenceforth the community could not have exposition of the Blessed Sacrament in their chapel without his express permission; and further that Benediction of the Blessed Sacrament would have to be held on different days from those it had previously been held on. As Mother St. Augustine recalled the interview, the bishop went on to say, "I am not acquainted with the rules of your Order. My relatives are among the Dominicans. But is not your Order originally a cloistered one? . . . [Yet] I see you have parochial schools in the city. This is not in accord with cloister. In my opinion, Sister, your Community would do well to resume its strict enclosure."[50]

In answer to the bishop's further inquiry, the superior assured him that the care of the schools had not interfered with the spiritual life of the community. "Monseigneur," she went on to say, "we undertook the work of the parochial schools at the direct request of . . . Bishop Dubuis, and with the written approbation of our Holy Father, the Pope." At this, the matter of the schools was apparently dropped.

In 1884, when several Jesuits came to begin Sacred Heart parish in Galveston, Gallagher informed the Ursulines that the Jesuits would also serve as chaplains to the Ursuline community and that the stipend paid for a chaplain would have to be increased to five hundred dollars. The sisters accepted this arrangement and got on well with the Jesuits. It was one of these priests who arranged for Father Ryan to visit the convent in 1885. Because of a ruling by their father-general in Rome, however, the Jesuits were no longer able to continue as chaplains to the sisters after September, 1886. The bishop told the community that since he had no one else to send as chaplain, he would serve in that capacity himself and would visit their chapel three days a week. For years the sisters had received Holy Communion frequently during the week, a practice frowned on by some nineteenth-century Catholics, and the bishop now informed the sisters they would have to receive the sacrament less often. This only worsened the estrangement between Gallagher and the Ursulines. After this difficulty, the superior went so far as to ask Rome for a "cardinal protector" for the Ursulines, a request that was eventually granted.[51]

The strained relationship with the bishop came to a head in the 1890s. On February 2, 1892, the feast of the Presentation, a feast of special importance to the Galveston community, the bishop informed the superior that the Galveston laity could no longer go to confession at the convent's exterior chapel nor attend mass there unless they were also active communicants of one of the local parishes. Gallagher believed that some of the laity used the chapel rather than becoming active in their local parish. Gallagher was unmoved when the superior objected that the exterior chapel had been erected for use by the laity in Bishop Dubuis's time. His ruling remained unchanged until the next year, when he informed the superior, "From henceforth, Reverend Mother, you must see to it that your exterior chapel is entirely closed to the public. You can have your chaplain, Father O'Connor, make the announcement tomorrow morning at Mass."[52] The next week, the bishop directed that all children's sodalities and other societies sponsored by the sisters must no longer meet in the chapel so that the members would be encouraged to attend their own parish churches. The superior, Mother Mary Joseph, informed the bishop she was writing her order's cardinal protector in Rome in a formal appeal against his action.[53]

In 1892 Gallagher received the title "bishop of Galveston" when it was relinquished by the aged Dubuis in France.[54] This action did not increase his authority, but it did provide added prestige since now Gallagher was administering the diocese in his own right rather than for somebody else too infirm and too distant to do so. The added prestige was helpful to Gallagher, since over the years he had displeased not only the Ursulines but others as well. The diocese had continued to grow and at least on the surface was doing well, but discontent was real.

Near the end of his diplomatic assignment, the apostolic delegate to the United States, Cardinal Francesco Satolli, announced he would tour several states in the South and West, and early in 1896 Gallagher invited Satolli to visit Galveston. In New Orleans, just before going to Galveston, he received a special-delivery letter from several Galveston laymen listing complaints against Bishop Gallagher's administration of the diocese.[55]

This communication is the first clear evidence that Satolli's visit to Galveston was to be anything other than pro forma, although the possibility that he was aware of frayed relations between the bishop and the Ursulines cannot be dismissed because of Mother Mary Joseph's appeal to Rome the previous February.[56]

Satolli arrived in Galveston by train at midday on Saturday, February 22. After a carriage procession to the cathedral, Satolli took the occasion of Washington's birthday to deliver an address in English, expressing his admiration for the United States and his hope that God would bless all Americans, Catholic and non-Catholic alike. This was in part an attempt to counter the activities of the fiercely anti-Catholic American Protective

Association, or A.P.A., which had stirred up resentment locally and nationally against having an apostolic delegate in the United States. Later that day the cardinal made calls at the Dominican convent, St. Mary's Infirmary, and St. Mary's Orphanage. Last of all he went to the Ursuline convent, where a short program was presented by the students of the academy.[57]

While the visit of the apostolic delegate to Galveston was certainly a highly significant event in the life of the diocesan church, the Ursuline sisters found even greater significance in the visit:

> Thank God! Yes, eternal thanks to our loving merciful God! The 'silver lining' of our cloud shone forth in all its splendor, Saturday evening, . . . when His Eminence, Cardinal Satolli, the Apostolic Delegate in America, entered our reception room. Never, perhaps, did human being receive a warmer welcome than we bestowed on our honored guest; for never did angel from high Heaven confer more heartfelt happiness than we experienced and which we treasure among our most hallowed remembrances.[58]

Satolli was accompanied during this and his other visits in the city by Bishop Gallagher. The sisters' Jesuit chaplain, whose sympathies seem to have been with the sisters in their conflict with the bishop, was also present at the Ursuline convent. When the guests visited the sisters' chapel, the chaplain suggested that they also visit the convent's exterior chapel on which so much of the controversy centered. As they entered this area, the chaplain said to Satolli, "Your Eminence, this part is closed to the public." The cardinal expressed admiration for the chapel's architecture, and then turned to Gallagher and said, "Look, Bishop, they have a double altar." The bishop made no response. The sisters saw favorable significance in the remark, and before leaving, Satolli promised he would celebrate mass in their chapel Monday morning.[59]

The next day, Sunday, Satolli celebrated a solemn pontifical mass at the cathedral with a choir accompanied by an orchestra. Various social events followed, concluding with dinner hosted by the Jesuits at the impressively large Sacred Heart Church. One of the guests was Rabbi Henry Cohen, who well into this century was one of the most revered religious figures in the state. The rabbi presented Satolli with a small book of quotations from the Talmud, and at the close of the meal, in an age not noted for ecumenism, Satolli asked the rabbi to offer a prayer. The meal closed with prayers in Hebrew, English, and Latin.[60]

True to his promise to Mother Mary Joseph, Satolli returned very early Monday morning to celebrate mass in the Ursuline chapel before his 7:30 departure for San Antonio.

During his Galveston visit Satolli approached Gallagher about the petition he had received in New Orleans. One of the grievances raised against the bishop was that he had closed the Ursulines' chapel to the laity. Gallagher was aware of the displeasure of some of the laity over this since in January, 1895, he too had received a petition to reopen the chapel. Satolli now made the same request, and Gallagher promised orally and in writing that the chapel would be reopened to the laity. Satolli went so far as to make this known to the Galveston laity before leaving the city. Satolli knew that his Monday morning celebration of mass in the Ursuline chapel was an obvious sign of his favor toward the position of the Ursulines and the laity on the use of this chapel, and to do this, he was willing to change his own schedule.[61]

Satolli and Gallagher also discussed the other complaints that had been made against the bishop: he caused priests to leave the diocese by his unkind treatment; he brought in priests of an arrogant temperament to replace them; both he and the newer priests came from a region where there was much prejudice against the people of the South; he addressed the laity in a peremptory manner; his interpretation and application of the rules regarding mixed marriages were too rigid; he made it too difficult to obtain a church burial; he treated the Ursulines in a spiteful manner; he had vastly increased the indebtedness of the diocese and of the cathedral parish; he had bought large tracts of "wild lands"; he had diverted funds for unwise investments; he took funds designated for one purpose and used them for other purposes; he had borrowed a large sum of money from the Sisters of Charity of the Incarnate Word that was not yet repaid; he had deprived the same community of an eight-thousand-dollar investment; and lastly, he had offended virtually all the adults in the diocese. An addendum to the list of grievances did say that the bishop had recently repaid to the nuns the borrowed money, but without interest.[62]

Satolli asked Gallagher to prepare a response to the charges, and the two agreed that the provincial archbishop, Francis Janssens of New Orleans, would conduct an investigation. Apparently during his train ride through western Texas en route to El Paso, Satolli wrote Janssens about the matter, and more extensive correspondence followed upon his return to Washington. The apostolic delegate put the matter entirely into Janssens's hands and promised his approval of whatever action the archbishop took to resolve the affair.[63]

Gallagher invited Janssens to visit Galveston in the course of his investigation, but this was declined out of concern that such a visit would only publicize the matter. Janssens advised the Galveston laity to be prepared to substantiate their charges as he proceeded with the investigation. The archbishop threw out the last charge in the petition—that Gallagher had offended every adult Catholic in the diocese—since it was obviously too vague to be taken seriously. He also concluded that some of the laity were looking back euphorically to Dubuis's administration, to the detriment of his successor. Even one of the petitioners, attorney J. Z. H. Scott, agreed that this was so. After the passage of a number of weeks and much correspondence between New Orleans and Galveston, Archbishop Janssens announced his findings: Gallagher did not force priests out of the diocese, although his cold and reserved manner may have encouraged some to leave; no evidence was found suggesting that the bishop brought abrasive priests into the diocese; the priests brought in by the bishop did not harbor sectional prejudices against the people of the diocese; the bishop did have difficulty understanding the people of the diocese, which had caused him to be too rigorous in regulating mixed marriages; there seemed to be nothing wrong with diocesan cemetery regulations; the bishop's conduct of diocesan finances was in order though he had acted unwisely when he increased the cathedral's debt; on matters of justice, the Sisters of Charity of the Incarnate Word had no real complaint, but they did want control of St. Mary's Orphanage returned to them; Gallagher seemed to favor the Dominicans sisters over the Ursulines; the bishop's reserved nature made him unpopular with both the laity and clergy.[64]

The charge about borrowing money from the Sisters of Charity of the Incarnate Word and denying other funds to them, Janssens found, was based on hearsay and misunderstanding of the facts. In a letter to Gallagher on May 6, Janssens wrote:

> With knowledge and consent of Mother Ausustine, you invested $3000 in land at Dallas for the purpose of an Infirmary, and $1500 in land in Galveston, on which stores were built; the former investment yields no revenue, and the other did not yield for some time; for which neither you nor anyone else is to be blamed; nor does the present Mother Superior complain about it,—but it seems that two Sisters *unauthorized* complained to some gentleman about this before the arrival of the Cardinal and so it was put in the list of charges.[65]

Similarly, it was found that no proof existed to indicate that the bishop had used a bequest to the orphanage of five thousand dollars (not eight thousand as alleged) for general diocesan expenses.[66]

For some time before the original list of charges was drawn up against the bishop, the Sisters of Charity of the Incarnate Word once again had lost full control over St. Mary's Orphanage. Janssens's advice to Gallagher on this point is contained in a letter of June 9, 1896:

> Sisters of asylums, in as far as I know, control everywhere their own affairs, or if not they, a Committee of gentlemen, with the Bishop or priest as President. You put yourself to much trouble and yet you satisfy neither the Sisters nor the public. Leaving it all in their hands, they will work much better and be more satisfied, the people will not have suspicions, will contribute better; and it will relieve you from

much anxiety. It is not good for a Bishop to enter into all the small details of administration, outside of that which especially belongs to his department.[67]

Obviously Janssens's advice in this letter extended to more than just the orphanage.

Gallagher's response was to organize a board of directors for the orphanage, consisting of Mother M. Benedict Kennedy, Thomas Goggan, Charles S. Ott, John A. Maurer, and Bernard Ganter, to which he turned over the orphanage's assets. This board agreed that the sisters would receive annual compensation for running the orphanage and, since the bishop wanted to relocate it, compensation for the sale of the old property. Although compensation for their years of maintenance of the property was soon forthcoming, the orphanage remained at the old site until the disastrous hurricane of 1900.[68]

Janssens's investigation resulted in his making several more recommendations to Bishop Gallagher. The Ursuline chapel, Gallagher was told, should be opened to use by the laity as in former times. Of course, the bishop had already assented to this while Satolli was in Galveston. Sometime after the cardinal's visit, Gallagher wrote Mother Mary Joseph to give his official permission for the reopening of the chapel to the laity: "Dear Reverend Mother: His Eminence, Cardinal Satolli, whom I promised, when he was here, to open your chapel, wishes me to do so without delay; and with his wish I glady comply. I am glad to have no further responsibility in the matter."[69] Gallagher was further advised to adopt a friendlier attitude toward the Ursulines.[70]

Over the years, Gallagher had served as both chaplain and confessor to the Dominicans, but Janssens advised him to appoint someone else to the position in order to avoid the appearance of showing favoritism to this particular order. Actually, several years before, some of the Dominicans themselves had sought to have another confessor available to them. With this recommendation the bishop was slower to comply, but in 1898 a new chaplain was appointed.[71]

Janssens also advised Gallagher to consult more with the diocesan consultors, especially in serious matters, and even while the investigation was in progress, Gallagher began to do so. Janssens also suggested that he try to overcome his cold, reserved nature and in this way become more open to both the laity and clergy. Again, the bishop exerted efforts to comply while the investigation was proceeding.[72] A related suggestion had especially happy results for the diocese of Galveston: the recommendation that the bishop appoint to the rectorship of St. Mary's Cathedral a priest who would work well with both the bishop and the cathedral laity and who possessed the financial acumen to reduce the cathedral's indebtedness. Gallagher's response was to appoint in August, 1896, Fr. James M. Kirwin, then studying at Catholic University of America in Washington, D.C., to this position. In his midtwenties, Kirwin had been ordained only a year. Like the bishop, he was a native of Ohio.[73]

To all appearances, Kirwin's appointment was an unlikely one, but a unique partnership resulted, one that lasted for the next twenty-two years and tended to compensate for Gallagher's reserved personality. The bishop and Kirwin, who in later years became the vicar-general, often went together for episcopal visitations. Gallagher performed the rites required of a bishop, and Kirwin usually delivered the sermon. On these public occasions, the two became so associated that whatever Gallagher lacked in manner was compensated in the warm, winsome ways of Father Kirwin. The public perception became that since Kirwin was warm and outgoing, then so must the bishop be also.[74]

If Gallagher showed himself "a man" in accepting the administration of the Galveston diocese fourteen years before, he did so again in what had to be one of the most difficult experiences of his life. Rather than circumventing the findings of Archbishop Janssens, he learned from this sobering experience and made genuine efforts to change conditions in the diocese. Perhaps the most telling of all, he was willing to share the attentions his office brought him with a priest whose personality traits were more winsome than his own. Until his death in 1918, whatever failings he possessed, to this important extent he was willing to put the interests of the diocese before his own ego.

The year 1900 found Galveston a growing port city, one of the four largest cities in Texas. The growth of the Catholic church there had matched that of the city in general. Some of the Catholic church buildings were among the architectural gems of the state, particularly the huge Sacred Heart Church and St. Patrick's with its lofty spire. There were about fifteen thousand Catholics in the city, and the estimated value of church-owned real estate on the island was about $1,001,900. Whatever difficulties Gallagher had in the early years of his administration, stagnation did not characterize church life and growth during this period. The year 1900, which began so well for the people of the diocesan see city, witnessed the worst natural disaster ever to befall Texas or the United States: the hurricane of September 8, 1900, killed possibly as many as six thousand people and destroyed many millions of dollars in property in Galveston and Southeast Texas. Many thousands of survivors were left homeless. About one thousand Catholics were numbered among the dead in Galveston, including ten Sisters of Charity of the Incarnate Word and ninety orphans of St. Mary's Orphanage.[75]

Despite the horrors of this disaster, the opening years of the new century would bode well for the future of Texas. The new oil industry bore signs of promise, and immigrants continued to arrive. Although Bishop Galla-

St. Joseph's Infirmary in Houston, 1887.
Courtesy Catholic Archives of Texas, Austin.

gher had long sought a native-born English-speaking clergy for his diocese, his hope was only partially fulfilled. Like his predecessors, he recruited many priests in Europe. In some ways this was fortunate, since Texas continued to be the destination of many non-English-speaking immigrants.[76] By 1900, the Galveston diocese, now confined to Southeast Texas and a portion of Central Texas, contained forty thousand Catholics in sixty-three churches served by sixty-four priests. The diocese was especially fortunate in having 320 sisters who staffed its twenty-eight parochial schools, seven girls' academies, and five hospitals. They far outnumbered the 11 brothers in the diocese who staffed three boys' schools. With the problems of the past behind them, the Catholics of the Galveston diocese stepped into the next century to meet its challenges with a renewed sense of unity and purpose. The once-resented bishop presided over his diocese for almost two more decades and grew increasingly beloved by his clergy and laity. Whether this was entirely the work of Monsignor Kirwin or not, for the long term good of the diocese it did not seem to matter.

TWELVE

Founding the Diocese of Dallas

O N July 15, 1890, Pope Leo XIII erected the new diocese of Dallas to consist of that part of Texas north and west of Lampasas, Coryell, McLennan, Freestone, Limestone, Anderson, Cherokee, Nacogdoches, and Shelby counties. This vast area included North Texas and the Panhandle and portions of El Paso County including the city of El Paso. Before this, all but the trans-Pecos portion had been in the diocese of Galveston. The city of El Paso had been part of the vicariate apostolic of Tucson since 1872.

Dallas, the new see city, began in 1846 as a small village, and in the early years, the small number of Catholics there were visited by the clergy of Nacogdoches, within whose parish they technically resided.[1] In 1873 the Houston and Texas Central Railway reached Dallas, connecting it with Houston and Galveston. This line had begun building prior to the Civil War but had gone no farther north than Millican, south of present-day Bryan, when the conflict brought construction to a stop. With the return of peace, construction began once more. After the line reached Dallas, another line was built north to the Red River at Denison where a connection was made with the Missouri, Kansas and Texas Railroad (Katy) which gave Dallas (and Texas) a rail connection with the north. Dallasites could receive a daily paper in the evening printed early the same day in Galveston, and they could read a two-day-old paper from Kansas City. For Texas in the 1870s this was nothing short of phenomenal.

With this kind of accessibility, Dallas became the unquestioned commercial center of North Texas and grew accordingly. In the 1880s, the Fort Worth and Denver, Texas and Pacific, and Santa Fe railroads gave Dallas and Fort Worth railway connections with California and every other major area of the country.

In 1872 the Catholic congregation in Dallas, reflecting the new wave of growth, was large enough to become a parish. Bishop Dubuis first sent Fr. Mathurin Pairier (or "Perrier") there to serve the new Sacred Heart parish, but the next year he was succeeded by Fr. Joseph Martiniere. For some years, Father Martiniere, like Pairier, had been visiting communities and army posts along the line of settlement. This was during the waning days of war-

Ursuline Convent nuns in Dallas, circa 1880.
Courtesy Catholic Archives of Texas, Austin.

fare between settlers and Indians on the Texas plains, and Martiniere narrowly missed death on several occasions. Once, after visiting the Catholics at Ft. Griffin, he came upon the mutilated bodies of travelers killed only minutes earlier.[2]

Martiniere was instrumental in arranging for a community of Ursulines to come to Dallas in January, 1874. Bishop Dubuis accompanied the sisters to Dallas, where they arrived on January 28, 1874.[3] They traveled by train from Galveston, a journey that not long before would have consumed weeks. After attending mass, the sisters went to their new convent only to find it "entirely empty, without a bed, chair, table or even a stove to keep out the January chill."[4] The sisters were given shelter by a local family, and in a few days their convent was furnished sufficiently for them to move in. They opened their school on February 2, 1874, making it the first Catholic school in the new diocese of Dallas.[5]

Although mass had been celebrated intermittently in the nearby town of Fort Worth since the 1860s by circuit-riding priests such as Fathers Pairier and Martiniere, it was in 1876 that the first parish, St. Stanislaus, opened there with a resident pastor, Fr. Thomas Loughrey. The parish's name was later changed to St. Patrick, today the cathedral of the Fort Worth diocese.

In 1885 the Sisters of St. Mary of Namur arrived in Fort Worth to open St. Ignatius Academy. Since the 1860s, this order had been operating a school in Waco. In the years ahead they founded two other schools in Fort Worth, two in Dallas, and one each in Denison, Sherman, and Wichita Falls. Also in 1885, ten Sisters of Charity of the Incarnate Word arrived from San Antonio to begin health care work in Fort Worth. They came at the invitation of the Texas and Pacific Railway Company to operate the hospital maintained there for their employees. When a fire broke out in the hospital that same year and the sisters singlehandedly rescued all the patients, they became the most heroic residents of the city. When in 1889 the railroad company decided to relocate its hospital facilities elsewhere, the sisters purchased the hospital from the company and founded St. Joseph's Hospital to serve the city.[6]

In 1889 Bishop Gallagher, the administrator of the diocese of Galveston, decided the time was more than ripe for a new division of the territory under his charge. Gallagher estimated that the Catholic population of the northern counties of Texas was fifteen thousand. There were now twenty-five churches in this area with about as many priests to work in them. The total population was estimated to be about one and a half million.[7]

At a meeting of the bishops of the province of New Orleans in March, 1890, Bishop Gallagher presented his case for establishing a Dallas-based diocese, and a petition to that effect was sent to Rome. In response the Vatican officially established the new diocese on July 15. The documents arrived in New Orleans and were forwarded by Archbishop Francis Janssens on August 16 to Bishop Gallagher in Galveston. Gallagher then convened a meeting of the priests of the new diocese and invited them to submit the names of three priests for consideration as their new bishop. From these nominees and some others offered by several provincial bishops, a smaller selection was made for submission to Rome at another bishops' meeting in New Orleans on October 1.[8]

Rome's decision fell upon the Reverend Thomas F. Brennan, the popular pastor of St. James's Church in Driftwood, Cameron County, Pennsylvania. Father Brennan was young to be a bishop, just thirty-seven years old. He was born in County Tipperary, Ireland. Brennan's father, James, was a classics teacher who earned his living as a private tutor. After James's death in 1865, Brennan came to the United States with his mother and brothers. He studied at St. Bonaventure's School in Allegheny, New York, then went to Europe in 1873 to study first in France and later at the University of Innsbruck, where he received a doctorate in divinity. Brennan was ordained to the priesthood in 1880 by the Prince-Bishop of Brixen, Austria, after which he spent a year studying canon law in Rome. Returning to the United States in 1881 to work in the diocese of Erie, he was assigned to assist his brother, James, who was then pastor of St. James's Church, Driftwood,

St. Joseph's Church in Marshall.
Church school boys with the Rev. Louis Granger, circa 1890.
Courtesy Catholic Archives of Texas, Austin.

Pennsylvania. The next year, he succeeded his brother as pastor and remained there until his appointment to the diocese of Dallas. During these years he went every fourth Sunday of the month to celebrate mass in a small church in the village of Bennezette, Pennsylvania.[9]

During his years as pastor of St. James's he visited Europe twice and North Africa at least once. In 1888 he acted as his bishop's delegate to Pope Leo XIII's jubilee and was made a monsignor at that time. It was on this occasion that he met the bishop of Natchez, Mississippi, Thomas Heslin. Heslin was so impressed with the energy, intelligence, and linguistic ability of Brennan that he nominated him for the new diocese of Dallas at the October, 1890, provincial bishops' meeting.[10]

On January 12, 1891, in answer to a letter from Bishop Gallagher, Brennan asked Gallagher to continue administering the new diocese until he could arrive on the scene himself. The letter was very solicitous and contained words that would later prove ironic: "I feel very happy to receive so good a letter from you. You will find me a very easy going man—no enthusiast. I will certainly need your assistance, at least in the beginning. The new diocese has been a portion of your solicitude for a long time and therefore I will be glad to go under your instructions for some time."[11]

On April 5, 1891, Brennan was consecrated a bishop in the cathedral in

The Rt. Rev. Thomas Francis Brennan, first bishop of Dallas, 1891–92.
Courtesy Catholic Archives of Texas, Austin.

Erie, Pennsylvania.[12] He arrived in Dallas in late April and, just as Bishop Heslin had foreseen, began his administration with a great show of energy. Soon he had a Catholic newspaper in operation, the *Texas Catholic,* based in Dallas. He became popular wherever he went, with Catholic and non-Catholic alike.

At the time Brennan was appointed to the new diocese, a controversy was raging in the American Catholic church over the question of what came to be called "Americanism." The chief spokesman of this ideology, a minority viewpoint among American bishops at the time, was Archbishop John Ireland of St. Paul, Minnesota. Other supporters included Archbishop James Cardinal Gibbons of Baltimore; Bp. John L. Spalding of Peoria, Illinois; Bp. John Keane of Richmond, Virginia, who later became rector of Catholic University of America; and Fr. Denis O'Connell, rector of the North American College in Rome. And although his tenure was brief and his surviving words are few, the name of Thomas F. Brennan must also be included among these. Building on ideas previously enunciated by Orestes Brownson and Isaac Hecker, the founder of the Paulists—ideas that included a more active role for the laity in the church and the concept that a new age was dawning in which an America guided by Catholics would be the hope of the world—the Americanists held, as Archbishop Ireland put it, that "the Church must herself be new, adapting herself in manner of life and in method of action to the conditions of the new order, thus proving herself, while ever ancient, to be ever new, as truth from heaven it is and ever must be."[13] The American church historian Jay P. Dolan, in commenting on Americanism, has written that Ireland

> also believed that just as America was the hope of the world, Catholics were the hope of America. Their mission was "to make America Catholic" and thereby solve "for the Church universal the all-absorbing problems with which religion is confronted in the present age." This was Ireland's ultimate goal: to reform Roman Catholicism throughout the world; for Ireland, this meant Europe, and both the model and agent of reform would be American Catholicism. It was precisely this ambitious, international program that did in Ireland and his liberal colleagues.[14]

In 1899, the Vatican issued a papal condemnation of Americanism.

In a letter published in the diocese in February, 1892, commemorating the four hundredth anniversary of Columbus's first voyage to the New World, Brennan echoes Ireland:

> America is the world's greatest blessing, the human family's hope and salvation. Without Columbus there would have been no Washington; without Washington there had been no America as the human family

has and holds America today, the citadel and temple of man's freedom, independence and happiness. The Fathers of American liberty laid the foundations of the fairest and mightiest nation ever raised and built by the hand of God. God's greatest blessing to mankind since the coming of Christ was the discovery of America.[15]

In a Thanksgiving Day address on November 26, 1891, he assured his hearers that "America is the hope of the world, the grandest expression and most powerful exponent of human freedom that ever was or could be."[16]

In a letter of October 28, 1891, to the Catholic Truth Society of St. Paul, Minnesota, the new bishop of Dallas discussed the church and America. The society was so taken with the letter that they published it for distribution in pamphlet form. The secretary of the society wrote that the letter "rivals in zeal and enthusiasm the address of our own Archbishop Ireland." Brennan wrote:

> "The truth will make you free" addresses itself with peculiar force to every Catholic heart in the liberty blessed land of America where our holy religion has such noble opportunities for expansion and consolidation if sustained in her efforts to emancipate the masses from the shackles that ignorance, prejudice and passion would fain place on their intellectual advancement and moral improvement, and as a necessary consequence, their material welfare and prosperity.
>
> What God did for a wicked, superstitious, and inhuman pagan world, He will more readily do at our instance by our efforts and labors, our prayers and our sacrifices, for a nation so free from the vices, superstitions, and inhumanities that degrade, enslave and decimate so large a portion of the whole world. . . . Catholic truth has secured for America in four hundred years a greater and more solid advancement than the old world has in fourteen centuries achieved.[17]

Brennan could also be outspokenly eloquent in defense of social justice. To the editor of the Jewish newspaper *Hebrew Standard*, on the horrors of recent Jewish pogroms in Russia, Brennan wrote: "By ancestry, citizenship and principle, I am a resolute foe of racial and religious prejudice . . . no government can set at defiance the public opinion of the civilized world. . . . I must confess myself, to a deep, warm and abiding kindly feeling for your people which registers me as an uncompromising antagonist of the persecution of the Hebrew people and a hearty cooperator in any and every expression or movement of sympathy in their regard."[18]

Brennan seems to have moved frequently about his vast diocese. Railroads had become almost commonplace in Texas, and Brennan used them to the fullest. In December, 1891, the bishop wrote the Hispanic congregation in Tascosa in the Panhandle that he was sending Fr. Francisco Grau

Interior of old Sacred Heart Cathedral, Dallas, circa 1891.
Courtesy Catholic Archives of Texas, Austin.

y Cruz to lead a mission for them and prepare them for confirmation. Brennan wrote to the congregation in Spanish and later preached in that language when he visited Tascosa in the spring.

At Christmas, 1891, Brennan officiated in Sacred Heart Cathedral in Dallas at the midnight mass, again the next morning at the 7:00 and 8:00 masses, and a fourth time at 10:30. Using two different texts, he preached two different sermons, one at midnight, the other at 10:30. Having recently instituted the Forty Hours Eucharistic devotion in the diocese, he and Bp. John Joseph Hennessy of Wichita, Kansas, participated in the closing of this devotion at the cathedral in January, 1892.

In early March the bishop was in Dennison, where the front page of the March 5, 1892, *Denison Herald* described him as "one of America's foremost divines in every branch of human knowledge . . . as a theologian he is profound, luminous and accurate. . . . As a speaker, Bishop Brennan is clear, thoughtful and impressive . . . his audiences are completely under his sway. . . . He has placed the whole diocese under the happy influence of a gentle but firm and orderly government."[19] On March 7 he dedicated a new church at Pilot Point and preached in both German and English. One listener, recalling the bishop's impressive style, said that "for more than a half hour

[he] held his auditors spellbound by his fearless exposition and unanswerable vindication of Catholic doctrine and practice. The Bishop never once assumed the tone of apology or defense."[20]

By April 2 Brennan was in Waxahachie, where he traded the Catholic church building and land to the Methodists in exchange for fifteen hundred dollars cash and 4½ acres of land. From there he went to the coal mining town of Thurber west of Fort Worth to visit the Catholics among the newly arrived immigrant workers. There was no church in Thurber yet, so a hall was hired. Brennan heard confessions, celebrated mass, and preached in Italian, Polish, and English. He also selected a site for a church and cemetery.

After Thurber, Brennan went on to El Paso, where he arranged for several Sisters of Mercy to go to Dallas, and on April 16 he began a tour of the Panhandle. Returning to Dallas by way of Austin, he welcomed the Sisters of Mercy to Dallas and on April 30 gave into their care the Oak Cliff Orphanage. These sisters then opened St. Mary's Academy for girls, which they operated in conjunction with the orphanage.

During the first week of May, Brennan visited Muenster and then Windthorst, where he blessed the cornerstone for a new church. In both places he preached in German. On July 10, he and Archbishop Janssens officiated at the dedication of the new St. Patrick's Church in Fort Worth. On August 7 he was back in Waxahachie to bless a new church built on the land he had arranged for just four months before. The trip to Waxahachie occurred just as Brennan was preparing to go to Rome for an *ad limina* visit, the required periodic visit a bishop makes to Rome to report on conditions within his diocese.[21]

During 1891 and 1892 the bishop of Dallas was on the move outside his diocese as well as in. On September 8, 1891, at the invitation of his patron, Bishop Heslin of Natchez, Brennan participated there in the consecration of the vicar apostolic of Indian territory, Theophile Meerschert. In October he went to Corpus Christi to visit Bishop Verdaquer, vicar apostolic of Brownsville, and conferred with Bishop Neraz of San Antonio as he passed through that city.[22] On January 27, 1892, Brennan went to Cullman, Alabama, for the blessing of a new abbot at St. Bernhard's Benedictine Abbey; from there he went to Little Rock for the silver jubilee celebration of Bp. Edward Fitzgerald.[23] He was becoming known throughout the American Church. The *Catholic Journal* of Memphis described him as "one of the most scholarly and zealous prelates in America. For years he studied in the leading seminaries of Germany and France, always carrying off the honors of his class . . . he speaks German as fluently as a German, French like an educated Parisian, and Italian as correctly as English; as a linguist, he has few superiors, for he is a master of seven different languages and speaks all of them with fluency."[24]

On April 19, 1892, in a sermon delivered in St. Mary's Church (now Cathedral) in Austin, Brennan included a review of Texas history and its heroes. The April 20 *Austin Statesman* showered praise on the bishop for his words and style of delivery: "The Bishop rose to the highest pitch of eloquence in extolling her [Texas'] glories and the praise of those who bled for her."[25] Praise from the general population continued to pour in for the new, young Catholic bishop.

In his first year as bishop, the number of priests increased by eleven; four additional religious communities were brought into the diocese; new churches were built in twelve places: Texarkana, Forney, Pilot Point, Muenster, Windthorst, Lindsay, Wichita Falls, Clarendon, Fort Worth, Waxahachie, and Denton. Five of these were erected for new congregations.[26] This was an impressive record, even for a man of Brennan's intelligence, energy, and exceptional eloquence in an eloquent age. But in spite of his able performance, things began to go wrong, so wrong that before the passing of another year, Brennan would no longer be bishop of Dallas.

Brennan was plagued with financial problems from the start. Times were hard in Dallas in 1891–92, and Brennan was faced with significant outstanding debts. He managed to go ahead and open an orphanage in Oak Cliff under the direction of the Sisters of Mercy in spite of an outstanding debt of twenty-five hundred dollars. There was, however, a larger debt. On the eve of Brennan's arrival, Fr. Joseph Blum, as pastor of Sacred Heart Church in Dallas, had entered into a real estate purchase to provide a new site for the parish located on Ross Avenue. He had borrowed thirty thousand dollars and bought an entire block, planning to pay for it with proceeds from what he thought would be a quick sale of the old property on Bryan Street. This action was approved by Bishop Gallagher, who still administered the area at the time. Soon, however, there was no market for real estate in Dallas and little or no chance of selling the old property. It is sometimes alleged that the financial crisis epitomized by this Ross Avenue debt was what caused Brennan to resign his diocese while in Rome in the fall of 1892.[27] But a man of Brennan's resourcefulness was not likely to give up in the face of such difficulty alone. Soon after his arrival in Dallas in 1891, he transferred Blum from Dallas to Muenster and informed Gallagher that he was arranging for the debt to be refinanced, hoping this would save the situation.[28]

As money continued to be tight, however, Brennan's resentment grew over the thirty-thousand-dollar debt. Barely three months after arriving in Dallas in 1891, Brennan chastized Gallagher over the Ross Avenue property: "All would be pleasant with us were it not for that Ross Avenue deal. You should have never signed either of the notes for Father Blum. Very fine for Moroney [the creditor]–now, they seem to have little sympathy for you."[29] Both bishops now made counter financial claims on each other. Six months later Brennan, evidently exasperated, wrote to Gallagher again about his action while Dallas was under his administration:

As I am making out a list of the annual collections, please send me account of the collection on the first Sunday of Lent, for the Indians and Negroes. Also for Good Friday . . . Also please explain how Mr. Ketcham could be transferred to the Indian Territory after he had been payed for by Dallas as well as Galveston. Half of the students payed for by diocesan funds are also *demanded*. If you can write to Fr. Martiniere, [that] you payed $1000. for Dallas since the division; and if you could last summer demand that I should *assume immediately* the foolish bargain contracted by you [the Ross Avenue property]; if you take away $600. from old Fr. Moore and then send him to Ennis; if you hold all the rented property of the diocese and use all collections heretofore taken in, for Galveston and Houston; if you refuse the demands of Fr. Martiniere for orphans . . . and state there was an orphanage in Dallas before I came, while I payed more than $2000. to finish building it—not yet even having the deed of it, I justly protest.[30]

Whatever justification Brennan may or may not have had in these matters, this kind of letter was hardly the ideal way for the junior prelate in the province to present his case—at least that was the position of Archbishop Janssens in New Orleans, who later wrote Gallagher that "Bp. Brennan is an impudent letter writer. He has not the least idea of delicacy of sentiment."[31]

As the work of Fr. James I. Tucek indicates, there was yet another financial question facing the bishop. Needing collateral security on the diocesan debt, Brennan apparently listed the Ursulines' school and other property as belonging in his name to the diocese. Mother M. Evangelist, the Ursuline superior, became aware of this when a banker inquired of her if indeed this property belonged to the bishop. When she voiced her protest to the bishop, he at first responded that the decretals of the Council of Baltimore directed that the ownership of all schools in a diocese be in the bishop's name and that they further stated that the bishop was the guardian and superior of all other church property, meaning here any other property the Ursulines owned. Mother Evangelist replied that according to the constitution of her order, which only the Vatican could change, this was impossible. She suggested that the bishop discuss the matter with Archbishop Janssens in New Orleans. To this, she recorded, Brennan responded that he had only been joking. Mother Evangelist was not amused, however. After consulting with some of the clergy and her fellow religious, she wrote a letter to Rome in which she mentioned the "sufferings" of her community and asked that the Vatican protect it "from the dangers which threaten us."[32]

For several months during 1892, Brennan began to pursue the idea that the time had come for Texas to become a separate ecclesiastical province with its own archbishop. He concluded that Dallas, although the newest Texas diocese, was the ideal provincial see; in other words, in his view he was the obvious choice for first archbishop of this new province. Brennan even enlisted the support of Gov. James Stephen Hogg, who wrote in a letter to the Cardinal Prefect of the Propaganda on July 28, 1892: "As a citizen of Texas and its Executive, I feel desirous of seeing its progress acknowledged and its growth promoted by the governing bodies of various Christian churches. Hence, I would rejoice to see a Catholic Archbishop in the person of the Right Reverend Dr. Brennan named for this State."[33]

In spite of his interest in the Hispanic Catholics at Tascosa, Brennan opposed San Antonio being named the archepiscopal see on the grounds that the Texas Catholic church would become too "foreignized" since the provincial see to the east, New Orleans, was French, and that to the west, Santa Fe, was Hispanic. It should not be Galveston either, however, as he explained in another brash letter to Bishop Gallagher, written from Rome on September 20, 1892:

> The Holy Father, *motu proprio*, has ordered the Propaganda to ask the bishops of the N. O. province why Texas should not be made a separate province and what they may have against Dallas. As you are only adm. apost. [administrator apostolic] of Galveston, your see will scarcely be put in the field. Now I am sure, next to your own, Dallas is dearest. Please consider the matter without prejudice and with a view to the future and the great impetus it would give to advancement.[34]

That he should have the temerity to write such a letter to Gallagher is startling in the degree of imprudence and resentment it demonstrates on the part of its author. It also demonstrates something else: that Brennan had no intention of resigning his see because of the diocese's debts; after all, he hoped to be "archbishop of Dallas."[35]

Brennan arrived in Rome during the *ferragosto*, the summer holiday when offices close and many leave the city to escape the heat. Brennan decided to make a short visit to the Holy Land and was back in Rome by September 20.[36]

Faced with Brennan's proposal, Gallagher now began to push the prospect of the Galveston diocese as the new metropolitan see. Before writing Gallagher from Rome that September, however, Brennan had written along the same lines to Archbishop Janssens. In his letter to Janssens, Brennan stated that he had personally urged the Pope to establish the new province. Shortly after receiving Brennan's letter, Janssens received an official inquiry from Rome as to his views on the possibility of forming the dioceses in Texas into a separate province. Janssens told Gallagher that he responded thus:

> 1. I have no objection, but see no good in it for religion & that I wrote to the Bishops interested that each might give his own ideas to the Propaganda.

2. That San Antonio should be the See.
3. That the Archbp. & Bps. of this Province [New Orleans] believe they made a mistake when placing the name of Msgr. B[rennan] second on the list of Dallas & may the Lord preserve Texas from ever having him as its Archbp.[37]

While Janssens was indifferent to the idea of a new province, except that he thought San Antonio ought to become its see city if there should be one, he was not indifferent to the thought of Brennan as the archbishop. Rome had not mentioned Dallas in the inquiry, but Brennan had in his letter from Rome. To make certain this would not happen, Janssens took the occasion to inform Rome that he and the other bishops of the province (one wonders if this included Heslin) regretted that Brennan was a bishop at all. Janssens also urged Gallagher to write Rome at once on this matter.[38]

It was on October 6 that Janssens informed Gallagher that he had sent this strongly worded message to Rome. The letter was sent, then, in either early October or late September, and no doubt was in Rome a number of days before November 17, the accepted date of Brennan's resignation of his diocese. However, other material as well was sent to Rome during this period. Janssens wrote on October 13, "I have had so many, and such serious charges against him, that I have felt compelled in conscience to bring them to the notice of the Propaganda."[39] Among the charges brought against Brennan, if not the bulk of them, were those contained in a document sent to New Orleans by some of the Dallas clergy and signed by Fr. Joseph Blum, the priest who had initiated the large Dallas debt, whom Brennan had sent to Muenster. Exactly how many priests initiated the charges is unclear. The charges were twelve in number and may be summarized: the bishop is a tyrant who suspends his best priests and uses "spies" to intimidate them; he is given to fits of anger even while holding the Blessed Sacrament, and "many" fear that he might become violent; his language is "rude and scandalous"; he approves of non-Catholic schools; he maintains that some seek the office of bishop by unscrupulous means; he is extremely prideful; the diocesan newspaper was founded only to glorify the bishop and one of his favorites; he has too freely given dispensations for mixed marriages without regard to church requirements; he is untruthful; it "seems" that he is not always virtuous; he has lost the love of the laity, clergy, and religious.[40]

The basis of these charges is unclear. That some of the clergy were alienated from their bishop is evident. Certainly Blum was. But Brennan could not have alienated all of them or the vast majority of the laity. Brennan was Irish and many of his clergy were French, but Gallagher, the bishop with whom relations were most strained, was not. The charge that he approved of non-Catholic schools probably stemmed from the Americanists' support of Archbishop Ireland's concept under which Catholic students were taught nonreligious subjects at public expense, with catechism taught at church expense near the end of the school day. It is unknown whether Brennan went as far as did the bishop of Little Rock, Edward Fitzgerald, who was satisfied for children to attend public schools as long as they attended catechism classes in their churches. Like most Americanists, he may simply have opposed the virtual excommunication of parents who did not send their children to church schools, a measure favored by some bishops at the time. However this may be, the charges indicate that some of Brennan's clergy were out of step with him and that perhaps the often winsome bishop had allowed abrasiveness to take hold of his relationship with some of them, as he had with Gallagher.[41]

There is a strong possiblity that the charges against Brennan were received in New Orleans before he left the diocese for Rome.[42] Archbishop Janssens may even have been aware of unrest among some of the clergy when he went to Dallas in July, 1892, to attend the dedication of St. Patrick's Church in Fort Worth. Father Blum, who by then had been sent to Muenster, also attended.[43] Confronted with this mass of complaints and charges, including the letter of Mother Evangelist, Brennan resigned the diocese of Dallas on November 17, 1892.[44]

Whatever part Brennan's Americanism may or may not have played in his troubles in Texas, obviously it had no direct bearing on Rome's action, since Bp. Edward Fitzgerald of Little Rock was appointed the administrator of the diocese until a new bishop was selected. It was not long, however, before Joseph Blum was back at Sacred Heart in Dallas and serving as vicar-general of the diocese.[45]

But what of Bishop Brennan? One account indicates that he was sent to Newfoundland, where he remained until called to Rome in 1904.[46] This does not seem to be the case, however. What apparently transpired was the following. Brennan was sent to Newfoundland as assistant to Bp. Thomas Power. This diocese was immediately subject to Rome, with no intervening provincial structure to participate in a bishop's selection. Rome wanted to place Brennan somewhere, and here was a place that seemed appropriate. Power died in 1893. It is unclear whether or not Brennan briefly succeeded him, although the *Catholic Directory* for 1894 does list him as bishop of the diocese. This information, reflecting the situation at the end of 1893, may have emanated only from Brennan. If indeed he was appointed bishop, it was again not to last. His tenure in St. John's, Newfoundland, was brief indeed. In 1894, a new bishop, M. F. Howley, was consecrated for St. John's. According to information in the Catholic Archives of Texas gleaned by Fr. Paul J. Foik, C.S.C., chairman of the Knights of Columbus Texas Historical Commission in 1932, Brennan was removed from St. John's, Newfoundland, "for cause" and called to Rome shortly after Howland's arrival. The recent research of Fr. James I. Tucek confirms this chronology. If the "cause" resulted from anything other than the problems related to Dallas, this remains unknown. According to Tucek, records of the diocese of St. John's Newfoundland, do not indicate that Brennan was ever there. One contemporary in St. John's wrote of his departure that "he left and we never heard from him again until we heard that he was in Rome."⁴⁷

For a time Rome considered sending him to work in a college in Constantinople (Istanbul), the capital of the Turkish Empire, but this never transpired. After his recall to Rome in 1894, he resided at the Grotta Ferrata Monastery until his death on March 21, 1916.⁴⁸ During 1913 and 1914, a young student in Rome, Laurence J. FitzSimon, later the third bishop of Amarillo, saw Brennan several times at various functions at Castel Gandolfo, the papal summer residence, and other places in and near Rome.⁴⁹ His long residence at the Grotta Ferrata Monastery might imply that he was under some form of penance. Years after Brennan's death, an elderly monk recalled only that "he was a holy man."⁵⁰

Whatever sentiments his fellow bishops and priests may have held toward him, and however justified his removal from two dioceses may have been, there were those who for long years cherished the fact that they had known Thomas Francis Brennan. The Mulry family of Bennezette, Pennsylvania, were among these. John Mulry offered his home to Brennan when he came each fourth Sunday during the 1880s to celebrate mass at the small parish church there. The two became fast friends, and Brennan was well liked by Mulry's children. When Brennan went to Europe and North Africa in 1887–88, he wrote Mulry of his adventures, and there was at least occasional correspondence with Mulry while Brennan was living at Grotta Ferrata Monastery. Mulry always credited Brennan with being the agent for what he believed was a miraculous cure he received during the time Brennan was his pastor in Bennezette.⁵¹

Others too remembered him with high praise. On April 8, 1891, the newly appointed bishop of Dallas visited his alma mater, St. Bonaventure's College in Allegheny, New York. Forty-two years later, Fr. J. F. Dugan still clearly remembered Brennan's remarks on that occasion, as did others. According to Dugan, "His remarks . . . are the talk of the older priests to this day. In a word Brennan was always *it*."⁵²

The circumstances surrounding Brennan's departure might have been catastrophic for a diocese as young as Dallas. That it was not is due to three factors: first, of course, is the organizational genius of the Roman Catholic Church, which with a few notable exceptions has been able to keep the structure functioning for a very long time though personalities come and go; second, with Brennan gone, the unrest among the disaffected faction of the clergy either ceased or was at least reduced to an innocuous level; third, the quality of leadership provided the diocese in the critical years immediately following Brennan's resignation contributed to a quick and complete recovery from the crisis. The latter factor is related to the first: when faced with a crisis such as this, Rome's course was exceptionally prudent. While searching for a new bishop, instead of temporarily returning the administration of the diocese to Bishop Gallagher, who was more familiar with it than any other neighboring bishop, Rome put the diocese in the care of the bishop of Little Rock.[53] Considering what the relationship between Gallagher and Brennan had become and some of the particular problems that had produced this, it would have been awkward for both Gallagher and the diocese of Dallas to have brought them together again.

Needing time to consult with the New Orleans provincial bishops, Rome did not announce a new bishop for Dallas until October 22, 1893. The appointment went to the pastor of All Saints Church in Chicago, Fr. Edward Joseph Dunn. Like Brennan, Dunn was born in County Tipperary, Ireland. He was forty-five in 1893, several years older than Brennan. After studying at St. Mary's of the Lake Seminary in Chicago, he went on to St. Mary's Seminary in Baltimore, where he was ordained to the priesthood on June 29, 1871. While his education for the priesthood was good, it was somewhat prosaic compared to that of his predecessor in Dallas. Between the time of his ordination and his appointment to the diocese of Dallas, Dunn worked successfully for over twenty years as a parish priest in the Chicago diocese.

Dunn was consecrated a bishop in his Chicago parish church on November 30, 1893, and was formally instituted as diocesan bishop in Dallas on January 17, 1894, exactly fourteen months after Brennan's resignation in Rome.

Three months after his investiture as bishop of Dallas, Dunn began consultations with Father Blum, who was once more rector of Sacred Heart pro-Cathedral, over the construction of a new Cathedral. Soon ground was broken for this project on the property on Ross Avenue at Pearl Street that had been purchased in the "foolish deal" contracted by Blum and approved by Gallagher years before. In spite of Brennan's fears, the property had not been foreclosed on after all. Four years later, the large building was completed and the cornerstone laid.[54]

Bishop Dunn's administration as bishop lasted for sixteen years. In spite of the controversy centering around Brennan, his short tenure had been quite productive for the diocese, and Dunn built well on this foundation. The *Texas Catholic,* the newspaper Brennan had begun, continued as an important apologist for the Catholic cause in North Texas. Additional religious orders entered the diocese. The Benedictines from New Subiaco Abbey in Arkansas came to the diocese in 1893 while it was in the care of the bishop of Little Rock. These Benedictine priests came to staff the parishes of Muenster, Lindsay, Windthorst, and Rhineland in North Texas, and Nazareth in the Panhandle.[55]

In 1895 several Olivetan Benedictine sisters from their community in Jonesboro, Arkansas, came to Sacred Heart Church in Muenster at the invitation of its pastor. They took over operation of the small parochial school, which later grew to contain all twelve grades.[56]

In 1896 Bishop Dunn helped arrange for members of the Sisters of Charity of St. Vincent de Paul to open a hospital in Dallas. Sr. Bernard Riordan came from Mobile, Alabama, to be the first superior of the new nursing community. Ground was broken for the hospital in November, 1896, on a five-acre site, and Sister Riordan began the supervision of its construction. Before the facilities opened in June, 1898, the sisters cared for the sick as best they could in a small cottage. St. Paul's hospital, named for St. Vincent de Paul, opened with a capacity for 110 patients. Four years later a school for nursing opened at St. Paul's.[57]

Bishop Dunn obtained several Sisters of Charity of the Incarnate Word from their San Antonio community in 1900 to go to Amarillo to open a hospital there. This order already operated St. Joseph's Hospital in Fort Worth. The medical profession and general public in Amarillo had asked that a hospital be opened there by a Catholic nursing order. Two city blocks were donated, and a two-story brick building with a capacity for ten patients was erected. Construction began in the fall of 1900, and the hospital opened on March 28, 1901. Amarillo was not Fort Worth, Dallas, or San Antonio, and frontier conditions still prevailed in the Panhandle: there were no telephones, electric lights, or paved streets. The hospital was named for St. Anthony. When the cornerstone was laid, there was no resident priest in Amarillo, so the officiant was Fr. David H. Dunne, the pastor of St. Mary's Church in Clarendon, located to the east on the Fort Worth and Denver Railway. Father Dunne began to visit the sisters at the new hospital and a small Amarillo congregation one Sunday a month, and two years later he moved there to be the resident pastor and hospital chaplain.[58]

By the end of the century the ten-year-old diocese contained about twenty-four thousand Catholics served by forty-four priests. There were forty churches and fifty-four mission stations where mass was occasionally celebrated though no church buildings existed there.[59]

THIRTEEN

1900

As the century ended, Texas' population now numbered just above 3 million, of whom approximately 202,000 were Catholics living in four distinct jurisdictions. The Native Americans who had dominated the land at the century's beginning were virtually gone from the Texas scene. In one sphere change was less drastic: Hispanic Texans were still the largest single Catholic ethnic group and continued to be concentrated in areas now included in either the diocese of San Antonio or the vicariate apostolic of Brownsville. These Catholics, whose spiritual roots ran deep in Texas, could have been better served by the Texas church, particularly in the Brownsville area, where the failure in leadership during the 1870s and 1880s had not yet been overcome (see table). To an important extent, however, this was offset, first, by a laity whose culture in its very nature expressed Catholic customs and values, and second, by the selfless efforts of priests and men and women religious who worked along the Rio Grande.

By 1900 the frontier era was over, though actual living conditions for some Texans were little changed from a century before. For many others, life had changed and technology afforded a safer, easier, less hostile environment. The age just past had brought out the best and the worst in those who experienced it. Through much of the nineteenth century, whether along the Rio Grande or in the woods of East Texas, the fundamental task of survival demanded stubbornness, a strength of will almost incomprehensible to a later generation, and an encompassing courage that reached out for a different tomorrow even when experience indicated it would be only a repetition of the sufferings of today.

Problems existed and all was not success. Some of the French clergy who entered Texas after 1840 were more attuned to the log cabin culture of the American settler than to that of the majority of Catholics who were Hispanic. A significant number of these clergy both learned and adapted, but when the oversized diocese of Galveston was divided in the 1870s, not enough care and insight went into submitting appropriate candidates to Rome to head the jurisdiction formed along the Rio Grande, and harm resulted.

Nor was the Texas church immune to another kind of ethnic conflict occurring when a large number of Irish Americans rose in the hierarchical

Catholic Population, 1900

Diocese	Catholic Population	Ratio of Resident Parochial Priests to Laity	Ratio of All Priests Serving in Diocese to Laity
Brownsville (Vicariate Apostolic)	63,000	1:4500	1:2863.6
Dallas	24,000	1:750	1:545.5
Galveston	40,000	1:952	1:625
San Antonio	75,000	1:1829	1:1027.4

SOURCE: *The Catholic Directory for 1901* (statistics for 1900), pp. 253–56, 300–303, 494–98, 552–54.

ranks after the Civil War and began to replace an older generation often representative of other ethnic groups. While tensions were not uncommon between bishops and religious superiors, the situation became more acute with the added dimension of ethnic rivalry, particularly since the Irish Americans tended to assume that as they were native-English speakers in a predominantly English-speaking nation, their approach to leadership was somehow more appropriate than that of others.

The story told in the preceding chapters is not one of perfect people who always got it right but rather the story of men and women who strived, in spite of their weaknesses and prejudices, to dedicate themselves to eternal ideals in service to others. All in all, the Catholic church thrived in frontier Texas. Often poor, its people were nevertheless a hearty lot who took their faith seriously and flourished spiritually. And this was in large part due to the determined priests and religious who led the frontier church. Though not perfect, when viewed in the perspective of when and where they labored, they tend to put later generations to shame.

The story is told of one priest at midcentury who set out to visit his scattered and isolated parishioners but encountered an Indian war party who tied him up and threw him over the back of a horse. Thus bound and periodically beaten over a space of six hours, he traveled with his captors over thirty miles of rough terrain to an encampment. On the verge of passing out, the priest managed to regain his composure and with great bravado was able to talk his way out of certain death.[1]

Lest we be tempted to judge them, we must first be certain to examine them and their accomplishments in the context of their time and place.

Notes

PREFACE

1. Robert E. Wright, O.M.I., "Catholic Diocesan Church of New Spain and Mexico (1700–1892)," in *The Handbook of Texas* (forthcoming).
2. Patrick Foley, "From Linares to Galveston: The Early Development of the Catholic Hierarchy in Texas," paper delivered before the Texas Catholic Historical Society, Austin, Nov. 15, 1989; Wright, "Catholic Diocesan Church"; Robert E. Wright, O.M.I., "The Parish of San Agustín, Laredo, 1760–1857," in Angel Sepúlveda Brown and Gloria Villa Cadena, *San Agustín Parish of Laredo: Marriage Book I, 1790–1857*.
3. Wright, "Catholic Diocesan Church."
4. Sr. Mary Angela Fitzmorris, *Four Decades of Catholicism in Texas, 1820–1860*, 37.
5. For a complete discussion of the vicars forane see Carlos Eduardo Castañeda, *Our Catholic Heritage in Texas*, VI, 311–17.
6. Ibid., 325–27.
7. Decree No. 276 of the Governor of the State of Coahuila and Texas, Apr. 18, 1834, in H. P. N. Gammel, *The Laws of Texas*, I, 363–64.
8. Decree No. 263 of the Governor of the State of Coahuila and Texas, 1834, in Gammel, I, 350.
9. Decree No. 272 of the Governor of the State of Coahuila and Texas, Mar., 1834, in Gammel, I, 358.
10. Castañeda, VI, 201–205, 329–30. The Spanish word *empresario* means "businessman."
11. Ibid., 214–17, 328–30.
12. Ibid.

CHAPTER ONE

1. Wright, "Catholic Diocesan Church"; Rachel Bluntzer Hebert, *The Forgotten Colony, San Patricio de Hibernia*, 119–21, 353; José Enrique de la Peña, *With Santa Anna in Texas: A Personal Narrative of the Revolution*, 186; Castañeda, VII, 24; Castañeda, VI, 329–30.
2. "The Unanimous Declaration of Independence Made by the Delegates of the People of Texas in General Convention at the Town of Washington on

the 2D Day of March, 1836," in Francis W. Johnson, *A History of Texas and Texans,* I, 390–93.
3. William Ransom Hogan, *The Texas Republic: A Social and Economic History,* 191–92; Samuel Harmon Lowrie, *Culture Conflict in Texas,* 53–58; John J. Linn, *Reminiscences of Fifty Years in Texas,* 283.
4. Fitzmorris, 36.
5. Louis Wiltz Kemp, *The Signers of the Texas Declaration of Independence,* 235–43; William M. Ryan, *Shamrock and Cactus,* 34–35; Félix D. Almaráz, Jr., *Governor Antonio Martínez and Mexican Independence in Texas: An Orderly Transition,* 7–11. For a thorough treatment of anticlericalism in this period, see Germán Valladares Alvarez, "Catolicismo y Anti-clericalismo en Valentín Gómez-Farías," Master's thesis, St. Mary's University, San Antonio, 1962, esp. pp. 102–10.
6. John Timon to Antoine Blanc, Jan. 17, 1839, Catholic Archives of Texas (Unless otherwise noted, the original or a photostatic copy of the original of all letters cited is to be found in the Catholic Archives of Texas, hereafter referred to as C.A.T.); Timon à Nozo, 9 Januier 1839, *Annales de l'Association de la Propagation de la Foi,* XII, 31; Jean Marie Odin, Diary 4, typescript copy, C.A.T.; Jean Marie Odin to Antoine Blanc, Aug. 24, 1840; Odin to Étienne, Aug. 28, 1840; Ralph Bayard, C.M., *Lone Star Vanguard: The Catholic Re-Occupation of Texas, 1838–1848,* 52, 133, 139; Castañeda, VII, 22, 27, 47, 51.
7. Kemp, 297–303; Eugene C. Barker, *The Life of Stephen F. Austin,* 227.
8. Ryan, 33–34; Kemp, 215–18; Odin, Diary, 10, 12.
9. Ryan, 35–36.
10. Castañeda, VI, 277.
11. William Stuart Red, *The Texas Colonists and Religion, 1821–1836,* 93.
12. Ibid.
13. Hogan, 191–92; *Texas Almanac, 1988–1989,* 63.
14. Stephen B. Oates, *With Malice toward None,* 6.

CHAPTER TWO

1. Linn, 15–16.
2. "Petition to the Most Reverend Archbishop and Right Reverend Bishops in Counsel [*sic*] Assembled in Baltimore," Mar. 20, 1837, copy in C.A.T.; Castañeda, VII, 6.
3. Bayard, 19; Castañeda, VII, 8 n. 15.
4. Henderson Yoakum, *History of Texas from Its First Settlement in 1865 to Its Annexation to the United States in 1846,* II, 224n.
5. Letter and plan of Count Farnesé, portions of which are quoted in Yoakum, II, 225–26; the original has been lost.
6. Houston to Count Farnesé, Aug. 5, 1837, in Amelia W. Williams and Eugene C. Barker, eds., *The Writings of Sam Houston, 1813–1863,* II, 135–37.

Notes to Pages 12–21 / 243

7. Bayard, 22.
8. "Catholics and Friends of Catholic Religion in Texas to His Holiness Pope Gregory XVI," Houston, Aug. 1, 1837, copy in C. A. T.; the location of the original is unknown.
9. Fransoni to Blanc, Jan. 16, 1838, in Fitzmorris, 42–43.
10. Fitzmorris, 41–42; Castañeda, VII, 10.
11. Bayard, 11.
12. Blanc to Timon, Mar. 30, 1838, condensed in Bayard, 15, 22–23.
13. Bayard, 3–13.
14. Ibid., 23–25.
15. Bruté to Timon, Dec. 7, 1838, condensed in Bayard, 27–28.
16. Bayard, 25.
17. Llebaría à Étienne, 15 Januier 1839, *Annales de l'Association de la Propagation de la Foi*, XII, 39–44.
18. Col. Edward Stiff, *The Texan Emigrant: Being a Narration of the Adventures of the Author in Texas*, 151–53.
19. Llebaría à Étienne, 15 Januier 1839, *Annales de l'Association de la Propagation de la Foi*, XII, 39–44.
20. Linn, 212–13.
21. Llebaría à Étienne, 15 Januier 1839, *Annales de l'Association de la Propagation de la Foi*, XII, 39–44.
22. Timon to Blanc, Dec. 28, 1838; Timon to Nozo, Dec. 29, 1838, *Archives of the Vincentian Motherhouse*, Paris, cited by Bayard, 38–39.
23. Llebaría à Étienne, 15 Januier 1839, *Annales de l'Association de la Propagation de la Foi*, XII, 39–44; Stiff, 62–63.
24. Stiff, 62–63.
25. Timon à Nozo, 9 Januier 1839, *Annales de l'Association de la Propagation de la Foi*, XII, 31–39.
26. Bayard, 43.
27. Timon à Nozo, 9 Januier 1839, *Annales de l'Association de la Propagation de la Foi*, XII, 31–39; Llebaría à Étienne, 15 Januier 1839, *Annales de l'Association de la Propagation de la Foi*, XII, 39–44.
28. Bayard, 48–49.
29. FitzGerald to Timon, Feb. 17, 1839.
30. Bayard, 49; Williston Walker, *A History of the Christian Church*, 581–82.
31. Timon à Nozo, 9 Januier 1839, *Annales de l'Association de la Propagation de la Foi*, XII, 31–39; Bayard, 50, 51, quotes from the complete version of the letter found in *Annales de la Congregation de la Mission*, V, 102.
32. Castañeda, VI, 335.
33. John Timon, *Barrens Memoir*, cited by Bayard, 44–45.
34. Harris County Courthouse records, cited by Bayard, 45n. 7.
35. Bayard, 51–53.
36. Ibid., 54, 63–64.

37. See Seymour V. Connor, *Texas: A History*, 172. Timon's figure is probably an overestimation by several thousand since in 1845, after the influx of many immigrants, the non-Indian population was between 125,000 and 150,000.
38. Timon à Nozo, 9 Januier 1839, *Annales de l'Association de la Propagation de la Foi*, XII, 31–39.
39. Stiff, 71.
40. Connor, 142–43.
41. Timon to Blanc, Mar. 12, 1839.
42. Bayard, 70.
43. Anduze to Blanc, Apr. 21, 1839; Joseph William Schmitz, S.M., *Texan Statecraft, 1836–1845*, 79.
44. Cited in Lina Trigg, "Father Michael Muldoon: The Story of an Early Pioneer Priest," Master's thesis, St. Mary's University, San Antonio, 1940.
45. Trigg, 36–38.
46. Jones to Muldoon, Jan. 10, 1842, quoted in Trigg, 44.
47. Trigg, 44–45. Hardly anything is known of Muldoon after he left Texas in the 1840s. There is the possibility that he died in a shipwreck traveling between New Orleans and Veracruz.
48. Bayard, 75.
49. Timon to Nozo, June 4, 1839, quoted in Bayard, 74.
50. Haydon to Timon, Mar. 15, 1839; James F. Vanderholt, "Father George W. Haydon," biographical essay, in C.A.T.; summary of biographical material in Loretto Motherhouse Archives, Nerinx, Kentucky, concerning "Rev. Edward Clarke," dated Aug. 10, 1944, in C.A.T.; John A. Lyons, *Bishops and Priests of the Diocese of Bardstown*, 37–39.
51. Bayard, 75.
52. Haydon to Blanc, Mar. 13, 1840.
53. Hogan, 229.
54. Haydon to Blanc, June 17, 1840.
55. Vanderholt, "Father George W. Haydon."
56. *The Guardian*, Louisville, Kentucky, Dec. 4, 1858.

CHAPTER THREE

1. Timon to Étienne, June 15, 1839.
2. Bayard, 80–85; Castañeda, VII, 31–33.
3. Timon to Blanc, Aug. 23, 1839; Bayard, 101–102.
4. Étienne to Timon, Dec. 19, 1839, quoted in Bayard, 104–105, 108.
5. Timon to Blanc, Aug. 23, 1839; Bayard, 102–103, 109.
6. Timon to Blanc, Mar. 12, 1839; Timon à Étienne, 15 Juin 1839.
7. Eccleston to Blanc, Apr. 8, 1839, a portion of which is in Sister Mary Benignus Sheridan, "Bishop Odin and the New Era of the Catholic Church in Texas, 1840–1860," diss., Saint Louis University, 1938, 91–92.
8. Odin to his sister, July 24, 1825, in Sheridan, 25. For Odin's early life, see

Patrick Foley, "Jean-Marie Odin, C.M., Missionary Bishop Extraordinaire of Texas," *Journal of Texas Catholic History and Culture* 1 (Mar., 1990): 44–48.
9. Odin to Rosati, Apr. 23, 1834, in Sheridan, 29–30.
10. For a sketch of Odin's life prior to his coming to Texas, see Sheridan, 10–41; see also Abbé Bony, *Vie de Monseigneur Jean-Marie Odin,* 11–40.
11. Odin Diary, 1.
12. Ibid.; Odin to Étienne, Aug. 28, 1840; Odin to Rosati, Aug. 27, 1840; Odin to Étienne, Apr. 11, 1841.
13. Odin to Étienne, Aug. 28, 1840; Odin to Rosati, Aug. 27, 1840; Odin to Étienne, Apr. 11, 1841; Castañeda, VII, 42–43.
14. Odin Diary, 2; Odin to Étienne, Aug. 28, 1840, and Apr. 11, 1841; Odin to Blanc, July 14, 1840.
15. Odin Diary, 3.
16. Ibid.; Odin to Étienne, Aug. 28, 1840, and Apr. 11, 1841; Odin to Blanc, July 14, 1840; Bayard, 129–30.
17. Odin Diary, 3; Odin to Étienne, Aug. 28, 1840, and Apr. 11, 1841; Odin to Blanc, July 14, 1840; Bayard, 129–30.
18. Odin to Étienne, Aug. 28, 1840; Félix D. Almaráz, Jr., "San Antonio's Old Franciscan Missions: Material Decline and Secular Avarice in the Transition from Hispanic to Mexican Control," *Americas* 44 (July, 1987): 1–22.
19. Castañeda, VII, 47; Odin Diary, 7.
20. Sheridan, 106.
21. Hobart Huson, "Jose Antonio Valdez," in Eldon Stephen Branda, ed., *The Handbook of Texas: A Supplement,* III, 1056.
22. Odin to Blanc, Aug. 24, 1840.
23. Odin Diary, 7; Castañeda, VII, 47.
24. Fidelia Miller Puckett, "Ramón Ortiz: Priest and Patriot," *New Mexico Historical Review* 25 (Oct., 1950): 265–95; Gilberto M. Hinojosa, "The Enduring Faith Communities: Spanish and Texas Church Historiography," *Journal of Texas Catholic History and Culture* 1 (Mar., 1990): 20–41. A forthcoming biography of Bishop Odin by Patrick Foley will contain another interpretation of some of the events in this chapter.
25. Odin to Joseph Rosati, Aug. 27, 1840.
26. Odin to Étienne, Aug. 28, 1840; Odin to Blanc, Aug. 24, 1840.
27. Odin Diary, 5; Odin to Blanc, Oct. 2, 1840.
28. Sheridan, 107–108.
29. Bayard, 134.
30. Odin Diary, 5.
31. Connor, 142–43.
32. Connor, 142–43, 240–47.
33. Odin to Blanc, Oct. 2, 1840.
34. Odin Diary, 6–7.

35. Odin to Étienne, Aug. 28, 1840.
36. Odin to Rosati, Aug. 27, 1840.
37. Odin to Blanc, Oct. 2, 1840; Odin to Étienne, Dec. 13, 1840.
38. Odin to Rosati, Aug. 27, 1840.
39. Odin Diary, 7–8.
40. Ibid., 8.
41. Ibid.
42. Odin to Étienne, Dec. 13, 1840.
43. Odin Diary, 9.
44. Odin to Étienne, Dec. 13, 1840; Odin Diary, 9; Bayard, 118–19.
45. Bayard, 162; Odin Diary, 10.
46. Odin Diary, 10.
47. Ibid.
48. Ibid., 11.
49. Ibid.
50. Ibid.
51. Ibid.; Timon to Blanc, Dec. 7, 1840; Timon to Étienne, December 8, 1840; Timon to Marcantonio Durando, Feb. 14, 1841; Fransoni to Lamar, July 18, 1840.
52. Odin Diary, 11.
53. Bayard, 157–58, 166, 172; Castañeda, VII, 53.
54. Bayard, 173.
55. Odin Diary, 11; Castañeda, VII, 59–60; Bayard, 176–78.
56. Odin to Fransoni, Dec. 15, 1840; Timon to Blanc, Jan. 15, 1841.
57. De Saligny to Timon, Jan. 18, 1841; Bayard, 179–80; Castañeda, VII, 60; Timon to Blanc, Apr. 28, 1841.
58. De Saligny to Timon, Jan. 18, 1841; Bayard, 179–80; Castañeda, VII, 60; Timon to Blanc, Apr. 28, 1841.
59. De Saligny to Timon, Jan. 18, 1841; Timon to Blanc, Apr. 28, 1841; H. N. P. Gammel, *The Laws of Texas*, II, 492–96.
60. Odin Diary, 12–13.
61. Ibid., 13.
62. Odin to Étienne, Apr. 11, 1841.
63. Odin Diary, 13; Bayard, 198; Odin to Étienne, Apr. 11, 1841.
64. Harriet Smither, ed., "Diary of Adolphus Sterne," *Southwest Historical Quarterly* 31 (July, 1927): 181–87; Odin Diary, 13.
65. Odin to Étienne, Apr. 11, 1841; Bayard, 196–203.
66. Odin Diary, 13; Bayard, 203.
67. Timon to Durando, Feb. 14, 1841.
68. Timon to De Saligny, Apr. 28, 1841; Timon to Blanc, Apr. 28, 1841.
69. Timon to Blanc, Apr. 14, 1841, Apr. 28, 1841, and May 4, 1841; Timon to Fransoni, May 10, 1841; Timon to Blanc, June 4, 1841.
70. Odin Diary, 15–16.

71. Ibid., 15–17; Odin to Blanc, May 9, 1841.
72. Timon to Blanc, July 27, 1841.
73. Odin to Blanc, July 8, 1841; Odin Diary, 17; Odin to Timon, Sept. 30, 1841.
74. Odin Diary, 17–18; Odin to Étienne, Feb. 7, 1841; Odin to Timon, Sept. 30, 1841.
75. Odin Diary, 18–19; Odin to Étienne, Feb. 7, 1842.
76. Odin Diary, 19–20; Odin to Étienne, Feb. 7, 1842.
77. Odin Diary, 20; Odin to Étienne, Feb. 7, 1842.
78. Odin Diary, 20; Odin to Étienne, Feb. 7, 1842.
79. Odin Diary, 20; Odin to Étienne, Feb. 7, 1842.
80. Odin Diary, 20; Odin to Étienne, Feb. 7, 1842.
81. Odin Diary, 21; Odin to Étienne, Feb. 7, 1842; Odin to Timon, Sept. 30, 1841.
82. Odin Diary, 21; Odin to Étienne, Feb. 7, 1842; Odin to Timon, Sept. 30, 1841.
83. Nicholas D. Labadie to Blanc, Jan. 2, 1842, and Jan. 23, 1842.
84. Odin to Blanc, Feb. 4, 1842.
85. Odin Diary, 21; Odin to Étienne, Feb. 7, 1842; Odin to Timon, Sept. 30, 1841.

CHAPTER FOUR

1. Bayard, 268–69; Odin Diary, 22.
2. Odin to Blanc, Feb. 4, 1842.
3. Connor, 149–53.
4. Odin to Blanc, July 4, 1842; Odin Diary, 23.
5. Odin to Étienne, March 28, 1842; Odin to Blanc, May 22, 1842; Odin to Blanc, Aug. 20, 1842; Odin to Rousselon, Dec. 10, 1842; Odin Diary, 28; W. Eugene Hollon and Ruth Lapham Butler, *William Bollaert's Texas*, 102.
6. Odin to Étienne, June 17, 1842.
7. Odin Diary, 23–25.
8. Ibid., 25–27, 30; Odin to Blanc, Sept. 19, 1842.
9. Odin to Blanc, Nov. 16, 1842; Castañeda, VII, 86–87.
10. Odin Diary, 30.
11. Bayard, 307–308; Castañeda, VII, 86–87; Odin to Blanc, July 24, 1843.
12. Odin to Blanc, Nov. 8, 1843; Bayard, 311; Odin to Blanc, Dec. 16, 1843.
13. Odin to Blanc, Jan. 8, 1844.
14. Bayard, 311–15; James F. Vanderholt, "Jean Pierre Ogé," in *Biographies of French Diocesan Priests in Nineteenth Century Texas;* Odin to Blanc, July 24, 1843.
15. Odin to Étienne, Jan. 12, 1844; Bayard, 327; Odin to Blanc, Dec. 10, 1844; Odin to Blanc, Jan. 6, 1845; Odin to Blanc, Jan. 25, 1845.
16. Odin to Blanc, May 18, 1844; Paquín to Timon, July 7, 1844 and Aug. 1,

1844; Labadie to Timon, Aug. 14, 1844; Brands to Timon, July 31, 1844, Aug. 8, 1844, and Sept. 4, 1844; *The Metropolitan Catholic Almanac and Laity's Directory for 1845,* 179; Odin Diary, 32.
17. Odin Diary, 31–32; Bobby D. Weaver, *Castro's Colony,* 42–43, 50–52; Odin to Blanc, Dec. 10, 1844.
18. Bayard, 340.
19. Timon to Sturchi, Jan. 12, 1845, cited by Bayard, 339–40; Odin to Blanc, Jan. 6, 1845; Odin to Blanc, Jan. 25, 1845; Castañeda, VII, 99; Odin Diary, 32–33.
20. Odin Diary, 33.
21. Bayard, 246–47, 365n. 23.
22. Ibid.; Odin to Étienne, Apr. 8, 1846. See also H. C. McKeown, *The Life and Labors of Most Reverend John Joseph Lynch, D.D.,* 1–69; Castañeda, VII, 104.
23. Odin Diary, 35; Odin to Fransoni, Sept. 12, 1845; Odin to Étienne, Sept. 23, 1845.
24. Odin to Blanc, Jan. 11, 1846; Odin Diary, 35.
25. Odin to the Society for the Propagation of the Faith, Lyon, Feb. 28, 1846, Mar. 9, 1846, and Mar. 17, 1846.
26. Odin to Étienne, Apr. 8, 1846; Odin to the Society for the Propagation of the Faith, Lyon, July 8, 1846.
27. Odin to Étienne, June 28, 1846, and July 21, 1846; Odin to the Society for the Propagation of the Faith, Lyon, July 8, 1846; Bayard, 369 n. 7, 377 n. 23.
28. Odin to "Monsieur," July 8, 1846; Odin to Blanc, July 4, 1846; *Le Propagateur Catholique,* June 27, 1846, quoted in Sheridan, 205.
29. Odin to Blanc, July 4, 1846; *Le Propagateur Catholique,* June 27, 1846, cited in Sheridan, 205; Odin to the Society for the Propagation of the Faith, Lyon, July 8, 1846.
30. Odin to "Monsieur," July 8, 1846.
31. Odin to Étienne, July 21, 1846.
32. Odin to the Society for the Propagation of the Faith, Lyon, July 8, 1846.
33. Odin to Étienne, June 18, 1846; Odin to Blanc, July 4, 1846; Odin to Étienne, July 21, 1846; Sheridan, 212.
34. Bayard, 370, 373–74.
35. Ferdinand von Roemer, *Roemer's Texas,* 213.
36. *The Catholic Almanac for 1847,* 190f.
37. Ibid.
38. S. M. Johnston, *Builders by the Sea: History of the Ursuline Community of Galveston, Texas,* 20–21; Sheridan, 211–14.
39. Bayard, 378–79.
40. Timon to Blanc, Mar. 29, 1847; Odin to Rousselon, Apr. 11, 1847.
41. Blanc to Odin, May 14, 1847; Timon to Blanc, Sept. 18, 1847; Blanc to Odin, Oct. 3, 1847.

42. Odin to Blanc, Aug. 3, 1846, and Sept. 6, 1846.
43. Blanc to Odin, Sept. 7, 1847; Odin to Blanc, Sept. 21, 1847; Castañeda, VII, 109; *Apostolicae sedis fastigio,* copy in C.A.T.
44. Odin to Blanc, Sept. 21, 1847, and Oct. 21, 1847; Bayard, 383.
45. Odin to Blanc, Dec. 21, 1847.

CHAPTER FIVE

1. Odin to Barnabo, Sept. 18, 1851; Odin to Blanc, Aug. 22, 1847, Jan. 18, 1849, and Mar. 18, 1849; Bernard Doyon, *The Cavalry of Christ on the Rio Grande,* 26; Gilberto Miguel Hinojosa, *A Borderlands Town in Transition: Laredo, 1755–1870,* 58; Odin to Blanc, May 26, 1853; Rev. Ernest J. Burrus, S.J., "A Brief Account of the El Paso Diocese," *Newsletter of the Texas Catholic Historical Society* II (Jan. 1987); Wright, "Catholic Diocesan Church."
2. *History of the Diocese of Galveston and St. Mary's Cathedral,* 103.
3. Emmanuel Domenech, *Missionary Adventures in Texas and Mexico: A Personal Narrative of Six Years' Sojourn in Those Regions,* 25.
4. Ibid., 176.
5. L. V. Jacks, *Claude Dubuis, Bishop of Galveston,* 103–106.
6. Domenech, 94–95.
7. Ibid., 190–94.
8. Doyon, 16–17.
9. Johnston, 56.
10. Fr. Alexander Soulerin, *Missions des O.M.I.* (1862), I, 454–67, quoted in Doyon, 18.
11. Ibid., 19.
12. Doyon, 21–24; Carmen Tafolla, "The Church in Texas," in Moíses Sandoval, *Fronteras: A History of the Latin American Church in the USA since 1513,* 185–86.
13. Castañeda, VII, 112–13; Odin Diary, 37.
14. Odin Diary, 37; Odin to Domenech, Dec. 28, 1850; Wright, "Parish of San Agustín," 16, 19, 20; Castañeda, VII, 113; José Bravo Ugarte, *Diócesis y Obispos de la Iglesia Mexicana, 1519–1965,* 66.
15. Ibid.; Domenech, 254, 262–77.
16. Odin to Domenech, Dec. 28, 1850; Sheridan, 234.
17. Odin to Domenech, Dec. 28, 1850.
18. Ibid.; Odin Diary, 37–38; Castañeda, VII, 114–15.
19. Odin to Étienne, Dec. 23, 1850; Odin to Blanc, Dec. 30, 1850.
20. Doyon, 27–30.
21. Odin to Domenech, Dec. 28, 1850.
22. Dubuis to Odin, Feb. 25, 1851; Odin to Blanc, Oct. 22, 1852; Sheridan, 313.
23. Dubuis to Odin, Feb. 25, 1851.
24. Domenech, 231.
25. Odin to Blanc, May 13, 1851; Domenech, 214–18, 220, 288.
26. Domenech, 364.

27. "Sister Ephrem's Diary," quoted in Sr. Mary Xavier Holworthy, *Diamonds for the King,* 17.
28. Wright, "Parish of San Agustín," 20; Hinojosa, *Borderlands Town in Transition,* 58–59, 79; James F. Vanderholt, "Claude Dumas," and "Louis-Marie Planchet," *Biographies of French Diocesan Priests in Nineteenth Century Texas;* Doyon, 69.
29. Doyon, 70–71; Tafolla, 185–87.
30. Odin to Blanc, Mar. 25, 1854; Odin to Blanc, July 29, 1854; P. F. Parisot, *The Reminiscences of a Texas Missionary,* 79–80; Domenech, 262–88; Wright, "Parish of San Agustín," 20; Puckett, 291; Odin to Blanc, Jan. 18, 1849; December 30, 1850; January 10, 1851; Gilberto Miguel Hinojosa, "The Enduring Hispanic Faith Communities: Spanish and Texas Church Historiography," *Journal of Texas Catholic History and Culture* (Mar. 1990): 34–35; Odin to Blanc, Nov. 22, 1857; Doyon, 77; Sheridan, 248; Odin to Rousselon, Feb. 23, 1861.
31. Parisot, 80–81; Chambodut to family, Nov. 28, 1854.
32. "Questionnaire for the Use of the Chancery Office, Archdiocese of San Antonio," copy in C.A.T.
33. Odin to Propagation of the Faith, Lyon, Aug. 25, 1852, and July 1, 1853; Odin to Fransoni, [no month or day], 1855.
34. Odin to Propagation of the Faith, Lyon, Aug. 25, 1852, Jan. 9, 1853, and July 1, 1853; Odin to Blanc, Sept. 10, 1852, Oct. 22, 1852, and Dec. 12, 1852; Joseph William Schmitz, *The Society of Mary in Texas,* 24–30.
35. Schmitz, *The Society of Mary,* 29–30.
36. Schmitz, *The Society of Mary,* 30, 44–48, 53; Dubuis to Odin, Jan. 22, 1853.
37. Dubuis to Odin, Dec. 5, 1855, Dec. 18, 1855, Mar. 24, 1856, May 9, 1856, May 24, 1856, Feb. 15, 1857, and July 15, 1857.

CHAPTER SIX

1. Rupert N. Richardson, Ernest Wallace, and Adrian N. Anderson, *Texas, the Lone Star,* 149; Odin to Blanc, Dec. 12, 1852.
2. Odin to Blanc, Nov. 27, 1856.
3. Parisot, 81–82; Odin to Blanc, Nov. 19, 1858.
4. Sr. Mary Monica La Fleur, C.C.V.I., "The Immigration Factor in the Growth of the Diocese of Galveston: 1841–1874," diss., University of Notre Dame, 1965, 64.
5. Ibid., 61–62; Henry Maresh, "The Czechs in Texas," *Southwestern Historical Quarterly* 50 (Oct., 1946): 234–40; Institute of Texan Cultures, *The Czech Texans,* 3.
6. Maresh, 234–40; Institute of Texan Cultures, 3–8, 10.
7. Institute of Texan Cultures, 15.
8. For a thorough discussion of early Polish settlement in Texas, see T. Lindsay Baker, *The First Polish Americans: Silesian Settlements in Texas,* and for the period in question, 3–63.

9. Odin to the Society for the Propagation of the Faith, Jan. 9, 1853; Baker, 6–8.
10. Baker, 60.
11. Ibid., 61.
12. Dubuis to Odin, Dec. 18, 1855; Baker, 31.
13. Baker, 61.
14. Ibid., 8–32, 104–105, 119–20; P. F. Parisot and C. J. Smith, *History of the Catholic Church in the Diocese of San Antonio, Texas*, 129–31.
15. Ibid., 56–57; Parisot and Smith, 187–88.
16. Baker, 57–58.
17. Ibid., 52.
18. Baker, 53–54, 59; Odin to President and Council of the Society for the Propagation of the Faith, Lyon, Aug. 7, 1857; Odin to Anstaett, Aug. 23, 1857.
19. Odin to Society for the Propagation of the Faith, Lyon, July 20, 1859.
20. Ibid.; Baker, 55.
21. Baker, 55.
22. See Baker, 58–59. Baker calculates 4.66 as the average family size of Silesians who immigrated to the United States based on figures in the 1860 census.
23. Baker, 67.
24. Castañeda, VII, 216; Baker, 61.
25. Odin to Society for the Propagation of the Faith, June 20, 1860.
26. Odin to the Society for the Propagation of the Faith, July 20, 1859.
27. Weninger to Odin, Mar. 27, 1859, Mar. 31, 1859, Apr. 4, 1859, Apr. 9, 1859, Apr. 15, 1859, Apr. 20, 1859, Apr. 26, 1859, May 8, 1859, May 12, 1859, June 8, 1859, and June 22, 1859; Sheridan, 269–72; Parisot and Smith, 111.
28. Castañeda, VII, 217–18.
29. Ibid., 218–19.
30. Ibid., 219.
31. Odin to Society for the Propagation of the Faith, June 18, 1856.
32. Ibid.
33. Jean Perrichone, *The Life of Bishop Dubuis, Apostle of Texas*, trans. Hectorine Piercey, 109–11; Jacks, *Claude Dubuis*, 144–45; *The Metropolitan Catholic Almanac and Laity's Directory for the United States for 1860*. 125.
34. Odin to Blanc, July 29, 1854.
35. Quoted in Fitzmorris.
36. *Texas State Gazette*, June 30, 1855, quoted in Fitzmorris, 84.
37. Arnoldo De León, *The Tejano Community, 1836–1900*, 28–29 (esp. quote of José Antonio Navarro); Arnoldo De León, *They Called Them Greasers*, 53.
38. Fitzmorris, 87–88.
39. James F. Vanderholt, "Antoine Borias," in *Biographies of French Diocesan Priests in Nineteenth Century Texas;* Odin to Society for the Propagation of the Faith, Feb. 14, 1856.

40. Odin to Blanc, Dec. 12, 1852; Odin to Society for the Propagation of the Faith, Lyon, June 24, 1854, and June 18, 1856.
41. Odin to Anstaett, July 18, 1857.
42. Odin to Anstaett, Oct. 3, 1857; Connor, 179.
43. De León, *They Called Them Greasers*, 50–53.
44. Ibid., 54–55.
45. Parisot, 97–99.
46. Parisot, 39–40; Perrichone, 103–104.
47. Parisot, 39.
48. Sheridan, 315; Dubuis to Odin, Feb. 13, 1856, Feb. 29, 1856, and Mar. 24, 1856.
49. Odin to Fransoni, [no month or day], 1855; Dubuis to Odin, Feb. 23, 1855, Mar. 8, 1855, Mar. 9, 1855; and June 12, 1855; Odin to the Society for the Propagation of the Faith, Lyon, Feb. 14, 1856; Fitzmorris, 89–90.
50. The term "synod" means "council," but in the Catholic Church the latter word by tradition is confined to worldwide conclaves of bishops presided over by the pope, such as the Second Vatican Council, and also for national or provincial assemblies of bishops, although today the term "conference" is generally used for these.
51. Chambodut, born at St.-Justen-Chevalet, France, in 1821, was a deacon studying at the seminary in Lyon in early 1846 when he volunteered as a Texas missionary during one of Odin's recruiting efforts in Europe. Arriving in Texas the same year, but after first completing his studies in St. Louis and being ordained to the priesthood, Chambodut worked in Nacogdoches and its environs until 1852. See the memoir by his niece, Mother Aloysia Chambodut, O.S.U., "Father Chambodut, the First Secular Priest Ordained for Texas: Biographical Sketch," Archives of the Ursuline Academy and Convent, Dallas.
52. "Minutes and Statutes of the First Synod of the Diocese of Galveston," in C.A.T.; James F. Vanderholt, "James Giraudon," in *Biographies of French Diocesan Priests in Nineteenth Century Texas;* Doyon, 73–74.
53. Odin to the Society for the Propagation of the Faith, July 12, 1858, July 20, 1859, and Mar. 1, 1860; Johnston, 87–90.
54. Odin to the Society for the Propagation of the Faith, Mar. 1, 1860, and June 20, 1860; *The Metropolitan Catholic Almanac and Laity's Directory for the Year 1857*, 250–51; *The Metropolitan Catholic Almanac and Laity's Directory for the United States for 1860*, 124–27.

CHAPTER SEVEN

1. Jean Marie Odin to the Society for the Propagation of the Faith, Lyon, Jan. 26, 1861.
2. "The Pope's Bull, and the Words of Daniel O'Connell," in *Official Proceedings of the Republican Convention Convened in the City of Pittsburg, Pennsylvania, on 22 February, 1856*.

3. Copy of "Bill of Sale of Clement and family," Jan. 9, 1847, in C.A.T.; Leonard R. Riforgiato, "John Timon and the Succession to the See of Baltimore in 1851," *Vencentian Heritage* 8 (1987): 31.
4. James F. Vanderholt, "Slavery and the Church," *East Texas Catholic*, Apr. 11, 1986; Peter Clarke, *A Free Church in a Free Society, The Ecclesiology of John England, Bishop of Charleston, 1820–1842*, 41, 394–96; Michael V. Gannon, *Rebel Bishop, The Life and Era of Augustin Verot*, 40–55.
5. Vanderholt, "Slavery and the Church"; Sr. Frances Jerome Woods, C.D.P., "Congregations of Religious Women in the Old South" in Randall M. Miller and John L. Wakelyn, eds., *Catholics in the Old South, Essays on Church and Culture*, 101, 112–14.
6. Odin to Joseph Anstaett, Sept. 10, 1861. Regarding pro-Confederate activity of clergy, see Cornelius M. Buckley, trans., *A Frenchman, a Chaplain, a Rebel: The War Letters of Père Louis-Hippolyte Gache, S.J.*
7. Conner, 194–95; campaign literature in possession of San Jacinto Monument and Museum, San Jacinto Battleground State Park, Texas.
8. Odin to Francis Patrick Kenrick, June 27, 1860.
9. Castañeda, VII, 121; Odin to Kenrick, June 27, 1860.
10. Castañeda, VII, 121.
11. Odin to Kenrick, Apr. 22, 1861.
12. Odin to Étiene Rousselon, Apr. 24, 1861; Odin to Kenrick, June 25, 1861.
13. Odin to John Baptist Purcell, June 25, 1861; Odin to Kenrick, June 25, 1861.
14. Castañeda, VII, 478–79.
15. For an account of Parisot's life, see Parisot.
16. Chambodut.
17. Sr. St. Marie to Odin, May 26, 1861, July 2, 1861, July 18, 1861, Aug. 6, 1861, Oct. 14, 1861, and Nov. 30, 1861.
18. Claude Marie Dubuis to Odin, Apr. 29, 1863.
19. Odin to Anstaett, Sept. 10, 1861.
20. Rev. Canisius J. Bluemel, O.S.B., pastor of Our Lady of the Lake Church, Mandeville, La., to Most Rev. Laurence FitzSimon, D.D., Bishop of Amarillo, Mar. 3, 1952.
21. Ibid.
22. Castañeda, VII, 123.
23. Samuel Carter, III, *The Final Fortress: The Campaign for Vicksburg, 1862–1863*, 26–33.
24. Odin to Rousellon, Sept. 22, 1862; Castañeda, VII, 123.
25. Perrichone, 112–14.
26. Ibid.
27. Connor, 198.
28. Perrichone, 116.
29. Ibid., 120.

30. Ibid., 120–21.
31. Ibid.
32. Dubuis to Odin, Apr. 29, 1863.
33. Ibid.
34. Ibid.
35. Connor, 198.
36. Chambodut.
37. Ibid.
38. Johnston, *Builders by the Sea*, 122.
39. Chambodut.
40. Perrichone, 133.
41. Johnston, 119–23.
42. Connor, 198.
43. Perrichone, 132.
44. Johnston, 123.
45. Dubuis to Odin, Oct. 2, 1863.
46. *Diocese of Galveston, Centennial, 1847–1947*, 76; Connor, 198.
47. Dubuis to Odin, Oct. 2, 1863, and Nov. 28, 1863; Connor, 199. For a discussion of Hispanic Texans in Union service, see Jerry D. Thompson, *Mexican Texans in the Union Army*.
48. Dubuis to Odin, Nov. 28, 1863.
49. Parisot, 101–102.
50. Mother M. Patricia Gunning, *To Texas with Love*, 86; Perrichone, 168–69.
51. Parisot, 107–108.
52. Odin to Martin John Spalding, Sept. 7, 1864; Thomas W. Spalding, *Martin John Spalding: American Churchman*, 161–62.
53. De León, *They Called Them Greasers*, 55; Hinojosa, *Borderlands Town in Transition*, 82–86.
54. Connor, 199–200.
55. Perrichone, 133.
56. Dubuis to Odin, Apr. 25, 1864; personal account of one of the missionaries, quoted in Perrichone, 133–35.
57. Dubuis to Odin, Nov. 10, 1864.
58. Dubuis to Odin, June 30, 1864, Sept. 20, 1864, Nov. 10, 1864.
59. Dubuis to Odin, Nov. 10, 1864.
60. Baker, 77.
61. Dubuis to Odin, Feb. 10, 1865.
62. Ibid.
63. Connor, 200, 210.
64. James F. Vanderholt, "C. L. M. Chambodut" in *Biographies of French Diocesan Priests in Nineteenth Century Texas*.
65. Connor, 210–11.

CHAPTER EIGHT

1. *Sadlier's Catholic Directory, Almanac, and Ordo for 1867*, 144–48.
2. Quoted in Felix Fellner, o.s.b., "Benedictine Pioneers in Texas," typescript #589, C.A.T.
3. An account of Benedictine work in Texas during the 1860s is given in Fellner.
4. Fellner, 595–601; Dubuis to Odin, Feb. 8, 1868.
5. Schmitz, *Society of Mary*, 49.
6. Reinbolt Report, Mar. 1, 1866, quoted in Schmitz, *Society of Mary*, 52; Odin to Anstaett, Jan. 15, 1866.
7. Schmitz, *Society of Mary*, 52–95.
8. Vanderholt, "C. L. M. Chambodut."
9. Louis Claude Marie Chambodut to Justine (niece), Apr. 20, 1866; Chambodut to Justine, Feb. 14, 1867.
10. Chambodut to Justine, Aug. 8, 1869.
11. De León, *They Called Them Greasers*, 56–57; De Leon, *The Tejano Community 1836–1900*, 30.
12. Fr. Adolph Bakanowski, as quoted in Baker, 84–85, a definitive history of the early Polish colonists in Texas.
13. Baker, 81, 200.
14. Chambodut to Justine, Apr. 20, 1866.
15. For the account of the founding of this order and their coming to Texas, see Baker, 78–81.
16. Dubuis as quoted in Baker, 79.
17. Ibid., 83.
18. Ibid., 89.
19. For a detailed discussion of the problem, see Baker, 81–98.
20. Quoted in Baker, 101–102.
21. Ibid., 105–106.
22. Ibid.; Vanderholt, "John M. Giraud, S.J."
23. Mary Loyola Hegarty, C.C.V.I., *Serving with Gladness: The Origin and History of the Congregation of the Sisters of Charity of the Incarnate Word, Houston, Texas*, 78–79.
24. Spalding, 194.
25. Odin to Spalding, Sept. 16, 1865.
26. Timon to Spalding, July 10, 1865, as quoted in Spalding, 197.
27. Spalding, 194–95.
28. Ibid., 199–200.
29. Ibid., and 204.
30. Dubuis to Odin, Apr. 30, 1866, and May 17, 1866.
31. Dubuis to Odin, Aug. 2, 1866.
32. Hegarty, 82–83.

33. Baker, 81; Hegarty, 139, 143-45.
34. Hegarty, 145-46.
35. Ibid., 147-48.
36. Spalding, 217.
37. Ibid., 218.
38. Ibid., 219.
39. Ibid., 236-37.
40. Ibid., 222.
41. Gunning, 100-102.
42. James F. Vanderholt, "Augustine Gardet," in *Biographies of French Diocesan Priests in Nineteenth Century Texas*.
43. *Diocese of Galveston, Centennial, 1847-1947*, 138.
44. Dubuis to Odin, Jan. 29, 1867; Hegarty, 210-11; James F. Vanderholt, "Joseph Querat," in *Biographies of French Diocesan Priests in Nineteenth Century Texas*.
45. Dubuis to Odin, Jan. 29, 1867.
46. Chambodut.
47. Anstaett to Odin, 1867, quoted in Hegarty, 155.
48. Dubuis to Odin, Mar. 2, 1867.
49. Ibid.; Spalding, 283.
50. Hegarty, 160-77.
51. Ibid.
52. Sister Mary Xavier, *Father Jaillet, Saddlebag Priest of the Nueces*, 30-31.
53. Doyon, 175.
54. This account follows that left by Mother St. Ange quoted in Gunning, 88-90.
55. Dubuis to Odin, Dec. 17, 1867; Gunning, 91-95.
56. Dubuis to Odin, Feb. 8, 1868, Mar. 19, 1868, and Apr. 3, 1868; Gunning, 92-94.
57. *Synodus Gemina Diocesana Galvestonensis Secunda*, 4, 6; Castañeda, VII, 126-28.
58. *Synodus Gemina Diocesana Galvestonensis Secunda*, 40-42; Doyon, 77; Castañeda, VII, 126-28.
59. Odin to Spalding, May 14, 1869.
60. Odin to Spalding, Feb. 19, 1870; Hegarty, 217-18.
61. Robert Giles, *Changing Times: Story of the Galveston-Houston Diocese*, 23.
62. Hegarty, 218; *History of the Diocese of Galveston and St. Mary's Cathedral*, 111.
63. Castañeda, VII, 312.
64. Hegarty, 202-13, 221-24; Gunning, 104, 125ff.
65. William Dunn, C.S.C., *The Finest Country in the World: The Brothers and Priests of Holy Cross in Texas, 1870-1983*, 1-2; Castañeda, VII, 261-62.
66. Dunn, *The Finest Country in the World*, 2-3; Dunn, *Saint Edward's University: A Centennial History*, 22.
67. Dunn, *The Finest Country in the World*, 5-6.

68. Ibid.
69. James F. Vanderholt, "Contributions of Religious Women," in *East Texas Catholic,* Apr. 11, 1986; Castañeda, VII, 321–22.
70. *The Catholic Directory,* 1873.
71. Castañeda, VII, 130–31.
72. Ernest J. Burrus, "A Brief Account of the El Paso Diocese," *Newsletter of the Texas Catholic Historical Society* II (Jan., 1987): 1–3; Wright, "Catholic Diocesan Church"; Castañeda, VII, 133.

CHAPTER NINE

1. *The Metropolitan Catholic Almanac and Laity's Directory for 1851,* 181; *The Metropolitan Catholic Almanac and Laity's Directory for 1856,* 222; *Sadlier's Catholic Directory, Almanac, and Ordo for 1866,* 159; *Sadlier's Catholic Directory, Almanac, and Ordo for 1868,* 199; *Archdiocese of San Antonio, 1874–1949,* 34–36; *San Antonio Express,* Feb. 6, 1927.
2. *Freeman's Journal,* Apr. 25, 1880.
3. Parisot and Smith, 77.
4. *Archdiocese of San Antonio, 1874–1949,* 35–36; Castañeda, VII, 26.
5. Castañeda, VII, 331–32; *Archdiocese of San Antonio, 1874–1949,* 34–35.
6. Castañeda, VII, 331–32.
7. Baker, 118–19.
8. Sister Angelina Murphy, *Mother Florence, a Biographical History,* 3–30; Castañeda, VII, 313–14.
9. Baker, 119–20.
10. Castañeda, VII, 319–20.
11. Parisot and Smith, 171.
12. Ibid., 97; Castañeda, VII, 305–307.
13. Schmitz, 81.
14. Ibid., 73, 81, 83–84, 87.
15. Rt. Rev. Anthony Dominic Pellicer, D.D., *Pastoral Letter,* 1879.
16. Castañeda, VII, 266–68; Vanderholt, "Augustin Gardet."
17. The Rt. Rev. Anthony Dominic Pellicer, D.D., *Pastoral Letter,* 1875.
18. Anthony Dominic Pellicer to J. C. Neraz, V.G., July 31, 1878, Sept. 6, 1878.
19. *Freeman's Journal,* Apr., 1880; *San Antonio Express,* Feb. 6, 1927.
20. *Archdiocese of San Antonio, 1874–1949,* 36.
21. Claude Jaillet, "Sketches of Catholicity in Texas," 1888, typescript copy in C.A.T.; Parisot, 26.
22. *Archdiocese of San Antonio 1874–1949,* 84; James F. Vanderholt, "John C. Neraz," in *Biographies of French Diocesan Priests in Nineteenth Century Texas; Synodus Gemina Diocesana, Galvestonensis Secunda,* 4, 6.
23. *Archdiocese of San Antonio, 1874–1949,* 84; C. M. Dubuis, *Circular to Our Clergy,* May 9, 1881.
24. Castañeda, VII, 270–71; *Archdiocese of San Antonio, 1874–1949,* 86–87.

25. Dunn, *The Finest Country in the World*, 8–11.
26. For an account of the bishop's relationship with the order, see Murphy, 24–96, the source of the information given in this chapter, pp. 177–80.
27. Murphy, 96, 137–38.
28. Parisot and Smith, 174; *Archdiocese of San Antonio, 1874–1974*, 20.
29. *Archdiocese of San Antonio, 1874–1974*, 18–19; Castañeda, VII, 233–34.
30. *Archdiocese of San Antonio, 1874–1974*, 19; Castañeda, VII, 233–34.
31. *Archdiocese of San Antonio, 1874–1974*, 20.
32. Parisot and Smith, 86, 88, 90.
33. Parisot, 150; Parisot and Smith, 90; *San Antonio Express*, Feb. 6, 1927.
34. Parisot and Smith, 88, 91, 93.
35. *Archdiocese of San Antonio, 1874–1974*, 22; Castañeda, VII, 234.
36. *The Catholic Directory, 1901* (statistics for the year 1900), 494–98.
37. Jay P. Dolan, *The American Catholic Experience*, 119–23; Fr. Barnabas Diekemper, "French Clergy on the Texas Frontier, 1837–1900," *East Texas Historical Journal* 21 (Fall, 1983): 33–37.

CHAPTER TEN

1. *The Metropolitan Catholic Almanac and Laity's Directory for 1856*, p. 222; *The Metropolitan Catholic Almanac and Laity's Directory for 1861*, p. 116; *Sadlier's Catholic Directory, Almanac, and Ordo for 1866*, p. 160; *Sadlier's Catholic Directory, Almanac, and Ordo for 1870*, p. 227; Castañeda, VII, 484–85.
2. Dominic Manucy to Society for the Propagation of the Faith, June 29, 1875; Jaillet, "Sketches of Catholicity in Texas."
3. *Freeman's Journal*, Mar. 23, 1875.
4. Ibid.; Gilbert M. Cruz, "The Vicariate Apostolic of Brownsville, 1874–1912: An Overview of Its Origins and Development," in *Essays in Honor of John Francis Bannon, S.J.*, ed. Russell Magnanhi, 9–10.
5. Parisot, 116.
6. Doyon, 201.
7. Dominic Manucy to James McMaster, Sept. 5, 1874.
8. Florent Vandenberghe to Aime Martinet, Dec. 12, 1874, quoted in Doyon, 200.
9. Vandenberghe to Joseph Fabre, Feb. 16, 1875, quoted in Doyon, 202.
10. Doyon, 202.
11. Parisot, 117–19.
12. Dominic Manucy to the Society for the Propagation of the Faith, Lyon, June 29, 1875, and Aug. 3, 1875; Castañeda, VII, 135; Claude Jaillet, "Historical Sketches," in *Biographies of French Diocesan Priests in Nineteenth Century Texas*, p. 11.
13. Manucy to Society for the Propagation of the Faith, Lyon, August 3, 1875.
14. Castañeda, VII, 135.

15. Doyon, 206.
16. Jaillet, "Historical Sketches," 10–11; Manucy to Society for the Propagation of the Faith, Lyon, June 29, 1875; Xavier, *Father Jaillet*, 13, 18, 40, 41.
17. Jaillet, "Historical Sketches," 11–12; James F. Vanderholt, "Peter Bard," in *French Diocesan Priests in Nineteenth Century Texas*.
18. Parisot, 122.
19. Ibid., 123.
20. Ibid., 123–32.
21. For a complete account of this journey, see Parisot, 120–33.
22. Jaillet, "Sketches of Catholicity in Texas."
23. Jaillet, "Sketches of Catholicity in Texas"; Xavier, 114–15; Castañeda, VII, 137.
24. Doyon, 142–52.
25. Sister Mary Xavier Holworthy, "History of the Diocese of Corpus Christi Texas," Master's thesis, St. Mary's University, 1939, 39.
26. Xavier, 115; Sister Mary Xavier, *A Century of Sacrifice*, 34–35.
27. Holworthy, "History of the Diocese of Corpus Christi, Texas," 37–38.
28. Years later in 1924, the girls' academy and boys' school were combined into the coeducational Incarnate Word Academy; see Gunning, 134.
29. Jaillet, "Sketches of Catholicity in Texas."
30. Holworthy, "History of the Diocese of Corpus Christi, Texas," 46.
31. Castañeda, VII, 404–405; Holworthy, "History of the Diocese of Corpus Christi, Texas," 47–48.
32. Castañeda, VII, 404–405; Holworthy, "History of the Diocese of Corpus Christi, Texas," 47–48.
33. Castañeda, VII, 387; Holworthy, "History of the Diocese of Corpus Christi, Texas," 48.
34. Holworthy, "History of the Diocese of Corpus Christi, Texas," 48; *South Texas Catholic*, Nov. 25, 1983.
35. *The Catholic Directory*, 1901, 552–54.

CHAPTER ELEVEN

1. C. M. Dubuis to Louis Chaland, Apr. 13, 1875, Apr. 17, 1875, July 13, 1875, and Sept. 6, 1875; C. M. Dubuis, *Pastoral Letter to Diocese of Galveston*, May 1, 1871, copies in C. A. T.
2. Raymond J. Clancy, "History of the Congregation of the Holy Cross," typescript, 22, in C. A. T.
3. Pierre Dufal to Dubuis, Oct. 29, 1878.
4. Signed affidavit of Claude M. Dubuis, Mar. 5, 1879, copy in C. A. T.; Edward Sorin to Dufal, Mar. 5, 1879.
5. Thomas T. McAvoy, C. S. C., to Raymond J. Clancy, C. S. C., May 2, 1945; Pierre Dufal to clergy of the diocese of Galveston, June 23, 1879.

6. Cardinal Giovanni Simeoni to Dufal, Dec. 9, 1879; McAvoy to Clancy, May 2, 1945; Clancy, 27.
7. Dufal to "Colleagues," Jan. 20, 1880.
8. Clancy, 28.
9. James F. Vanderholt, "Claude M. Dubuis," in *Biographies of French Diocesan Priests in Nineteenth Century Texas.*
10. "Power of Attorney," Apr. 30, 1881, in Diocese of Galveston-Houston Archive, hereafter referred to as G.-H.A.
11. *Southern Messenger,* July 12, 1894, copy in C.A.T.
12. C. M. Dubuis, *Circular to Our Clergy,* May 9, 1881, in G.-H.A.
13. Giles, 27.
14. *Catholic Directory,* 1881, 216.
15. N. J. Perché to Priests and Catholics of the Diocese of Galveston, Dec. 20, 1881.
16. John Quinlan to N. A. Gallagher, Dec. 26, 1881; J. B. Purcell to N. A. Gallagher, Oct. 29, 1878, in G.-H.A.
17. Perché to the "Reverend Priests and Catholics of the Diocese of Galveston," Dec. 20, 1881, copy in C.A.T.; Theodore Buffard, Circular Letter to the Clergy, Dec. 25, 1881, in C.A.T.
18. John Quinlan to Gallagher, Dec. 26, 1881.
19. Anthony M. Truchard to Gallagher, Dec. 27, 1881.
20. Anthony M. Truchard to Gallagher, Dec. 27, 1881.
21. William Henry Elder to Gallagher, Jan. 4, 1882, in G.-H.A.
22. Jean Louis Bussant to Elder, Jan. 4, 1882; Elder to Gallagher, Jan. 9, 1882, both in G.-H.A.
23. Louis Chaland to Gallagher, Jan. 6, 1882, in G.-H.A.
24. John J. Delaney and James Edward Tobin, *Dictionary of Catholic Biography,* 788.
25. James A. McMaster to Nicholas A. Gallagher, Jan. 6, 1882, in G.-H.A.
26. McMaster to Gallagher, Jan. 7, 1882, in G.-H.A.
27. Louis Chaland to Gallagher, Jan. 6, 1882, in G.-H.A.
28. Theodore Buffard to Gallagher, Jan. 5, 1882.
29. Truchard to Gallagher, Jan. 9, 1882, in G.-H.A.
30. Theodore Buffard to Francis X. Leray, Feb. 9, 1882.
31. Truchard to Gallagher, Jan. 9, 1882, in G.-H.A.
32. Gallagher to the Clergy of the Diocese of Galveston, Mar. 3, 1882, in G.-H.A.
33. Hegarty, 279; Sheila Hackett, O.P., *Dominican Women in Texas,* 59.
34. Dubuis to Gallagher, Apr. 3, 1882.
35. Delaney and Tobin, 457; James F. Vanderholt, "Gentle Giant from Ohio," *East Texas Catholic,* Apr. 23, 1982; Castañeda, VII, 480–81; Nicholas A. Gallagher file in C.A.T.
36. *Sadlier's Catholic Directory, Almanac and Ordo for 1883,* 314–16; *1884,* 300–302, 515; *1885,* 209–10, 353, 354; *1887,* 211–13; *1893,* 295–97.

37. James F. Vanderholt, "Anthony M. Truchard," in *Biographies of French Diocesan Priests in Nineteenth Century Texas*.
38. Hegarty, 279–82.
39. Hegarty, 282.
40. Hegarty, 284.
41. Hegarty, 285–87.
42. Hackett, 52, 61–62.
43. Hackett, 63.
44. Johnston, 182; Hackett, 66–67.
45. Hackett, 67, App. 10, 679; Johnston, 185–86.
46. Hackett, 64.
47. Elinore McDonough as quoted in Hackett, 65.
48. Hackett, 60.
49. Johnston, 184–85.
50. Annals of the Ursuline Convent, Galveston, as quoted in Johnston, 178.
51. Johnston, 191–92.
52. As quoted in Johnston, 203.
53. Johnston, 203.
54. *History of the Diocese of Galveston and St. Mary's Cathedral*, 113.
55. Hegarty, 311; Cardinal Satolli's visit to Galveston and San Antonio is thoroughly examined and described in Raymond C. Mensing, Jr., "A Papal Delegate in Texas, The Visit of His Eminence Cardinal Satolli," *East Texas Historical Journal* 20 (Fall, 1982): 18–27.
56. Johnston, 203; Mensing, "A Papal Delegate in Texas," 19.
57. Mensing, "A Papal Delegate in Texas."
58. Annals of the Ursuline Convent, as quoted in Johnston, 207.
59. Ibid., 207–208.
60. Mensing, "A Papal Delegate in Texas," 20–21.
61. Johnston, 208; Mensing, "A Papal Delegate in Texas," 21; *Galveston Daily News*, Feb. 23, 1896.
62. Mensing, "A Papal Delegate in Texas," 21; Hegarty, 311.
63. Mensing, "A Papal Delegate in Texas," 21; Hegarty, 311.
64. Mensing, "A Papal Delegate in Texas," 22–23.
65. As quoted in Hegarty, 312.
66. Ibid.
67. Ibid.
68. Ibid., 312–14.
69. As quoted in Johnston, 208.
70. Mensing, "A Papal Delegate in Texas," 24–25.
71. Hackett, 93–94; Mensing, "A Papal Delegate in Texas," 24.
72. Mensing, "A Papal Delegate in Texas," 24.
73. Giles, 41; Vanderholt, "Gentle Giant from Ohio"; Hackett, 94.

74. Vanderholt, "Gentle Giant from Ohio"; Monsignor Anton J. Frank, "Homily on Anniversary of Death of Monsignor James M. Kirwin," Jan. 24, 1980, in author's possession.
75. Account regarding Catholic churches written by the Reverend James M. Kirwin, in Clarence Ousley, ed., *Galveston in Nineteen Hundred*, 97–116.
76. Pastoral Letter by the Rt. Rev. Nicholas A. Gallagher, Feb. 2, 1902, in C.A.T.

CHAPTER TWELVE

1. *The Metropolitan Catholic Almanac and Laity's Directory for the United States for 1860*, 125.
2. James F. Vanderholt, "Joseph Martiniere" and "Mathurin Pairier," in *Biographies of French Diocesan Priests in Nineteenth Century Texas*; Castañeda, VII, 137–38.
3. "Annals of the Ursuline Convent," Galveston, as quoted in Johnston, 146.
4. Castañeda, VII, 297.
5. Ibid., 297–98.
6. William R. Hoover, *St. Patrick's: The First 100 Years*, 5–7; Castañeda, VII, 381–83.
7. Nicholas A. Gallagher, "Information about the New See of Dallas, Texas," handwritten notes in C.A.T.
8. Most Reverend Fraancis Janssens to Rt. Rev. Nicholas A. Gallagher, Mar. 4, 1890, and Aug. 16, 1890, both in G.-H.A.
9. The Reverend Paul J. Foik, C.S.C., to Mr. J. D. Hackett, Mar. 16, 1932; Joseph Bernard Code, *Dictionary of the American Hierarchy*, 29; *Sadlier's Catholic Directory*, 1882, 296, 1890, 245; Joseph G. O'Donohoe, "Life of Bishop Brennan, First Bishop of Dallas," typescript in C.A.T.; M. F. Byrne to Rev. J. G. O'Donohoe, Feb. 7, 1933.
10. O'Donohoe, 2.
11. Brennan to Gallagher, Jan. 12, 1891.
12. *The Southern Messenger*, May 1, 1891; Brennan to Janssens, Feb. 18, 1891.
13. Dolan, 308–309.
14. Ibid., 309.
15. O'Donohoe, 7.
16. Ibid., 5.
17. Ibid., 4.
18. Ibid., 3.
19. Ibid., 7.
20. Ibid., 8.
21. Ibid., 9.
22. *St. Mary's Weekly Review*, Oct. 24, 1891.
23. O'Donohoe, 6.

24. *The Catholic Journal,* Aug. 22, 1891.
25. O'Donohoe, 8.
26. Ibid., 9.
27. Castañeda, VII, 141; O'Donohoe, 11.
28. Brennan to Gallagher, July 10, 1891, in G.-H.A.
29. Brennan to Gallagher, July 10, 1891, in G.-H.A.
30. Brennan to Gallagher, Jan. 15, 1892, in G.-H.A.
31. Janssens to Gallagher, Oct. 13, 1892, in G.-H.A. The use of "archbishop" in addressing Gallagher is a mistake; the letter's presence in the Galveston-Houston Archive leaves little doubt that it was meant for Gallagher.
32. James I. Tucek, *A Century of Faith: The Story of the Diocese of Dallas,* 38.
33. Gov. James Stephen Hogg to the Cardinal Prefect of the Propaganda, July 28, 1892, quoted in Tucek, 40.
34. Brennan to Gallagher, Sept. 20, 1892, in G.-H.A.
35. *Catholic Directories,* 1893 to 1903 state that he resigned in 1892; those from 1904 to present give the date as November 17, 1892.
36. Tucek, 40–41.
37. As quoted in Janssens to Gallagher, Oct. 6, 1892, in G.-H.A.
38. Janssens to Gallagher, Oct. 6 & Oct. 13, 1892, in G.-H.A.
39. Janssens to Gallagher, Oct. 13, 1892, in G.-H.A.
40. Photostatic copy of charges, written in Latin and attested to by Father Joseph Blum, in C.A.T.
41. Dolan, 271–76.
42. An unsigned, undated fragment of a letter exists which is probably from Janssens to Brennan indicating that the archbishop has received a list of accusations that he considers vague and for which he has requested substantiation on the part of the accusers. Photostat in C.A.T.
43. O'Donohoe, 9.
44. *The Official Catholic Directory, 1987,* 237.
45. *Sadlier's Catholic Directory, 1893,* 252–53.
46. *The Catholic Encyclopedia,* IV, 605.
47. Tucek, 43–44.
48. Foik to Hackett, Mar. 16, 1932.
49. "Historical Note on Bishop Brennan," undated typescript attributed to Bishop Laurence J. FitzSimon, in C.A.T.
50. Tucek, 44.
51. Brennan to Mulry, Mar. 17, 1911. When Brennan first visited the Mulry house, John Mulry was near death. When Brennan administered the rites for the sick, he said, "If ever there was a man cured, I will cure you." See Sara V. Mulry to Joseph G. Donohoe, May 28, 1933.
52. J. F. Dugan to O'Donohoe, Mar. 14, 1933.
53. *Sadlier's Catholic Directory, 1893,* 252.

54. O'Donohoe, 11; Thomas P. Cloherty, "History of the Diocese of Dallas" in G.-H.A.
55. Cloherty, 9; Castañeda, VII, 222.
56. Castañeda, VII, 340–41.
57. Ibid., 394–95.
58. Ibid., 383–85.
59. *The Catholic Directory,* 1901, 253–56.

CHAPTER THIRTEEN

1. Perrichone, 116.

Bibliography

Almaráz, Félix D., Jr. *Governor Antonio Martínez and Mexican Independence in Texas: An Orderly Transition*. San Antonio: Bexar County Historical Commission, 1979.

———. "San Antonio's Old Franciscan Missions: Material Decline and Secular Avarice in the Transition from Hispanic to Mexican Control." *Americas* 44 (July, 1987): 1–22.

Alvarez, Germán Valladares. "Catolicismo y Anti-clericalismo en Valentín Gómez-Farías." Master's thesis, St. Mary's University, San Antonio, 1962.

Annales de l'Association de la Propagation de la Foi, volume 12. Lyon: Association de la Propagation de la Foi, 1840.

Archdiocese of San Antonio, 1874–1949. San Antonio: Archdiocese of San Antonio, 1974.

Baker, T. Lindsay. *The First Polish Americans: Silesian Settlements in Texas*. College Station: Texas A&M University Press, 1979.

Barker, Eugene C. *The Life of Stephen F. Austin*. Austin: University of Texas Press, 1980.

Bayard, Ralph, C.M. *Lone Star Vanguard: The Catholic Re-Occupation of Texas, 1838–1848*. St. Louis: Vincentian Press, 1945.

Bony, Abbé. *Vie de Mgr. Jean-Marie Odin: Missionaire Lazariste, Archeveque de la Nouvelle-Orleans*. Paris: Imprimerie de D. DuMoulin et Cie., 1896.

Branda, Eldon Stephen, ed. *The Handbook of Texas: A Supplement*, volume 3. Austin: Texas State Historical Association, 1976.

Buckley, Cornelius M., trans. *A Frenchman, a Chaplain, a Rebel: The War Letters of Pere Louis-Hippolyte Gache, S.J.* Chicago: Loyola University Press, 1981.

Buffard, Theodore. Circular Letter to the Clergy, Galveston, December 25, 1881, in Catholic Archives of Texas, Austin.

Burrus, Ernest J., S.J. "A Brief Account of the El Paso Diocese," *Newsletter of the Texas Catholic Historical Society* 11 (January, 1987): 1–3.

Carter, Samuel, III. *The Final Fortress: The Campaign for Vicksburg, 1862–1863*. New York: St. Martin's Press, 1980.

Castañeda, Carlos Eduardo. *Our Catholic Heritage in Texas*, 7 volumes. Austin: Von Boeckmann-Jones, 1958.

Catholic Almanac for 1847, The. Baltimore: Fielding Lucas, Jr., 1847.

Catholic Directory, 1901, The. Milwaukee: M. H. Wiltzius and Co., 1901.

Catholic Encyclopedia, The. New York: Encyclopedia Press, 1908.

Chambodut, Mother Aloysia, O.S.M. "Father Chambodut, the First Secular Priest Ordained for Texas: Biographical Sketch." In archives of the Ursuline Convent and Academy, Dallas.

Clancy, Raymond J. "History of the Congregation of the Holy Cross," typescript 22, n.d., in Catholic Archives of Texas, Austin.

Clarke, Peter. *A Free Church in a Free Society: The Ecclesiology of John England, Bishop of Charleston, 1820-1842.* Rome: Pontifical Gregorian University, 1980.

Cloherty, Thomas P. "History of the Diocese of Dallas." Paper presented to the Diocese of Galveston-Houston on the eightieth anniversary of the Diocese of Dallas, 1971. Typescript in Galveston-Houston Archives.

Code, Joseph Bernard. *Dictionary of the American Hierarchy.* New York: Longmans, Green and Co., 1940.

Connor, Seymour V. *Texas: A History.* Arlington Heights: Ill.: AHM Publishing Corporation, 1971.

Cruz, Gilbert R. "The Vicariate Apostolic of Brownsville, 1874-1912: An Overview of Its Origins and Development," in *Essays in Honor of John Francis Bannon, S.J.,* edited by Russell Magnanhi. Marquette: Northern Michigan University Press, 1982.

Delaney, John J., and James Edward Tobin. *Dictionary of Catholic Biography.* Garden City, N.J.: Doubleday and Co., 1961.

De la Peña, José Enrique. *With Santa Anna in Texas: A Personal Narrative of the Revolution.* College Station: Texas A&M University Press, 1975.

De León, Arnoldo. *The Tejano Community, 1836-1900.* Albuquerque: University of New Mexico Press, 1982.

―――. *They Called Them Greasers.* Austin: University of Texas Press, 1983.

Diekemper, Fr. Barnabas. "French Clergy on the Texas Frontier, 1837-1900," *East Texas Historical Journal* 21 (Fall, 1983): 29-37.

Diocese of Galveston, Centennial, 1847-1947. Houston: Centennial Book Committee, 1947.

Dolan, Jay P. *The American Catholic Experience.* Garden City, N.Y.: Doubleday & Company, 1985.

Domenech, Emmanuel. *Missionary Adventures in Texas and Mexico: A Personal Narrative of Six Years' Sojourn in Those Regions.* London: Longman, Brown, Green, Longman, and Roberts, 1858.

Doyon, Bernard, O.M.I. *The Cavalry of Christ on the Rio Grande.* Milwaukee: Bruce Press, 1956.

Dubuis, C[laude] M[arie]. *Circular to Our Clergy.* May 9, 1881. San Antonio, 1881. In Galveston-Houston Archive.

―――. *Pastoral Letter to Diocese of Galveston.* Galveston, 1870.

―――. *Pastoral Letter to Diocese of Galveston,* May 1, 1870. Copy in Catholic Archives of Texas, Austin.

Dunn, William, C.S.C. *The Finest Country in the World: The Brothers and Priests of*

Holy Cross in Texas, 1870–1983. Notre Dame, Indiana: Province Archives Center, 1985.

———. *Saint Edward's University: A Centennial History.* Austin: Saint Edward's University Press, 1986.

Fellner, Felix, O.S.B. "Benedictine Pioneers in Texas." Typescript #589 in Catholic Archives of Texas, Austin.

Fitzmorris, Sister Mary Angela. *Four Decades of Catholicism in Texas, 1820–1860.* Washington, D.C.: Catholic University of America, 1926.

Foley, Patrick. "Jean-Marie Odin, C.M., Missionary Bishop Extraordinaire of Texas," *Journal of Texas History and Culture* 1 (March, 1990): 42–60.

Frank, Anton J. "Homily on Anniversary of Death of Monsignor James M. Kirwin." Annunciation Church, Houston, January 24, 1980. Copy in author's possession.

Gallagher, Nicholas A. "Information about the New See of Dallas, Texas." Handwritten notes [apparently in Gallagher's hand] in Catholic Archives of Texas, Austin.

———. *Pastoral Letter.* Galveston, February 2, 1902.

Gammel, H. P. N. *The Laws of Texas, 1822–1897.* Volume I. Austin: Gammel Book Company, 1898.

Gannon, Michael V. *Rebel Bishop: The Life and Era of Augustin Verot.* Milwaukee: Bruce Publishing Co., 1964.

Giles, Robert. *Changing Times: Story of the Galveston-Houston Diocese.* Houston: Texas Catholic Herald, 1972.

Gunning, Mother M. Patricia. *To Texas with Love.* Austin: Best Printing, 1971.

Hackett, Sheila, O.P. *Dominican Women in Texas.* Houston: D. Armstrong Company, 1986.

Hebert, Rachel Bluntzer. *The Forgotten Colony, San Patricio de Hibernia.* Burnet, Texas: Eakin Press, 1981.

Hegarty, Mary Loyola, C.C.V.I. *Serving with Gladness: The Origin and History of the Congregation of the Sisters of Charity of the Incarnate Word, Houston, Texas.* Milwaukee: Bruce Publishing Company, 1967.

Hinojosa, Gilberto Miguel. *A Borderlands Town in Transition: Laredo, 1755–1870.* College Station: Texas A&M University Press, 1983.

———. "The Enduring Hispanic Faith Communities: Spanish and Texas Church Historiography," *Journal of Texas Catholic History and Culture* 1 (March, 1990): 20–41.

History of the Diocese of Galveston and St. Mary's Cathedral, compiled by the faculty of St. Mary's Seminary. La Porte, Texas, 1922.

Hoffman's Catholic Directory. Volumes for 1895–1900. Milwaukee: Hoffman Bros. Co.

Hogan, William Ransom. *The Texas Republic: A Social and Economic History.* Norman: University of Oklahoma Press, 1946.

Hollon, W. Eugene, and Ruth Lapham Butler, eds. *William Bollaert's Texas*. Norman: University of Oklahoma Press, 1956.
Holworthy, Sister Mary Xavier. *Diamonds for the King*. San Antonio: Clegg Publishing Company, 1945.
———. "History of the Diocese of Corpus Christi, Texas." Master's thesis, St. Mary's University, 1939.
Hoover, William R. *St. Patrick's: The First 100 Years*. Fort Worth: St. Patrick Cathedral, 1988.
Institute of Texan Cultures. *The Czech Texans*. San Antonio: Institute of Texan Cultures, 1978.
Jacks, L. V. *Claude Dubuis, Bishop of Galveston*. St. Louis: B. Herder Book Co., 1946.
Jaillet, Claude. "Historical Sketches," in *Biographies of French Diocesan Priests in Nineteenth Century Texas,* edited by James F. Vanderholt, San Antonio, 1978.
———. "Sketches of Catholicity in Texas." Typescript copy of a report made to the American Historical Society, 1888, in Catholic Archives of Texas.
Johnson, Francis W. *A History of Texas and Texans,* volume 1. Chicago: American Historical Society, 1914.
Johnston, S. M. *Builders by the Sea: History of the Ursuline Community of Galveston, Texas*. New York: Exposition Press, 1971.
Kemp, Louis Wiltz. *The Signers of the Texas Declaration of Independence*. Houston: Anson Jones Press, 1944.
La Fleur, Sister Mary Monica, C.C.V.I. "The Immigration Factor in the Growth of the Diocese of Galveston: 1841-1874. Dissertation, University of Notre Dame, 1965.
Linn, John J. *Reminiscences of Fifty Years in Texas*. Austin: Steck Company, 1935.
Lowrie, Samuel Harmon. *Culture Conflict in Texas*. New York: AMS Press, 1967.
Lyons, John A. *Bishops and Priests of the Diocese of Bardstown*. Louisville: Privately printed, 1976.
McComb, David G. *Texas: A Modern History*. Austin: University of Texas Press, 1989.
McKeown, H. C. *The Life and Labors of Most Reverend John Joseph Lynch, D.D.* Montreal: James A. Sadlier, 1886.
Maresh, Henry. "The Czechs in Texas," *Southwestern Historical Quarterly* 50 (October, 1946): 234-40.
Mensing, Raymond C., Jr. "A Papal Delegate in Texas: The Visit of His Eminence Cardinal Satolli," *East Texas Historical Journal* 20 (Fall, 1982): 18-27.
Metropolitan Catholic Almanac and Laity's Directory, The. For various years. Baltimore: Fielding Lucas, Jr., 1845, 1851; Lucas Bros., 1856, 1857; John Murphy and Co., 1860, 1861.
"Minutes and Statutes of the First Synod of the Diocese of Galveston." [1858] Typescript copy of original, printed edition. Copy in Galveston-Houston Archives.
Murphy, Sister Angelina. *Mother Florence, A Biographical History*. Smithstown, New York: Exposition Press, 1980.

Oates, Stephen B. *With Malice toward None.* New York: Harper and Row, 1977.
O'Donohoe, Joseph G. "Life of Bishop Brennan, First Bishop of Dallas." N.d. Typescript in Catholic Archives of Texas, Austin.
Ousley, Clarence, ed. *Galveston in Nineteen Hundred.* Atlanta: William C. Chase, 1900.
Parisot, P. F., O.M.I. *The Reminiscences of a Texas Missionary.* San Antonio: Press of Johnson Bros. Printing Co., 1899.
———, and C. J. Smith, O.M.I. *History of the Catholic Church in the Diocese of San Antonio, Texas.* San Antonio: Carrico & Bowen, 1897.
Pellicer, The Rt. Rev. Anthony Dominic, D.D. *Pastoral Letter.* San Antonio: Herald Publishing Co., 1875.
———. *Pastoral Letter.* San Antonio: J. S. Penn & Bro., 1879.
Perrichone, Jean. *The Life of Bishop Dubuis, Apostle of Texas,* translated by Hectorine Piercey, 1978. Typescript translation of French work published in Lyon, 1899, copy in Galveston-Houston Archives.
"Pope's Bull, and the Words of Daniel O'Connell, The" in *Official Proceedings of the Republican Convention Convened in the City of Pittsburg, Pennsylvania, on 22 February, 1856.* New York: New York Republican Committee, 1856.
Puckett, Fidelia Miller. "Ramón Ortiz: Priest and Patriot," *New Mexico Historical Review* 25 (October, 1950): 265–95.
Red, William Stuart. *The Texas Colonists and Religion, 1821–1836.* Austin: E. L. Shettles, 1924.
Richardson, Rupert N., Ernest Wallace, Adrian N. Anderson. *Texas, the Lone Star State.* Englewood Cliffs, New Jersey: Prentice-Hall, 1970.
Riforgiato, Leonard R. "John Timon and the Succession to the See of Baltimore in 1851," *Vencentian Heritage* 8 (1987): 27–42.
Roemer, Ferdinand von. *Roemer's Texas,* translated by Oswald Mueller. San Antonio: Standard Printing Company, 1935.
Ryan, William M. *Shamrock and Cactus.* San Antonio: Southern Literary Institute, 1936.
Sadlier's Catholic Directory, Almanac, and Ordo, volumes for 1866, 1867, 1868, 1870, 1881, 1883, 1884, 1885, 1887, 1893. New York: D. and J. Sadlier.
Schmitz, Joseph William, S.M. *The Society of Mary in Texas.* San Antonio: Naylor, 1951.
———. *Texan Statecraft, 1836–1845.* San Antonio: Naylor, 1941.
———. *Thus They Lived: Social Life in the Republic of Texas.* San Antonio: Naylor, 1935.
Sheridan, Sister Mary Benignus. "Bishop Odin and the New Era of the Catholic Church in Texas, 1840–1860." Dissertation, Saint Louis University, 1938.
Smither, Harriet, ed. "Diary of Adolphus Sterne," *Southwest Historical Quarterly* 31 (July, 1927): 181–87.
Spalding, Thomas W. *Martin John Spalding: American Churchman.* Washington, D.C.: Catholic University of America Press, 1973.

Stiff, Col. Edward. *The Texan Emigrant: Being a Narration of the Adventures of the Author in Texas.* Waco: Texian Press, 1968.
Synodus Gemina Diocesana Galvestonensis Secunda. New Orleans: Propagateur Catholique, 1869. Copy in Catholic Archives of Texas, Austin.
Tafolla, Carmen. "The Church in Texas," in *Fronteras: A History of the Latin American Church in the USA since 1513*, edited by Moíses Sandoval. San Antonio: Mexican American Cultural Center, 1983.
Texas Almanac, 1988–1989. Dallas: Dallas Morning News, 1987.
Thompson, Jerry D. *Mexican Texans in the Union Army.* El Paso: Texas Western Press, 1986.
Trigg, Lina. "Father Michael Muldoon: The Story of an Early Pioneer Priest." Master's thesis, St. Mary's University, San Antonio, 1940.
Tucek, James I. *A Century of Faith: The Story of the Diocese of Dallas.* Dallas: Taylor Publishing Company, 1990.
Ugarte, José Bravo. *Diócesis y Obispos de la Iglesia Mexicana, 1519–1965.* Mexico City: Editorial Jus, 1965.
Vanderholt, James F. *Biographies of French Diocesan Priests in Nineteenth Century Texas.* San Antonio: Privately printed, 1978.
———. "Contributions of Religious Women," *East Texas Catholic*, April 11, 1986.
———. "Father George W. Haydon." 1984. Biographical essay in Catholic Archives of Texas, Austin.
———. "Gentle Giant from Ohio," *East Texas Catholic*, April 23, 1982.
———. "Slavery and the Church," *East Texas Catholic*, April 11, 1986.
Walker, Williston. *A History of the Christian Church.* New York: Charles Scribner's Sons, 1945.
Weaver, Bobby D. *Castro's Colony.* College Station: Texas A&M University Press, 1985.
Williams, Amelia W., and Eugene C. Barker, eds. *The Writings of Sam Houston, 1813–1863*, volume 2. Austin: Jenkins, 1970.
Woods, Sister Frances Jerome, C.D.P. "Congregations of Religious Women in the Old South," in *Catholics in the Old South: Essays on Church and Culture*, edited by Randall M. Miller and John L. Wakelyn. Macon, Georgia: Mercer University Press, 1983.
Wright, Robert E., O.M.I. "Catholic Diocesan Church of New Spain and Mexico (1700–1892)," essay prepared for the revised *Handbook of Texas.* Austin: Texas State Historical Association, forthcoming.
———. "The Parish of San Agustín, Laredo, 1760–1857," in *San Agustín Parish of Laredo: Marriage Book I, 1790–1857*, edited by Angel Sepúlveda Brown and Gloria Villa Cadena. San Antonio: Privately printed, 1989.
Xavier, Sister Mary, I.W.B.S. *A Century of Sacrifice.* Corpus Christi, 1953.
———. *Father Jaillet, Saddlebag Priest of the Nueces.* Corpus Christi, 1948.
Yoakum, Henderson. *History of Texas from Its First Settlement in 1685 to Its Annexation to the United States in 1846*, volume 2. Austin: Steck Company, 1935.

Index

abolitionists, 7–8, 121–22
Academy of the Sacred Heart, Waco, 162
Adelsverein, the, 71, 78
administration: of El Paso County, 165; of religious orders, 178–80; of St. Mary's Infirmary, 208–10; of St. Mary's Orphanage, 218–19; of Texas Catholic Church, 118–19, 160–61, 165, 168, 194, 200–11
Alamo, the, 44, 51–53, 66, 95, 117–18
Alamo Church, 51–53
Almaráz, Félix D., Jr., 39
Amarillo, 238
Americanism, 227–28, 234–35
Ami de la Religion, L', 15
Anduze, Abbé N. B., 26–29, 31
Anglos: Catholic, 21–22, 56–57, 111, 189–90, 196; and Civil War, 148. *See also* immigrants; *names of people*
annexation: of California, 73–74; of New Mexico, 73–74; of Oregon, 73; of Texas, 6, 9, 20, 24, 66, 73, 76–77, 82
Annunciation of the Blessed Virgin Mary Church, St. Hedwig, 106
Anstaett, Fr. Joseph, 81, 126, 161; quoted, 158
anti-Catholicism, 100, 138; American, 4, 7, 10, 55, 215–16; in Brownsville, 185, 188–89; Know-Nothing, 111–16; and Reconstruction, 147–48
anticlericalism, 4–8, 110, 168
Apodaca Loreto, Bp. Salvador, 91
Archconfraternity of the Immaculate Heart of the Blessed Virgin Mary, 119
atheism, Fourierist, 110
Aubert, Mother St. Joseph, 175
Austin, 24, 47–48, 113, 163
Austin County, 78, 103
Austin Statesman, 231
authority, ecclesiastical, 10, 32, 39–40, 82–83

Bakanowski, Fr. Adolph, 145–50
Baker, T. Lindsay: *The First Polish Americans: Silesian Settlements in Texas,* 104–105, 108, 145, 147–48
Bandera, 105–106, 108
Banks, Nathaniel P., 134–37
Bard, Pierre, 191–92
Barzynski, Fr. Vincent, 146–47, 149–50
Bastrop, 53
Baunach, Fr. Peter, 110, 140, 142
Bayard, Ralph, 14
Bayou La Fourche, 15, 26, 36
Belaunzarán y Ureña, Bp. José María, 91
Bellaclas, John B., 161
bells, church, 41–43, 62, 148, 184, 192
Benavides, Santos, 115, 135
Benedictine Order, 109–10, 140, 162, 237–38
Bexar County, 78, 115
Bittowski, Fr. Joseph, 103
blacks: and Catholic Church, 152, 154–55, 180–82, 213; education of, 122, 173, 213; and Reconstruction, 144–45
Blanc, Archbishop Antoine, of Galveston, 34; as archbishop of New Orleans, 101, 123; as bishop of New Orleans, 10, 12–15, 21, 27–28, 31–32, 57–58, 64–65, 83
blockade, Civil War, 123–26, 132, 136
Blum, Fr. Joseph, 231, 234–35, 237
Boehns, Bro. Michael, 110
Borias, Antoine, 113–14
boundaries: of Brownsville vicariate, 184; of Dallas diocese, 222; disputed, 81–83; of Galveston diocese, 161, 200; of San Antonio diocese, 163, 165; of Texas, 3, 24, 77; U.S.–New Spain, 12–13
Boundary Statute of 1836, 24, 82
Brands, John, 70–71, 73
Brazoria, 78, 79, 120
Brazos de Santiago, 76, 92, 135, 138

271

Brazos River, 59, 69
Brennan, Bp. Thomas F.: as bishop of Dallas, 224–36; quoted, 225, 227–28, 231–32, 263n.51
Bretault, Fr. Jean, 192–93
Brothers of Mary. *See* Society of Mary
Brownson, Orestes, 206, 227
Brown's Settlement, 29, 47, 60, 63, 78–79
Brownsville, 77, 89–92, 94, 129, 132, 134–35, 160; education in, 120, 155, 163; Oblates in, 95–98, 119, 163, 185, 187–90, 195
Brownsville, vicariate of, 165–66, 168, 184–99
Buffalo Bayou, 18, 55, 85
Buffard, Fr. Stephen (Etienne Marie), 161, 181, 191
Buffard, Fr. Theodore, 201, 203–11
Burnet, David G., 9, 19–20, 49–52, 57
Bussant, Fr. Jean Louis, 206, 209–11

Caballero, Fernando, 196
California, 73–74, 77, 82
Calvo, Fr. Miguel, 35–39, 42–44, 46, 60, 68, 72, 80, 93
Camargo, Mexico, 91, 95, 97
Canopus, see of, 210
"Cart War," 114–15
Cashin, Sr. Mary Rose, 211
Castro, Henri, 71–72
Castroville, 72, 78, 81, 85–90, 92; priests for, 104, 107; religious orders in, 110, 170, 177–80
Catholic Church: and Civil War, 122; and Confederacy, 122–23; and European immigration, 70–72; and jurisdictional boundaries, 83; and Mexican Revolution, 3–4; and Mexico, 12–13; and Republic of Texas, 10–13, 49; and slavery, 126; and Texas Church, 28; and Texas prefecture, 31–32. *See also* Vatican
Catholic Church, in Texas, 9, 81; and blacks, 180–82, 213; and Civil War, 134–35, 140, 142; growth of, 120; and Mexican clergy, 97–98; in 1900, 239–40; reorganization of, 6, 9–23, 28–30, 160–61, 165; and resignation of Bishop Brennan, 236–37; and slavery, 121–22. *See also* prefecture apostolic; vicariates apostolic; *names of dioceses*
Catholic Church, Mexican, 8, 12–13, 91, 188; and Texas, 9, 32, 83, 97–98
Catholic Church, U.S.: and Americanism, 227; and blacks, 152, 154–55; and Know-

Catholic Church, U.S. (*cont.*)
Nothing party, 111–12; and Reconstruction, 151–52; and Texas, 10, 34, 58, 69, 75
Catholic Journal, 230
Catholics: black, 180–81; Czech, 101–103; Hispanic, 61–62, 92–93, 239; Mexican, 101; and slavery, 121–22; in Texas, 3–4, 6, 8–12, 21–22, 56, 121–22. *See also* population, Catholic
Catholic Truth Society, 228
Chaland, Fr. Jacques, 191
Chaland, Fr. Louis, 161, 191, 201, 203, 205, 207–10
Chambodut, Fr. Louis Claude Marie, 79, 81, 111, 124–25, 161, 252n.51; and Civil War, 130–31, 144; as diocesan chancellor, 119, 162; as vicar general, 156, 158
Chanche, Bp. John, 65
Chandy, Fr. Jean Pierre, 26, 32
Chandy, Fr. Pierre, 208, 210
Chanrion, Fr. Anthony, 79, 81
Chanzelle, Fr. Matthew, 79
chapels: in Brownsville vicariate, 192, 195; numbers of, 120, 140; rural, 91, 97; Ursuline, 214–18
Chapolard, Emile, 191
Charbonnel, Bp. Armand de, 127
Chazelle, Matthew, 81, 85
Cherokee Indians, 25
churches: in Brownsville vicariate, 194–96; building of, 17, 20, 59, 75, 88–89, 96, 105–106, 140–42, 150, 181–83; consecration of, 174; in Dallas diocese, 231; damage to, 57, 111; disputes over, 113–14; in Galveston, 59, 63–64, 69, 220; for German settlers, 78; in Goliad, 113–14; in Houston, 63, 69; inadequacy of, 84; location of, 78; numbers of, 120, 140, 238; ownership of, 52–53; in Republic of Texas, 17, 29; in Texas vicariate, 78–79. *See also names of churches*
Cinquin, Mother St. Pierre, 172
civil rights, and Reconstruction, 144–45
Civil War, 108, 110, 113, 121–39, 222
Clarendon, 238
Claretians. *See* Sons of the Immaculate Heart of Mary
Clarke, Fr. Edward, 28–30, 47, 181
Claudiopolis, see of, 58
clergy, Catholic: in Dallas, 234; in Galveston, 160–61, 200–11; Mexican, 94–95, 97–98; secular, 41; and slavery, 7–8; and syn-

clergy, Catholic (*cont.*)
  odal decrees, 118. *See also names of individuals*
clergy, Protestant, 6–7, 10, 23, 54
climate: of Texas, 18–19, 21, 38, 54–56, 67, 69, 72, 107, 159–60, 220; and travel, 35–36, 38, 59–60
Cohen, Henry, 216
Coleto, 3, 106, 150
Coleto Creek, 38, 58, 63
colonization, xi–xii, 4, 78
Comanche, 51, 53
Comanche Indians, 25–26, 87; conflict with, 38, 43–44, 46–47, 58, 90–91; fear of, 63
communications: during Civil War, 124–26, 137–38; and railroad expansion, 222
communities: German, 111, 112; immigrant, 78; Polish, 104–106, 108, 112, 145–50, 169–70; rural, 63, 69, 89–90, 95, 97, 103
Compromise of 1850, 3, 82
Confederacy, 126–27, 129–30, 132, 135, 138–40, 144, 147; and Catholic Church, 122, 140, 142
Confederate supporters, 135; civil rights for, 144–45
Confederate troops, 122, 129–30, 132, 134–35, 138–39
conflict: over Church property, 53, 113–14, 116–18; between clergy, 178–80, 200–20, 231–35, 240; over education, 169–70; ethnic, 57, 113–16, 145–49, 240; Indian-settler, 25–26, 37–38, 43, 46–47, 58, 62–63, 65, 86, 90–91, 223; in Mexico, 150; Mexico-France, 26; North-South, 112–13, 213; political, 112; religious, 41–42, 113–14; Republic of Texas–Mexico, 65–67; over slavery, 100, 112–13, 115, 121. *See also* rebellion
Congregation of the Evangelization of Peoples, 205
Congregation of the Holy Cross, 162–65, 178, 200–201
Congregation of the Mission. *See* Vincentian Order
Congregation of the Resurrection, 146–47, 152–53
Congregation of the Sisters of Charity of the Incarnate Word. *See* Sisters of Charity of the Incarnate Word
Connobio, Fr. Félix de, 134
consecration: of Bishop Brennan, 225–26; of Bishop Dubuis, 127; of Bishop Dunn, 237; of Bishop Forest, 181; of Bishop Gallagher, 208–10; of Bishop Manucy, 184, 187; of Bishop Meerschert, 230; of Bishop Neraz, 175, 177, 201; of Bishop Odin, 65, 83; of Bishop Pellicer, 166; of Bishop Verdaquer, 196; of churches, 174
Considerant, Victor, 110–11
constitution: of Republic of Texas, 6–7, 11; of State of Texas, 7; U.S., 144; Ursuline, 232
Constitutional Union party, 123
controversy: and Bishop Manucy, 188–89; and church ownership, 52–53. *See also* conflict
convents: Dominican, 212–13, 216; Sisters of Charity of the Incarnate Word, 156; Sisters of Divine Providence, 156, 178–80; Sisters of Mercy, 212; Sisters of the Incarnate Word and Blessed Sacrament, 135, 155–57, 162; Ursuline, 89, 98–99, 116, 130, 132, 154, 156, 175, 216, 223
Córdova, Vicente, 25
Corpus Christi, 68, 77, 78, 92, 143, 159, 162, 190, 194–96
corruption: alleged, 215–18; and land titles, 115; of local government, 94, 114; of loyalist priests, 39–41
Cortina, Juan, 115–16
council, use of term, 252n.50
Council of Trent, 118
Councils of Baltimore, 10, 118; and Church property, 232; Fifth, 69; Seventh, 89; Sixth, 75, 80
crime: and Civil War, 136, 138–39; in Houston, 18–19; and Texas army, 68. *See also* outlaws
culture: European, 72; Hispanic, 61–62, 183
Cummings Creek, 78, 92

Daingerfield, William, 31, 48
Dallas, 110–11, 222–23, 229–31, 238
Dallas, diocese of, 83, 222–38
D'Asti, Fr. Augustine, 156
Daughters of the Cross, 122
Davis, Edmund J., 134, 145, 164–65
Davis, Jefferson, 122, 135
de la Garza, Fr. Refugio, 3, 21, 29, 39–42, 68
De León, Arnoldo: *They Called Them Greasers*, 115
de Mazenod, Bp. Charles, 93, 95

274 / *Index*

Democratic party, 73, 112–13, 121, 123, 145, 164
de Saligny, Alphonse Dubois, 36, 48, 50–51
de Zavala, Lorenzo, 5, 9
D'Hanis, 85–86, 104, 110
Díaz de León, Fr. José Antonio, 3, 20, 22, 47, 81
Diekemper, Fr. Barnabas, 183
Dirstyn, John, 106
disease, 84, 87; tuberculosis, 140, 142. *See also* epidemics
Dolan, Jay P., quoted, 227
Domenech, Emmanuel, 85–88, 93–95, 97; quoted, 88
Dominican Order: and Bishop Gallagher, 212–13, 218–19
Donado, Benedict, 196
Dowling, Richard, 134, 159
Doyle, Mary, 163
Dubina, 103
Dubourge, Bp. Louis, 34
Dubuis, Bp. Claude Marie: as bishop of Galveston, 122, 128–29, 132, 134, 136–38, 149–56, 158–65, 168, 170–71, 175, 177, 222–23; and Brownsville vicariate, 185; as missionary pastor, 85–86, 88–89, 93, 98, 111, 116, 119, 124–27; quoted, 137; recruitment by, 127, 140, 142–43, 146–47, 151, 191; retired, 200–203, 207–10, 215
Dufal, Bp. Pierre, 200–201, 203, 207
Dugan, Fr. J. F., quoted, 236
Dumas, Fr. Claude, 96
Dunn, Bp. Joseph Edward, 237–38
Dunne, Fr. David H., 238

Eccleston, Archbishop Samuel, 34, 57, 69
economy, of Texas, 65, 68, 112, 129
ecumenism, 216
Edel, Bro. Andrew, 99–100, 142–43
education: for blacks, 122, 213; Catholic, 43, 57–58, 62, 78–79, 98–100, 119–20, 122, 155, 162–64, 168–71, 173, 177, 221; conflict over, 113, 169–70, 234–35; in San Antonio diocese, 181–82; seminary, 173–74, 177. *See also* schools; *names of institutions*
Edward, David: *The History of Texas*, 15
Elder, Archbishop William Henry, 123, 135, 206
elections: in Texas, 9, 24, 113, 164; U.S., 73, 122; of women religious, 179–80, 211
El Mexicano de Tejas, 145
El Paso, 3, 83, 122, 230

El Paso County, 83, 97, 165
El Paso del Norte, 41, 97
England, Bp. John, 122
epidemics, 109; cholera, 37, 87–88, 137; influenza, 192; smallpox, 180; typhoid, 137; yellow fever, 71, 81, 137, 155, 158–59
Escude, Josephine. *See* Mary Ange of Jesus, Sr.
Estany, Fr. Eudald, 35–37, 43, 46–47, 60, 63, 72
Etienne, Jean-Baptiste, 15
Europe: clergy from, 93, 95, 127, 140, 143, 146, 152–53, 165, 221; immigration from, 104; and Texas missionary work, 74–75. *See also names of countries*
expansionism: railroad, 108–109, 151, 184; U.S., 73–74, 77, 82

factionalism, in Galveston diocese, 200–11
farmers, immigrant, 102–103, 107
Farnesé, Comte de, 10–12
Fauvre, Claude, 191
Federalism, Mexican, 4–6, 65–66
Feltin, Fr. Nicholas, 156, 163, 178
Feltin, Mother St. Andrew, 170, 178–80
Ferdinand VII, 5
festivals, religious, 61–62, 95, 119, 149–50
finances: alleged misuse of, 217–18; of Catholic schools, 113, 117, 156, 171; of Dallas diocese, 230–31; hospital, 198; and Texas mission work, 74, 187, 189. *See also* fundraising
First Polish Americans, The: Silesian Settlements in Texas (Baker), 104–105, 108, 145, 147–48
First Vatican Council, 161–62, 200
Fitzgerald, Bp. Edward, 177, 209, 230, 235, 237
Fitzgerald, Fr. James, 80, 87
FitzSimon, Bp. Laurence J., 236
Foik, Fr. Paul J., 235
food: and Civil War, 129, 137; shortage of, 67, 85–86, 103
Forest, Bp. John Anthony, 180–83, 191
forts, 6, 85, 87, 124, 126
Fort Worth, 222–24
Fourier, Charles, 110
"Fourierists," 110–11
France: and Civil War, 127, 129, 134, 138; immigration from, 110; recruitment in, 99, 126, 146, 152, 159, 165, 170, 190; and Republic of Texas, 26–27, 31, 48; retirement to,

France (*cont.*)
211; Society of Mary in, 143; and Texas missionary work, 74–75
Francis, Bro. Charles, 143, 173
Franciscan Order, x, 62, 81, 103–105, 107–108, 117, 156
Fransoni, Cardinal Giacomo, 12–15, 49, 57
Fredericksburg, 78, 86, 94, 103–104, 107, 110, 140
Freeman's Journal, 185, 206
Frías, Timoteo, 96
fundraising: for church building, 54, 100; in Europe, 74–75; for Galveston diocese, 150; hospital, 158; for missionary work, 36, 118

Gallagher, Rt. Rev. Nicholas A.: and Bishop Brennan, 224–25, 231–35, 237; and Galveston diocese, 203–20
Galveston, 16–18, 23, 54–55, 62, 68, 70; churches in, 59, 63–64, 68–69, 75, 78; and Civil War, 124, 126–27, 129–30, 132, 137–39; disease in, 71, 81, 84, 137, 158–59; hospitals in, 152–54, 156, 158–59; living conditions in, 65, 84, 144–45; in 1900, 220; orphanages in, 162; politics in, 111, 113; religious orders in, 78–79, 89, 92–93, 211–20
Galveston, diocese of, 80–83; during Civil War, 121–39; conflict in, 200–20; division of, 200, 222, 240; first synod of, 118–19; growth of, 101–21, 118, 140; and Reconstruction, 140–65
Galveston Daily News, quoted, 153–54
García, José Trinidad, 90, 96, 98
Gardet, Fr. Augustine, 156
Garesche, Julius, 89, 94
Gaudet, Fr. Augustin, 89, 119, 161
Gaye, Fr. Jean-Marie, 96
Gelot, Bro. Paul, 89
Germany, recruitment in, 103–104, 170
Gibbons, Archbishop James Cardinal, 227
Giraud, Fr. Jean, 150–51
Giraudon, Fr. Jacques, 92–93, 119
Goliad, 3, 22, 37–38, 40, 60, 66, 113–15
Gonnard, Fr. Jean, 159
Gonzales, 46–47, 79
government, local: corrupt, 94, 114; of San Antonio, 117–18
government, Mexican: and Catholic Church, 37, 39, 91, 98, 168, 188; and Texas, 9, 65–67, 76–77, 83

government, of Republic of Texas: and annexation, 76; and Church property, 45, 48–53, 57, 114
government, of State of Texas, 76, 164–65
government, Spanish: and Church property, 50
government, U.S.: and Alamo buildings, 117–18; and Reconstruction, 143, 152; and Texas boundaries, 82–83
Granger, Rev. Louis, 225
Grau y Cruz, Fr. Francisco, 228–29
Gregory XVI, 12, 35, 64, 75, 80
Grotta Ferrata Monastery, Rome, 236
Guadalupe River, 47, 63
Gutiérrez de Lara, Bernardo, 5

Harrington, Mother St. Pierre, 132–33
Haydon, George W., 28–30, 40, 70; quoted, 30
Hearne, 162
Hebrew Standard, 228
Hegarty, Sr. Mary Loyola, quoted, 211
Helena, 115, 148
Hennessy, Bp. John Joseph, 229
Heslin, Bp. Thomas, 225, 227, 230, 234
Hidalgo, Padre Miguel, 5
Hinojosa, Gilberto M., 41
Hispanics: in Brownsville vicariate, 184; Catholic, 3–5, 21–22, 56, 61–62, 239; and Civil War, 135; prejudice against, 90, 100, 112–15, 187–88; and Reconstruction, 145; schools for, 169; and slavery, 115; and Texas army, 68
History of Texas, The (Edward), 15
Hiver, Mother Angelique, 152–53
Hoermann, Fr. Alto, quoted, 110
Hogg, James Stephen, quoted, 233
Holy Rosary School, Galveston, 213
hospitals: in Brownsville vicariate, 198; in Civil War, 130, 132; in Dallas diocese, 238; in Galveston, 152–54, 156, 158–59; need for, 20–21, 109, 162; and railroads, 162, 224; and religious orders, 171; in San Antonio, 168. *See also names of hospitals*
Hostyn, 103
housing: for priests, 84–85, 135; for Ursuline sisters, 98. *See also* convents
Houston, Sam, 9, 66–67, 123; and Catholic Church, 11–14, 20, 48–51, 112; policies of, 23–25, 69, 73, 116; quoted, 11–12
Houston, 18–21, 25, 54–56, 62, 79, 92;

Houston (*cont.*)
    churches in, 63, 69, 78; in Civil War, 137; living conditions in, 23, 84, 159; Ursuline Order in, 156
Houston and Texas Central Railway Company, 108, 162, 222
Howley, Bp. M. F., 235
hurricanes, 159–60, 220
Hurth, Fr. Peter, 177

Immaculate Conception Church, Brownsville, 184–85, 195
immigrants: civil rights for, 145; and Civil War, 132, 134, 140, 147; Czech, 101–103, 145, 147, 181; European, 37, 70–72; Fourierist, 110–11; and Galveston population, 158; German, 51, 54, 70–71, 74, 76, 78, 101, 103–104, 108–109, 112, 132, 134, 140, 145, 151; Irish, 76, 101, 108–109, 111, 121, 151; Mexican, 101, 158, 165; Polish, 101, 103–104, 112, 145–46, 169; poverty of, 72, 103; prejudice against, 111–12; and Reconstruction, 145–50; and Texas army, 68; U.S., xi, 4, 16–17, 23, 28–29, 37, 55, 151
immigration: and Catholic population, 47, 100, 151, 155, 183; European, 101–11, 165
Incarnate Word Academy, San Antonio, 171
Indianola, 114–15, 158
Indians: fear of, 37–38, 43–44, 46–47, 62–63, 86–87, 90, 92, 97; in 1900, 239; and priests, 240; raids by, 105, 174; and Republic of Texas, 24–26, 59, 65
Indian Territory, 25, 230
invasion: during Civil War, 125; Mexican, 66–68
Ireland, Archbishop John, 227–28, 234
Ireland: recruitment in, 74, 99, 170, 211–12
Irish. *See* immigrants; Texans, Catholic

Jacquet, Fr. J. M., 210
Jaillet, Fr. Claude, 190–92, 194, 196
Janssens, Archbishop Francis, 181, 217–20, 224, 232–35, 263n.42
Jesuits, 76, 109–10, 136; in Galveston, 210–11, 214, 216; Mexican, 168, 173–74
Johnson, Andrew, 143–44, 155
Johnston, Sr. S. M., quoted, 132
Juárez, Benito, 150, 158
Justine, Sr., 156

Kansas-Nebraska Act (1854), 112
Karnes, Henry W., 41–42
Karnes County, 105, 147–49
Katolicka Jednota Texaska, 103
Keane, Bp. John, 227
Keller, Fr. Bonaventura, 104
Kelly, Fr. James, 3
Kenrick, Archbishop Francis Patrick, 74, 124
Keralum, Fr. Pierre, 96
Kerr, James, 19, 47, 60
Kiowa Indians, 86–87
Kirwin, Fr. James M., 220
Knights of Columbus Texas Historical Commission, 235
Know-Nothing party, 111–15, 120
Koenig, Bro. Nicholas, 99

Labadie, Nicholas, 17, 55
labor, railroad, 108–109, 151
Lagier, Fr. Jean, 189
Laignoux, Bro. John Baptist, 99
laity: and Americanism, 227; and education, 169–70; in Galveston, 215, 217–19; relations with, 53, 183, 187–88, 215, 234; and Texas Revolution, 9. *See also names of individuals*
Lamar, Mirabeau B., 9, 29, 48; and Catholic Church, 19–20, 49–50; policies of, 23–27, 31, 59, 65–66
land: donated to Church, 57, 73, 163, 198; for European colonists, 71–72, 105–106; purchased by Church, 58, 73, 107, 218, 231; theft of, 115; title to, 94
language: English, 185, 211–12, 221, 229, 240; French, 211; German, 103, 109, 170, 229–30; Polish, 170; Spanish, 185, 196, 229
Laredo, 3, 67, 83, 90–91, 96, 120, 195; as vicariate headquarters, 196, 198
Lauth, Fr. John, 177
Lavaca County, 70, 78–79
Lavaca River, 60, 63–64; settlement on, 46–47, 78, 92, 181
law: anti-Church, x–xi; Church, 41–42, 119, 151, 160; Texas, 164; U.S., 94, 115
"lay trusteeism," 53
legislation: and Church property, 48–51
legislature, Texas state, 114, 164
Leona River, 85, 90
Leo XIII, 201, 222, 225
Leray, Bp. Francis X., 208
Lerdo de Tejada, Sebastián, 168

Liberty, 79, 119
Linares, see of, 12
Lincoln, Abraham, 121–22, 124, 143, 206
Linn, John J., 6, 10, 19, 29, 37; quoted, 9
Linnville, 37, 43
Lipan Apache Indians, 38, 86–87
litigation: and Church property, 117–18
Llebaría, Fr. Juan Francisco, 15–21, 35, 40
Loughrey, Fr. Thomas, 223
Louisiana: recruitment in, 26, 136
Louis Philippe, King, 74–75
Ludwig, King of Bavaria, 110, 142
Lynch, Fr. John, 74, 80
Lynchburg, 55, 69
Lyonnet, Bp. Jean Paul, 127

McMaster, James Alphonsus, 185, 206–209
McSweeney, William, 191
Magevny, Mother Agnes, 213
Magruder, John B., 130, 132, 138, 144
Malloy, Fr. John Thomas, 3, 37
Malone, Sr. Mary Clare, 211
Maloney, Richard J., 180–81
Manucy, Bp. Dominic, 166, 175, 184–96, 210; quoted, 185, 187
Marín de Porras, Bp. Primo Feliciano, 12
Martín de León Colony, 37, 47
Martínez: Polish community in, 106, 108, 147. *See also* St. Hedwig
Martiniere, Fr. Claude, 191
Martiniere, Fr. Joseph, 191, 222–23
Mary Angela, Sr., 162
Mary Ange of Jesus, Sr., 153, 159
Mary Augustine, Sr., 211–12
Mary Blandine of Jesus, Mother, 153, 159
Mary Euphrosine, Mother, 164
Mary Evangelist, Mother, 232, 235
Mary Joseph, Mother, 215, 219
Mary Joseph of Jesus, Sr., 153
Mary Louise, Sr., 156
Mary of the Cross, Sr., 156
Mary Paul, Sr., 156
mass-stations, location of, 78
Matagorda Bay, 23, 129
Matamoros, Mexico, 91, 94, 129, 138, 159
Mathelin, Mary. *See* Mary Blandine of Jesus, Mother
Mauclerc, Bro. Xavier, 99
Maximilian, 150, 158
Medina River, 5, 71–72
Meerschert, Theophile, 230

Menard, Michel, 6, 16–17, 48, 55
Menard, Peter, 16–17, 55
Menthe, Bro. Joseph, 89
Menzl, Rev. Bohumir, 103
Mercy Hospital, Laredo, 198
Mescens, Fr. Dominic, 104
Methodists, 6, 230
Metton, Elisa. *See* St. Augustine, Sister
Mexican Congress, 82
Mexicans, in Rio Grande Valley, 101
"Mexican Texan Club," 145
Mexico: church-state relations in, 4–5, 9, 12–13, 91, 168, 188; and Civil War, 125, 134; conflict within, 150, 158; and hurricane of 1867, 160; relations with France, 26–27; and Republic of Texas, 48, 59, 65–68; after Spanish independence, 13; and United States, 76–77, 82; and U.S. slavery, 115
Meyer, Rev. A. J., 203, 207–208
Miconleau, Fr. Anthony, 159
Mier, 67
militia, of Republic of Texas, 61–62, 66–68
missionaries: Benedictine, 109–10, 140, 142; for Brownsville vicariate, 190–92; Franciscan, 103–105; need for, 9–10, 12, 21–23; Protestant, 23; recruitment of, 89, 126–27; Vincentian, 35–36, 49–51; volunteer, 15, 26, 28–30, 74–75. *See also* priests; *names of missionaries; names of religious orders*
missionary work, 34–35; difficulties of, 60, 62–63; Vincentian, 70–71
Mission Concepción, 45, 51, 117, 142–43
Mission Espíritu Santo, 38
Mission Nuestra Señora de la Purísima Concepción de Acuña, 99
Mission Refugio, 39
missions: New Mexico, 83; Texas, 39, 44–45, 62, 78, 86, 92, 168; ownership of, 114, 117–18. *See also* mission stations; *names of missions*
Mission San Antonio de Valero. *See also* Alamo, the
Mission San Bernardo, 90
Mission San Francisco de la Espada, 45–46, 78, 168–69
Mission San José, 39, 62, 78; and Benedictines, 140, 162
Mission San Juan Bautista, 90
Mission San Juan Capistrano, 44–46, 78, 110
mission stations: Benedictine, 140; in Brownsville vicariate, 191, 195–96, 198–99;

mission stations *(cont.)*
  numbers of, 120, 238; in San Antonio diocese, 183
mission tours, 34–35; of Bishop Brennan, 228–31; of Bishop Dubuis, 132, 134, 155–56, 158, 161; of Bishop Manucy, 189–90, 192–93; of Bishop Odin, 34–35, 46–48, 51, 53–64, 68, 78, 90–92, 101–102; of Bishop Pellicer, 174; of Bishop Timon, 51, 53–57; Jesuit, 109
Missouri, 13–15, 75, 78, 81, 85, 107
Mobile, 36, 74
Mobile, diocese of, 166, 184
Moczygemba, Fr. Leopold Bonaventure Maria, 103–105, 107–108
Monclus, Ramón, 196
Monterrey, diocese of, 9, 11–12, 91
Monthly Review of St. Mary's Church, 181
Montreal: recruitment in, 89
Morgan's Point, 30, 79
Muenster, 237–38
Muher, Bro. Boniface, 163
Muldoon, Fr. Miguel, 27–28, 103, 244n.46
Muller, Fr. Anthony, 104
Mulry, John, 236, 263n.51
Murphy, Margaret Healy, 180–81

Nacogdoches, 22, 56–57, 58, 78, 92, 164; priests for, 81, 150, 175
Nagle, James, 158
Nash, James P., 159
Natchitoches, 57
National Intelligencer, 28
Navarro, José Antonio, 5–6, 19, 65, 145; quoted, 113
Nazareth Academy, Victoria, 155, 171, 173
Neraz, Bp. Jean Claude, 161; as bishop of San Antonio, 175–81, 201, 209–10, 230
New Braunfels, 78, 86, 92, 103, 110; churches in, 140, 142; priests for, 104, 107
Newfoundland, see of, 235
New Mexico: Texas sovereignty over, 65; and Treaty of Guadalupe Hidalgo, 82–83; and U.S.-Mexico war, 77
New Orleans, 15–16, 36, 58, 65; and annexation, 74; in Civil War, 126–27, 137; meeting of bishops in, 160; Ursuline Order in, 78, 79, 87, 98
New Orleans, province of, 118, 122–24, 203, 205, 208–209, 232
newspapers: and Bishop Brennan, 228–31;

newspapers *(cont.)*
  Catholic, 185, 206–207, 227, 234, 237; and Catholic Church, 42, 55, 116, 178; and Catholic schools, 173; and female religious orders, 153–54; and Galveston hospital, 158, 159; Jewish, 228; Polish, 108; Republican, 145; and Texas politics, 112, 145
New York, 69, 74
Noyer, Marie. *See* St. Angela, Sr.
Nozo, Jean Baptiste, 14–15, 31–32
Nuevo Laredo, 96
Nuevo León: separatists in, 65
nuns. *See* women religious
nursing: need for, 109; and religious orders, 152–53, 159, 170–71; for yellow fever, 159

Oak Cliff Orphanage, 230–32
Oblates of Mary Immaculate, 125, 134–35, 160, 180–81, 192, 194–95; in Brownsville, 89–90, 95–98, 119, 163, 185, 187–90, 195; withdrawal of, 92–93, 107
O'Connell, Fr. Denis, 227
Odin, Archbishop Jean Marie, 6; as archbishop of New Orleans, 123–27, 151–52, 155, 161; as bishop of Galveston, 80–85, 89–100, 103–104, 107, 113–15, 117–19, 121–22; letters of, 77, 93, 101, 110–11, 121, 124, 152, 161; quoted, 35, 38, 44, 54, 56, 59–60, 63, 68, 91–92, 102, 107, 109, 122, 129; as vicar apostolic, 58, 64, 67–80; as vice prefect, 32–51, 53–64
Ogé, Jean Pierre, 70–71, 75
Old Stone Fort, Nacogdoches, 56
Olivetan Benedictine sisters, 237–38
Olivier, Fr. Frigomer, 96
Order of Friars Minor Conventual, 104, 108
Order of Friars Minor Observant, 104
Order of the Immaculate Conception of the Virgin Mary, 169–70
Order of the Incarnate Word and Blessed Sacrament, 152–53
Oregon, 73
orphanages: in Galveston, 162; in Laredo, 198; in San Antonio, 143, 168
Ortiz, Ramón, 41, 97
Our Lady of Guadalupe: chapel dedicated to, 91–92; feast day of, 61–62
Our Lady of Guadalupe Church, Laredo, 198

Our Lady of Guadalupe Church, Victoria, 29, 37, 60, 78
Our Lady of Guadalupe Seminary, Seguin, 173–74
Our Lady of Loretto Church, Goliad, 38
Our Lady of Refuge Church, Refugio, 78
Our Lady of the Lake University, San Antonio, 177
outlaws, 63, 90, 147–48

Padey, Charles, 81
Pairier, Fr. Mathurin, 222–23
Palmito Ranch, 138
Panna Maria, 105–108, 147–49, 169–70
Paquín, Joseph, 26, 32, 70–71
parishes: colonist, 72; creation of, 198; of Fort Worth, 223; of Galveston, 55, 70, 213; of Houston, 54–55; after Independence, 3; of Laredo, 90, 96, 196; Mexican, 97; records of, 18; of San Antonio, 68, 73, 110, 150, 168
Parisot, Fr. Pierre F., 102, 124–25, 185, 195; memoirs of, 192–93
Pease, Elisha M., 113, 115, 145
Pellicer, Bp. Anthony Dominic, 166–67, 169–71, 174–75, 184
Pennsylvania, 109–10, 140, 142
Perche, Archbishop Napoleon J., 203, 205, 208–209
Pereda, Sr. Tereza, 175
Peter, Joseph, Senior, 103
petitions: and Bishop Gallagher, 215–18; for Dallas diocese, 224
Philadelphia, 75, 111
Pius IX, 80, 105, 127, 158, 165
Plana, Luis, 196
Planchet, Louis-Marie, 96
Plum Creek, battle at, 43–44
Point Isabel, 76, 77, 89
Poland, 103–104, 146
politics, of Texas, 164–65; and Know-Nothing party, 111–13; and Reconstruction, 145; and slavery, 122–23
Polk, James Knox, 73–74
population: of Brownsville vicariate, 184; of Gonzales, 47; of Houston, 18; Polish immigrant, 108; of Republic of Texas, 21; of Texas, 101, 239
population, Catholic: in Brownsville vicariate, 189–90, 195–96, 198–99, 239; centers of, 83, 92–93; of Dallas diocese, 239; of East Texas, 150–51; of Galveston, 70; of Galveston diocese, 220–21, 239; and immigration, 101, 151, 155, 165; of Nacogdoches, 56; of North Texas, 224; of Republic of Texas, 21–22, 73; rural, 90; of San Antonio diocese, 183, 239
Portier, Bp. Michael, 65
Potard, Sr. Joseph, 164
poverty, immigrant, 72, 103
Power, Bp. Thomas, 235
Praha, 103
preachers, self-styled, 10, 23
prefecture apostolic, of Texas, 31–64
prejudice: ethnic, 48, 111–14, 145–48, 187–88, 228; against Hispanics, 57, 68, 90, 94, 100, 187–88; and North-South conflict, 213; racial, 228; religious, 10. *See also* anti-Catholicism; anticlericalism
Presbyterians, 54
Presidio, 83, 165
Presidio del Río Grande, 90
Presidio La Bahía, 38, 40
priests: circuit-riding, 223; diverse duties of, 88; as educators, 169; Franciscan, 156; French, 134, 175, 183, 211; German, 78, 104; houses for, 84–85; Irish, 78, 240; Jesuit, 109–10; loyalist, 39–40, 48; Mexican, 94–95, 97; need for, 67, 70, 73, 93, 190; numbers of, 79, 120, 140, 165, 199, 231; Oblate, 95–96; Polish, 103–108, 145–49, 156; recruitment of, 74–75; in Republic of Texas, 26–30; retirement of, 211; skills of, 96; training of, 173; for U.S. army, 76; unsatisfactory, 75, 96. *See also names of individuals*
processions, religious, 42–43, 61–62, 91–92, 184–85
Propaganda, the, 205, 233–34
property, Church ownership of, 37, 39, 41, 45, 48–53, 64, 114, 116–18, 232. *See also* land: *names of properties*
Protestants, 6, 10, 23, 54, 101–102
Przysiecki, Fr. Julian, 108, 146
publications, Catholic, 181, 230. *See also* newspapers
Puig, Michael, 196
Purcell, Archbishop John Baptist, 123–24

Querat, Fr. Joseph, 156–57
Quihi, 85, 140
Quinlan, Bp. John, 205

railroads, 74; in Civil War, 137; and diocese travel, 60, 168, 228–29; expansion of, 108–109, 151, 165, 184, 222; hospitals for, 162, 224
Rancho de Don Carlos de la Garza, 40, 58, 63–64, 78
Rancho de la Palma, 95
rebellion: of 1838, 25; Fredonian, 6; of Galveston clergy, 203–10; Hispanic, 115–16; at Medina River, 5; Pueblo, 83. *See also* war
Reconstruction, 7, 139, 140, 143–50, 151–52, 165, 173
recruitment, 89, 98–99; of Benedictines, 109–10; in Canada, 89; during Civil War, 136; in Europe, 74–75, 93, 95, 103–104, 127, 140, 143, 146, 152–53, 165, 170, 191, 221; in France, 126, 152, 159, 165; of seminarians, 74–75, 146, 159; of women religious, 74–75, 89, 99, 155, 170, 211–12; in U.S., 26, 109–10, 136
refugees: Jesuit, 168, 173; Mexican, 101, 150, 188–89
Refugio, 22, 29, 78, 92, 196, 198
religious foundations: in Galveston diocese, 161–65; and health care, 152–53. *See also names of foundations; names of orders*
religious orders: administration of, 161, 178–80; in Brownsville vicariate, 196, 198; conflict with, 178–80; in Dallas diocese, 238–39, 331; and education, 177; and nursing, 170–71; in San Antonio diocese, 168–69, 182. *See also names of orders*
Renard, Madeleine. *See* St. Ursula, Sr.
Republican party, 121, 143–45, 165
Republic of the Rio Grande, independence of, 65–66
Reynosa, 91, 94–95, 98
Rheinbolt, Fr. John N., 143
Richard, Rev. Pierre, 141, 191
Richmond, 29, 59, 79, 109, 126, 130
Rio Grande, 67, 76, 82
Rio Grande City, 91, 95, 134, 195
Rio Grande Valley: Catholics in, 83; and Civil War, 134–35; hurricane in, 159–60; Mexican immigrants in, 101, 158, 165; missionaries in, 89–98, 101–102, 192–93. *See also names of settlements*
Riordan, Sr. Bernard, 238
Robards, William, 163
Roemer, Ferdinand von, quoted, 78
Rollando, Fr. Bartholomew, 81

Roma, 91, 95, 195
Rosati, Bp. Joseph, 31, 34
Rosecrans, Bp. S. H., 210
Rosecrans, Sr. Imelda, 213
Rossadowski, Fr. Anthony, 108
Rossberger, Bro. Norbert, 110
Roudet, Bro. Pierre, 96
Roussin, Lucine. *See* Mary Joseph of Jesus, Sr.
Ruiz, Francisco, 5–6
Ryan, Abraham Joseph, 213–14
Rzeppa, Emanuel, 169–70

Sabine Pass, 69, 130, 134
Sacred Congregation for the Propagation of the Faith, 12
Sacred Heart Academy, Galveston, 212
Sacred Heart Cathedral, Dallas, 229
Sacred Heart Church, Dallas, 231
Sacred Heart Church, Muenster, 237–38
St. Ambroise, Sister, 79
St. Ange, Mother, 155; quoted, 160
St. Angela, Sister, 79
Saint Arsene, Sr. Josephin Blin de, 79
St. Augustine, Mother, 214
St. Augustine, Sister, 79
St. Bruno, Sister, 79
St. Chantal, Sister, 89
St. Claire, Mother, 155–56
St. Edward's College, Austin, 163, 177
St. Francisville, 107
St. Hedwig, 106, 147, 150
St. Ignatius Academy, Fort Worth, 224
St. James, fiesta for, 95
St. John's, Canada, 235–36
St. Joseph's Church, Fagan Settlement, 78
St. Joseph's College, Bardstown, 28
St. Joseph's College, Brownsville, 163, 185
St. Joseph's College, Victoria, 177
St. Joseph Seminary, Victoria, 196
St. Joseph's Hospital, Fort Worth, 224, 238
St. Joseph's Orphanage, San Antonio, 168, 171
St. Joseph's School, Corpus Christi, 196
St. Joseph's School, San Antonio, 170
St. Louis' Church, Castroville, 78, 140
St. Marie, Sister, 125
St. Mary-of-the-Barrens College, 26
St. Mary-of-the-Barrens Seminary, 13, 26, 32, 34–35, 47, 79
St. Mary's Academy, Dallas, 230

St. Mary's Cathedral, Galveston, 80–81, 83, 130, 132, 138, 209
St. Mary's Church, Austin, 230–31
St. Mary's Church, Brown's Settlement, 78
St. Mary's Church, Clarendon, 238
St. Mary's Church, Fredericksburg, 110
St. Mary's Church, Galveston, 69–70, 71, 73, 78, 79–80
St. Mary's Church, Krakow, 105
St. Mary's Church, Lavaca County, 70
St. Mary's Church, Praha, 103
St. Mary's Church, San Antonio, 100, 140
St. Mary's College, San Antonio, 120, 173
St. Mary's College and Seminary, Galveston, 107, 120, 137, 162–63
St. Mary's Infirmary, Galveston, 208, 210–11, 216
St. Mary's Institute, San Antonio, 142–43
St. Mary's of the Immaculate Conception Church, Austin, 156
St. Mary's Orphanage, Galveston, 212, 216–20
St. Mary's University, San Antonio, 99, 173
St. Mary's Weekly Review, 181
St. Michael's Church, San Antonio, 106
St. Patrick's Cathedral, Fort Worth, 223
St. Patrick's Church, Corpus Christi, 194–96
St. Patrick's Church, Fort Worth, 223, 230, 235
St. Patrick's Church, Galveston, 209
St. Paul's Hospital, Dallas, 238
St. Peter's Church, Cummings Creek, 78
St. Peter's Church, New Braunfels, 104
Sts. Peter and Paul Church, Fredericksburg, 140
St. Stanislaus, Sister, 79
St. Thomas, Sister, 89
St. Ursula, Sister, 79
St. Vincent, Pennsylvania, 109
St. Vincent de Paul, 13
St. Vincent de Paul Church, Houston, 69, 71, 78, 84, 134, 156
Sala, Bro. Ramón, 35–38, 46
Salado Creek, battle at, 66
San Antonio, 3, 21–22, 25–26, 29, 68, 90, 92; anti-Catholicism in, 116–18; and Cart War, 114–15; Catholics in, 73, 83, 92–93; cholera in, 87–88; churches in, 78; in Civil War, 137; educational facilities in, 98–100, 120, 173; hospital for, 162; Indian conflict in, 86; and Know-Nothing party, 112; Mexi-

San Antonio *(cont.)*
can occupation of, 66, 68; parochial life in, 100; pastoral work in, 38–46; Polish community in, 106, 108, 150; proposed archdiocese of, 31; as provincial see, 234; religious festivals in, 60–62; religious orders in, 98–99, 110, 142–43
San Antonio, diocese of, 163, 165–83, 239
San Antonio Express, 173
San Antonio Messenger, 181
San Antonio River, 63; settlements on, 72
San Augustine, 57, 78
San Diego: priests for, 190–92
San Elizario, 3, 83
San Felipe de Austin, 54, 63
San Fernando Cathedral, San Antonio, 166, 168, 175, 177
San Fernando Church, San Antonio, 3, 6, 29, 39–42, 58, 78, 98, 100; conflict over, 116–17; repairs to, 41, 44, 60–61
San Francisco de Paula Church, San Diego, 192
San Jacinto battlesite, 8–10, 17–18, 27, 40, 66, 102
San Patricio, 3, 22, 78, 92, 196
Santa Anna, Antonio López de, 9–10, 66–67
Santa Fe: attack on, 77; diocese of, 83
Santa Fe Expedition, 6, 67
Santa Gertrudis Church, Victoria County, 78
Santa Rita, 90–91, 95
Santa Rosa Hospital, San Antonio, 162
Sarry, Fr. Matthew, 161
Satolli, Cardinal Francesco, 215–17, 219
Savoye, Stephane, 191
scandals, public, 178–79
Schmidtbauer, Fr. Columban, 142
Schneider, Father, 70–71, 75
schools: boys', 99–100, 120, 140, 163, 177; in Brownsville, 160; building of, 181–82; Catholic, 64, 119–20, 140, 142–43, 155–56, 162–64, 168–71, 173, 177; convent, 96, 98–99; funding of, 113, 117; in Galveston, 213; in Galveston diocese, 221; girls', 79, 98–99, 119–20, 140, 156, 163; in North Texas, 162; ownership of, 232; in Panna Maria, 108; parochial, 79, 156, 168; public, 113, 169–71, 235; in San Antonio, 168; Ursuline, 78–79, 89
Scott, L. Z. H., 217

secession, 113, 123–24, 135
Second Plenary Council of Baltimore, 151–55, 160
secularization, of Texas missions, 39
Seguín, Juan N., 38, 48
Seguin, 46, 79; seminary in, 173–74
seminarians: arrival of, 78; recruitment of, 74–75, 146, 159; Spanish, 196. *See also names of individuals*
seminaries, 162, 173, 177, 195
Sentinel, 42
separatists, Mexican, 65–66
Servants of the Sacred Heart of Jesus and of the Poor, 198
settlers. *See* immigrants
Sheridan, Sr. Mary Benignus, quoted, 40, 43
Sherman, Sidney, 132
Sherman, Sidney, Jr., 132
shortages: in Civil War, 125; of clothing, 86; of food, 67, 85–86, 103, 137; of religious supplies, 149
sickness: among settlers, 59–60
Sisters of Charity, Mexican, 188–89
Sisters of Charity of St. Vincent de Paul: and nursing, 238
Sisters of Charity of the Incarnate Word, 153; and Bishop Gallagher, 217–18; and education, 170–71; in Galveston, 208–209, 212; and nursing, 156, 158–59, 198, 224, 238; orphanage of, 162; in San Antonio, 168
Sisters of Divine Providence, 156, 178–80; and education, 168, 170, 177–78
Sisters of Mercy, 198; and education, 169, 212–13, 230–31
Sisters of Our Lady of Victory School, 182
Sisters of St. Mary of Namur, 162, 224
Sisters of the Holy Ghost, 181
Sisters of the Immaculate Conception, 106
Sisters of the Incarnate Word and Blessed Sacrament, 96, 120, 134–35; and education, 155–56, 162, 168, 171, 195–96; in Galveston, 211–12
slavery: abolition of, 7–8, 139, 143; and Catholic Church, 100, 121–22, 126; conflict over, 115, 121; in Texas, 73, 82, 84, 112–13
Smith, John W., 41–42
Society for the Propagation of the Faith, 74–75, 109, 110, 118, 121

Society of Mary, 99–100, 117; and education, 120, 177; and Reconstruction, 142–43
Society of St. Joseph, 182
Socorro, 83
Solemn Benediction, permission for, 119
Somervell, Alexander, 66–67
Sons of the Immaculate Heart of Mary, 182
Sorin, Fr. Edward, 162–63
Souchon, Fr. Michael, 175
Soulerin, Fr. Alexander, 89
Southern Messenger, 181
Spain: recruitment in, 196
Spalding, Archbishop Martin John, 151–52, 154, 161
Spalding, Bp. John L., 227
Spillard, Fr. Daniel, 163
Spohn Hospital, 198
Spring Creek, 56, 79
Stehle, Nicholas, 49–51, 53, 59
Sterne, Adolphus, 56
Strasbourg, Bishop of, 70, 75
synod: Galveston diocese, 118–19, 160–61, 165, 175; use of term, 252n.50

Tamaulipas, Mexico, 65, 91
Tascosa, 228–29
Taylor, Zachary, 77
Telegraph and Texas Register, 55
Telmon, Fr. Pierre, 89–90
Texan navy, 59, 66
Texans, Catholic, 3–4, 8; Irish, 3, 9–10. *See also names of individuals*
Texas: diocesan status for, 75, 80–81; as ecclesiastical province, 232–34; in 1900, 220–21, 239–40; and Reconstruction, 144
Texas, Republic of: Church reorganization in, 9–23, 28–30; creation of, 3–6; diplomatic recognition of, 9, 11–12, 20, 27, 31, 49, 65; invaded by Mexico, 65–66; and Mexican Church, 32; as prefecture apostolic, 31–64; as vicariate apostolic, 58, 64–81
Texas Catholic, 227, 237
Texas Congress, 23–24, 48–51, 65–66, 76
Texas Declaration of Independence, 4–6
Texas Rangers, 66, 90; and Indians, 24, 26, 43, 47, 87
Texas Revolution, 3–6, 40, 132; and Catholic Church, 40, 92

Texas State Gazette, 112
Texas Supreme Court, 118, 164
They Called Them Greasers (De León), 115
Thurber, 230
Timon, Bp. John, 6, 13–23, 26, 28; as bishop of Buffalo, 80, 83, 152, 162; as prefect apostolic, 31–32, 49–51, 53–57, 58; and slavery, 122; as vicar apostolic, 114; as Vincentian provincial supervisor, 32, 34, 65, 72–74
trade: and Church property, 230; in Dallas, 222; slave, 122; U.S.–Mexico, 65
transportation: in Civil War, 136–37; for immigrants, 104–106; and missionary travel, 60, 74, 85, 137, 174, 192–93
travel: by boat, 35–37, 55, 59, 69, 104, 127, 147, 153; in caravans, 37–38; immigrant, 104–105; missionary, 59–63, 147, 189–93; by railroad, 222–23; rigors of, 35–38, 46–47, 55–56, 59–63, 69, 92, 101, 168; wartime, 91, 127, 129, 136–37
treaties: Adams-Onis, 13; of Guadalupe Hidalgo, 82
Trouard, Mother Marie, 98
Truchard, Fr. Anthony, 205–10
Tucek, Fr. James, 232, 235–36
Tucson: as vicariate apostolic, 83, 165, 222
Twohig, John, 105, 107
Tyler, John, 73–74

Union: Texan support for, 135, 140, 148
Union Army, 125–26, 129–30, 132, 134–36
Union Navy, 124–26, 130, 132
United States: immigration from, 151; and Republic of Texas, 9, 20, 24; and Texas annexation, 73–74; and Treaty of Guadalupe Hidalgo, 82; and war with Mexico, 76–77
Urrea, José, 3, 40
Ursuline Academy, 130
Ursuline Order, 98, 154, 168; and Bishop Gallagher, 213–19; and Civil War, 125, 130, 132, 137; in Dallas, 223; dissidents of, 119; and education, 119–20, 171, 196; in Galveston, 77–79, 81, 89; in Houston, 156; and Know-Nothing party, 116; in Laredo, 175; property of, 232; recruitment among, 74, 89
U.S. Army, 75–77, 148–49. *See also* Union Army
U.S. Congress: and annexation, 73–74; and Reconstruction, 144

U.S. Constitution: and Reconstruction, 144

Valdéz, Fr. José Antonio, 3, 21, 29, 39–40
Vandenberghe, Fr. Florent, 187–88
Van Hamins, Napoleon, 53
Van Ness, Cornelius, 51–52
Vásquez, Rafael, 66, 68
Vatican: and Americanism, 227; appointments of, 57, 166, 175, 182, 200–201, 203, 207, 224, 237; and black evangelism, 155; and Catholic Church in Texas, 10–13, 28, 31–32, 165, 222, 224, 232–35, 237; and Mexican Church, 13; and Plenary Council of Baltimore, 160; and Sisters of Divine Providence, 180; and Ursuline Order, 214–15, 232
Velasco, 78
Verdaquer de Prat, Bp. Pedro, 196–99, 230
Verdet, Fr. Jean-Maurice, 96, 98, 119
Verea y González, Bp. Francisco de P., 97–98
Verot, Bp. Augustine, 122, 155
vicariates apostolic: Brownsville, 165–66, 168, 184–99; Indian Territory, 230; Texas, 58, 64–81; Tucson, 83, 165, 222
Victoria, 3, 22, 29, 37, 43, 46–47, 58, 60, 62–64, 114; cholera in, 87; Church in, 78; Mexican occupation of, 66; Polish community in, 107; and Republic of Rio Grande, 65; schools in, 155–56, 171, 173
Vincentian Order: missionary work of, 13–15, 21, 26, 31–32, 34–35, 49, 70–71, 72–74, 79; and slavery, 121–22; withdrawal of, 92–93, 98
violence: anti-Catholic, 111–12; ethnic, 68, 111–13, 115, 147; Indian-settler, 43, 86–87, 90–91; and local government, 94; and Reconstruction, 145–49, 165; and slavery, 100; and volunteer militia, 68, 78
volunteers: army, 67–68, 75–76; missionary, 15, 74–75, 190–91
voting rights, 144, 147

Waco, 162, 224
Walter, Sr. Florence, 179–80
war: of La Reforma, 101; threat of, 65–68, 76; U.S.–Mexican, 76–77, 82, 91, 114, 117. *See also names of wars*
Washington-on-the-Brazos, convention at, 4–6, 9
Waxahachie, 230

Wendel, Fr. Aemilian, 110
Weninger, Fr. Francis Xavier, 109–10
Wharton, William H., 27
Wimmer, Abbot Boniface, 109, 142
Woll, Adrián, 66–67
women religious: charitable works of, 79, 152–54, 156, 158–59, 162–64, 168–71; and Civil War, 125, 130, 132, 134–37; and diocese administration, 208–209; dissident, 119; need for, 67; recruitment of, 74–75, 89, 99, 155, 170, 211–12; in San Antonio, 98–99,

women religious (*cont.*)
168. *See also names of individuals; names of orders*
Wyer, Fr. Lawrence, 177

Ylla, Amelio, 196
Yorktown, 106, 150
Ysleta, 3, 83

Zubiría y Escalante, Bp. José López de, 83
Zwiardowski, Felix, 146–47, 149, 169–70

Through Fire and Flood was composed into type on a Compugraphic digital phototypesetter in ten point Galliard with two points of spacing between the lines. Galliard italic was selected for display. The book was designed by Cameron Poulter, typeset by Metricomp, Inc., printed offset by Thomson-Shore, Inc., and bound by John H. Dekker & Sons, Inc. The paper on which this book is printed carries acid-free characteristics for an effective life of at least three hundred years.

TEXAS A&M UNIVERSITY PRESS : COLLEGE STATION

www.ingramcontent.com/pod-product-compliance
Lightning Source LLC
Chambersburg PA
CBHW030307080526
44584CB00012B/475